OXFORD MONOGRAI
INTERNATIONAL I

General Editor: Professor Ian Browni.. ᴄ..,
Emeritus Professor of Public International Law in
the University of Oxford and Fellow of All Souls College, Oxford.

THE RESPONSIBILITY OF STATES
FOR INTERNATIONAL CRIMES

OXFORD MONOGRAPHS IN
INTERNATIONAL LAW

The aim of this series of monographs is to publish important
and original pieces of research on all aspects of public international law. Topics which are given particular prominence are
those which, while of interest to the academic lawyer, also have
important bearing on issues which touch the actual conduct of
international relations. None the less the series is wide in scope
and includes monographs on the history and philosophical
foundations of international law.

The Responsibility of States
for International Crimes

NINA H. B. JØRGENSEN

OXFORD
UNIVERSITY PRESS

OXFORD

UNIVERSITY PRESS

Great Clarendon Street, Oxford OX2 6DP

Oxford University Press is a department of the University of Oxford.
It furthers the University's objective of excellence in research, scholarship,
and education by publishing worldwide in

Oxford New York

Athens Auckland Bangkok Bogotá Buenos Aires Calcutta
Cape Town Chennai Dar es Salaam Delhi Florence Hong Kong Istanbul
Karachi Kuala Lumpur Madrid Melbourne Mexico City Mumbai
Nairobi Paris São Paulo Taipei Tokyo Toronto Warsaw

Oxford is a registered trade mark of Oxford University Press
in the UK and in certain other countries

Published in the United States
by Oxford University Press Inc., New York

British Library Cataloguing in Publication Data
Data available

Library of Congress Cataloging in Publication Data
Jørgensen, Nina H. B.
The responsibility of states for international crimes/Nina H.B. Jørgensen.
p. cm. – (Oxford monographs in international law)
Includes bibliographical references and index.
1. International offenses. 2. Government liability (International law)
I. Title. II. Series.

K5301 .J67 2000   341.7′7–dc21   00–057433

ISBN 0–19–829861–7

ISBN 0–19–925800–7 (pbk)

Typeset in Times
by J&L Composition, Filey, North Yorkshire
Printed in Great Britain
on acid-free paper by
T.J. International, Padstow, Cornwall

To my parents

Editor's Preface

This book is the successful outcome of a well-sustained and complex pattern of research. The subject-matter calls for the necessary articulation of several different areas of law and legal theory, some of which are themselves problematical and still in the formative stage. The topicality of the question of State crimes is obvious and it must rank high on any agenda of the codification and progressive development of international law. Dr Jørgensen has provided a comprehensive and scholarly guide to a very difficult area.

Blackstone Chambers   IAN BROWNLIE
Temple
15 June 2000

Preface

This book is based on my D.Phil. thesis, *State Responsibility for the Commission of Crimes against International Law* (University of Oxford, Hilary Term 1998), which I prepared for publication after qualifying as a barrister in June 1999.

The choice of subject was motivated initially by visits to the Hiroshima Memorial Museum (1988), Dachau Concentration Camp (1990) and Yad Vashem Holocaust Museum, Jerusalem (1993), and by the subsequent preparation of an undergraduate dissertation on 'The Case for a Permanent International Criminal Tribunal in the Light of the Ad Hoc International Tribunal for the Former Yugoslavia'. In 1995 I had the opportunity to visit the International Criminal Tribunal for the Former Yugoslavia in The Hague, and in 1996 I visited the International Criminal Tribunal for Rwanda in Arusha. Some of the research was conducted during a short internship at the International Human Rights Law Institute, De Paul University, Chicago, which resulted in an invitation to attend the Meeting of Experts on the Establishment of an International Criminal Court at the International Institute of Higher Studies in Criminal Sciences, Siracusa.

Despite the increasing concern for individuals and the role of the individual in the international legal system, the state is still the pivotal actor in that system, and this fact may risk becoming obscured by all the current attention on individual criminal responsibility. State crimes are the most serious of all crimes; they belong in a category of their own, beyond Dante's 'Ninth Circle' where the betrayers of their own kindred cause the devil himself to weep tears of bewilderment. It would seem that this is justification enough for undertaking a detailed examination of the concept of state criminality in an effort to discover whether international law is impotent in an area where the need for its vitality is self-evident. A further justification is the adoption by the International Law Commission of Article 19 of Part I of the Draft Articles on State Responsibility on first reading in 1980. Draft Article 19 attempts to embody the notion of state crimes, but since it has been the topic of considerable controversy, it may not survive the second reading of the Draft Articles. However, this will not necessarily impede the development of the concept of state criminality in international law, and the questions it raises are consequently both important and urgent. This is highlighted by the 1996 Judgment of the International Court of Justice in the *Case Concerning the Application of the Convention on the Prevention and Punishment of the Crime of Genocide* (Preliminary Objections) between Bosnia-Herzegovina and Yugoslavia.

I wish to express my gratitude first and foremost to my D.Phil. Supervisor, Professor Ian Brownlie, for his limitless advice and for his time and patience. Like the wisest of teachers he did not persuade me to 'enter the house of his wisdom' but rather led me to the threshold of my own mind. I also wish to extend my thanks to the examiners of my thesis, Professor Christopher Greenwood, London School of Economics, and Professor Derrick Wyatt, University of Oxford, for an inspiring *viva voce* examination and for their report; to Professor James Crawford, Director at the Cambridge Research Centre for International Law, for making International Law Commission material available to me and for his detailed comments on the entire thesis; to Professor M. Cherif Bassiouni, President of the International Human Rights Law Institute, De Paul University, for his generosity in Chicago and Siracusa; to Professor John Dugard, University of Leiden, for valuable and encouraging discussions on 'state criminality' and for introducing me to the Cambridge Research Centre for International Law during his time as Director; to Professor Malcolm Evans, University of Bristol, for his advice and continued support; to Justice Richard Goldstone for meeting me at the International Criminal Tribunal for the Former Yugoslavia; to Sir Francis Vallat and the Hague Academy of International Law for the award of a scholarship enabling me to attend the courses of the Academy in Public International Law in 1995; to Mr Arthur Th. Witteveen, International Court of Justice, for sending me extensive material on the *Case Concerning the Application of the Genocide Convention*; to the librarians at the Bodleian, Codrington, Social Studies and Nuffield College libraries in Oxford, Gray's Inn Library in London, the Nobel Institute, Human Rights Institute and Foreign Ministry libraries in Oslo, and the University of Tel Aviv Law Library; to the Norwegian Research Council (Norges forskningsråd) for its financial support during the process of updating and amending the original text; to the staff of Oxford University Press for their careful preparation of the text for publication; to the Principal and governing body at Linacre College for awarding me a Domus Studentship; and to the staff and members of the College for making Linacre a home. Finally, I wish to thank my parents and my sister for all their moral and practical support.

NHBJ

London, January 2000

Foreword

At the time this book was completed in 1999 the International Law Commission's Draft Articles on State Responsibility were in a state of flux and in the process of being revamped. This process was completed in 2001. The final Draft Articles on the Responsibility of States for Internationally Wrongful Acts were taken note of in a Resolution of the United Nations General Assembly adopted without a vote on 12 December 2001.[1] The Articles thereby lost the word 'Draft' and were annexed to the Resolution, which reserved to a later session of the General Assembly the question of their future adoption by way of a convention or declaration.

Predictably, Article 19, which purported to define the concept of international crimes of state but failed to do so adequately, did not survive the second reading of the Draft Articles. Anticipating such an outcome, the aim in this book was to place Article 19 squarely in its historical context, to explore ways in which the concept of state criminal responsibility had already permeated international law and to consider possibilities for its development in the future. Since this development may well be affected by the Articles on the Responsibility of States for Internationally Wrongful Acts, it seems appropriate to preface the paperback edition of this book with what is effectively a postscript describing briefly how the story ended in the International Law Commission. The previous Appendix III is now replaced by the final version of the Articles. In all other respects the text remains unchanged.

Article 19 was debated vigorously in the ILC in 1998 but it was decided not to take a vote on its deletion, as a significant majority in favour of deletion could not be guaranteed.[2] Consideration of the Article was therefore put to one side[3] to allow time for the concept of state crimes, or at least some of the values embodied in it, to be reworked and recast in terms that would be acceptable to states and attract a consensus. According to the Special Rapporteur, a genuine regime of criminal responsibility for states would need to contain five elements: proper definitions, a procedure for investigation, a system of due process, sanctions consequential upon a determination on behalf of the international community that a crime had been committed, and a system by which the state could purge its guilt and expunge the record.[4] But

---

[1] A/RES/56/83, 28 January 2002.

[2] See J. Crawford, *The International Law Commission's Articles on State Responsibility, Introduction, Text and Commentaries*, (Cambridge University Press, 2002), 27.

[3] See Report of the ILC on the work of its fiftieth session (1998), GAOR, 53rd session, A/53/10, para. 331.

[4] First Report on State Responsibility by J. Crawford, Special Rapporteur, A/CN.4/490/Add.3, 24 April 1998, para. 91.

it seemed that even the supporters of Article 19 did not envisage a full-scale penal regime for states and an alternative solution needed to be found. Since the existence of obligations *erga omnes* was generally accepted, one solution was to replace Article 19 with a notion of serious breaches of obligations to the international community as a whole. The resulting compromise involved the deletion of Article 19 and the concept of state crimes but the inclusion of special consequences in Part II of the Draft Articles applicable to breaches of obligations *erga omnes*.[5] The proposed section read as follows:[6]

Chapter III: Serious breaches of essential obligations to the international community

Article 41

Application of this Chapter

1. This Chapter applies to the international responsibility arising from an internationally wrongful act that constitutes a serious breach by a State of an obligation owed to the international community as a whole and essential for the protection of its fundamental interests.
2. A breach of such an obligation is serious if it involves a gross or systematic failure by the responsible State to fulfil the obligation, risking substantial harm to the fundamental interests protected thereby.

Article 42 [51, 53]

Consequences of serious breaches of obligations to the international community as a whole

1. A serious breach within the meaning of article 41 may involve, for the responsible State, damages reflecting the gravity of the breach.
2. It entails, for all other States, the following obligations:
    (a) Not to recognize as lawful the situation created by the breach;
    (b) Not to render aid or assistance to the responsible State in maintaining the situation so created;
    (c) To cooperate as far as possible to bring the breach to an end.
3. This article is without prejudice to the consequences referred to in Chapter II and to such further consequences that a breach to which this Chapter applies may entail under international law.

Under the scheme of the Draft Articles, all states would be entitled to invoke responsibility for breaches of obligations owed to the international community as a whole, irrespective of their seriousness.[7]

Article 42(1) proved to be controversial even though it was understood not to refer to punitive damages and it was subsequently deleted. It was also felt that the notion of obligations to the international community as a whole was

---

[5] See Provisional Summary Record of the 2662nd Meeting, A/CN.4/SR.2662, 4 September 2000.   [6] A/CN.4/L.600, 11 August 2000.
[7] A/CN.4/L.600, 11 August 2000, Article 43.

too general and, moreover, that it referred to the invocation of responsibility rather than the status of the breach. A new solution was therefore found in the concept of peremptory norms (*jus cogens*).[8] The revised and final Chapter III on serious breaches of obligations under peremptory norms of general international law contains the following articles:

Article 40

Application of this chapter

1. This chapter applies to the international responsibility which is entailed by a serious breach by a State of an obligation arising under a peremptory norm of general international law.
2. A breach of such an obligation is serious if it involves a gross or systematic failure by the responsible State to fulfil the obligation.

Article 41

Particular consequences of a serious breach of an obligation under this chapter

1. States shall cooperate to bring to an end through lawful means any serious breach within the meaning of article 40.
2. No State shall recognize as lawful a situation created by a serious breach within the meaning of article 40, nor render aid or assistance in maintaining that situation.
3. The article is without prejudice to the other consequences referred to in this part and to such further consequences that a breach to which this chapter applies may entail under international law.

There is no list of examples of serious breaches of obligations under peremptory norms and the Chapter is described as providing a 'framework for progressive development'[9] through state practice and judicial decisions. However, the Commentary to Article 40 includes as examples of *jus cogens* the norms prohibiting aggression, slavery, genocide, racial discrimination, apartheid, torture, and the suppression of the right to self-determination. These largely overlap with the examples given in the old Article 19, which are cited in a footnote. In order for Article 40 to come into play, two requirements must be met. First, the obligation breached must be peremptory, and second, the breach must fulfil a criterion of seriousness. The particular consequences of such a breach differ only slightly from those put forward by Special Rapporteur Riphagen in relation to international crimes in 1982.[10] In the context of international crimes, these consequences constituted an unambitious and soft regime. They are uncontroversial as minimum requirements under Article 41 and are probably applicable to breaches of all peremptory norms.

[8] See Report of the ILC on the work of its fifty-third session (2001), GAOR, 55th session, A/56/10, para. 49.   [9] Crawford, (n. 2 above), 38.
[10] (1982) *YrbkILC*, vol. 2, pt. 1, 48, para. 150, Article 6.

The decision to abandon Article 19 was a pragmatic and a political one, aimed at furthering the likelihood of unanimous acceptance of the Draft Articles by states. The action by the Commission did not involve the rejection of the concept of state crimes as a matter of principle. Rather, it was felt that a full elaboration of the topic fell outside the scope of the state responsibility agenda. Part I of the Draft Articles 'now proceeds on the basis that internationally wrongful acts of a State form a single category and that the criteria for such acts (in particular the criteria for attribution and the circumstances precluding wrongfulness) apply to all, without reference to any distinction between "delictual" and "criminal" responsibility'.[11]

Acceptance of the Articles as they now stand does not exclude the possibility of the development in the future of a regime that properly describes certain acts as crimes in the context of an organizational and institutional structure for the implementation of state criminal responsibility. Indeed, it is possible that a category of state crimes could develop out of Article 40 and be subject to a *lex specialis* regime under Article 55. The Special Rapporteur agrees that 'crimes of State, if they exist, would be a paradigm example of wrongs viv-à-vis the international community as a whole',[12] and he highlights embryonic practice in relation to aggression and genocide.[13] Taking a different tack, he suggests that excluding the possibility for the future of applying the notion of corporate criminal responsibility to the state as a legal entity might constitute a 'reversion to the discredited idea of the State as being above [international] law'.[14]

The terrorist attacks in the United States on 11 September 2001 brought state sponsored terrorism and new forms of organizational crime into focus. In an unpredictable world it could be dangerous to close the door on the concept of state crime when it has the potential to contribute towards international justice and world order. In terms of achieving these goals, the International Criminal Court, which came into operation on 1 July 2002, may be the most important international institution to be established since the creation of the United Nations. But does a system built on complementarity[15] and the responsibility of natural persons answer all the needs of a complete system of international criminal justice? The ICC, particularly when it deals with cases of genocide and eventually aggression, may well find that state and individual criminal responsibility are complementary. The resignation of the Dutch cabinet on 16 April 2002 in response to the publication of a report by the Netherlands Institute for War Documentation implicating Dutch troops in the genocidal[16] massacre at Srebrenica in 1995, suggests how

---

[11] Crawford, (n. 2 above), 37.   [12] Ibid, 18.   [13] Ibid, 19.   [14] Ibid.

[15] According to this principle the ICC will only be able to exercise jurisdiction if national courts are unable or unwilling to prosecute.

[16] General Krstic was convicted of genocide before the International Criminal Tribunal for the Former Yugoslavia in relation to the mass executions of Bosnian Muslim men in Srebrenica between 11 July and 1 November 1995. Case IT-98-33, Judgment (Trial Chamber), 2 August 2001.

mature democracies can share in the responsibility for international crimes. It is also notable that the European Court of Justice recently imposed a 'penalty payment' on a state for its persistent failure to comply with its obligations as a member of the European Union.[17]

It is debatable to what extent the difficulties associated with the normative distinctions contained in Article 19 have been eliminated in the final Articles of 2001. How does an 'international crime' differ normatively from a serious (i.e. gross and systematic) breach of an obligation under a peremptory norm of international law? And who decides if a breach is gross and systematic? Can it simply be inferred that we are faced with such a breach if all states refuse to recognize the resulting situation as lawful, and cooperate in bringing the breach to an end? What role should the organized international community play? The 'genie' of state crimes may well be back in its bottle as far as the Articles on State Responsibility are concerned, but whether deliberately, inadvertently, or inevitably, it would seem that the ILC left the lid off.

Nina H. B. Jørgensen

The Hague, April 2002

---

[17] *Commission of the European Communities v. Hellenic Republic*, Case C-387/97, [2000] ECR I-5047.

Contents

Abbreviations

AC	Appeal Cases, England and Wales
A/CN.4	Symbol for documents of the International Law Commission
AJIL	*American Journal of International Law*
All ER	All England Reports, England and Wales
Annual Digest	*Annual Digest of Public International Law Cases*
BYIL	*British Yearbook of International Law*
CLR	Commonwealth Law Reports, Australia
CMLR	Common Market Law Reports
DLR	Dominion Law Reports, Canada
Draft Code	Draft Code of Offences against the Peace and Security of Mankind
ECOSOC	United Nations Economic and Social Council
ECR	European Court of Justice Reports
GA	General Assembly
Hague *Recueil*	*Recueil des Cours de l'Académie de Droit International*
HL	House of Lords, United Kingdom
ICC	International Criminal Court
ICJ Pleadings	International Court of Justice: Pleadings, Oral Arguments, Documents
ICJ Reports	Reports of Judgments, Advisory Opinions, and Orders of the International Court of Justice
ICLQ	*International and Comparative Law Quarterly*
ILA	International Law Association
ILC	International Law Commission
ILM	*International Legal Materials*
ILO	International Labour Organization
ILQ	*International Law Quarterly*

ILR   International Law Reports
IMT   International Military Tribunal
Int. Enc. Comp. L.   *International Encyclopaedia of Comparative Law*

International   M. O. Hudson (ed.), *International Legislation:*
   Legislation   *A Collection of Texts of Multipartite International Instruments of General Interest* (9 vols., Washington, DC, 1914–45)

Keesing   *Keesing's Record of World Events* (continuation of *Keesing's Contemporary Archives*).

Law Reports   Law Reports of Trials of War Criminals
   UNWCC   published by the United Nations War Crimes Commission
LNOJ   *League of Nations Official Journal*
LNTS   *League of Nations Treaty Series*
LQR   *Law Quarterly Review*

Nuremberg   *Trial of the Major War Criminals before the*
   Judgment   *IMT*, Nuremberg, 14 November 1945–1 October 1946, *Official Documents* (1947), vol. i, *Judgment*, 171
NY   New York
NZLR   New Zealand Law Reports

OR   Official Records

PCIJ   Permanent Court of International Justice Reports, Series A, Judgments and Orders (1922–30); Series A/B, Advisory Opinions, Judgments and Orders (1931–40); Series B, Advisory Opinions (1922–30)

RGDIP   *Revue Générale de Droit International Public*
RIAA   United Nations, *Reports of International Arbitral Awards*

SC   Security Council
Suppl.   Supplement

UKTS   *United Kingdom Treaty Series*
UNTS   *United Nations Treaty Series*

UNWCC   United Nations War Crimes Commission

Whiteman's *Digest*   M. M. Whiteman, *Digest of International Law*
                           (15 vols., Washington, DC, 1963–73)
WLR   Weekly Law Reports, England and Wales

YrbkILC   *Yearbook of the International Law Commission*
YrbkUN   *Yearbook of the United Nations*

Table of Cases

C. European Court of Human Rights

D. European Court of Justice

E. Inter-American Court of Human Rights

F. International Arbitral Awards, Decisions of Mixed Claims Commissions and Other Decisions

G. International Military Tribunals

Judgment of the IMT for the Trial of German Major War Criminals, Nuremberg, 30 September and 1 October 1946, Cmd. 6964, London: His Majesty's Stationery Office.
Trial of the Major War Criminals before the IMT, Nuremberg, 14 November– 1 October 1946, *Official Documents* (1947), vol. 1, *Judgment*, 171.
The Trial of German Major War Criminals, Opening Speeches of the Chief Prosecutors (1946), London: His Majesty's Stationery Office.
The Trial of German Major War Criminals, Speeches of the Chief Prosecutors at the Close of the Case Against the Individual Defendants (1946), London: His Majesty's Stationery Office.
The Trial of German Major War Criminals, Speeches of the Chief Prosecutors at the Close of the Case Against the Indicted Organizations (1946), London: His Majesty's Stationery Office.
Trial of German Major War Criminals, Proceedings of the IMT, pts. 1–22 (1947–9).
Transcript of the Proceedings of the IMT for the Far East, *Judgment*, text produced by the Far Eastern Commission (November 1948), Bodleian Law Library, Oxford (Internat 580 I 62.7a).
B. V. A. Röling, and C. F. Rüter (eds.), *The Tokyo Judgment: The IMT for the Far East*, 29 April 1946–12 November 1948, 2 vols. (1977).

Table of International Treaties
and Other Documents

List of International Law
Commission Documents

I. GENERAL

Survey of International Law in Relation to the Work of the ILC, Memorandum submitted by the Secretary-General, A/CN.4/1/Rev.1 (1949).

Report of the Ad Hoc Working Group of Experts Under Commission Resolution 8 (XXVII), Study Concerning the Question of Apartheid from the Point of View of International Penal Law, E/CN.4/1075 (15 February 1972).

Jus Cogens, by A. Jacovides, Outlines prepared by members of the Commission on selected topics of international law, A/CN.4/454 (1993).

II. FORMULATION OF THE NUREMBERG PRINCIPLES

Formulation of the principles recognized in the Charter of the Nuremberg Tribunal and in the Judgment of the Tribunal, A/CN.4/415, (1949) *YrbkILC*, Summary Records of 17th, 25th–29th, 31st and 35th meetings.

Report to the General Assembly, ibid. 282–3.

Report by J. Spiropoulos, Special Rapporteur, A/CN.4/22 (1950) *YrbkILC*, vol. 2, 181–95.

Report of the ILC covering its second session, ibid. 374–8 (for list of Principles).

Observations of Member States (1951) *YrbkILC*, vol. 2, 104–9.

III. DRAFT CODE OF CRIMES AGAINST THE PEACE AND SECURITY OF MANKIND

Report by J. Spiropoulos, Special Rapporteur, A/CN.4/25 (1950) *YrbkILC*, vol. 2, 253–78.

Mémorandum présenté par le Secrétariat, by V. V. Pella, A/CN.4/39, ibid. 278–362 (English translation as separate document).

Second Report by Spiropoulos, A/CN.4/44 (1951) *YrbkILC*, vol. 2, 43–69.

Report of the ILC covering the work of its third session, ibid. 133–7 (for 1951 Draft Articles).

Troisième rapport, A/CN.4/85 (1954) *YrbkILC*, vol. 2, 112–22.

Report of the ILC covering the work of its sixth session, ibid. 149–52 (for 1954 Draft Articles).

First Report on the Draft Code of Offences against the Peace and Security of

Mankind, by D. Thiam, Special Rapporteur, A/CN.4/364 (1983) *YrbkILC*, vol. 2, pt. 1, 137–52.

Analytical paper prepared pursuant to the request contained in paragraph 256 of the report of the Commission on the work of its thirty-fourth session, A/CN.4/365 (1983).

Second Report, A/CN.4/377 (1984) *YrbkILC*, vol. 2, pt. 1, 89–100.

Third Report, A/CN.4/387 (1985) *YrbkILC*, vol. 2, pt. 1, 63–83.

Fourth Report, A.CN.4/398 (1986) *YrbkILC*, vol. 2, pt. 1, 53–86.

Fifth Report, A/CN.4/404 (1987) *YrbkILC*, vol. 2, pt. 1, 1–10.

Sixth Report, A/CN.4/411 (1988) *YrbkILC*, vol. 2, pt. 1, 197–204.

Seventh Report, A/CN.4/419 (1989) *YrbkILC*, vol. 2, pt. 1, 81–90.

Eighth Report, A/CN.4/430 and Add.1 (1990) *YrbkILC*, vol. 2, pt. 1, 27–39.

Ninth Report, A/CN.4/435 and Add.1 (1991) *YrbkILC*, vol. 2, pt. 1, 37–44.

Report of the ILC on the work of its forty-third session, ibid. pt. 2, 79–107 (1991 Draft Code, text and commentary).

Comments and observations of governments on the Draft Code adopted on first reading by the ILC at its forty-third session, 1991, A/CN.4/448 (1993).

Twelfth Report by Thiam, A/CN.4/460 (1994).

Thirteenth Report, A/CN.4/466 (1995).

Titles and texts of articles on the Draft Code of Crimes against the Peace and Security of Mankind adopted by the ILC at its forty-eighth session (1996), A/CN.4/L.532.

IV. INTERNATIONAL CRIMINAL COURT

Historical Survey of the Question of International Criminal Jurisdiction. Memorandum submitted by the Secretary-General to the International Law Commission, A/CN.4/7/Rev.1 (1949).

Report to the General Assembly (1949) *YrbkILC*, 283.

'Question of International Criminal Jurisdiction', Report by R. J. Alfaro, Special Rapporteur, A/CN.4/15 (1950) *YrbkILC*, vol. 2, 1–18.

Report by E. Sandstrøm, Special Rapporteur, A/CN.4/20, ibid, 18–23.

Tenth Report on the Draft Code of Crimes against the Peace and Security of Mankind by D. Thiam, Special Rapporteur, A/CN.4/442 (1992) *YrbkILC*, vol. 2, pt. 1, 51–8.

Eleventh Report, A/CN.4/449 (1993).

Report of the ILC on the work of its forty-sixth session (1994) *YrbkILC*, vol. 2, pt. 2, 18–87 (1994 Draft Statute).

Comments of governments on the report of the Working Group on a draft statute for an ICC, A/CN.4/458 (1994).

Report of the ILC on the work of its forty-sixth session, 1994. Topical summary of the discussion held in the Sixth Committee of the GA during its forty-ninth session, prepared by the Secretariat, A/CN.4/464/Add.1 (1995).

V. LAW OF TREATIES

Second Report on the Law of Treaties, by Sir Humphrey Waldock, Special
Rapporteur, A/CN.4/156 and Adds. 1–3 (1963) *YrbkILC*, vol. 2, 36–94.
Report of the ILC on the work of its eighteenth session (1966) *YrbkILC*, vol.
2, 177–274 (draft articles with commentary).

VI. STATE RESPONSIBILITY

'International Responsibility', Report by F. V. Garcia-Amador, Special
Rapporteur, A/CN.4/96 (1956) *YrbkILC*, vol. 2, 173–231.
Second Report, A/CN.4/106 (1957) *YrbkILC*, vol. 2, 104–30.
Third Report, A/CN.4/111 (1958) *YrbkILC*, vol. 2, 47–73.
Fourth Report, A/CN.4/119 (1959) *YrbkILC*, vol. 2, 1–36.
Fifth Report, A/CN.4/125 (1960) *YrbkILC*, vol. 2, 41–68.
Sixth Report, A/CN.4/134 and Add.1 (1961) *YrbkILC*, vol. 2, 1–54.
Summary of the discussions in various UN organs and the resulting deci-
sions: working paper prepared by the Secretariat, A/CN.4/165 (1964)
YrbkILC, vol. 2, 125–32, and Supplement (1969) *YrbkILC*, vol. 2, 114–24.
Note by R. Ago, Special Rapporteur (1967) *YrbkILC*, vol. 2, 325–7.
Digest of the decisions of international tribunals relating to state responsi-
bility, prepared by the Secretariat, A/CN.4/169, ibid. 132–71, and Supple-
ment A/CN.4/208, ibid. 101–13.
First Report by Ago, A/CN.4/217 and Add.1 (1969) *YrbkILC*, vol. 2, 125–56.
Second Report, A/CN.4/233 (1970) *YrbkILC*, vol. 2, 177–97.
Third Report, A/CN.4/246 and Adds. 1–3 (1971) *YrbkILC*, vol. 2, 199–274.
Fourth Report, A/CN.4/264 and Add.1 (1972) *YrbkILC*, vol. 2, 71–160.
Fifth Report, A/CN.4/291 and Adds. 1–2 (1976) *YrbkILC*, vol. 2, pt. 1, 3–54.
Report of the ILC on the work of its twenty-eighth session, ibid. pt. 2,
69–122 (Draft Articles, text and commentary).
Sixth Report by Ago, A/CN.4/302 and Adds. 1–3 (1977) *YrbkILC*, vol. 2, pt.
1, 3–43.
Seventh Report, A/CN.4/307 and Adds. 1–2 (1978) *YrbkILC*, vol. 2, pt. 1,
31–243.
Eighth Report, A/CN.4/318 and Adds. 1–4 (1979) *YrbkILC*, vol. 2, pt. 1,
3–66, and Adds. 5–7 (1980) *YrbkILC*, vol. 2, pt. 1, 13–70.
Observations and comments of governments on Part I, A/CN.4/328 and
Adds. 1–4 (1980) *YrbkILC*, vol. 2, pt. 1, 87–129.
Preliminary report on the content, forms and degrees of international
responsibility (Part 2 of the draft articles on state responsibility) by W.
Riphagen, Special Rapporteur, A/CN.4/330, ibid. 107–29.
Comments of governments on Part I, A/CN.4/342 and Adds. 1–4 (1981)
YrbkILC, vol. 2, pt. 1, 71–8.

Second Report by Riphagen, A/CN.4/344, ibid. 79–101.

Comments of governments on Part I, A/CN.4/351 and Adds. 1–3 (1982) *YrbkILC*, vol. 2, pt. 1, 15–21.

Third Report by Riphagen, A/CN.4/354 and Adds. 1–2, ibid. 22–50.

Fourth Report, A/CN.4/366 and Add.1 (1983) *YrbkILC*, vol. 2, pt. 1, 3–24.

Fifth Report, A/CN.4/380 (1984) *YrbkILC*, vol. 2, pt. 1, 1–4.

Sixth Report, A/CN.4/389 (1985) *YrbkILC*, vol. 2, pt. 1, 3–19.

Seventh Report, A/CN.4/397 and Add. 1 (1986) *YrbkILC*, vol. 2, pt. 1, 1–19.

Comments and observations of governments, A/CN.4/414 (1988) *YrbkILC*, vol. 2, pt. 1, 1–5.

Preliminary report on state responsibility by G. Arangio-Ruiz, Special Rapporteur, A/CN.4/416 and Add. 1, ibid. 6–43.

Second Report, A/CN.4/425 and Add. 1 (1989) *YrbkILC*, vol. 2, pt. 1, 1–58.

Third Report, A/CN.4/440 and Add. 1 (1991) *YrbkILC*, vol. 2, pt. 1, 1–35.

Fourth Report, A/CN.4/444 and Adds. 1–4 (1992) *YrbkILC*, vol. 2, pt. 1, 1–49.

Fifth Report, A/CN.4/453 and Adds. 1–3 (1993).

Report of the ILC on the work of its forty-fifth session (1993), GAOR, 48th session, A/48/10.

Topical summary of the discussion held in the Sixth Committee of the GA during its 48th session prepared by the Secretariat, A/CN.4/457 (1993).

Sixth Report by Arangio-Ruiz, A/CN.4/461 and Adds. 1–2 (1994).

Seventh Report, A/CN.4/469 and Adds. 1–2 (1995).

Report of the ILC on the work of its forty-seventh session (1995), GAOR, 50th session, A/50/10, A/50/402.

Eighth Report, A/CN.4/476 and Add. 1 (1996).

Part One of the draft articles on state responsibility as adopted by the Commission on first reading at its thirty-second session in 1980 and text and titles of Parts Two and Three of the draft articles on state responsibility as provisionally adopted by the Drafting Committee on first reading at the forty-eighth session in 1996, A/CN.4/L.524 (1996).

Comments and observations received from governments, A/CN.4/488 (1998).

First Report on state responsibility by J. Crawford, Special Rapporteur, A/CN.4/490 and Adds. 1–3 (1998).

Report of the ILC on the work of its fiftieth session (1998), GAOR, 53rd session, A/53/10.

Topical summary of the discussion held in the Sixth Committee of the GA during its fifty-third session prepared by the Secretariat, A/CN.4/496 (1999).

Second Report by Crawford, A/CN.4.498, and Adds. 1–4 (1999).

Historical Introduction to the Concept of State Criminality

I

International Criminal Responsibility
in the Two World Wars

1. INTRODUCTION

The universal sense of mankind recognizes that in the present state of civilization peace is the normal condition of the world's peoples and war is the abnormal condition.[1]

In the years preceding the outbreak of the First World War, the sentiment that war was inevitable began to change as a liberal peace movement gained influence. The work of Henry Dunant inspired the adoption of a series of conventions regulating the conduct of hostilities;[2] societies devoted to peace, such as the Inter-Parliamentary Union, evolved in Western nations; and Alfred Nobel established a prize for those who made a significant contribution to peace. The peace movement proclaimed an idea that had been prominent since the Enlightenment of the eighteenth century, namely that methods could be devised of restricting or even abolishing war. The 'solution to war' appeared to lie in the strengthening of international law, and in particular in the notion of international criminal responsibility.

At the outbreak of the First World War in 1914, international law permitted each sovereign state to be the sole judge of its motives or justification for engaging in war. 'International law has ... no alternative but to accept war, independently of the justice of its origin, as a relation which the parties to it may set up if they choose, and to busy itself only in regulating the effects of the relation.'[3] This view marked the abandonment of the notion that wars may be just or unjust which goes back to ancient times, when the question was essentially a theological matter. The Just War (*bellum justum*) theory, as developed by writers such as St Augustine and Grotius, stated that war was illegal unless undertaken for a 'just cause', which generally involved a wrong received or a right illegally denied. Since the end of the First World War, resort to armed force

---

[1] C. Phillipson, *International Law and the Great War* (1915), 2.

[2] The first of these was the 1864 Geneva Convention for the Amelioration of the Condition of the Wounded in Armies in the Field. Efforts were made to codify the laws of war at the Hague Conference of 1899 which was convened by Tsar Nicholas II. It was also agreed to establish the machinery of a Permanent Court for the voluntary settlement of disputes between states by arbitration, but this machinery was never invoked. The laws of war were further codified at the Hague Conference of 1907. Proposals for obligatory arbitration were discussed but were not accepted.　　　　　　　　　　　　[3] W. E. Hall, *International Law*, 8th edn. (1924), 82.

in international relations has required a legal justification, and the view-point has been advanced that a war of aggression is a matter of grave international delinquency.

Traditionally, international law has been concerned with the activities of states, and it would seem that the concept of illegal war was at first discussed primarily in relation to the collective responsibility of the state. During the First and Second World Wars, crimes of a gravity never before equalled were committed and condoned by the state, and the intangibility of the state bureaucratic apparatus gave rise to the question of the criminal responsibility of the physical persons representing the state and acting in its name. In his report of 7 June 1945 to the US President, the US Chief Prosecutor of the German Major War Criminals, Justice Robert Jackson, stated that there can no longer be accepted

the paradox that legal responsibility should be the least where the power is the greatest. We stand on the principle of responsible government declared some three centuries ago to King James by Lord Chief Justice Coke, who proclaimed that even a king is still 'under God and the law'.[4]

The criminal responsibility of states, individuals, governments, and organizations were all notions that received considerable attention in the aftermath of each of the two world wars and three possible systems were advocated: first, that of the exclusive responsibility of states; second, that of the cumulative responsibility of states and individuals; and finally, that of the exclusive responsibility of individuals.

2. THE FIRST WORLD WAR

(a) The Treaty of Versailles and the Plan for Postwar Prosecutions

On the first day of the First World War, Wilhelm II wrote in a letter to the Austrian Emperor, Francis Joseph:

Everything must be drowned in fire and blood. It is essential to kill men and women, children and old men, not to leave standing a single house or a single tree. By these terrorist methods, the only methods capable of frightening such a degenerate people as the French, the war will be ended in less than two months; while if I take considerations of humanity into account, the war will last several years.[5]

The horrors of the First World War reawoke a general feeling of disillusionment and scepticism regarding the value and efficacy of international law as

---

[4] Report to the President from Justice Robert H. Jackson, Chief Counsel for the US in the Prosecution of Axis War Criminals, 7 June 1945; (July 1945) 39 *AJIL Suppl.* 178, 182.

[5] Quoted in A. N. Trainin, *Hitlerite Responsibility under Criminal Law* (1944), 18.

a means of preventing and controlling wars. During the hostilities, Phillipson wrote: 'The main problem to which men and nations should devote themselves is how to fortify [international law] by such potent sanctions as will make its violations not merely dishonourable, but unprofitable to an offending member of the community of States.'[6] The situation provided an opportunity to test the worth of many rules, and revealed the existence of a variety of problems for which international law offered no solution.

During the course of the First World War, the Allied governments failed to reach agreement concerning postwar prosecutions. They only acted together on this matter once, when on 28 May 1915 a joint declaration was issued threatening to punish Turkish officials responsible for the massacre of Armenians in the Ottoman Empire.[7] In any event, a crushing defeat of the enemy did not seem imminent and the material objectives of the war overshadowed ambitious schemes of reform. As soon as victory seemed likely, the Allied Powers renewed their earlier pledges to punish war criminals, and when Germany asked for an armistice on 4 October 1918, the French Government declared:

Conduct which is equally contrary to international law and the fundamental principles of all human civilization will not go unpunished . . . the authors and directors of these crimes will be held responsible morally, judicially, and financially. They will seek in vain to escape the inexorable expiation which awaits them.[8]

The Allies met with some difficulties when they attempted to translate policy into law at the Paris Peace Conference which convened on 18 January 1919. A Commission on the Responsibility of the Authors of the War and the Enforcement of Penalties was created on 25 January 1919 to study questions concerning the origins of the war, and the establishment of a tribunal to try those accused of committing crimes. After considerable disagreement, the Commission presented its report to the Peace Conference on 29 March 1919.[9] It had been necessary to consider whether launching a war of aggression was an international crime and whether a state's leaders could be held personally culpable. Allied citizens had looked to the Napoleonic precedent of 1815 and argued that Wilhelm II deserved to be punished in a similar way. Napoleon was found to be an 'Enemy and Disturber of the tranquillity of the World' and banished to St Helena, where he was imprisoned as a preventive measure in the interest of preserving the peace.[10] But in dealing with the

---

[6] Phillipson, *International Law and the Great War*, vi.

[7] See UNWCC, *History of the United Nations War Crimes Commission and the Development of the Laws of War* (1948), 35.   [8] *The Times*, 7 Oct. 1918; *New York Times*, 5 Oct. 1918.

[9] Printed in (1920) 14 *AJIL* 95.

[10] The decision to banish Napoleon was made by the British Government, and on 2 Aug. 1815 a treaty was drawn up between Great Britain and the Great Powers authorizing his imprisonment. There was no attempt to try Napoleon for waging war. See I. Brownlie, *International Law and the Use of Force by States* (1963), 51.

Kaiser, the Allied leaders proposed to establish a new precedent employing judicial institutions and framing policy in terms of criminal law.

It was the bold intention of Part VII of the Treaty of Versailles entitled 'Sanctions' to deal with the question of the criminal responsibility of Wilhelm II and his accomplices. Article 227 states:

The Allied and Associated Powers publicly arraign William II of Hohenzollern, formerly German Emperor, for a supreme offence against international morality and the sanctity of treaties. A special tribunal will be constituted to try the accused, thereby assuring him the guarantees essential to the right of defence . . . In its decision the tribunal will be guided by the highest motives of international policy, with a view to vindicating the solemn obligations of international undertakings and the validity of international morality. It will be its duty to fix the punishment which it considers should be imposed. The Allied and Associated Powers will address a request to the Government of the Netherlands for the surrender to them of the ex-Emperor in order that he may be put on trial.

Articles 228 and 229 contained German recognition of the right of the Allies to bring to trial before national or international military tribunals persons accused of having committed acts in violation of the laws and customs of war (of which the Commission had listed thirty-two categories),[11] and an undertaking by the German Government to hand such persons over to the Allies for trial. Similar provisions to those of the Treaty of Versailles were inserted in the Peace Treaty of St Germain, concluded with Austria, and the Treaty of Neuilly, concluded with Bulgaria. The Treaty of Sèvres, which completed the system by anticipating that those responsible for the massacres committed during the war in Turkey would be brought before an international tribunal, never came into force. The Treaty of Lausanne, which replaced the Treaty of Sèvres, omitted all mention of war crimes, and was accompanied by a 'Declaration of Amnesty' for all offences between 1 August 1914 and 20 November 1922.[12]

The Commission had concluded that a war of aggression could not be considered an act directly contrary to positive law entailing personal responsibility. However, it stated in its 'Conclusions': 'It is desirable that for the future penal sanctions should be provided for such grave outrages against the elementary principles of international law.'[13] Articles 227–9 of the Versailles Treaty were evidence of changes in moral, political, and legal attitudes towards international violence and it has been argued by Kelsen[14] that the true reason for demanding the trial of the Kaiser was that he was viewed as the main author of the war, and resorting to this war was considered to be a crime. In Kelsen's opinion, Article 227 speaks of 'an offence against interna-

---

[11] (1920) 14 *AJIL* 114–15. See also *History of the UNWCC*, 34–5. Crimes against humanity were not included in the list.   [12] Ibid. 45.
[13] (1920) 14 *AJIL* 120.   [14] H. Kelsen, *Peace Through Law* (1944), 89.

tional morality' in order to avoid the phrase 'a violation of international law'; but, he argues, if a legal norm (one established by an international treaty) attaches punishment to an offence against morality, which is to be inflicted upon the offender by a court, the offence assumes *ex post facto* the character of a violation of law. Alternatively, the process could be viewed as an attempt to convict a state in the person of its titular head,[15] or even as a venture forced upon the Allies by public opinion which they never intended to carry out. The main difficulty was that the proposed trial lacked a firm legal basis, but Article 227 did prove to have some value as a precedent.

(b) The Failure of Postwar Prosecutions and the Leipzig Trials[16]

The provisions of the peace treaties relating to postwar prosecutions had no practical outcome. The Allies failed to come up with an effective solution in Paris for arranging the surrender of the Kaiser by the Netherlands. Allied disunity caused delay, and when a formal demand for the delivery of the Kaiser was prepared on 15 January 1920, Dutch resistance was expected. On 23 January 1920 the Dutch declared their refusal to hand over the Kaiser on the basis that the Netherlands had always been a land of refuge for the vanquished in international conflicts. A second formal demand for the Kaiser was made on 14 February 1920, and the Allies made it clear that at the very least they expected precautionary measures to be taken in keeping the ex-Emperor far away from the scene of his crimes. On 16 March 1920, Queen Wilhelmina interned the Kaiser in the province of Utrecht as an 'alien dangerous to the public tranquility'.[17] The Dutch claimed that such a measure was unprecedented and showed how far they had gone to meet Allied demands. Despite a feeling in Allied countries that justice had not been served, the British Prime Minister, Lloyd George, dismissed as futile the idea of the French Prime Minister, Millerand, that proceedings could be conducted in the Kaiser's absence.[18]

Attempts to organize the trials of Wilhelm's accomplices were also in vain. On 3 February 1920, Millerand sent Baron Lersner, the President of the German Peace Delegation in Paris, a letter giving a list of persons who should be handed over to the Allied Powers according to Article 228 of the Versailles Treaty. In all, the Allied Powers demanded that Germany should hand over

---

[15] See Brownlie, *International Law and the Use of Force by States*, 53.

[16] See generally J. F. Willis, *Prologue to Nuremberg* (1982), 98–147, and C. Mullins, *The Leipzig Trials* (1921).

[17] Graham to Curzon, 17 Mar. 1920, *Documents on British Foreign Policy*, 1919–39, 1st series, ix (1960), 716–17. For the text of the decree of internment, see Willis, *Prologue to Nuremburg*, 111.   [18] Ibid. 112.

854 persons, including such eminent figures as Admiral von Tirpitz, Hindenburg, General von Mackensen, former Reich Chancellor von Bethmann-Hollweg, Ludendorff, Crown Prince Rupprecht of Bavaria, and the Duke of Württemberg. A total of several thousand people had originally been proposed, but it had occurred to certain members of the British and French Governments that there were political reasons why the list should be reduced. In Lord Birkenhead's view, the vindication of the 'moral law of the world'[19] made it highly desirable that a certain number of those who had committed atrocities should be punished, and it was felt that the Germans might hand over a smaller number willingly even if they would not consent to handing over a large number. The result was an arbitrary curtailment of the list.

Despite the fact that Lersner had previously received a categorical instruction to accept and forward to Berlin a Note of this kind if it were presented, he returned the letter to Millerand. Meanwhile a movement against the surrender of war criminals was developing in Germany. A law adopted on 13 December 1919 provided for the trial before the Supreme Court at Leipzig of persons accused of war crimes. Interested powers were invited to send observers to attend the trial. The Allies ultimately agreed to this compromise on 17 February 1920.

It was not until 23 May 1921 that the Leipzig court heard its first case. Sergeant Karl Heynen, charged with the brutal treatment of British prisoners of war in the Münster camp, was sentenced to ten months' imprisonment, with a special British mission led by Sir Ernest Pollock as witness.[20] General Stenger, accused of giving an order for the shooting of French prisoners, was acquitted on the ground that no written instructions for the execution of the order were discovered, despite it being established beyond a doubt that such an order had been issued. In protest, France followed the Belgian example and recalled its mission from Leipzig. In general, the war crimes trials at Leipzig proved unsatisfactory to the Allies, with most trials resulting in acquittals despite strong evidence of guilt. Those who were convicted faced disproportionately low sentences, and the German press and public judged all its war criminals to be heroes.

The British gradually lost interest in the issue of punishing war criminals, but Prime Minister Briand was persuaded by French public opinion to establish an Inter-Allied Commission on the Leipzig Trials which eventually met on 6–7 January 1922.[21] The Commission recommended that the Allies repudiate the compromise arrangement for German trials and require the surrender of the accused to Allied tribunals under Articles 228–30 of the Versailles Treaty.[22] Further trials then took place at Leipzig in an effort by Chancellor

---

[19] *Documents on British Foreign Policy*, 1919–39, 1st series, ii (1948), 886.
[20] (1923–4) 2 *Annual Digest*, 431; (1922) 16 *AJIL* 633.
[21] See Willis, *Prologue to Nuremburg*, 139–40.   [22] Ibid. 140.

Wirth to forestall new Allied demands. But at a meeting of the Conference of Ambassadors on 26 July 1922, Poincaré, who replaced Briand, put forward a policy of ending the German trials in order to place Germany in breach of the Versailles Treaty. Since the British were opposed to any explicit recognition of a German default or any application of sanctions, it was agreed to send a joint Allied Note to Germany criticizing the trials and reserving all formal rights under Articles 228–30.[23] This resulted in the prosecution and trial *par contumace* by the French of more than 1,200 Germans by December 1924. The Belgians tried approximately eighty cases. The Locarno Treaty of 1925 improved relations with Germany; however, the French policy of denying visas to condemned Germans continued until 1929.[24]

(c) War Guilt and Postwar Reparations

Responsibility for the First World War was found to rest first on Germany and Austria, secondly on Turkey and Bulgaria. This accusation was not included in the Peace Treaty of Versailles. However, Article 231 of the Treaty, designed to justify a financial claim for all damage caused to the Allies by Germany's aggression, was viewed by many Germans as a 'war-guilt' clause: [25]

The Allied and Associated Governments affirm and Germany accepts the responsibility of Germany and her Allies for causing all the loss and damage to which the Allied and Associated Governments and their nationals have been subjected as a consequence of the war imposed upon them by the aggression of Germany and her Allies.

Similar clauses appeared in Article 177 of the Treaty with Austria and Article 161 of the Treaty with Hungary.[26] The inclusion of a 'war-guilt' clause in the Paris Settlement marked a break from the practice of inserting amnesty clauses in peace treaties which avoided drawing a distinction between victors and vanquished.[27]

It then became necessary to determine the precise legal consequences of war guilt, and in the peace treaties following the First World War there was a clear attempt to link the obligation to pay reparations with responsibility for waging aggressive war. As early as 1914, Asquith had declared: 'We shall never sheathe the sword . . . until Belgium recovers in full measure all and more than all that she has sacrificed.'[28] Lloyd George has argued that such an indemnity, involving more than mere restoration, contained a punitive element.[29] When the war was nearing its conclusion, armistice negotiations

---

[23] Ibid. 141–2.   [24] Ibid. 142–5.
[25] See P. M. Burnett, *Reparation at the Paris Peace Conference* (1940), i, p. xi: 'In the light of subsequent developments it may be that this Article was the most important single article in the Treaty.'
[26] 112 *British and Foreign State Papers* 317, 384, and 113 *British and Foreign State Papers* 486, 539 respectively.   [27] See A. Osiander, *The States System of Europe 1640–1990* (1994), 299.
[28] D. Lloyd George, *The Truth about the Peace Treaties*, i (1938), 440.   [29] Ibid.

took place on the basis of President Wilson's speeches in 1918 and his 'Fourteen Points'. The Fourteen Points made no direct reference to reparation, and in his speech of 11 February 1918 Wilson declared that there would be no 'punitive indemnities'.[30] While these may have been his own sentiments, he treated them as the principles of the 'court of mankind'.[31] Nevertheless, when the Fourteen Points came to be interpreted in the American Commentary of 28 October 1918, it was stated that reparation was due for all damage caused by acts contrary to international law, such as the illegal invasion of Belgium, which was 'illegitimate and therefore all the consequences of that act are of the same character'.[32] Secretary of State Lansing transmitted the Allied conditions for the acceptance of the armistice to Germany on 5 November 1918 in the form of a memorandum which included the following qualification:

Further, in the conditions of peace, laid down in his address to Congress of 8 January, 1918, the President declared that invaded territories must be restored as well as evacuated and freed. The Allied Governments feel that no doubt ought to be allowed to exist as to what this provision implies: By it they understand that compensation will be made by Germany for all damage done to the civilian population of the Allies and their property by the aggression of Germany by land, by sea, and from the air.[33]

It is notable that a reference was made to 'aggression'. This was to ensure that all the Allies would receive reparation rather than just those who were the victim of an invasion, and an affirmation of German war guilt was not intended. But it was clear that certain of the Allies wished to find moral and legal bases for the obligation to make reparation, apart from the armistice agreement. There was talk both of a moral and of an equitable responsibility of Germany for the consequences of aggression, and also of a legal principle requiring reparation to be made for war damage.

Germany asserted that it would only accept the obligation to make reparation independently of the question of responsibility for the war,[34] but the Allies replied in a Note of 20 May 1919 that: 'It is only possible to conceive of such an obligation if its origin and cause is the responsibility of the author of the damage'.[35] Temperley states that Article 231 imposed a moral and not a financial responsibility on Germany,[36] and Article 232 acknowledged that Germany did not have the resources to make reparation for all war damage. The British view was that although the indemnity which Germany and its allies should in justice pay was the total cost of the war to the Allied Powers, Germany would only be required to pay to the upmost limit of her capacity. Thus, the moral obligation extended further than the legal obligation.

---

[30] H. W. V. Temperley (ed.), *A History of the Peace Conference of Paris*, ii (1920), 43, n. 1.
[31] Ibid.   [32] Burnett, *Reparation*, 3–4.
[33] G. A. Finch, 'The Peace Conference of Paris', (1919) 13 *AJIL* 159, 164.
[34] A. M. Luckau, *The German Delegation at the Paris Peace Conference* (1941), 241–2.
[35] Ibid. 254.   [36] Temperley, *History*, 73.

At the time of the First World War the legal effects of waging a war of aggression were unclear, although there was a general desire to punish Germany. Eagleton states that 'world opinion was rapidly swinging round to the idea of penalizing the state which starts a war by attacking' another state.[37] In a discussion in the Imperial War Cabinet on the question of reparations, Sir Robert Borden 'agreed that it would be for the peace of the world that a Power which had broken that peace should be punished'.[38] In his election statement Lloyd George proclaimed:

You may depend upon it that the first consideration in the minds of the Allies will be the interests of the people upon whom Germany has made war, *and not the interests of the German people who have been guilty of this crime against humanity.*[39]

Despite the fact that the legal basis for translating policy into practice was not in place, the Allies held Germany responsible for waging a war of aggression—an act which was increasingly being thought of as an international crime. The attempt to obtain reparation from Germany to its upmost capacity, together with the plan to try Kaiser Wilhelm, appears to go beyond liability to pay compensation for ordinary wrongful acts.

(d) The Covenant of the League of Nations

The 1919 Covenant of the League of Nations imposed certain limitations upon resort to war and was intended to bring an end to the anarchy of international politics. At the time, the idea had been developing that a war of aggression affected not only the state attacked, but all other states concerned in the maintenance of international order. By the time the League of Nations was established, the 'right' of third parties to give their support to the country unjustly attacked had become a duty. Article 16 of the Covenant states:

Should any Member of the League resort to war in disregard of its covenants under Articles 12, 13 or 15, it shall *ipso facto* be deemed to have committed an act of war against all other Members of the League.

The latter:

. . . undertake immediately to subject it to the severance of all trade or financial relations, the prohibition of all intercourse between their nationals and the nationals of the covenant-breaking state, and the prevention of all financial, commercial or personal intercourse between the nationals of the covenant-breaking state and the nationals of any other state, whether a member of the League or not.

Article 16 also provides for other serious sanctions:

It shall be the duty of the Council in such case to recommend to the several Governments concerned what effective military, naval or air force the Members of the League shall severally contribute to the armed forces to be used to protect the covenants of the League.

---

[37] 'An Attempt to Define Aggression', (1950) *International Conciliation*, no. 264, 583, 589.
[38] See Lloyd George, *Truth*, 479.   [39] Ibid. 467 (emphasis added).

The question arose in the literature whether resort to war, contrary to the League Covenant, represented a crime, and whether the sanctions provided by Article 16 represented the punishment for that crime.[40] An affirmative answer was given by Wehberg, who was of the opinion that:

> Les mesures économiques et militaires qu'il convient de prendre contre un gouvernement qui a commencé une guerre défendue ne doivent pas être seulement une sorte de garantie pour l'État attaqué; elles doivent en même temps assurer la punition de l'agresseur.[41]

Wehberg asserted that the elements of Article 16 rested on the idea of punishment for a crime. A similar interpretation was offered by Bourquin, who argued that Article 16 provided for a 'game of sanctions' amounting to

> . . . le déclenchement d'une reaction sociale, réaction d'ordre économique imposée en principe à tous les membres de la société et qui tend . . . à réaliser le 'blocus' de l'État coupable, réaction . . . d'ordre militaire, enfin, expulsion éventuelle de la Société, prononcée par le Conseil, à charge du membre en rupture de Pacte.[42]

Cohn[43] proposed that the purport of Article 16 was in the nature of criminal law, although he went on to argue that Article 16 was inadequate to prevent future wars since its elements were so ambiguous.[44] In particular, he pointed out that while the presupposition of a penalty in criminal law was the guilt of the person to be punished, Article 16 did not explain which elements should be decisive for determining the guilt of the covenant-breaking state and did not deal with the problem of collective guilt. Consequently, the idea of punishment which he argued was inherent in Article 16 could not be applied. Kunz suggested that Article 16 'présuppose le délit du recours illégal à la guerre et stipule des sanctions',[45] while Brueck went so far as to say: 'Article 16 contains a whole system of sanctions. It is the "criminal code" of the League of Nations.'[46] Brownlie, on the other hand, has suggested that Article 16 provided for police measures rather than modes of punishment.[47] While this is probably true, Article 16 would seem to have contained at least a punitive element.[48] Whatever the possibilities contained in Article 16, they were never comprehensively put into effect. This was in the interest of keep-

---

[40] See Trainin, *Hitlerite Responsibility*, 30–1.

[41] H. Wehberg, 'La Problème de la mise de la guerre hors la loi', (1928–IV) 24 Hague *Recueil* 146, 166.

[42] M. Bourquin, 'Règles générales du droit de la paix', (1931–I) 35 Hague *Recueil* 1, 181.

[43] G. Cohn, *Kriegsverhütung und Schuldfrage* (1931), 48 ff.

[44] See review by U. Kersten, (1931–2) *Harvard Law Rev.*, vol. 45, 1286–8.

[45] J. L. Kunz, 'L'Article XI du Pacte de la Société de Nations', (1932–I) Hague *Recueil* 678, 758.

[46] O. Bruck, *Les Sanctions en droit international* (1933), 101; quoted in Trainin, *Hitlerite Responsibility*, 31.   [47] *International Law and the Use of Force by States*, 153.

[48] See also L. Kopelmanas, 'The Problem of Aggression and the Prevention of War', (1937) 31 *AJIL* 244, 251–2, esp. 251, n. 28.

ing the peace which might be contradicted by the launching of a war of sanction, and states were also keen to protect their own economies from the effects of the application of sanctions.

(e) State Practice 1920–1939[49]

Article I of the draft Treaty of Mutual Assistance[50] sponsored by the League of Nations in 1923 stated that 'aggressive war is an international crime' and that the parties would 'undertake that no one of them will be guilty of its commission'. About half the twenty-nine states to which the draft Treaty was submitted were in favour of accepting the text; the principal objection lay in the difficulty of defining acts which would constitute aggression rather than in any doubt as to the perceived criminality of aggressive war.

The Preamble to the League of Nations 1924 Protocol for the Pacific Settlement of International Disputes (Geneva Protocol), after 'recognizing the solidarity of the members of the international community', declared that 'a war of aggression constitutes a violation of this solidarity and is an international crime'.[51] The Protocol advanced the formula that if a state went to war rather than accepting compulsory arbitration of a dispute, it would be considered an aggressor and face sanctions imposed by members of the League, unless the League unanimously decided otherwise. The Protocol did not receive the ratifications necessary for it to come into effect, but all forty-eight members of the League recommended its ratification in the Assembly and it was signed by nineteen states. Both the draft Treaty of Mutual Assistance[52] and the Geneva Protocol[53] provided for the payment of reparation by the aggressor. In the latter it was stipulated that the expense of repressing aggression, as well as reparation for loss or damage suffered by individuals, 'shall be borne by the aggressor up to the extreme limit of its capacity'. Given that both instruments describe aggression as an international crime, it could be argued that the payment of reparation to the limit of a state's capacity is part of the punishment for the crime. This interpretation is consistent with the debate on reparations following the First World War.[54]

In 1925 the League Assembly adopted a resolution denouncing aggression

---

[49] The developments referred to in this section were cited in the Nuremberg Judgment as evidence of state practice supportive of the contention that aggressive war was an international crime. See *Nuremburg Judgment*, 219–22.

[50] *LNOJ* 1923, Special Suppl. no. 16; see Eagleton, 'Attempt', 620.

[51] *LNOJ* 1924, Special Suppl. no. 24, Annex 18, 136–40; (1922–4) 2 *International Legislation*, no. 128, 1378.   [52] Article 10.

[53] Article 15.   [54] See section 2(c) above.

as an international crime.[55] Subsequently, at its Eighth Assembly in 1927, a further resolution was adopted unanimously by the League:

(1) That all wars of aggression are, and shall always be, prohibited.
(2) That every pacific means must be employed to settle disputes of every description, which may arise between states.

The Assembly declares that the states Members of the League are under an obligation to conform to these principles.[56]

Once again, in the Preamble, a war of aggression was stigmatized as an international crime. Brownlie argues that this resolution could be understood to create legal obligations for members of the League.[57] Other organizations took similar action. The Pan American Conference, for example, meeting at Havana in 1928, affirmed that 'war of aggression constitutes an international crime against the human species'.[58]

In 1927, the French Prime Minister, Briand, proposed that the US and France agree to outlaw resort to war in their disputes. In his reply, the US Secretary of State, Kellogg, suggested that a multilateral agreement would make a more significant contribution to world peace. In 1928, the Covenant of the League of Nations was supplemented by the General Treaty for the Renunciation of War (Kellogg–Briand Pact).[59] Its aim was to achieve a comprehensive prohibition of war as an instrument of national policy. Article I states:

The High Contracting Parties solemnly declare in the names of their respective peoples that they condemn recourse to war for the solution of international controversies, and renounce it as an instrument of national policy in their relations with one another.

Under Article II it is agreed 'that the settlement or solution of all disputes or conflicts of whatever nature or of whatever origin they may be, which may arise among them, shall never be sought except by pacific means'. The background to the adoption of the Pact makes it clear that the negotiators and signatories intended a legal obligation to be the result, and no state subsequently challenged this aspect.[60] The Pact had a significant effect on state practice; it was reaffirmed in subsequent agreements and became an issue in some subsequent conflicts.[61] It seems that a customary rule limiting the use of force had emerged by 1939. The dec-

[55] 25 Sept. 1925, Resolutions of the Sixth Assembly, 21.
[56] 24 Sept. 1927, *LNOJ* 1927, Special Suppl. no. 53, 22 (Annex 9).
[57] *International Law and the Use of Force by States*, 72.
[58] Sixième Conférence Internationale Américaine, Acte Finale (Havana, 1928), 178; see (1928) 22 *AJIL* 356–7.   [59] *UKTS* 29 (1929); 94 *LNTS* 57.
[60] See Brownlie, *International Law and the Use of Force by States*, 82–3.   [61] Ibid. 76–80.

larations that aggressive war was an international crime could only have referred to state responsibility during this period, even though the precise application of international law in this field had yet to be worked out.[62] Virtually the whole of the international community at that time (sixty-three states) were bound by the Treaty when war broke out in 1939.

3. THE SECOND WORLD WAR

(a) Allied Declarations and Warnings, and Public Opinion

Beginning early in the Second World War various declarations and warnings revealed the intention of the Allies to punish those guilty of committing atrocities. On 25 October 1941, while the US was still neutral, President Franklin Roosevelt called attention to the acts of the Nazis in occupied territories.[63] Prime Minister Winston Churchill was quick to associate the British Government with Roosevelt's statement, and added that retribution should be one of the major purposes of the war.[64]

In Molotov's first Note of 25 November 1941, informing all governments with which the Soviet Union had diplomatic relations of the atrocities committed by German troops, he pointed out that the Soviet Government held the 'criminal Hitlerite Government of Germany'[65] responsible for the inhuman acts of the German military and civil authorities.

The first Inter-Allied Declaration on war crimes was signed at St James's Palace, London, on 13 January 1942 by the governments in exile of Belgium, Czechoslovakia, France, Greece, Luxemburg, Netherlands, Norway, Poland, and Yugoslavia. The signatories pointed out

that international law, and in particular the Convention signed at the Hague in 1907 regarding the laws and customs of land warfare, do not permit belligerents in occupied countries to commit acts of violence against civilians, to disregard the laws in force, or to overthrow national institutions.[66]

They placed 'among their principal war aims the punishment, through the channel of organized justice, of those guilty of or responsible for these crimes, whether they have ordered them, perpetrated them or participated in them'.[67]

The Moscow Declaration of German Atrocities was signed by Stalin, Roosevelt, and Churchill on 2 November 1943. The three leaders proclaimed that at the time of the granting of any armistice to a new German

---

[62] This view is supported by M. O. Hudson, in *International Tribunals, Past and Future* (1944), 180.   [63] See *History of the UNWCC*, 87–8.

[64] Ibid. 88.   [65] Ibid. 89.

[66] Quoted in Whiteman, *Digest*, xi (1968), 874; and see *History of the UNWCC*, 90.

[67] Ibid.

Government, the German officers and men, and members of the Nazi Party who had been responsible for or taken a consenting part in any atrocities, would be sent back to the countries in which their deeds were done and be judged and punished. Those major criminals whose offences had no particular geographical location would be punished in accordance with a joint decision of the Allied Governments.[68]

The US issued a number of warnings concerning war crimes during the period 1942–5. On 1 February 1945 the Acting Secretary of State announced that proposals had been worked out to provide 'for the punishment of German leaders and their associates for their responsibility for the whole broad criminal enterprise devised and executed with ruthless disregard of the very foundation of law and morality'.[69]

The Potsdam Declaration of 26 July 1945, made by the US, the UK and China, and later adhered to by the Soviet Union, stated with respect to Japan: 'We do not intend that the Japanese shall be enslaved as a race or destroyed as a nation but stern justice shall be meted out to all war criminals including those who have visited cruelties upon our prisoners.'[70]

Meanwhile, the question arose as to where precise responsibility for the war actually lay. The press discussed whether only the Nazis were guilty of the war, or the leaders of the German army as well, or the entire German people for failing to revolt against the dictatorship of Hitler. Lord Vansittart,[71] a prominent British diplomat at the time, considered that the German people had demonstrated its complete viciousness and incapacity for peaceful coexistence with other peoples through the birth of militaristic junkerdom and aggressive Hitlerism. As a result, the country ought to be punished severely and abandoned forever as a penalized nation. The term 'Vansittartism' derives from the doctrine that the conduct of German war leaders from the time of the Franco-German War (1870–1) had the whole-hearted support of the German people, and that Germany needed to be permanently demilitarized to ensure against future aggression.[72] However, Vansittart's advice was never taken, and he was regarded by Neville Chamberlain as a hindrance to the British Government's efforts to reach a settlement with Hitler. In the United States the Treasury Secretary, Henry Morgenthau, devised a plan providing for the complete deindustralization of Germany as a means of eliminating Germany's war potential and penalizing the civilian population for embracing authoritarian and militaristic practices.[73] Less severe judges proposed that the German people be deprived of its

---

[68] *Department of State Bulletin*, 9 (228), press release, 6 Nov. 1943, 310–11.
[69] Ibid. 12 (293), 4 Feb. 1945, 154–5.   [70] Ibid. 13 (318), 29 July 1946, 137–8.
[71] See Trainin, *Hitlerite Responsibility*, 71.
[72] *Encyclopaedia Britannica, Micropaedia*, x (1983), 355.
[73] See C. Eisenberg, *Drawing the Line: The American Decision to Divide Germany, 1944–1949* (1996), 32–51.

rights for a definite period only, during the course of a complete system of re-education conducted by the United Nations. More moderate opinion felt that it would be sufficient to abolish the Nazi regime in Germany.

Trainin[74] wrote an influential book in 1944 asserting the criminal responsibility of the Nazi leadership for the war and related excesses, and demanding the trial and punishment of the 'Hitlerite criminals'.[75] He raised the question whether a state can bear criminal responsibility in addition to political and material responsibility. He referred to Levit, Saldaña, and Pella, who favoured the criminal responsibility of a state. But he pointed to the 'criminal intangibility of the state'[76] and argued that the criminal responsibility of persons acting in the name of the state had to be sought via the judicial process, while the destruction of the Third Reich would take place through military force.

(b) The United Nations War Crimes Commission and the London Agreement

In 1942 the US and the UK announced their agreement upon the proposal to establish a United Nations Commission for the Investigation of War Crimes. On 7 October 1942, the Lord Chancellor announced to the House of Lords:

The Commission would direct its attention in particular to organized atrocities; atrocities perpetrated by, or on the orders of Germany in occupied France should be included. The investigation should cover war crimes of offenders irrespective of rank. The aim would be to collect material, supported wherever possible by depositions or other documents, to establish such crimes, especially where they were systematically perpetrated, and to name and identify those responsible for their perpetration.[77]

President Roosevelt released a statement to the press on the same day, adding: 'It is not the intention of this Government or of the Governments associated with us to resort to mass reprisals'; 'the number of persons eventually found guilty will undoubtedly be extremely small compared to the total enemy populations', but 'it is our intention that just and sure punishment shall be meted out to the ringleaders responsible for the organized murder of thousands of innocent persons'.[78]

During October 1943, the representatives of seventeen Allied nations, including all the major powers except the Soviet Union, met in London and established the UN War Crimes Commission. The role of the Commission was to formulate and implement the general measures necessary to ensure the detection, apprehension, trial, and punishment of persons accused of war crimes.[79]

---

[74] *Hitlerite Responsibilty.*   [75] Ibid. 9.   [76] Ibid. 74.
[77] *The Times*, 8 Oct. 1942; G. A. Finch, 'Retribution for War Crimes', (1943) 37 *AJIL* 81, 84.
[78] *Department of State Bulletin*, 7, 10 Oct. 1942, 797; Finch, 'Retribution'.
[79] See *History of the UNWCC*.

On 8 August 1945, at the conclusion of the war, an agreement for the Prosecution and Punishment of the Major War Criminals of the European Axis
was signed in London by the US, the Provisional Government of France, the
UK, and the Soviet Union 'acting in the interests of all the United
Nations'.[80] The Charter for an International Military Tribunal for the trial of
the major Axis war criminals whose offences had no particular geographical
location was annexed to the London Agreement as an integral part thereof.
The Charter listed three categories of crimes falling within the jurisdiction of
the Tribunal for which there was to be individual responsibility: crimes
against peace (planning, preparing for, initiating, or waging a war of aggression or a war in violation of international treaties, agreements or assurances
or participating in a common plan or conspiracy for the accomplishment of
any of the foregoing); war crimes (violations of the laws or customs of war,
such as murder, ill-treatment, or deportation of the civilian population of
occupied territory, murder or ill-treatment of prisoners of war or persons on
the seas, killing of hostages, plunder of public or private property, wanton
destruction of cities, towns, or villages, or devastation not justified by military necessity); and crimes against humanity (murder, extermination, enslavement, deportation, and other inhumane acts committed against any civilian
population, either before or during a war, or persecutions on political, racial,
or religious grounds in execution of or in connection with any other war
crime). The Charter specified that the official position of a defendant as head
of state or as a responsible government official would not free him from
responsibility or mitigate his punishment. Neither would the fact that a
defendant acted pursuant to the order of his government or a superior free
him from responsibility, but this might be considered in mitigation of punishment. The Tribunal could declare any group or organization to be criminal in character, with the result that any national, military or occupation
courts of any signatory state could subsequently bring individuals to trial for
membership therein, and the criminal nature of the group or organization
could not be questioned.[81]

(c) The International Military Tribunal at Nuremberg

The first session of the Tribunal took place in Berlin on 18 October 1945,
under the presidency of the Soviet member, General Nikitchenko. An indictment was lodged against twenty-four former Nazi leaders, and six groups or
organizations were charged with being criminal in nature. One defendant,
Ley, committed suicide on 25 October 1945, and on 15 November 1945 the
Tribunal ruled that Krupp could not be tried because of his physical and

---

[80] 82 *UNTS* 279–84; (1945) 39 *AJIL Suppl.* 257.
[81] For a more complete account of the responsibility of organizations, see Chapter 3 below.

mental condition. The Trial opened in Nuremberg on 20 November 1945, under the presidency of the British member, Lord Justice Sir Geoffrey Lawrence. The reading of the Judgment of the Tribunal with regard to the twenty-two defendants and the six groups or organizations was concluded on 1 October 1946. Three defendants were acquitted (Schacht, Von Papen, and Fritsche); twelve were sentenced to death by hanging (Goering, Ribbentrop, Keitel, Kaltendrunner, Rosenberg, Frank, Frick, Streicher, Sauckel, Jodl, Seyss-Inquart, and Bormann); three were sentenced to life imprisonment (Hess, Funk, and Raeder); and four were sentenced to imprisonment for terms ranging from ten to twenty years (Doenitz, Schirach, Speer, and Neurath). The Tribunal declared three of the indicted organizations to be criminal (the 'Leadership Corps' of the Nazi Party, the SS, and the Gestapo), which meant that those who became or remained members after 1 September 1939 could be tried.

(d) Selected Legal Questions Dealt with at Nuremberg

One of the main defence contentions at Nuremberg was that aggressive war did not constitute a crime at the time the alleged criminal acts were committed, and that there could be no punishment without a pre-existing law (*nullum crimen sine lege, nulla poena sine lege*). The Tribunal rejected this argument, holding that aggressive war had been a crime under international criminal law at least since the Kellogg–Briand Pact of 1928. The rejection of the defence contention that international law did not provide for the punishment of individuals but was concerned only with the actions of sovereign states had a less obvious justification. The labelling of aggression as an international crime initially made reference to the responsibility of the state as a collectivity. However, it was argued, for example, by General Rudenko, Chief Prosecutor for the Soviet Union, that '[w]hen the subject of International Law, i.e., a state, violates the principles of International Law, certain consequences of an international character are entailed, but in no case does it entail the criminal responsibility of the state'.[82] The argument that individuals could not be held responsible for acts of state was decisively rejected in the Judgment of the Nuremberg Tribunal: 'Crimes against international law are committed by men, not by abstract entities, and only by punishing individuals who commit such crimes can the provisions of international law be enforced.'[83] Finally, with regard to the 'Law as to the Common Plan or Conspiracy', the Tribunal implicated a large number of Germans and rejected the defence argument that common planning cannot exist where there is complete dictatorship:

---

[82] *Trial of German Major War Criminals: Proceedings of the IMT*, 29 July–8 Aug. 1946, pt. 20 (1949), 32.   [83] *Nuremberg Judgment*, 223.

Hitler could not make aggressive war by himself. He had to have the co-operation of statesmen, military leaders, diplomats and business men. When they, with knowledge of his aims, gave him their cooperation, they made themselves parties to the plan he had initiated. They are not to be deemed innocent because Hitler made use of them, if they knew what they were doing.[84]

(e) Trials under Control Council Law No. 10

Control Council Law No. 10[85] was enacted on 20 December 1945, to give effect to the terms of the Moscow Declaration and the London Agreement and Charter, and to establish a uniform legal basis in Germany for the prosecution of war criminals other than those dealt with by the International Military Tribunal. Twelve trials under Control Council Law No. 10 were held between 1946 and 1948 before the Tribunals set up at Nuremberg under the US Military Government Ordinance No. 7. These cases demonstrate the difficulties of implicating masses of Germans, including the whole state system under the Nazis, while avoiding the charge of collective punishment. For example in the trial of Josef Altstötter et al. (Justice Case),[86] the tribunal traced the rapid degeneration of the judiciary under the Third Reich. Once the judicial system had been distorted and perverted into a mechanism of the dictatorship, the legal machinery was used to commit the crimes charged in the indictment.

The charge, in brief, is that of conscious participation in a nationwide governmentally organized system of cruelty and injustice, in violation of the laws of war and of humanity, and perpetrated in the name of law by the authors of the Ministry of Justice and through the instrumentality of the courts.[87]

All the defendants were judges, prosecutors, or ministerial officers. Ten of the sixteen accused were found guilty of war crimes and/or crimes against humanity and/or membership of criminal organizations. The case of Carl Krauch et al. (IG Farben Case)[88] concerned twenty-four directors and officers of IG Farbenindustrie. In its judgment, the tribunal stated:

The defendants now before us were neither high public officials in the civil government nor high military officers. Their participation was that of followers and not leaders. If we lower the standard of participation to include them, it is difficult to find a logical place to draw the line between the guilty and the innocent among the great mass of German people. It is, of course, unthinkable that the majority of Germans should be condemned as guilty of committing crimes against peace. This would amount to a determination of collective guilt. . . .[89]

---

[84] *Nuremberg Judgment*, 226.
[85] *Department of State Bulletin*, 15 (384), 10 Nov. 1946, 862; and see Whiteman, *Digest*, 895–934.   [86] Law Reports UNWCC, vol. 6, 1–110.
[87] Ibid. 49–50.   [88] Ibid. vol. 10, 1, 1–68.   [89] Ibid. 39.

All of the accused were found not guilty of committing crimes against peace and participating in the conspiracy.

(f) The International Military Tribunal at Tokyo[90]

On 19 January 1946, the Supreme Commander for the Allied Powers in Japan, US General of the Army Douglas MacArthur, issued under the authority of the Declaration of the Moscow Conference,[91] a Proclamation establishing an International Military Tribunal for the Far East for the trial of the major war criminals in that area.[92] The Tribunal ultimately consisted of judges derived from the eleven nations responsible for its establishment (Australia, Canada, China, France, India, the Netherlands, New Zealand, the Philippines, the Soviet Union, the UK, and the US). The trial began in Tokyo on 3 May 1946. It lasted more than two years, the judgment being delivered on 4–12 November 1948. The twenty-eight defendants were charged with crimes against peace, murder, other conventional war crimes, and crimes against humanity. Two of the accused died during the course of the trial (Matsuoka and Nagano), and one was declared unfit to stand trial (Okawa). Seven of the defendants were sentenced to death (Dohihara, Hirota, Hagaki, Kimura, Matsui, Muto, Tojo). Togo was sentenced to imprisonment for twenty years, and Shigemutsu to seven. The remaining sixteen defendants were sentenced to life imprisonment (Araki, Hashimoto, Hata, Hiranuma, Hoshino, Kaya, Kido, Koiso, Minami, Oka, Oshima, Sato, Shimada, Shiratori, Suzuki, Umezu).

The Tribunal dealt with the defence contentions that aggressive war was not a crime under international law and that war was the act of a nation for which there was no individual responsibility under international law by expressing its unqualified adherence to the relevant opinions of the Nuremberg Tribunal. In relation to the first contention, some judges preferred to invoke natural law arguments, rather than resting their conclusions on the legal effect of the Kellogg–Briand Pact. Justice Bernard spoke of war as 'a crime in the eyes of reason and universal conscience'.[93] Justice Pal[94] dissented from all theories advanced to support the thesis that aggressive war was a crime:

[90] Transcript of the Proceedings of the International Military Tribunal for the Far East, *Judgment*, text produced by the Far Eastern Commission (Nov. 1948), Bodleian Law Library, Oxford (Internat. 580 I 62.7a); B. V. A. Röling and C. F. Rüter (eds.), *The Tokyo Judgment: The International Military Tribunal for the Far East, 29 April 1946–12 November 1948* (2 vols, 1977).

[91] *Department of State Bulletin*, vol. 13, 16–26 Dec. 1945, 1029.

[92] See *Trial of Japanese War Criminals*, Dept. of State Publication 2613, Far Eastern Series 12, 39–44, for Charter of the International Military Tribunal for the Far East, as Amended, 26 Apr. 1946. Also in Dept. of State, *A Decade of American Foreign Policy: Basic Documents 1941–1949*, rev. edn. (1985), 433. [93] Röling and Rüter, *The Tokyo Judgment*, 483, 490.

[94] Dissenting Opinion published as *International Military Tribunal for the Far East, Dissentient Judgment of Justice Pal* (1953).

no category of war became a crime in international life up to the date of commencement of the world war under our consideration. The Pact of Paris did not affect the character of war and failed to introduce any criminal responsibility in respect of any category of war in international life ... War itself, as before remained outside the province of law, its conduct only having been brought under legal regulations. No customary law developed so as to make any war a crime. International Community itself was not based on a footing which would justify the introduction of the conception of criminality in international life.[95]

In relation to the question whether there was individual responsibility for aggressive war, Justice Bernard again invoked natural law and claimed that 'the individual cannot shelter behind the responsibility of the community the responsibility which he incurred by his own acts'.[96] In contrast, Justice Pal held that individuals constituting the government and functioning as its agents could not be held criminally responsible under international law for their acts. He felt that the international community had not yet reached the stage where it was practicable to utilize the judicial process for judging and punishing either states or individuals.[97]

(g) The Emperor of Japan

The most conspicuous omission from the list of defendants at the Tokyo Tribunal was the Emperor of Japan. Arguably, Hirohito played a less important role in the Second World War than Wilhelm had in the First World War, but he was *de jure* sovereign and had taken part in wartime decision-making. The Emperor's name did appear on the initial list of war criminals, and several countries, including the UK and the Soviet Union, urged his prosecution. The choice was between an aggressive policy which would involve the complete abolition of the Emperor system or proceeding cautiously and giving the Japanese the framework within which they could work out their own destiny.[98] Some Japanese argued that if the Emperor had sufficient power to stop the war, he had had the authority to prevent it.[99] However, there was considerable doubt as to the Emperor's power to act independently of the advice of his counsellors and the dominant military clique which represented the current of public opinion. More importantly, General MacArthur warned that the destruction of the Emperor could cause Japan to disintegrate and spark off a long-term vendetta of revenge amounting to guerrilla warfare, and military government would have had to be instituted throughout Japan.[100]

---

[95] *International Military Tribunal for the Far East, Dissentient Judgment of Justice Pal* (1953) 70.   [96] Röling and Rüter, *The Tokyo Judgment*, 490.
[97] Pal, Dissentient Judgment, 71–105.
[98] The Acting Political Advisor in Japan (Atcheson) to President Truman, Tokyo, 4 Jan. 1946, *Foreign Relations of the US* (1946), viii: *The Far East* (1971), 90.   [99] Ibid.
[100] General of the Army Douglas MacArthur to the Chief of Staff, United States Army (Eisenhower), Tokyo, 25 Jan. 1946; *Foreign Relations of the US* (1946), 396.

It is unclear at what date the Emperor's name was struck from the list. This decision was clearly political, as it would apparently have been easy to ensure his conviction on all the counts of the indictment. He had in fact offered to 'bear sole responsibility for every political and military decision made and action taken by [his] people in the conduct of the war',[101] and it was somewhat anomalous that he was granted immunity while many of his accomplices suffered the death penalty.

(h) Adoption of the Nuremberg Principles

In Resolution 95 adopted on 11 December 1946, the United Nations General Assembly took note 'of the Agreement for the establishment of an International Military Tribunal for the prosecution and punishment of the major war criminals of the European Axis . . . and of the Charter annexed thereto, and of the fact that similar principles have been adopted in the Charter of the International Military Tribunal for the trial of the major war criminals in the Far East', and affirmed 'the principles of international law recognized by the Charter of the Nuremberg Tribunal and the Judgment of the Tribunal'.[102]

Under General Assembly Resolution 177(II), paragraph (a), of 21 November 1947, the newly established International Law Commission (ILC) was directed to 'formulate the principles of international law recognized in the Charter of the Nuremberg Tribunal and in the judgment of the Tribunal'. The ILC undertook a preliminary consideration of the topic at its first session, and appointed Jean Spiropoulos as Special Rapporteur.[103] At its second session, the ILC considered Spiropoulos' report[104] and adopted a formulation of the Nuremberg principles.[105] In discussions in the Sixth (Legal) Committee relating to Principle I, according to which 'any person who commits an act which constitutes a crime under international law is responsible therefor and liable to punishment', there were differing opinions as to the possible criminal responsibility of a state, but the concept was rejected since it seemed that a state could be regarded as responsible only in a civil and administrative sense.[106] These specific adoptions of the Nuremberg principles helped to confirm the validity of the postwar prosecutions, and individual responsibility for international crimes is now an integral part of positive international law.

---

[101] Emperor's statement to General MacArthur at their first meeting, in D. MacArthur, *Reminiscences* (1964), 288.

[102] These principles were also affirmed in the trials before the national courts of the Allies of approximately 6,500 Germans and 6,000 Japanese for breaches of international law committed during the war. Many of the cases are reported in the *Annual Digest*.

[103] See (1949) *YrbkILC*, 282–3.   [104] A/CN.4/22.

[105] See Report of the ILC Covering its Second Session, (1950) *YrbkILC*, vol. 2, 374.

[106] See (1964) *YrbkILC*, vol. 2, 128.

(i) War Guilt[107] and Postwar Reparations

As a result of the Crimean Conference[108] it was determined that Germany should make reparation in kind for damage caused to the Allied nations in the war to the 'greatest extent possible'.[109] A similar obligation appeared in the Potsdam Declaration,[110] which provided for the complete de-Nazification of Germany and stated that 'the German people have begun to atone for the terrible crimes committed under the leadership of those whom in the hour of their success, they openly approved and blindly obeyed'.[111] Regarding reparations, the Declaration went on to say that 'the German people cannot escape responsibility'.[112] Japan was also required to pay reparation for the consequences of Japanese aggression.[113] Japanese reparations were to be made through the transfer of property and goods or of such existing capital, equipment, and facilities as were not necessary for a peaceful Japanese economy.[114]

The first consideration in assessing the amount of reparations due following the Second World War was the extent of responsibility for participation in it which could be diminished by early withdrawal from the war against the United Nations and the declaration of war on Germany. Therefore, there was a direct link between war guilt and the obligation to make reparations. The amount of reparation payments varied in accordance with the willingness of certain members of the United Nations to forgo claims, the economic situation of the claimant, the desire to promote economic recovery in ex-enemy states, and the capacity of the ex-enemy states to meet demands.[115] Whatever its original aims, the application of the scheme for reparation payments was cut back. This reflected the growing tension between East and West which marked the beginning of the

---

[107] For a German perspective on war guilt, see A. Jodl, 'A Short Historical Consideration of German War Guilt', in *Nazi Conspiracy and Aggression*, viii (1946), 662–9: 'The mass of the people considers war as fate just like sickness and death. People never influence its outbreak and have no insight whether it was unavoidable or not.'

[108] *Department of State Bulletin*, 12, 11 Feb. 1945, 213; (1945) 39 *AJIL Suppl.* 103, 104–5.

[109] Ibid. 104.   [110] Ibid. 245.   [111] Ibid. 247–8.

[112] Ibid. 251.

[113] US Initial Post-Surrender Policy for Japan, 6 Sept. 1945, pt. 4, section 4; Basic Initial Post-Surrender Policy, Directive to Supreme Commander for the Allied Powers for the Occupation and Control of Japan, 1 Nov. 1945, pt. 2, para. 28; printed in Department of State, *A Decade of American Foreign Policy*, 415, 419 and 419, 429 respectively.

[114] The original reparation policy for Japan included the punitive aim of suppressing the Japanese economy to the level of a 'minimum civilian standard of living', but the terms of the 1951 Treaty of Peace were less harsh. See T. Ito, 'Japan's Settlement of the Post-World War II Reparations and Claims', (1994) *Japanese Annual of International Law*, no. 37, 38, 41.

[115] See Brownlie, *International Law and the Use of Force by States*, 744, esp. n. 1; and see Statement by F. R. McCoy, 'US Responsibility on the Far Eastern Commission, 12 May 1949: Japanese Reparations and the Level of Industry', in Dept. of State, *A Decade of American Foreign Policy*, 452.

Cold War, and rendered any strategy of isolating Germany and Japan politically unwise.

The demand for reparations following the Second World War did not appear to contain a significant punitive factor, although the various statements to the effect that the German population was collectively responsible for the results of aggression indicate that the payment of reparations was part of the punishment for what was by then generally considered to be a crime. One difference between the response to aggression in the First and Second World Wars is that in the latter case the question of war guilt was dealt with mainly in the trials of the major war criminals, which implicated a very large number of individuals, while in the former case the desire to impose some form of punishment could ultimately only be achieved through the payment of reparations.

4. CONCLUSION

It seemed more expedient to talk of individual criminal responsibility after the Second World War, although it would seem that, in the case of Germany, given the number of people tried as individuals or members of criminal organizations, the entire state apparatus was in effect condemned. Kennan's view is that:

In the Nuremberg trials, beyond the trials of the Nazi war criminals, there was a shadow trial of all those Germans who gave their acceptance of the laws of the German state as their excuse for not protesting against crimes against humanity.[116]

Telford Taylor finds it 'quite legitimate to say that all Germans shared a "collective political responsibility" for the sins and shortcomings of the Third Reich',[117] although he distinguishes this from moral responsibility and legal guilt. Nevertheless, he maintains that there was 'extensive moral responsibility virtually throughout German society for the laws and practices of the Nazis',[118] even if this fell short of legal guilt.[119] Taylor also describes the most significant feature of the Nazi crimes as being that they were carried out by the state itself, or in conformity with state policies. He contrasts this with the situation in Japan, where, he argues, few of the actions charged as criminal in the Tokyo War Crimes Trials were based on matters of state policy, being performed instead on an individual basis.

---

[116] *New York Review of Books*, 24 Apr. 1969, quoted in T. Taylor, 'Guilt, Responsibility and the Third Reich', *Churchill College Overseas Fellowship Lectures* 6 (1970), 7.   [117] Ibid. 8.
[118] Ibid. 9.
[119] See also D. J. Goldhagen, *Hitler's Willing Executioners: Ordinary Germans and the Holocaust* (1996).

In the Nuremberg Trials themselves the notion of the criminal responsibility of the state was not ignored, and the Trials were clearly viewed by those conducting them as a condemnation of all that Nazi Germany represented at the time. Sir Hartley Shawcross, Chief Prosecutor for the UK, indicated in his Opening Speech before the Nuremberg Tribunal that criminal responsibility should fall on the state, but that in order to avoid the difficulty of collective punishment it was preferable to punish those directly responsible for the criminal conduct of their state.

There is not anything startlingly new in the adoption of the principle that the State as such is responsible for its criminal acts . . . In fact . . . the immeasurable potentialities for evil inherent in the State in this age of science and organization would seem to demand, quite imperatively, means of repression of criminal conduct even more drastic and more effective than in the case of individuals.[120]

François de Menthon, the French Chief Prosecutor, went as far as to say:

it is necessary that, after having premeditated, prepared and launched a war of aggression . . . after having thereupon piled up the most odious crimes in the course of the war years, Nazi Germany shall be declared guilty and her rulers and those chiefly responsible punished as such.[121]

Donnedieu de Vabres, the French member of the Tribunal, has expressed the view that all that prevented the principle of the criminal responsibility of the state from being applied was the suspension of German sovereignty as a result of the unconditional surrender and total occupation of Germany.[122]

It must be emphasized that acceptance of individual criminal responsibility under international law is very much a result of the post-Second World War trials. When the question of war crimes trials arose after the First World War, Allied leaders were sceptical, and President Wilson pointed out:

up to the present time, responsibility for international crimes has been solely a collective responsibility . . . If you declare that crimes, recognized as such within each country, when committed during an international conflict, can be punished in future by an international court, you will be substituting individual responsibility for collective responsibility, which alone has been recognized in the past. But you cannot act pursuant to that principle before it has been recognized.[123]

Mullins, who was one of the British observers at the Leipzig Trials, has suggested that 'Germany's war criminals were part of the system which produced and encouraged them, and the condemnation of that system is of greater

---

[120] *The Trial of German Major War Criminals: Opening Speeches of the Chief Prosecutors* (1946), 57–8.   [121] Ibid. 90.

[122] *Revue de Droit Pénal et de Criminologie*, 10 (1947), 882; see also 'Le Procès de Nuremberg devant les principes modernes du droit pénal international', (1947–I) 70 Hague *Recueil* 480, 559–73, esp. 561.

[123] Conversation between Wilson, Clemenceau, Lloyd George, and Orlando, 2 Apr. 1919, in P. Mantaux, *Paris Peace Conference 1919: Proceedings of the Council of Four* (1964), 90–3.

importance than the fate of any individual wrongdoers'.[124] Nevertheless, it is apparent that after the Second World War, individual criminal responsibility under international law for acts of state became well established while state criminal responsibility, although a key issue, was increasingly viewed as an unworkable concept, and consequently took a back seat.

[124] Mullins, *The Leipzig Trials*, 15.

2

Efforts to Codify and Develop the Law Relating to International Criminal Responsibility

I. INTRODUCTION

The Nuremberg and Tokyo Trials generated much critical literature.[1] While English and American jurists emphasized the Nuremberg Tribunal's moral mandate and the need to satisfy world public conscience, German jurists condemned the fact that no individuals from the Allied side were indicted and that no judge from Germany or a neutral country was appointed to the Tribunal.[2] They also regarded the Allies as being motivated by interests such as future security and power rather than the advancement of international law, and this view was partly shared by some English and American historians.[3]

The ideals of the interwar period had led to a drive to create a code of international criminal law of universal application and a court before which the developing rules could be applied impartially. No such system was in place by the end of the Second World War, and the lessons of Nuremberg informed subsequent efforts to advance international criminal law. This meant an emphasis on individual criminal responsibility until in 1976 the International Law Commission resurrected the early interest in the notion of state criminal responsibility.

[1] For a summary of some of the criticisms of the Nuremberg Trial see K. R. Chaney, 'Pitfalls and Imperatives: Applying the Lessons of Nuremberg to the Yugoslav War Crimes Trials', in D. O. Friedrichs, *State Crime*, ii. (1998), 70–81. For criticisms of the Tokyo Trial see e.g. R. H. Minear, *Victor's Justice: The Tokyo War Crimes Trial* (1971); B. V. A. Röling and A. Casesse, *The Tokyo Trial and Beyond: Reflections of a Peacemonger* (1993).

[2] See H. Ehard (Minister-President of Bavaria), 'The Nuremberg Trial Against the Major War Criminals and International Law', (1949) 43 *AJIL* 223, 243: 'In our evaluation of the Nuremberg trial we should not be misled by the unworthy wish for a milder judgment of the crime, but only by the desire for an ever-increased perfection of the law and the longing for the final and universal victory of law over might', ibid. 225. See also H. Kraus, 'The Nuremberg Trial of the Major War Criminals: Reflections After Seventeen Years', (1963–4) 13 *De Paul Law Rev.* 233; C. Haensel, 'The Nuremberg Trial Revisited', ibid. 248; O. Kranzbuhler, 'Nuremberg Eighteen Years Afterward', (1964–5) 14 *De Paul Law Rev.* 333; W. E. Benton and G. Grimm, *Nuremberg: German Views of the War Trials* (1955).

[3] See e.g. B. F. Smith, *Reaching Judgment at Nuremberg* (1977).

2. IDEAS FOR AN INTERNATIONAL CRIMINAL CODE AND COURT

(a) The Advisory Committee of Jurists, 1920[4]

In 1920, the Council of the League of Nations appointed an Advisory Committee of Jurists to frame the Statute of a Permanent Court of International Justice. In the Committee, Baron Descamps of Belgium proposed the establishment of a 'High Court of International Justice' to try those responsible for offences against international public order and the universal law of nations. Lord Phillimore, the British member, also favoured the establishment of such an institution, believing it would impartially contribute to the League's ability to repress international crimes. The League Assembly took the view that if certain crimes were in future to be brought within the scope of international penal law, a criminal department might be set up in the Permanent Court of International Justice, but the Assembly felt that consideration of the problem was premature.[5] The idea seemed radical at a time when only states were considered to be subjects of international law, although no mention was made of the possible criminal responsibility of states in this context.

(b) The International Law Association, 1922–1926

The International Law Association took up the question of creating an international criminal court at its conference in Buenos Aires in 1922,[6] and decided that the matter was both urgent and essential in the interest of justice. A detailed plan was submitted by Professor Hugh Bellot in Stockholm in 1924,[7] which was subsequently referred to a Special Committee. The Special Committee, in reporting back to the Association at the Vienna Conference in 1926,[8] declared that the creation of a permanent international criminal court was both expedient and practicable.[9] It was proposed to establish such a court in addition to and distinct from the Permanent Court of International Justice at the Hague, to exercise a separate jurisdiction in cases of states and individuals charged with violations of international obligations

---

[4] See R. J. Phillimore, 'An International Criminal Court and the Resolutions of the Committee of Jurists', (1922–3) *BYIL* 79.

[5] *Historical Survey of the Question of International Criminal Jurisdiction* (1949), 12. See also Report on the Question of International Criminal Jurisdiction by Alfaro, RJ, A/CN.4/15, (1950) *YrbkILC*, 2, 3–4.

[6] See H. H. L. Bellot, 'Permanent International Criminal Court', in ILA, *Report of the Thirty-First Conference*, Buenos Aires, 24–30 Aug. 1922, 63–86.

[7] Bellot, 'Statute for the Permanent International Criminal Court', in ILA, *Report of the Thirty-Third Conference*, Stockholm, 8–13 Sept. 1924, 75–111.

[8] 'Report of the Permanent International Criminal Court Committee', in ILA, *Report of the Thirty-Fourth Conference*, Vienna, 5–11 Aug. 1926, 106–225 and 279–309.   [9] Ibid. 109.

of a penal character; violations of any treaty, convention, or declaration regulating the methods and conduct of warfare; and violations of the laws and customs of war generally accepted as binding by civilized nations. The Court was to have the power to order a guilty state to pay to the complaining state a pecuniary penalty; an indemnity for any damage done; or a sum by way of indemnity to any subject or citizen of the complaining state who proved loss or injury caused by the act or default of the defendant state or of any subject or citizen of that state.

(c) The Inter-Parliamentary Union, 1924–1925

The Inter-Parliamentary Union discussed the question of an international criminal court at conferences in Berne in 1924 and Washington in 1925. A permanent committee was created to make a study of the social, political, economic, and moral causes of wars of aggression in order to find practical solutions for the prevention of that crime, and to prepare a first draft of an 'International Legal Code'. These resolutions were based on a report presented by Pella which was accompanied by an annex laying down certain fundamental propositions of international criminal law, such as the penal responsibility of individuals as well as of states.[10]

(d) The Association Internationale de Droit Pénal, 1926–1928

In 1926, the International Association of Penal Law, presided over by Pella, held its first International Congress of Penal Law in Brussels. The Congress took as the basis for its discussions reports prepared by Pella and Donnedieu de Vabres. A resolution was passed recommending that the Permanent Court of International Justice be empowered to deal with criminal matters, and that it should have competence to 'hear all cases for penal responsibilities against states consequent upon an unjust aggression and for violations of international law',[11] and also cases against individuals arising from the crime of aggression and all violations of international law committed in times of peace or war. The crimes coming within the jurisdiction of the Court were to be defined by international conventions which would also prescribe the penal sanctions to be imposed by the Court. Sentences upon states would be enforced by the Council of the League of Nations, while those upon individuals would be implemented by a state chosen and supervised by the Council.

---

[10] Union interparlementaire, *Compte rendu de la XXIIIe Conférence*, Washington, 1925, 46–50; full text of resolution and annex in *Historical Survey of the Question of International Criminal Jurisdiction*, 70; see also Report by Alfaro, 4.

[11] *Premier congrès international de droit pénal: Actes du congrès*, 634. Full text of resolution in *Historical Survey of the Question of International Criminal Jurisdiction*, app. 6; and see Report by Alfaro, 4–5.

A committee was set up by the Congress to prepare a draft statute of an international criminal court, and Pella was charged with this task at its first meeting in 1927. In 1928, Pella's draft was adopted by the Association and communicated to the governments represented at the Congress and to the League of Nations. Pella revised his draft in 1946,[12] and in 1947 the fifth International Congress of Penal Law recommended once more the establishment of a permanent international criminal court.[13] The Association was to remain actively seized of the matter.[14]

(e) The Terrorism Convention, 1937

Some attention was paid to the elaborate draft codes and statutes for an international criminal law and court in the mid-1930s. The murder of the Yugoslav King, Alexander, and the French Minister for Foreign Affairs, Barthou, by Croatian nationalists at Marseilles on 9 October 1934 prompted the preparation of an International Convention against Terrorism by the League of Nations in 1937.[15] Article I of the Convention reaffirms 'the duty of every state to refrain from any act designed to encourage terrorist activities directed against another state and to prevent the acts in which such activities take shape'. The Convention is, however, framed in terms of individual responsibility. Linked to the Terrorism Convention, and dependent upon its entry into force, was a Convention for the Creation of an International Criminal Court for the trial of persons accused of having committed acts of terrorism.[16] The Terrorism Convention was only ratified by India, and never came into force.[17]

(f) The Institut de Droit International, 1948 and 1952

In 1948, the Institut de Droit International took up discussion of the topic of an international criminal court.[18] In 1952 a report presented by Donnedieu de Vabres[19] recommended that an international criminal court be established by a General Assembly resolution to judge crimes against international law committed by heads of state, government agents, and their accomplices; crimes involving the responsibility of one state towards other states; and

---

[12] Full text in V. V. Pella, *La Guerre-crime et les criminels de guerre* (1946), 129–44.

[13] See *Revue Internationale de Droit Pénal* (1948), vol. 19.

[14] See *Nouvelles Études Pénales* (1993), vol. 10, and *Revue Internationale de Droit Pénal* (1996), vol. 67.

[15] Convention for the Prevention and Punishment of Terrorism, (1935–7) 7 *International Legislation*, 862.

[16] Convention for the Creation of an International Criminal Court, ibid. 878.   [17] Ibid. 862.

[18] *Annuaire de l'Institut de Droit International*: Session de Bruxelles, Donnedieu de Vabres, Rapporteur, (1948) vol. 42, 222–38.

[19] *Annuaire de l'Institut de Droit International*: Session de Sienne, (1952) vol. 44(I), 361.

crimes the repression of which represented an international interest. The report was based on the responses of members of the Institute to a questionnaire which revealed divergent attitudes towards the establishment of an international criminal court and to the relevance of state criminality. It was decided not to include the direct responsibility of states for crimes, even though 'Une sanction judiciaire visant ces hautes personnes morales qui sont les sujets traditionnels et directs du droit international serait le complément logique d'un système de sécurité collective gouverné par ce droit'.[20] Finch observed that he was not convinced of the practicability of establishing an international criminal court for the trial of individuals, as crimes against peace and humanity were already punishable by national courts and any nation which declined or omitted to do so was in fact a participant in the crime. He recommended the establishment of a tribunal before which the guilty governments themselves could be charged with these violations of international law. He suggested that the tribunal should be 'vested with the power to pronounce judgment *ex parte* and submit the justice of its judgment to the bar of the public opinion of the world'.[21] In the opinion of François, 'une responsabilité pénale de l'État ne paraît pas exclue',[22] although Ross took the opposite view. The issue was not taken any further by the Institute.

3. THE GENOCIDE CONVENTION, 1948

(a) Background to the Adoption of the Genocide Convention

In 1933, Raphael Lemkin submitted a proposal to the fifth International Conference for the Unification of Criminal Law held in Madrid to declare the destruction of racial, religious, or social collectivities a crime under international law. Lemkin envisaged the creation of two new international crimes: the crime of barbarism and the crime of vandalism. His proposal went as follows:

Whosoever, out of hatred towards a racial, religious, or social collectivity, or with a view to the extermination thereof, undertakes a punishable action against the life, bodily integrity, liberty, dignity, or economic existence of a person belonging to such a collectivity, is liable, for the crime of barbarity . . .

   Whosoever, either out of hatred towards a racial, religious or social collectivity, or with a view to the extermination thereof, destroys its cultural or artistic works, will be liable for the crime of vandalism.[23]

---

[20] *Annuaire de l'Institut de Droit International*: Session de Sienne, (1952) vol. 44(I), 368.
[21] Ibid. 420.   [22] Ibid. 368, n. 1.
[23] 'Terrorisme', in *Actes de la Ve Conférence internationale pour l'unification du droit pénal* (Paris, 1935), 48–56; see also R. Lemkin, 'Genocide as a Crime under International Law', (1947) 41 *AJIL* 145–51.

It is significant that this proposal was not accepted. As Sir Hartley Shawcross declared during a discussion on genocide in the UN General Assembly on 22 November 1946, the failure of the proposal made it impossible to punish some of the Nazi crimes after the Second World War, as there was an insufficient basis in existing international law to do so.[24] The Nuremberg Charter was interpreted narrowly so that genocidal acts committed before the outbreak of the war were not punishable offences. Hence no precedent could be established to the effect that a state is prohibited from destroying groups of its own citizens.

In 1944, in his book *Axis Rule in Occupied Europe*, Lemkin coined the term 'genocide' which derived from the Greek word *genos*, meaning race, nation, or tribe, and the Latin *cide*, meaning killing. Lemkin described genocide as signifying a coordinated plan of different actions, aimed at the destruction of the essential foundations of the existence of the nation or group as an entity, where the actions involved were directed against individuals in their capacity as members of the group, and the goal was the eventual annihilation of the group itself. These actions traversed the political, social, cultural, economic, and biological fields, the field of physical existence, the religious field and the moral field.

Having traced the means of committing genocide during the Second World War, Lemkin urged the amendment of the Hague Regulations of 1899 and 1907 to include, first, every action infringing upon the life, liberty, health, corporal integrity, economic existence, and honour of a group of people when that action was committed because they belonged to a particular national, religious, or racial group; and second, every policy aimed at the destruction or the aggrandizement of one such group to the prejudice or detriment of another.[25] The concept of genocide was accepted in Article 6(c) of the Nuremberg Charter, and the word was first used in the indictment of 8 October 1945 whereby the major German war criminals were alleged to have conducted 'deliberate and systematic genocide, viz. the extermination of racial and national groups, against the civilian populations of certain occupied territories in order to destroy particular races and classes of people and national, racial or religious groups'.[26] The concept was also employed in the subsequent trials of Nazi war criminals which took place under Control Council Law No. 10 and in the national courts of the Allies.[27]

Lemkin's work provided the impetus for the unanimous adoption by the

---

[24] UN Official Records of the First Part of the First Session of the General Assembly, Sixth Committee, Legal Questions, Summary Records of Meetings, 2 Nov.–13 Dec. 1946, 22nd Meeting, 102.   [25] R. Lemkin, *Axis Rule in Occupied Europe* (1944), 92–3.

[26] *Trial of the Major War Criminals Before the IMT*, Nuremberg, 14 Nov.–1 Oct. 1946, *Official Documents* (1947), vol. 1, 43–4.

[27] Law Reports of Trials of War Criminals, United Nations War Crimes Commission (1947–9), vol. 6, 48; vol. 7, 7 and 24; vol. 13, 2–3, 6, 112–14; vol. 15, 122–3.

General Assembly of Resolution 96(1) of 11 December 1946, according to which it was agreed:

Genocide is a denial of the right of existence of entire human groups, as homicide is the denial of the right to live of individual human beings; such denial of the right of existence shocks the conscience of mankind, results in great losses to humanity ... and is contrary to moral law and to the spirit and aims of the United Nations.

The General Assembly therefore affirmed:

genocide is a crime under international law which the civilized world condemns, and for the commission of which principals and accomplices—whether private individuals, public officials or statesmen, and whether the crime is committed on religious, racial, political or any other grounds—are punishable.

In the same Resolution, the Economic and Social Council was requested to embark upon the drawing up of a Convention on Genocide. On 28 March 1947, the Council adopted Resolution 47 (IV) which instructed the Secretary-General:

(a) to undertake, with the assistance of experts in the field of international and criminal law, the necessary studies with a view to drawing up a draft convention in accordance with the resolution of the General Assembly; and (b) after consultation with the General Assembly Committee on the Development and Codification of International Law and, after reference to all Member Governments for comments, to submit to the next session of the Economic and Social Council a draft convention on the crime of genocide.[28]

A UN ad hoc Committee on Genocide was subsequently established by the Economic and Social Council and entrusted with the task of preparing a draft convention on the crime of genocide.[29] The Committee met from 5 April to 10 May 1948, and adopted a draft convention which was reported to the Economic and Social Council,[30] and transmitted to the Third Session of the General Assembly.[31] Following consideration of the draft in the Sixth Committee of the General Assembly, the text of a Convention on the Prevention and Punishment of the Crime of Genocide was unanimously approved by the Assembly in 1948 and proposed for signature and ratification.[32] The Convention[33] entered into force on 12 January 1951.

In discussions by the General Assembly in plenary meeting,[34] prior to the adoption of the Convention, there was disagreement over the second part of Article VI, which provided that perpetrators of genocide could be tried 'by such international penal tribunal as may have jurisdiction with respect to

---

[28] (1947–8) *YrbkUN*, 595.   [29] ECOSOC Resolution 117 (VI).
[30] See Report of the Committee and the Draft Convention drawn up by the Committee, E/794, 24 May 1948, and E/794/Corr. 1, 10 June 1948; (1947–8) *YrbkUN*, 597–9.
[31] ECOSOC Resolution 153 (VII).   [32] Resolution 260A(III), 9 Dec. 1948.
[33] 78 *UNTS* 277; see Appendix 1 below.   [34] See (1948–9) *YrbkUN*, 957.

those Contracting Parties which shall have accepted its jurisdiction'. The Soviet delegation felt that this provision infringed upon the sovereignty of states; but several other delegations pointed out that genocide could be perpetrated by a state, or by individuals who might be representatives or agents of a state, and therefore the punishment of the crime could not be left to the state in which the alleged genocidal acts took place, as provided in the first part of Article VI. However, the principle of universal jurisdiction was abandoned by the ad hoc Committee on the basis that it would violate the sovereign rights of states. A further reason, highlighted by Robinson, was that 'since Genocide involves or may involve the responsibility of a State, the principle of universal repression would result in making courts of foreign States the judge of the conduct of a foreign government, which could provoke international tension'.[35] These arguments have been surpassed by customary law which defines genocide as a crime of universal jurisdiction.[36]

(b) State Responsibility under the Genocide Convention

The question arose during the preparation of the Genocide Convention as to whether it should make provision for the responsibility of states for genocide directly, in addition to their responsibility for the failure to prevent or punish acts of genocide. The *travaux préparatoires* indicate that the final version of the Convention was intended to deal exclusively with individual criminal responsibility, although the ambiguous wording of Article IX has been subjected to scrutiny in the literature both contemporaneously with the adoption of the Convention and subsequently. The question has attained renewed relevance in the light of the case before the ICJ concerning allegations by Bosnia-Herzegovina of genocide committed by Yugoslavia (Serbia-Montenegro).[37]

The UN Sixth (Legal) Committee spent fifty-one meetings discussing the draft Convention on Genocide and considered a number of amendments.[38] Early in the debate, the UK proposed an amendment to Article V:

[35] N. Robinson, *The Genocide Convention: A Commentary* (1960), 31–2.

[36] See Advisory Opinion in *Reservations to the Convention on the Prevention and Punishment of the Crime of Genocide*, (1951) ICJ Reports 15, 23, in which the Court refers to the 'universal character both of the condemnation of genocide and of the co-operation required "in order to liberate mankind from such an odious scourge" ', and Judgment on Preliminary Objections in *Application of the Convention on the Prevention and Punishment of the Crime of Genocide (Bosnia and Herzegovina v. Yugoslavia (Serbia and Montenegro))*, (1996) ICJ Reports, para. 31, in which '[t]he Court notes that the obligation each State . . . has to prevent and to punish the crime of genocide is not territorially limited by the Convention'.

[37] *Case Concerning the Application of the Genocide Convention*, Order on Provisional Measures, (1993) ICJ Reports 3, Judgment on Preliminary Objections, (1996) ICJ Reports. See further Chapter 17 below.

[38] See Official Records of the Third Session of the General Assembly, Part I, Sixth Committee, Legal Questions, Summary Records of Meetings, 21 Sept.–10 Dec. 1948, (hereinafter Summary Records); (1948–9) *YrbkUN*, 953–7.

Criminal responsibility for any act of genocide as specified in Articles II and IV shall extend not only to all private persons or associations, but also to states, governments, or organs or authorities of the state or government, by whom such acts are committed. Such acts committed by or on behalf of states or governments constitute a breach of the present Convention.[39]

The UK argued that the fact to be established was the penal responsibility of the state or the government itself, or even the organs or authorities of the state or government, which included heads of state and public officials.[40] It argued further that even though it was not possible to imagine the punishment in its proper sense of states and governments, as they could not be brought before their own courts, states could nevertheless be brought before an international court which would have the power to order the cessation of genocidal acts. Those in favour of the amendment pointed out that because of the complex structure of the modern state, acts could often not be imputed to an individual but only to a whole system. No penal sanction was envisaged, but it was argued that other sanctions could be instituted against states, such as the dissolution of a criminal police or the seizure of material goods and financial resources belonging to the responsible government. It was also suggested that a provision for holding states responsible for the crime of genocide would bring out the close relationship between the question of genocide and the maintenance of peace, and might also act as a deterrent to states.

The amendment was rejected by twenty-four votes to twenty-two.[41] The main opposition arguments were that the only punishment which could be imposed on states would be material reparations, which were unlikely to have the desired deterrent effect as they would be paid by the taxpayer. Reference was also made to the model of the Nuremberg Trials which, it was argued, had been more significant than a moral condemnation of the German state.

The UK also submitted an amendment to Article VII, providing for the punishment of genocide by national tribunals or by an international tribunal:

Where the act of genocide as specified by articles II and IV is, or is alleged to be the act of a state or government itself or of any organ or authority of the state or government, the matter shall, at the request of any other party to the present Convention, be referred to the ICJ, whose decision shall be final and binding.[42]

It was felt that this amendment had already been implicitly rejected by the rejection of the amendment to Article V and it was withdrawn, even though some representatives were adamant that the Convention should deal separately with the responsibility of individuals and states.

---

[39] A/C.6/236, 16 Oct. 1948.   [40] 92nd Meeting, Summary Records, 302.
[41] 96th Meeting, ibid. 355.
[42] A/C.6/236/Corr.1; see 99th and 100th Meetings, Summary Records, 392–4.

Subsequently, Article IX of the Convention became the British target for including state responsibility in the Convention. In its original form, this article stated that disputes relating to the interpretation or application of the Convention should be submitted to the ICJ, provided that no dispute were submitted to the Court involving an issue which had been referred to and was pending before, or had been passed upon by, a competent international criminal tribunal. The Committee subsequently adopted[43] by twenty-three votes to thirteen, with eight abstentions, a joint amendment to Article IX (then Article X) submitted by the UK and Belgium,[44] and further amended by India,[45] according to which any dispute between the contracting parties relating to the interpretation, application, or fulfilment of the Convention, including disputes relating to the responsibility of a state for any of the acts enumerated in Articles II and IV, should be submitted to the ICJ at the request of any of the contracting parties. The Soviet Union and Poland raised objections, but by way of explanation the UK representative, Fitzmaurice, stated that it was necessary to take into consideration the enormous practical difficulties of bringing rulers and heads of state to justice, except perhaps at the end of a war. As a result, the UK delegation felt that a provision to refer acts of genocide to the ICJ, and the inclusion of the idea of the international responsibility of states or governments, was imperative in order to establish an effective convention on genocide.[46] The US Representative, Maktos, was more sceptical, and he:

did not share the opinion of the United Kingdom representative that genocide could be committed by juridical entities, such as the state or the government; in reality, genocide was always committed by individuals. It was one of the aims of the Convention on genocide to organize the punishment of that crime. It was necessary to punish perpetrators of acts of genocide, and not to envisage measures such as the cessation of imputed acts or payment of compensation.[47]

Fitzmaurice confirmed that the responsibility envisaged in the joint amendment 'was civil responsibility, not criminal responsibility'.[48] This was also the view of the French representative, Chaumont, who 'was in no way opposed to the principle of the international responsibility of states as long as it was a matter of civil, and not criminal responsibility'.[49] This opinion was shared by Demesmin of Haiti.[50]

In its ratification of the Convention, the Philippines stated that it did not consider Article IX 'to extend the concept of state responsibility beyond that recognized by the generally accepted principles of international law'.[51] The

---

[43] 104th Meeting, Summary Records, 447.   [44] A/C.6/258.   [45] A/C.6/260.
[46] (1948–9) *Yrbk UN*, 955–6.   [47] 93rd Meeting, Summary Records, 319–20.
[48] 103rd Meeting, ibid. 440; see also Fitzmaurice, 104th Meeting, ibid. 444.
[49] 103rd Meeting, ibid. 431.   [50] Ibid. 436.
[51] Quoted in M. O. Hudson, 'The Twenty-Ninth Year of the World Court', (1951) 45 *AJIL* 1, 34.

US President, in presenting the Convention for the advice and consent of the Senate on 16 June 1949, felt it necessary to endorse a recommendation by the acting Secretary of State that such action be taken 'with the understanding that Article IX shall be understood in the traditional sense of responsibility to another state for injuries sustained by nationals of the complaining state in violation of principles of international law, and shall not be understood as meaning that a state can be held liable in damages for injuries inflicted by it on its own nationals'.[52] The literature contemporaneous with the adoption of the Genocide Convention conforms to this standpoint.

One of the earliest commentaries, which appears in the *Yale Law Journal*,[53] stresses the link between Article VIII, under which states can call upon organs of the UN for the prevention and suppression of genocide, and Article IX. According to this commentator, the Security Council could have a potential case of genocide referred to it either directly under Article VIII, or a state disputing the Convention's interpretation, application, or fulfilment might refer the matter to the Security Council from the ICJ as provided by Article 94(2) of the UN Charter. The Security Council could then adopt measures against the wrongdoing state provided the alleged genocide threatened international peace and security.

Kunz[54] describes the Genocide Convention as old-fashioned and traditional, but declares its main innovation to be that genocide committed by a state against its own citizens is made a matter of international concern. He writes:

The crimes under Article II and III are 'crimes under international law', but not crimes against international law. These crimes are defined by international law; but individuals are only under a duty if and when the states enact the corresponding domestic legislation. The Convention gives criminal jurisdiction under its domestic law to the state in the territory of which the act was committed; in addition, as the Sixth Committee stated, Article VI 'does not affect the right of any state to bring to trial before its own tribunals any of its nationals for acts committed outside of the state'.[55]

Kunz goes on to say that states alone are *internationally* responsible for genocide, but under the general conditions of state responsibility and not under criminal law.

Graven gave a course at the Hague Academy in 1950[56] in which he analysed the debate in the Sixth Committee on the nature of the state responsibility envisaged in the draft convention. He argued that the fundamental notion of the Convention was that all those responsible for acts of genocide

---

[52] Quoted in Hudson, 'The Twenty-Ninth Year of the World Court', (1951) 45 *AJIL* 1, 34, n. 52.
[53] 'Genocide: A Commentary on the Convention', (1948–9) *Yale Law Journal*, 58, 1142.
[54] J. L. Kunz, 'The United Nations Convention on Genocide', (1949) 43 *AJIL* 738.
[55] Ibid. 745.
[56] J. Graven, 'Les Crimes contre l'humanité', (1950–1) 76 Hague *Recueil* 429, 507–11.

should be punished. He pointed to the argument of the UK Government in the Sixth Committee that in reality the state or government itself was responsible, although he accepted that in the result only physical persons could be punished under the Convention.

In Hudson's[57] opinion:

read as a whole, the Convention refers to the punishment of individuals only; the punishment of a state is not adumbrated in any way, and it is excluded from Article V by which the parties undertake to enact punitive legislation. Hence the 'responsibility of a state' referred to in Article IX is not criminal liability. Instead it is limited to the civil responsibility of a state, and such responsibility is governed, not by any provisions of the Convention, but by general international law.

Sibert goes further in denying that the Convention even imposes civil responsibility on states.[58]

Subsequent doctrine relating to the Genocide Convention does not differ radically from the early doctrine just outlined. Robinson, in his detailed commentary on the Convention, states that Article IX was regarded by the members of the Committee as involving civil responsibility.[59] However, he goes on to say that the definition of civil responsibility in this context is by no means clear, and he raises the question whether it should be understood in the traditional sense of responsibility of the state that is in breach of its obligations to another state for injuries sustained by nationals of that state or in a broader sense. In other words:

If Genocide is a crime under an international Convention and if such crimes, when committed by a government in its own territory against its own citizens, are a matter of international concern, why should not the State responsible for acts of Genocide against its own nationals be liable for the reparation of the civil damages caused, just as it is responsible for the criminal prosecution of those who have perpetrated these acts against nationals of another State? This would seem to be the logical conclusion of the civil responsibility of the State. It would obviously be up to the International Court of Justice to decide how far the responsibility goes.[60]

More recently, Shaw has commented on the drafting of Article IX as follows:

Of particular interest is the provision relating to the question of jurisdiction over state responsibility for genocide. This was included in an attempt to make the Convention more effective, although considerable opposition was expressed on the grounds of the controversial and vague nature of state responsibility in areas of international criminal law. The majority took the view that it was rather an issue of civil responsibility involving liability to pay damages. The question of states having to compensate their

---

57 Hudson, 'The Twenty-Ninth Year of the World Court', (1951) 45 *AJIL* 1, 33–4.
58 M. Sibert, *Traité de droit international public: le droit de la paix* (1951), i. 446.
59 *The Genocide Convention*, 99–106.   60 Ibid. 104, and see further Chapter 17 below.

own nationals under an international legal rule also caused some interest in this connection, but without clarification or determination.[61]

The position seems to be that Article IX refers to the ordinary civil responsibility of states, although in the preparation of the Convention some states
clearly wished it to go further, or for state responsibility to be the subject of
a definitive article. Article IX deals with the enforcement of the Convention,
rather than the substantive law, which may explain Sibert's statement that the
Convention does not deal directly with state responsibility. This, in Graven's
opinion, is a considerable flaw, which can be explained on the basis that:

'puisque la convention est un document de droit pénal et non de droit civil' il était
inutile d'y prévoir une responsabilité et des réparations pécuniaires à la charge des
Gouvernements, alors qu'on n'avait 'pas l'intention de les punir'.[62]

He goes on to say:

C'est, selon nous, sinon une erreur du point de vue pratique et dans la situation du
droit pénal et public actuelle, du moins un obstacle théorique extrêmement regrettable
au progrès nécessaire du droit international.[63]

In a Study of the Question of the Prevention and Punishment of the Crime
of Genocide, prepared for the UN Sub-Commission on Prevention of
Discrimination and Protection of Minorities by Ruhashyankiki in 1978, it
was noted that at the present stage in the development of international
criminal law, 'the state can bear only political responsibility for international
crimes'[64] such as genocide. The Revised and Updated Report on the same
question, prepared in 1985 by Whitaker,[65] went further in asserting that a
state's collective responsibility, including sometimes liability for damages and
restitution, was not necessarily excluded by the application of individual
responsibility. Whitaker recommended that upon a revision of the Convention, consideration should be given to including provision for a state's responsibility for genocide together with reparations, although he does not examine
the nature of the proposed state responsibility.[66]

The establishment of a Convention dealing with the crime of genocide is
significant, since by its nature genocide cannot be committed by individuals
acting alone. Clearly, the international community was concerned to make
provision for the prevention and punishment of genocide while the horrors of
the Second World War were still fresh in the minds of governments and the
general public; and the promotion of the concept of individual criminal
responsibility under international law seemed appropriate in the light of the

---

[61] M. N. Shaw, 'Genocide and International Law', in Y. Dinstein (ed.), *International Law at a
Time of Perplexity: Essays in Honour of Shabtai Rosenne* (1989), 818.
[62] Graven, 'Les Crimes contre l'humanité', 511.   [63] Ibid.
[64] E/CN.4/Sub.2/416, 4 July 1978, 38.   [65] E/CN.4/Sub.2/1985/6, 2 July 1985.
[66] Ibid. 26.

Nuremberg Tribunal's declarations on the matter. The Convention is, therefore, very much a reflection of the mood prevalent in the late 1940s, but does not entirely dismiss the notion of state responsibility for genocide, which was the topic of considerable discussion. The time now seems ripe to bring the Genocide Convention up to date. Conventions are tools, and if they are to be effective, they will need to be interpreted in a manner which keeps them apace with developments in international law.[67]

4. STRUCTURE, FUNCTIONS, AND THE THREE-TIER WORK OF THE INTERNATIONAL LAW COMMISSION

In 1947, the UN established the International Law Commission (ILC) as a subsidiary organ of the General Assembly,[68] which began to function in 1949. The ILC is composed of thirty-four members 'who shall be persons of recognized competence in international law'.[69] Members represent the principal legal systems of the world, and sit as individuals rather than as representatives of their governments. According to Article I of its Statute, the ILC 'shall have for its object the promotion of the progressive development of international law and its codification'. The former expression refers to the preparation of draft conventions on subjects which have not yet been regulated by international law, or in regard to which the law has not yet been sufficiently developed in the practice of states, while the latter expression means the more precise formulation and systematization of rules of international law in areas where there has already been extensive state practice, precedent, and doctrine.[70] The ILC has a good record of producing drafts which are acceptable to governments, as its membership combines technical qualities and experience of government work, and reflects a variety of political standpoints.

By Resolution 260B(III) of 9 December 1948, the General Assembly invited the ILC 'to study the desirability and possibility of establishing an international judicial organ for the trial of persons charged with genocide or other crimes over which jurisdiction will be conferred upon that organ by international conventions', and requested it also 'to pay attention to the possibility of establishing a Criminal Chamber of the International Court of Justice'. At its first session in 1949, the ILC appointed Mr Alfaro and Mr Sandstrøm as Special Rapporteurs. Their reports were considered at the ILC's second session.[71] Alfaro proposed that 'the jurisdiction of the international organ of criminal justice be exercised over states as well as over

---

[67] See Chapter 17 below for an analysis of state responsibility under the Genocide Convention in contemporary international law.   [68] GA Resolution 174(II), 17 Nov. 1947.
[69] Article 2, Statute of the ILC.   [70] Article 15, Statute of the ILC.
[71] See Report of the ILC Covering its Second Session, (1950) *YrbkILC* 2, 364, 378–9.

individuals', and '[t]hat all crimes for which states or individuals be tried by the international judicial organ be defined in an International Penal Code'. [72]

A majority in the ILC voted that the establishment of an international criminal tribunal was both desirable and possible. The creation of a criminal chamber in the International Court of Justice was not recommended, as this would have necessitated an amendment of the Statute of the Court which, in Article 34, provides that only states may be parties in cases before the Court.

By contrast, Sandstrøm[73] argued that the time for an international criminal court was not yet ripe, and his position reflected the consensus of the world community in 1950. France was the only state among the Security Council's permanent members to support the idea of an international criminal court. However, as no state wished to be responsible for obstructing the course of such an idea, the debate continued, and in 1951 the Special Committee of the General Assembly appointed to draft the Statute for the Formulation of an International Criminal Tribunal completed its task.[74] It became apparent that many states were still unwilling to surrender any portion of their sovereignty to such a tribunal. A new Committee acted to save the project and a revised Statute was completed in 1953,[75] which allowed more flexibility and voluntary participation on the part of states. In the 1951 Committee, a majority felt that the proposed court should not have jurisdiction over states, and this was reflected in Article 25 of the Draft Statute.[76] This particular debate was not reopened in 1953, although the responsibility of corporations and other legal entities was discussed.[77] By Resolution 898(IX) of 14 December 1954, the General Assembly tabled the International Criminal Tribunal project until such time as the project on a Draft Code of Offences against the Peace and Security of Mankind was finalized.[78]

By Resolution 177(II), paragraph (b), of 21 November 1947, the General Assembly requested the ILC to prepare a draft code of offences against the

---

[72] A/CN.4/15, (1950) *YrbkILC* 2, 17.   [73] A/CN.4/20, (1950) *YrbkILC* 2, 18.

[74] Draft Statute for an International Criminal Court (Annex to the Report of the Committee on International Criminal Jurisdiction, 1–31 Aug. 1951), UN Doc A/2136 (1952), 7 GAOR Suppl. No. 11, 21.

[75] Revised Draft Statute for an International Criminal Court (Annex to the Report of the 1953 Committee on International Criminal Jurisdiction, 27 July–20 Aug. 1953), UN Doc A/2645, 9 GAOR Suppl. No. 12, 23.

[76] Report of the Committee on International Criminal Jurisdiction (n. 74 above), 10. A proposal was also made to the effect that the court should be competent to decide the civil responsibility of an accused for the commission of criminal acts and award damages. A state could then be held jointly liable for the payment of damages. Reference was made to the lacuna in the system of war crimes trials after the Second World War in so far as there had been no possibility of obtaining a judicial decision regarding the responsibility of Germany to pay damages to victims, ibid. 11.

[77] Report of the 1953 Committee on International Criminal Jurisdiction (n. 75 above), 13.

[78] The Rome Statute of the International Criminal Court was adopted by the United Nations Diplomatic Conference of Plenipotentiaries on 17 July 1998, A/CONF.183/9, (1998) 37 *ILM* 999.

peace and security of mankind, indicating clearly the place to be accorded to the Nuremberg Principles. At its first session the ILC appointed Mr Spiropoulos Special Rapporteur for the topic, and he presented his working paper to the ILC at its second session.[79]

The idea of a 'code of offences against the peace and security of mankind' has its roots in correspondence between Justice Biddle and President Truman at the conclusion of the trial before the Nuremberg Tribunal.[80] In a report to President Truman of 9 November 1946, Justice Biddle suggested that the time had come to 'set about drafting a code of international criminal law'. He also considered that this was an opportune moment for advancing the proposal that the UN 'reaffirm the principles of the Nuremberg Charter in the context of a general codification of offences against the peace and security of mankind'. He believed such action would not only 'perpetuate the vital principle that war of aggression is the supreme crime' but also 'afford an opportunity to strengthen the sanctions against the lesser violations of international law and to utilize the experience of Nuremberg in the development of those permanent procedures and institutions upon which the effective enforcement of international law ultimately depends'.

The ILC dealt briefly with the question of state responsibility in the context of the Draft Code, but Spiropoulos remarked that although the concept of the criminal responsibility of states had been much discussed in theory, there had been no relevant precedent in international practice. As a result, he concluded: 'following international practice up to this time, and particularly in the view of the pronouncements of the Nuremberg Tribunal, the establishment of the criminal responsibility of states—at least for the time being—does not seem advisable.'[81] It seems that according to the Draft Code, the responsibility of a state was equivalent to the individual responsibility of the members of the government.

The ILC submitted its approved text of a Draft Code to the General Assembly in 1954.[82] However, the Code lacked a definition of aggression, and the General Assembly decided in Resolution 897(IX) of 4 December 1954 to postpone further consideration of the Draft Code until the Special Committee on the question of defining aggression had submitted its report.[83] It was not until 1981 that the ILC reconsidered the Draft Code of 1954.[84]

The codification work relating to international criminal responsibility was, therefore, split between several separate committees dealing with its

---

[79] A/CN.4/25, (1950) *YrbkILC* 2, 253.

[80] *Department of State Bulletin*, 15 (386), 24 Nov. 1946, 954–7.

[81] A/CN.4/25, (1950) *YrbkILC* 2, 261. See also the debate in the Commission, ibid. vol. 1, 105–6.   [82] For text of draft see (1954) *YrbkILC* 2, 151.

[83] A definition of aggression was adopted by a General Assembly consensus resolution in 1974 (Resolution 3314 (XXIX), 14 Dec. 1974).

[84] New Draft Codes were elaborated in 1991 and 1996. For a more complete discussion of the Draft Codes see Chapter 12 below.

substantive aspects (the Draft Code and the definition of aggression) and its enforcement aspects (the international criminal tribunal). Clearly these projects were linked, and arguably there was little point in dividing the tasks if the goal was to produce quickly an international criminal code and a statute for an international criminal court. Such a strategy may have been designed to ensure that states would not be placed in the position of making a final political decision on a legal product which none of them really desired. In the mid-1950s, few states were willing to subordinate their sovereignty to an international criminal tribunal, or to surrender their political and military leaders to be tried by such a tribunal, or to accept that one day their very state could be held criminally responsible.

5. THE APARTHEID CONVENTION, 1973

The UN was concerned to promote the elimination of all forms of racial discrimination from its inception. By the 1970s international concern was growing over the armed struggle of the black South African majority against apartheid, and the repressive reactions of the white South Africans in power. In 1973 the International Convention on the Suppression and Punishment of the Crime of Apartheid was adopted by the UN.[85] The statement that apartheid is a crime against humanity which appears in Article I is deduced from a number of international instruments and resolutions which preceded the Convention, and furnishes a good example of the evolution of international law in this sphere and in the realm of international criminal responsibility generally. Article 6(c) of the Nuremberg Charter includes in its definition of crimes against humanity 'persecutions on ... racial ... grounds'. The 1948 Universal Declaration of Human Rights[86] proclaims that all human beings are born free and equal in dignity and rights, and that everyone is entitled to all the rights and freedoms set out therein, without distinction of any kind, in particular as to race, colour, or national origin.

Article 3 of the 1966 International Convention on the Elimination of All Forms of Racial Discrimination[87] emphasizes that 'states parties particularly condemn racial segregation and apartheid and undertake to prevent, prohibit and eradicate all practices of this nature in territories under their jurisdiction'. The same year the General Assembly condemned as a crime against humanity the policies of apartheid as a whole.[88] This formulation had earlier appeared in resolutions concerning the South-West African and Southern

---

[85] GA Resolution 3068(XXVIII), 30 Nov. 1973; repr. in (1974) 13 *ILM* 50.
[86] GA Resolution 217A(III), 10 Dec. 1948.   [87] *UKTS* 77 (1969).
[88] GA Resolution 2202A(XXI), 16 Dec. 1966.

Rhodesian questions.[89] In the 1968 Convention on the Non-Applicability of Statutory Limitations to War Crimes and Crimes Against Humanity,[90] 'inhuman acts resulting from the policy of apartheid' are once again described as crimes against humanity. It is not specified in any of these international instruments which of its elements makes apartheid a crime against humanity. It seems to have evolved in tune with considerations of public policy and as a reflection of public outrage.

Article V of the Apartheid Convention provides that individuals accused of apartheid may be tried by an 'international penal tribunal having jurisdiction with respect to those States Parties which shall have accepted its jurisdiction'. In 1980 the Ad Hoc Working Group of Experts on South Africa of the Commission on Human Rights commissioned M. Cherif Bassiouni to prepare a draft statute for such an international penal tribunal. This was duly prepared and accepted by the Working Group.[91] In his report, Bassiouni argued that the principle of responsibility embodied in the Apartheid Convention was much too narrow under Article III and under international law, and should include *inter alia* state responsibility. Bassiouni maintained:

While International Criminal Law contemplates only the punishment of individuals, the responsibility of corporate entities and that of the state can be deemed to be a quasi-criminal responsibility for which fines and punitive damages are the appropriate remedies.[92]

It was also specified in the report that apartheid is a crime of state policy. Article V of the proposed 'International Penal Tribunal for the Suppression and Punishment of the Crime of Apartheid and Other International Crimes' provided that the Tribunal would be competent to investigate, prosecute, adjudicate, and punish any person or *legal entity* accused or guilty of the crimes listed.[93] Article XXI, part 6, provided that a state was 'responsible for any crime committed on its behalf, behest or benefit by a person in authority'. In addition, 'conduct is attributed to a state if it is performed by persons or groups acting in their official capacity, who under the domestic law of that state possess the authority to make decisions for the state or any political subdivision thereof or possess the status of organs, agencies or instrumentalities of that state or a political subdivision thereof'.[94] The failure of a state to fulfil its obligations under the Convention would constitute an 'international offence'. Article XXI also made provision for the collective

---

[89] GA Resolution 2074(XX), 17 Dec. 1965.

[90] GA Resolution 2391(XXIII), 9 Dec. 1968; (1969) 8 *ILM* 68.

[91] Report of M. C. Bassiouni to the Ad Hoc Working Group of Experts for the Commission on Human Rights, UN Doc E/CN/4/1426, (1981), reprinted in part as M. C. Bassiouni and D. H. Derby, 'Final Report on the Establishment of an International Criminal Court for the Implementation of the Apartheid Convention and Other Relevant International Instruments', (1981) 9 *Hofstra Law Rev* 523.   [92] Ibid. 540.

[93] Ibid. 548 (emphasis added).   [94] Ibid. 562–3.

responsibility of groups or organizations. Article XXIV dealt with penalties and specified that states could be liable to pay fines. The Commission on Human Rights circulated the draft to member states in 1981, but no further progress was made.

The Apartheid Convention has not proved to be an effective addition to the list of instruments dealing with racial non-discrimination. The main purpose of the Convention was probably to enable international jurisdiction to be extended to all states, thus opening up the possibility of bringing to trial the individuals responsible for creating and maintaining the apartheid regime, or even the government as an organization. Under Article X, the UN Commission on Human Rights is empowered to prepare, on the basis of reports from UN organs and from states parties, 'a list of individuals, organizations, institutions and representatives of states who are alleged to be responsible for the crimes enumerated in Article II of the Convention'. Extensive lists of accused persons and organizations have been compiled, but the establishment of a Truth and Reconciliation Commission in South Africa has meant that any action under the Apartheid Convention is unlikely. This poor prognosis for the Apartheid Convention is underlined by the fact that it has been dropped from the Draft Code of Offences against the Peace and Security of Mankind.[95]

6. THE CODIFICATION OF STATE RESPONSIBILITY

(a) The International Law Commission's Mandate and Early Work

It is intrinsic in all social relations, including international relations, that the violation of a legally binding obligation creates legal responsibility.[96] The rules on state responsibility are concerned with the incidence and consequences of violations of international law.

On 7 December 1953, the General Assembly adopted Resolution 799(VIII) requesting the ILC to undertake the codification of the principles of international law governing state responsibility. The text of the Resolution was as follows:

Request for the codification of the principles of international law governing state responsibility . . .
The General Assembly,
Considering that it is desirable for the maintenance and development of peaceful

---

[95] See Chapter 12 below, and compare the Draft Code of 1991 with those of 1995 and 1996. Article 7(1)(j) of the Rome Statute of the International Criminal Court, A/CONF.183/9, recasts the crime of apartheid as a crime against humanity.

[96] See I. Brownlie, *Principles of Public International Law*, 4th edn. (1990), 432 ff.

relations between states that the principles of international law governing state responsibility be codified,

Noting that the ILC at its first session included the topic 'state responsibility' in its provisional list of topics of international law selected for codification,

Requests the ILC, as soon as it considers it advisable, to undertake the codification of the principles of international law governing state responsibility.

This text threw little light on the exact scope of the codification, but the ILC felt that the expression 'state responsibility' could not be literally and narrowly construed. At an early stage the ILC, in conformity with Article 18 of its Statute, had surveyed the whole field of international law with a view to selecting topics for codification. In the relevant memorandum submitted by the Secretary-General, it was stated that the codification of the rules on state responsibility 'must take into account the problems which have arisen in connection with recent developments such as the question of the criminal responsibility of states as well as that of individuals acting on behalf of the state'.[97] Such novel features of state responsibility were referred to only incidentally in considering the suitability of the topic for codification, but it was inevitable that the existence of these features would become a central problem when the topic was studied in depth. The ILC went so far as to say that it was necessary to do something more than 'to codify'; traditional law needed to be changed and adapted so that it would reflect the profound transformations that had occurred in international law.[98]

The first Special Rapporteur on state responsibility, Mr Garcia-Amador, brought his first report before the ILC in 1956. Garcia-Amador considered the extent to which criminal responsibility under international law was segregated and distinct from civil responsibility. He was of the opinion that, particularly since the Second World War, the idea of international criminal responsibility had become so well defined and so widely acknowledged that it must be admitted as one of the consequences of the breach or non-observance of certain international obligations, and thus should not be ignored in the codification of state responsibility.[99]

In Garcia-Amador's opinion, international law distinguished 'merely wrongful' acts from 'punishable acts'.[100] In speaking of punishable acts, he was referring to 'crimes under international law' committed by individuals who are organs of the state and acting as such, rather than international crimes committed by the states themselves. However, he may have seen in the punishment of the individual a form of responsibility of the state of which

---

[97] A/CN.4/1/Rev. 1, *Survey of International Law in Relation to the Work of Codification of the ILC* (1949), 57.

[98] See Report on International Responsibility by F. V. Garcia-Amador, A/CN.4/96; (1956) *YrbkILC* 2, 173, 176.

[99] Ibid. 182–3. See also the debate in the Commission (General Discussion on State Responsibility), (1956) *YrbkILC* 1, 228–48, esp. 239–45.   [100] Ibid.

the individual is an agent.[101] He subsequently submitted to the ILC a draft limited to the question of state responsibility for injuries to aliens.

Between 1960 and 1962, in the Sixth Committee of the General Assembly, the delegations of the Soviet Union and other Socialist countries, and many developing countries, consistently criticized the Draft Articles drawn up by Garcia-Amador.[102] They felt that the codification of state responsibility for violations of the fundamental principles of international law was an urgent matter, and they referred specifically to obligations in connection with the maintenance of international peace and security, aggression and other infringements of territorial integrity, independence and sovereignty of states, and the right of peoples to self-determination.

In response to these criticisms, the ILC set up a Sub-Committee on the codification of state responsibility.[103] It was agreed that the codification should concern only the rules defining the conditions for the existence of an internationally wrongful act and its consequences (secondary rules), and not the rules laying down obligations the violation of which may be the cause of responsibility (primary rules). The Sub-Committee's report recommended that the ILC 'give priority to the definition of the general rules governing the international responsibility of the state'.[104] Listed as one of the points to be considered in the programme of work proposed by the Sub-Committee was the 'possible distinction between international wrongful acts involving merely a duty to make reparation and those involving the application of sanctions. Possible basis for such a distinction.'[105] The ILC unanimously approved the Sub-Committee's work, and appointed Roberto Ago as Special Rapporteur on state responsibility.

In 1973 the ILC began to prepare the Draft Articles on State Responsibility. Article 1, entitled 'Responsibility of a State for its Internationally Wrongful Acts', established that '[e]very internationally wrongful act of a state entails the international responsibility of that state'. This was designed to state a basic principle 'capable of encompassing in itself all the various possible cases'.[106] One such case would be 'a distinct and more serious category of internationally wrongful acts, which might perhaps be described as international crimes'.[107] In this context the term 'sanction' was used to 'describe a measure which, although not necessarily involving the use of

[101] See further Chapter 12 below, s. 5.
[102] See e.g. speeches by the delegations of the Soviet Union (A/C.6/SR.651, paras. 9–10 and SR. 657, para. 31; A/C.6/SR.717, para. 36); Romania (SR. 653, paras. 9–10); Hungary (SR. 654, paras. 12–13.); see also J. H. H. Weiler, A. Cassese, and M. Spinedi (eds.), *Crimes of State: A Critical Analysis of the ILC's Draft Article 19 on State Responsibility* (1989), 12–13.
[103] (1962) *YrbkILC* 2, 188–91.
[104] Report by R. Ago, Chairman of the Sub-Committee on State Responsibility, A/CN.4/152; (1963) *YrbkILC* 2, 227, 228.   [105] Ibid.
[106] Report of the ILC on the Work of its Twenty-Fifth Session, A/CN.4/272; (1973) *YrbkILC* 2, 155, 172.   [107] Ibid. 172.

force, is characterized—at least in part—by the fact that the purpose is to inflict punishment'.[108]

In 1976 Ago emphasized the growing tendency since the Second World War to single out among international obligations a restricted set of obligations to which a special regime of responsibility needed to be attached in order to safeguard the fundamental interests of the international community as a whole. He spoke of, on the one hand, a 'heavy', severe kind of international responsibility for violations of the basic principles of international law where the main emphasis and concern of the modern approach to the question of international responsibility should be placed and, on the other hand, a less severe kind of international responsibility for other breaches of international obligations which often result in agreed solutions and are to be seen in close relation to the question of dispute settlement.[109] His proposed Draft Article 18 stated:[110]

2. The breach by a State of an international obligation established for the purpose of maintaining international peace and security, and in particular the breach by a State of the prohibition of any resort to the threat or use of force against the territorial integrity or political independence of another State, is an 'international crime'.
3. The serious breach by a State of an international obligation established by a norm of general international law accepted and recognized as essential by the international community as a whole and having as its purpose:
(a) respect for the principle of the equal rights of all peoples and of their right of self-determination; or
(b) respect for human rights and fundamental freedoms for all, without distinction based on race, sex, language or religion; or
(c) the conservation and the free enjoyment for everyone of a resource common to all mankind is also an 'international crime'.
4. The breach by a State of any other international obligation is an 'international delict'.

The Drafting Committee unanimously agreed to crystallize these ideas, with some alterations and changes in emphasis, in Draft Article 19,[111] which reads as follows:

1. An act of a state which constitutes a breach of an international obligation is an internationally wrongful act, regardless of the subject-matter of the obligation breached.
2. An internationally wrongful act which results from the breach by a state of an international obligation so essential for the protection of fundamental interests of the international community that its breach is recognized as a crime by that community as a whole constitutes an international crime.

---

[108] Ibid. 175.
[109] See Fifth Report on State Responsibility by Roberto Ago, Special Rapporteur, A/CN.4/291 and Add. 1 and 2; (1976) *YrbkILC* vol. 2, pt. 1, 3.   [110] Ibid. 54.
[111] (1976) *YrbkILC*, vol. 2, pt. 2, 95–6.

3. Subject to paragraph 2, and on the basis of the rules of international law in force, an international crime may result, *inter alia*, from:

(a) a serious breach of an international obligation of essential importance for the maintenance of international peace and security, such as that prohibiting aggression;

(b) a serious breach of an international obligation of essential importance for safeguarding the right of self-determination of peoples, such as that prohibiting the establishment or maintenance by force of colonial domination;

(c) a serious breach on a widespread scale of an international obligation of essential importance for safeguarding the human being, such as those prohibiting slavery, genocide and apartheid;

(d) a serious breach of an international obligation of essential importance for the safeguarding and preservation of the human environment, such as those prohibiting massive pollution of the atmosphere or the seas.

4. Any internationally wrongful act which is not an international crime in accordance with paragraph 2 constitutes an international delict.

The ILC completed the first reading of Part I of the Draft Articles on State Responsibility in 1980 and provisionally adopted thirty-five draft articles dealing with the origin of international responsibility.[112] It decided to postpone consideration of the regime of responsibility under which a state guilty of an international crime would be placed until it began work on Part II of the Draft Articles.[113]

(b) The Method of Defining Crimes of State in Draft Article 19

The ILC had three options available to it when it came to choosing a method of designating which acts could be characterized as international crimes of state.[114] An exhaustive list of those acts could be drawn up, or the criterion for determining such a list could merely be indicated, or an intermediate path could be followed. The method of drawing up an exhaustive list was discarded because it would not have permitted the definition of international crimes to be progressively adapted to the future evolution of international law, and would have involved the ILC in defining the content of the primary obligations the breach of which entailed state responsibility. Another less openly stated reason was that it was difficult to reach agreement on a complete list of international crimes. The method of indicating a general criterion

---

[112] (1980) *YrbkILC*, vol. 2, pt. 2, 30–4.

[113] Between 1980 and 1996, Willem Riphagen (Special Rapporteur, 1980–6) and Gaetano Arangio-Ruiz (Special Rapporteur, 1987–96) produced reports dealing with Parts II and III of the Draft Articles. The ILC completed the first reading of Parts II and III in 1996. See Report of the ILC on the Work of its Forty-Eighth Session, GAOR, Fifty-First Session (1996), Suppl. No. 10 (A/51/10), 125–51. See further Chapter 13 below, s. 5.

[114] See Commentary to Draft Article 19, (1976) *YrbkILC*, vol. 2, pt. 2, 119–20.

for identifying international crimes was also rejected, as it did not take sufficient account of the need to be able to determine easily whether at a given moment a certain act was an international crime. The ILC eventually adopted an intermediate path. It decided to take as a basic criterion that used in Article 53 of the Vienna Convention on the Law of Treaties[115] relating to norms of *jus cogens*, and then added some concrete indications and examples in order to facilitate the determination of the acts in question.

The basic criterion appears in paragraph 2 of Article 19 and establishes that for the purposes of the Draft Articles, the violation of an international obligation is to be considered a wrongful act coming within the category of particularly serious internationally wrongful acts, or international crimes, and will as a result entail the special regime of responsibility indicated in the second part of the Draft Articles, if it can be established that the international community as a whole recognizes it as such. In the opinion of the ILC, the system of giving only a basic criterion for determining the obligations in question would encourage the crystallization of international practice and jurisprudence in the field, while at the same time being flexible enough not to be an obstacle to the development of the legal conscience of states.[116]

Paragraph 2 has two aspects. It also states that only a breach of an obligation 'essential for the protection of fundamental interests of the international community' will qualify as an international crime. This phrase injects the definition with an inductive element which complements the basic criterion. The international community as a whole is responsible for judging whether the obligation is essential and, accordingly, whether its breach is of a criminal nature.

Paragraph 3 indicates the areas of international law more likely to involve obligations whose breach is recognized by the international community as a whole as a crime. These are areas containing rules aimed at: the maintenance of international peace and security; the safeguard of the right of self-determination of peoples; the safeguard of the human being; and the safeguard and preservation of the human environment. Examples are supplied for each of the areas mentioned of breaches currently recognized as crimes by the international community as a whole. These are aggression, the establishment or maintenance by force of colonial domination, slavery, genocide, apartheid, and massive pollution of the atmosphere or the seas.

The breaches mentioned in paragraph 3 do not constitute an exhaustive list of international crimes. This appears clearly from the use of *inter alia* in the text of the paragraph, and was specifically stressed in the commentary which states that the ILC, in giving examples of international crimes, in no way intended to imply that international law then in force recognized no other

---

[115] See Chapter 5 below, s. 2.   [116] (1976) *YrbkILC*, vol. 2, pt. 2, 119.

crimes, or that it might not recognize them in the future.[117] The Special Rapporteur recognized that the list was already dated, and that crimes such as colonialism, slavery, and apartheid might soon disappear. On the other hand, the crimes referred to in sub-paragraph (d), such as depriving human beings of their environment, taking away their sources of supply, and causing climatic changes, could be the crimes of the future. In addition there are potentially many acts that qualify for inclusion in sub-paragraph (c), for example the massacre of prisoners of war, the deportation of populations, and crimes referred to in the conventions on humanitarian law.

In order to determine whether at a given moment other acts are to be regarded as international crimes for the purposes of the Draft Articles, the basic criterion set out in paragraph 2 must be applied: it must be established whether the international community as a whole recognizes them as particularly serious wrongful acts entailing a special regime of responsibility. The list of examples in paragraph 3 is not, in a true sense, a part of the definition, and it was perhaps added to ensure that the definition would at least extend to the wrongful acts mentioned.

(c) Critique of Draft Article 19[118]

Criticisms of Article 19 have been concerned as much with the concept of international crimes embodied in the Article as with its precise wording. Nevertheless a few comments may be made regarding the suitability of Article 19 as an international criminal law framework.

First, paragraph 2 is circular and, when read together with paragraph 3, the definition of state crime could be said to amount to no more than the following: if an act 'is so serious that the international community as a whole stigmatizes that act as criminal, then it is to be accounted a crime'.[119]

Second, while paragraph 2 is concerned with the importance of international norms, paragraph 3 does not frame fundamentality in terms of those norms, but in terms of seriousness. This leads to a confusion of the gravity of the norm with the gravity of the breach.

Third, paragraph 3 refers to unspecified rules of international law in force and does not explain fully what role these rules play in applying the general definition in paragraph 2. The phrase 'may result' also lacks specificity.[120]

---

[117] (1976) *YrbkILC*, vol. 2, pt. 2, 120.

[118] See esp. First Report on State Responsibility by James Crawford, Special Rapporteur, A/CN.4/490/Add.1, 24 Apr. 1998, paras. 46–50, and Report of the ILC on the Work of its Fiftieth Session, GAOR, Fifty-Third session (1998), Suppl. No. 10 (A/53/10), paras. 202–331.

[119] Ibid. para. 50. However, the definition of crimes is no more circular than the definition of *jus cogens* in Article 53 of the Vienna Convention on the Law of Treaties, and it has been argued by G. Abi-Saab, 'The Uses of Article 19', (1999) *EJIL* 10, no. 2, 339, 341, that Article 19 is an improvement on Article 53 as the cause rather than the effect is at the basis of the definition.

[120] 'First Report on State Responsibility' (n. 118 above), para. 49.

Fourth, the non-exhaustive list of vague terms in paragraph 3 fails to illuminate the substantive nature of the crimes mentioned, and it is questionable whether it is appropriate in the first place to list examples.[121] The individual sub-paragraphs are rife with the term 'such as', and with qualifying adjectives like 'essential', 'widespread', and 'massive'. Arguably this language is not specific enough for defining the highest level of responsibility, particularly as it may not be a court which makes the determination.[122] Sub-paragraph (a) is perhaps too broad and could be limited to prohibiting aggression, unless the dividing line between lawful and unlawful uses of force becomes clearer. The prohibition of forcible colonial domination in sub-paragraph (b) is becoming increasingly out of date and could possibly be replaced by more current obligations for safeguarding the right of self-determination. Sub-paragraph (c) deals appropriately with slavery, genocide, and apartheid, and could include torture as state policy,[123] but it may not need to go beyond this given the rapid developments and emergence of multilateral treaties in the human rights field. With regard to paragraph (d), it cannot be determined from Article 19 whether a given case of pollution of the seas, for example, constitutes an international crime or merely a public-law violation which may be best dealt with under the treaties and agencies dealing with such problems. A possible candidate for inclusion in a separate sub-paragraph of paragraph 3 is state-sponsored terrorism, and the use of nuclear weapons could also be listed. Finally, there is no mention of the mental element for a crime, but this is perhaps an aspect of the primary rule.

In general, it seems that the ILC took care not to make the definition of crimes too broad, while allowing scope for future developments, but the end result proved to be less than satisfactory. It is notable that Draft Article 19, as adopted by the Commission, differs significantly from Ago's original proposal which was broader in its scope yet more specific in its content. Crawford has commented that Ago's proposal 'is better read as an attempt to express the notion of obligations *erga omnes*'[124] and he points to the fact that the term 'international crime' appeared in inverted commas. It would seem that the members of the ILC were keen to go a step further and attempt to describe a genuine concept of crime.

---

[121] Cf. Abi-Saab, 'The Uses of Article 19', who states that 'the examples were probably provided in order to demonstrate that the category is not moot or purely hypothetical and that several of its species are evident and recognizable in international practice'.

[122] See further Chapter 15 below.

[123] R. H. Higgins queries its omission in *Problems and Process: International Law and How We Use It* (1994), 168.

[124] 'First Report on State Responsibility' (n. 118 above), para. 51, n. 33.

(d) The International Law Commission's 1998 Position on Draft Article 19

At its forty-ninth session in 1997, the ILC appointed James Crawford as
Special Rapporteur on the topic of state responsibility and established a
Working Group to address matters concerning the second reading of the
topic.[125] The ILC's aim is to complete the second reading by the end of the
quinquennium (2001).

In his First Report on State Responsibility,[126] Crawford revisited the question of a distinction between criminal and delictual responsibility. He concluded, on the basis of the comments received by governments,[127] that Article
19 was generally viewed as an exercise of development rather than codification, that the terminology of crimes was widely felt to be potentially misleading, and that the definition of state crimes in Draft Article 19 needed
further clarification.[128]

Crawford considered various possible future approaches to the concept of
state criminal responsibility in the Draft Articles.[129] These included maintaining the status quo; replacing the concept of state crime by a new concept
of 'exceptionally serious wrongful acts'; elaborating a full-scale punitive
regime of state criminal responsibility; rejecting the concept of state crime
completely, both within the Draft Articles and in international law; and
simply excluding the concept from the ambit of the Draft Articles.[130]
Crawford favoured the fifth option, believing that the subject required separate treatment.[131] This would not preclude the development of the concepts
of obligations *erga omnes* and *jus cogens* in the context of the second reading
of Part II in particular.[132] It was also emphasized by Crawford that his recommendation was without prejudice 'to the notion of "international crimes
of States" and its possible future development, whether as a separate topic
for the Commission, or through State practice and the practice of the competent international organizations'.[133]

7. CONCLUSION

The aim of this chapter has been to trace attempts, successful or otherwise,
to develop and codify the law relating to international criminal responsibility
which touched upon, or dealt in detail with, the concept of state criminality.
The adoption by the ILC of a distinction between crimes and delicts is clearly

[125] Report of the ILC on the Work of its Fiftieth Session, GAOR, Fifty-Third session (1998),
Suppl. No. 10 (A/53/10), 111.   [126] A/CN.4/490 and Adds. 1–3.
[127] Crawford recognized that these comments could not be regarded as representative of the
views of the international community as a whole.
[128] 'First Report on State Responsibility' (n. 118 above), paras. 52–60.
[129] A/CN.4/490/Add. 3, 11 May 1998, paras. 76–101.   [130] Ibid. paras. 76–99.
[131] Ibid. para. 100.   [132] Ibid. paras. 87 and 101.   [133] Ibid. para. 101.

a landmark but it must be treated in its historical context. It is a significant, but somewhat limited,[134] aspect of the concept of state criminality's journey through history and into present-day international law. Further aspects of this journey will be considered once the concept's intellectual feasibility and juridical status in contemporary international law have been established.

[134] The reference here is to the inherent limitations of Article 19 which have been discussed above, to the limited remit of the Draft Articles on State Responsibility, and to the limited chance of survival of the concept of state criminality in the final Draft. On these latter two aspects see also Chapter 13 below, s. 5, and Chapter 16 below, s. 7.

PART II

Juridical Status of the
Concept of State Criminality

3

The Concept of Criminal Organizations

1. ORIGINS OF THE CONCEPT OF CRIMINAL ORGANIZATIONS

The crimes committed during the Second World War contained certain unparalleled features which called for innovative methods of prosecution. As the Secretaries of State and War and the Attorney-General wrote in a Memorandum to President Roosevelt on 22 January 1945:

The criminality of the German leaders and their associates does not consist solely of individual outrages, but represents the result of a systematic and planned reign of terror . . . We are satisfied that these atrocities were perpetrated in pursuance of a premeditated criminal plan or enterprise which either contemplated or necessarily involved their commission.[1]

The Allied Powers faced the challenge of devising or adapting a legal mechanism to deal with the type of organized criminality which had been carried out by the German state apparatus and numerous willing participants between 1933 and 1945, while taking care not to condemn the German people as a whole.

An American solution to this problem was first engineered in September 1944 by Colonel Murray Bernays, who felt it was important to understand the perverse ideology behind Nazi criminality:

The ordinary thug does not defend on the ground that thuggery is noble, he only contends that the police have arrested the wrong man. Behind each Axis war criminal, however, lies the basic criminal instigation of the Nazi doctrine and policy. It is the guilty nature of this instigation that must be established, for only then will the conviction and punishment of the individuals concerned achieve their true moral and juristic significance.[2]

Bernays' proposed plan consisted of two phases. First, a special international tribunal would establish that the Nazi Government, its party, and other agencies such as the Gestapo, SS, and SA were guilty of conspiracy to commit murder and other violent crimes. The tribunal would also try individual representatives of these organizations, who would have the guilt of the organization imputed to them and be prosecuted on the basis of membership alone. According to the second phase, every member of an organization held to be

---

[1] See Dept. of State, *Report of Robert H. Jackson, United States Representative to the International Conference on Military Trials* (1949), 4–5.

[2] B. F. Smith (ed.), *The American Road to Nuremberg: The Documentary Record 1944–1945* (1982), Document 16, 35.

criminal would be subject to arrest, trial, and punishment in the national courts of the Allies, proof of membership being sufficient to establish guilt. This plan was not explicitly endorsed by President Roosevelt, but when Truman took over the presidency, Bernays' proposals were approved in their refined version and presented to the Allies at the London Conference in June 1945.

Initially it seemed that international law was not sufficiently developed to accommodate the American plan, and the notions of conspiracy and criminal organizations proved to be very controversial, in particular because conspiracy was a common law concept which also constituted the doctrinal underpinnings of the criminal organizations idea. Parallel to discussions on the political plane, the issue was considered in depth in the UN War Crimes Commission. A draft recommendation was prepared by the Legal Committee in July and August 1944, which declared *inter alia* the right of the Allied occupying authorities in Germany to disband the SA, SS, and Gestapo, intern its members, and 'make membership in them henceforth a crime and punish it as such'.[3] It was felt that the topic required further study and the debate was reopened by the French representative to a special Sub-Committee established under the chairmanship of Lord Wright in December 1944. A new French memorandum was submitted in March 1945, stating that the principle of individual guilt could not be applied to the entirely new phenomenon of mass criminality, and that a novel procedure was required to ensure that war criminals would not escape punishment solely on account of the difficulty of proving their individual guilt.

French law provided two possible solutions. The first was the reversal of the burden of proof to invoke a presumption of guilt. Second, individuals could be held guilty of voluntary membership in an 'association' of criminals as provided for in the French Penal Code (Articles 265–7). Most members agreed in principle with the proposal, but specific responses ranged from that of the Dutch delegate, who expressed unease over the concept of collective responsibility, to that of the Czech delegate, who thought the evidence already collected warranted an outright declaration that membership in the Gestapo, SS, and similar bodies was in itself a war crime. The matter was adjourned pending a full report by the Commission's legal Secretariat on the facts and the legal conclusions deriving from them. Following the submission of the Report in May 1945, the French representative produced a draft recommendation which was adopted by the Commission on 16 May, and read as follows:

The United Nations War Crimes Commission, having ascertained that countless crimes have been committed during the war by organized gangs, Gestapo groups, SS or military units, sometimes entire formations, in order to secure the punishment of all the guilty, makes the following recommendation to the member Governments:

[3] UNWCC, *History of the United Nations War Crimes Commission and the Development of the Laws of War* (1948), 291–2.

(a) to seek out the leading criminals responsible for the organization of criminal enterprises including systematic terrorism, planned looting and the general policy of atrocities against the peoples of the occupied states, in order to punish all the organizers of such crimes;

(b) to commit for trial, either jointly or individually all those who, as members of these criminal gangs, have taken part in any way in the carrying out of crimes committed collectively by groups, formations or units.[4]

Section (a) was intended to avert fears over the concept of collective responsibility by pointing to the responsibility of the leading criminals, while section (b) implied the possibility of holding individuals guilty of membership in a criminal organization as such.

2. THE NUREMBERG CHARTER

It was left to the Nuremberg Charter and Tribunal to establish a logically consistent and just theory of criminal organizations on the basis of the recommendations of the Commission. The main source of international law on the matter is contained in Articles 9–11 of the Nuremberg Charter which provide:

Article 9

At the trial of any individual member of any group or organization the Tribunal may declare (in connection with any act of which the individual may be convicted) that the group or organization of which the individual was a member was a criminal organization.

After receipt of the Indictment the Tribunal shall give such notice as it thinks fit that the prosecution intends to ask the Tribunal to make such declaration and any member of the organization will be entitled to apply to the Tribunal for leave to be heard by the Tribunal upon the question of the criminal character of the organization. The Tribunal shall have the power to allow or reject the application. If the application is allowed, the Tribunal may direct in what manner the applicants shall be represented and heard.

Article 10

In cases where a group or organization is declared criminal by the Tribunal, the competent national authority of any Signatory shall have the right to bring individuals to trial for membership therein before national, military or occupation courts. In any case the criminal nature of the group or organization is considered proved and shall not be questioned.

Article 11

Any person convicted by the Tribunal may be charged before a national, military or occupation court, referred to in Article 10 of this Charter, with a crime other than of membership in a criminal group or organization and such court may, after convicting

---

4 Ibid. 296.

him, impose upon him punishment independent of and additional to the punishment imposed by the Tribunal for participation in the criminal activities of such group or organization.

Thus, the Nuremberg Tribunal was empowered to declare that an indicted group or organization was criminal, which meant that in subsequent proceedings the criminal nature of the group or organization could not be challenged, and on this basis an individual could be prosecuted for the crime of 'membership' therein. It did not appear to be the intention of the Charter that once an organization was declared criminal, all its members were automatically guilty of membership, although the wording of the Charter did not eliminate the possibility.

Six groups or organizations were indicted by the prosecutors for the US, France, the UK, and the Soviet Union: the Cabinet of the Nazi Government (Reich Cabinet), the Leadership Corps of the Nazi Party, the SS (*Schutzstaffeln*), the Gestapo, the SA (*Sturmabteilungen*), and the General Staff and High Command of the German Armed Forces. The groups or organizations were charged on all counts under the Charter, namely crimes against peace, including as a separate crime conspiracy to prepare, initiate, or wage aggressive wars; war crimes and crimes against humanity. In principle, the organizations were indicted as a whole and the charges related to all their members. The Prosecution did, however, make certain explicit exclusions in respect of the Gestapo, the Leadership Corps, and the SA.

3. PROSECUTION ARGUMENTS AT NUREMBERG

The prosecutors faced the task of developing a precise and complete theory of collective criminality and liability, as distinguished from individual criminality and liability. The theory was presented along three lines of reasoning. The first issue was the concept of collective criminality. Justice Jackson attempted to demonstrate that the Charter did not introduce an entirely new legal concept, by pointing to the legislation of several different countries which allowed for the prosecution of members of collective bodies found to be criminal.[5] For example, in the US the Smith Act of 1940 made it a felony to be a member of any organization which advocated the overthrow of the US Government by force or violence. In the UK, the British India Act No. 30 of 1836 provided that 'whoever was proved to have belonged to a gang of thugs' was to be punished with 'imprisonment for life with hard labour'.[6] German law itself provided the most striking examples. The German Penal Code of 1871 made the 'participation in an organization, the existence, con-

---

[5] See *Trial of German Major War Criminals: Proceedings of the IMT*, 27 Feb.–11 Mar. 1946, (hereinafter *Proceedings of the IMT*), pt. 8 (1947), 41–3.   [6] Ibid. 42.

stitution, or purposes of which are to be kept secret from the Government, or in which obedience to unknown superiors or unconditional obedience to known superiors is pledged' subject to punishment. In 1924, German courts declared the entire Nazi Party to be a criminal organization, and in 1927 and 1928 the German Communist Party was declared criminal and sentences were pronounced against its Leadership Corps. Following this analysis, Jackson laid down five essential tests of collective criminality:[7]

(1) The group or organization must be 'some aggregation of persons associated in identifiable relationship with a collective, general purpose'[8] or with a 'common plan of action'.[9] The notions of 'group' or 'organization' are non-technical. They 'mean in the context of the Charter what they mean in the ordinary speech of the people'. The term 'group' is used 'as a broader term, implying a looser or less formal structure or relationship than is implied in the term organization'.[10]

(2) Membership in such group or organization 'must be generally voluntary',[11] that is 'the membership as a whole, irrespective of particular cases of compulsion against individuals or groups of individuals within the organization must not have been due to legal compulsion'.[12]

(3) 'The aims of the organization must be criminal in that it was designed to perform acts denounced as crimes in Art. 6 of the Charter',[13] that is crimes against peace, war crimes or crimes against humanity.

(4) 'The criminal aims or methods of the organization must have been of such character that its membership in general may properly be charged with knowledge of them.'[14]

(5) 'Some individual defendant must have been a member of the organization and must be convicted of some act on the basis of which the organization was declared to be criminal.'[15]

The second point was the legal nature of the declaration of criminality. Jackson emphasized that the Tribunal was only empowered to try natural persons, and could not impose a sentence on the group or organization as such. The only issue was the collective criminality of the organization or group, and the judgment would be declaratory. Third, the question remained as to the effect of a declaration of criminality. One effect was that the criminal nature of the group or organization could no longer be challenged. It was also suggested that the declaration created a rebuttable presumption of guilt and thereby reversed the burden of proof.

---

[7] See *History of the UNWCC*, 305.   [8] *Proceedings of the IMT*, pt. 8, 45.

[9] *Trial of German Major War Criminals: Speeches of the Prosecutors at the Close of the Case Against the Indicted Organizations* (1946), 62.   [10] *Proceedings of the IMT*, pt. 8, 47.

[11] Ibid. 45.   [12] *Speeches of the Prosecutors*, 62.   [13] *Proceedings of the IMT*, pt. 8, 46.

[14] Ibid.   [15] Ibid.

4. DEFENCE ARGUMENTS AT NUREMBERG

The defence arguments[16] were numerous but related essentially to the novelty of the idea of criminal organizations, and the fact that the law in this respect was retrospective and not supported by the precedents referred to by the prosecution. It was also argued that the indicted organizations had already been dissolved by the Allied authorities and could not, therefore, be the object of a declaration of criminality. Following from this it was maintained that the task of declaring an organization to be criminal was that of a legislator and not a tribunal, and permitting the declaration to serve as law for the subsequent courts was contrary to the principles of modern justice. In addition, the defence maintained that the concept of guilt could only apply to individuals and not to groups, although this was inconsistent with the argument used elsewhere that only the state should bear responsibility under international law for aggressive war. Perhaps the most important defence argument, and the one which caused most concern to the Allies, was the point that as the membership of the indicted organizations composed many millions of individuals, the declarations of criminality would certainly affect the innocent. Defence counsel Dr Kubuschok argued:

to declare an organization criminal means the outlawing and branding as criminal, not only of the organization as such, but, above all, of each individual member. Such a declaration, therefore, means a final sentencing of each individual member to a general loss of honour. The effect of this outlawing and branding is unavoidable and ineradicable, especially if that verdict is pronounced by so important a Court as the International Military Tribunal before the forum of the world. The effect of the outlawing would apply to each member of the organization and would cling to him, regardless of whether the subsequent proceedings . . . were carried out against the individual members or not.[17]

It was also contested that the indicted organizations were criminal in the sense of the Charter, or that some of them were groups or organizations in the first place.

5. THE NUREMBERG JUDGMENT

The Judgment of the Tribunal constituted a third formative link in the development of the concept of criminal organizations following upon the law of the Charter and the combined arguments of the prosecution and defence. The Tribunal first established the general rule that there was a crime of

---

[16] *Proceedings of the IMT*, pt. 8, 61–127. For an interesting account of the defence arguments and the response of the prosecution see R. E. Conot, *Justice at Nuremberg* (1983), 455–66.

[17] *Proceedings of the IMT*, pt. 8, 61–2.

'membership' in an organization declared to be criminal, but emphasized that this was 'a far-reaching and novel procedure. Its application, unless properly safeguarded, may produce great injustice.'[18] The Tribunal went on to affirm that the thesis behind the Charter was that a declaration of group criminality would not result in an unqualified, indiscriminate, and automatic collective penal responsibility of all its members, and this had also been the approach of the prosecution. With reference to its own discretionary power in making declarations of criminality, the Tribunal declared:

This discretion is a judicial one and does not permit arbitrary action, but should be exercised in accordance with well-settled legal principles, one of the most important of which is that criminal guilt is individual and that mass punishment should be avoided. If satisfied of the criminal guilt of any organization or group, this Tribunal should not hesitate to declare it to be criminal because the theory of 'group criminality' is new, or because it might be unjustly applied by some subsequent tribunals. On the other hand, the Tribunal should make such declaration of criminality as far as possible in a manner to ensure that innocent persons will not be punished.[19]

The Tribunal also advanced a definition of a criminal group or organization:

A criminal organization is analogous to a criminal conspiracy in that the essence of both is co-operation for criminal purposes. There must be a group bound together and organized for a common purpose. The group must be formed or used in connection with the commission of crimes denounced by the Charter. Since the declaration with respect to the organizations and groups will, as has been pointed out, fix the criminality of its members, that definition should exclude persons who had no knowledge of the criminal purposes or acts of the organization and those who were drafted by the State for membership, unless they were personally implicated in the commission of acts declared criminal by Article 6 of the Charter as members of the organization. Membership alone is not enough to come within the scope of these declarations.[20]

A final issue concerned the allocation of the burden of proof in subsequent cases of personal guilt, and although the Tribunal seemed to delegate this task to the competent courts in subsequent proceedings, the wording used by the Tribunal indicates that it regarded the burden as resting on the prosecution, which to some extent frustrated the scheme for streamlined mass trials. As a result of unease over the concept of collective guilt, the Tribunal proceeded with caution and declared criminal only the Leadership Corps of the Nazi Party, the Gestapo, and the SS, although the Soviet Judge, Nikitchenko, voted to hold all of the indicted organizations criminal.

---

[18] *Trial of the Major War Criminals before the IMT*, Nuremberg, 14 Nov. 1945–1 Oct. 1946, (1947), *Nuremberg Judgment*, 171, 256.   [19] Ibid.
[20] Ibid.

6. THE SUBSEQUENT PROCEEDINGS

The concept of criminal organizations was a key feature of the subsequent Nuremberg proceedings under Law No. 10 of the Allied Control Council for Germany. Article II, paragraph 1(d) of the Law provided that 'Membership in categories of a criminal group or organization declared criminal by the International Military Tribunal' was recognized as a crime.[21] One of the main issues addressed in the subsequent proceedings was whether the prosecution or the defence was to bear the onus of proof in relation to tests of personal guilt. In certain cases it was explicitly ruled by the competent courts that the burden of proof remained on the prosecution.[22] While this seemed to be the general approach, in other cases the court was willing to assume knowledge on the part of defendants of the criminal purposes of the organization.[23]

Another important question was whether the competent courts could declare criminal certain groups or organizations which had not been found to be such by the Nuremberg Tribunal. An affirmative answer was provided in Article 4, paragraph 2, of the Polish War Crimes Decree of 1944.[24] The Polish courts declared organizations such as the leadership of the German civil administration in the so-called Central Government, officials of the administration of the Lodz ghetto, and members of the concentration camp staff at Auschwitz[25] to be criminal. The 'organization of a concentration camp' was stated to include the authorities, the administration, and the personnel of a camp, with the exception of the inmates, who under compulsion were performing various administrative functions.[26] A considerable number of trials led to the conviction of accused persons for membership in criminal organizations. A case which may be cited as typical of the jurisprudence created on these occasions is that of Karl Brandt et al. (Medical Case).[27] Brandt and eight other defendants were found guilty of membership in the SS, and they were consequently held to be implicated in the commission of war crimes and crimes against humanity. Similarly, in the trial of Josef Altstötter et al. (Justice Case),[28] the chief defendant, Altstötter, was found guilty on the count of membership only, it having been proved that he had knowledge of the criminal purposes and acts of the SS and voluntarily remained a member.

---

[21] Law Reports UNWCC, vol. 10, 59.   [22] See ibid. and vol. 13, 58–60 and 62.
[23] Ibid. vol. 15, 151–3.   [24] Ibid. vol. 7, 86–7.
[25] Ibid. 20–4, and vol. 14, 40–8.   [26] Ibid. vol. 7, 21.
[27] Trials of War Criminals before the Nuremberg Military Tribunals under Control Council Law No. 10, Nuremberg, Oct. 1946–Apr. 1949 (1950–3), vols. I and II, 3, 180.
[28] Ibid. vol. III, 3, 1029.

7. THE INTERNATIONAL MILITARY TRIBUNAL FOR THE FAR EAST

The concept of criminal organizations is mentioned in the Charter of the International Military Tribunal for the Far East, but there are no provisions corresponding to those of the Nuremberg Charter. Article 5 simply provides that the 'Tribunal shall have the power to try and punish war criminals who as individuals or as members of organizations' are prosecuted for offences falling within its competence. The question whether organizations could be declared to be criminal under the Charter was left unanswered by the Tribunal, as the prosecutors did not indict any of the groups or organizations to which the Japanese defendants belonged.

8. EVALUATION

It is significant that in the national law of various Allied countries, provisions dealing with criminal groups or organizations either were already in existence prior to the enactment of the Nuremberg Charter or were introduced in order to respond to the type of collective criminality evidenced by Nazi activities.[29] These provisions tend to be more far-reaching than those of the Nuremberg Charter, with the crime of membership in a criminal organization often entailing automatic punishment. An illustration is the French Ordinance of 24 August 1944, which extended certain provisions of the French Penal Code to enemy or quisling criminal groups or organizations. Article 2 states that by way of interpretation, '[o]rganizations or undertakings of systematic terrorism are regarded as representing an "association of malefactors" as provided in Article 265 and subsequent articles of the Penal Code'.[30] The notion of criminal organizations was also adopted by the US military commissions in their 'Regulations governing the Trial of War Criminals' in the 'China Theatre' of operations. These regulations formed part of general American military law and, in line with the attitude of Jackson and the US military Government in Germany, the crime of membership expressly operated by means of a rebuttable presumption of guilt.[31]

At a conservative estimate, around 7,000,000 individuals belonged to the organizations indicted at Nuremberg. Kubuschok felt that it could be said 'with great certainty that the Indictment will actually include a very considerable part of the adult male German population'.[32] Thus, the potential scope of the theory of criminal organizations was vast, and could have led to

---

[29] See generally *History of the UNWCC*, 324–32.   [30] Ibid. 327.
[31] Article 16(e) of the Regulations; see *History of the UNWCC*, 331.
[32] *Proceedings of the IMT*, pt. 8, 62.

the punishment of millions of individuals. Although the German Government or state itself was not indicted, the organizations were in fact the essence of the German state at the time, and the German people followed this aspect of the Nuremberg proceedings with anxiety. The judges faced difficulties both with the complications inherent in each of the organizations, and with general doubt about the justice of prosecuting organizations at all.[33]

During the proceedings various ways of eliminating the idea of collective guilt were considered, such as exempting certain sub-groups from the overall ruling of criminality, or specifying a time period during which the organizations were to be considered criminal. It was also suggested that precise rules be established to be used by the occupation courts in the subsequent proceedings which would include fixed penalties for each category of members. Judge Biddle, who in January 1945 had been one of the three US Cabinet members to sign the paper recommending to Roosevelt that a trial system based on the prosecution of criminal organizations should be used, desired to repudiate the whole approach by September 1946.[34] On the other hand, his European counterparts realized that public opinion made it impossible to brush aside the question of criminal organizations. In the result, the approach of the Tribunal was so guarded that in theory the occupation authorities were left with the unrealizable task of prosecuting several million individuals, and of having to prove in each case that the defendant was a knowledgeable and voluntary member of a criminal organization. Nevertheless, the formula ensured that the worst threats to the civil liberties of individual members of organizations were overcome while ensuring that the underlying moral purpose was achieved. It has been said:

> Judicial pronouncement of the major Nazi structures as criminal organizations was to have a great symbolic, moral, political and ideological significance. The condemnation of Nazism as a political movement, as a system of ideological propositions and, most of all, as a state practice—in short, as a multi-faceted social phenomenon, was the major goal.[35]

The Nuremberg Tribunal faced many difficulties in relation to the possible criminality of organizations, and devised a pragmatic and just method of dealing with them.[36] It has been said that 'organization trials seemed to offer

---

[33] See further B. F. Smith, *Reaching Judgment at Nuremberg* (1977), 160–70.

[34] Ibid. 161.

[35] S. Pomorski, 'Conspiracy and Criminal Organization', in G. Ginsburgs and V. N. Kudriavtsev (eds.), *The Nuremberg Trial and International Law* (1990), 213, 225.

[36] For a contrasting view see H. Kelsen, 'Will the Judgment in the Nuremberg Trial Constitute a Precedent in International Law?', (1947) 1 *ILQ* 153, 165–6, who condemns the theory of organizational criminality as being primitive and inconsistent with the London Charter's establishment of the principle of individual responsibility for crimes against peace. However, the notion is included in Article I(2) of the 1973 Apartheid Convention: 'The States Parties to the present Convention declare criminal those organizations, institutions and individuals committing the crime of apartheid.' Somewhat surprisingly, organizational criminality is not a feature of the 1948 Genocide Convention.

the only effective means for punishing thousands of Nazi collaborators who might otherwise have escaped justice, and, at the same time, for segregating potentially dangerous elements of the population from a mass of passive or non-Nazi Germans'.[37] Since Nuremberg it would seem that a declaratory judgment of criminality may be made against an organization, although this does not mean that the organization itself is liable, and the theory of organizational criminality differs in this crucial respect from that of corporate criminality.[38] In a sense, the notion of organizational criminality goes further in making each individual within an organization susceptible to punishment, rather than directing the punishment towards the organization as a legal entity. The question is whether the Nuremberg principle can be taken further to include the possibility of a declaratory judgment of criminality against the state as an organization. Given the magnitude of a state, it would be absurd to try each and every citizen for a crime of the state, even if this would be the only true way of segregating the innocent from the guilty. Perhaps such dramatic action does not seem so inconceivable when it is remembered that over 100,000 Rwandans are awaiting trial for the 1994 massacres in their country, but the justice of this may be queried.

The lesson from Nuremberg seems to be that a declaration of criminality against an organization such as a state need not expose the entire population to the threat of punishment, but enables the members of the government and significant numbers of key criminals to be tried individually, preferably by an international tribunal. To take a practical example, if the International Criminal Tribunal for Rwanda had been endowed with the jurisdiction to declare that the Rwandan Government and groups which instigated the 1994 massacres were criminal organizations, and could specify the maximum penalty for membership, it might have encouraged fairer and swifter trials in Rwandan courts where thousands of 'minor' criminals face a long wait in custody and qualify potentially for the death penalty. This illustrates the point that the notion of group criminality is not necessarily a formula for injustice if the institutions are in place to enable it to operate effectively.

9. THE CRIMINALITY OF GOVERNMENTS

Proceeding from the idea that the state is a fiction, Drost rejects the concept of the criminal responsibility of a state under international law, but believes that it is possible to imagine a criminal government:

The criminal state is juridically speaking a nonsense; the criminal government, on the contrary, a juristic reality and challenge of the first order. The state is amoral; many

---

[37] H. Leventhal, 'The Nuernberg Verdict', (1947) 60 *Harvard Law Rev.*, 857, 901.
[38] See Chapter 4 below.

a government immoral. The punishability of the state is both a legal and a practical impossibility. Governments could and should be punished, if the international legal order were to provide the implementation of penal justice.[39]

Drost envisages the individual responsibility of the members of the government.

At a relatively early stage in the deliberations of the UN War Crimes Commission it was suggested by the Dutch representative that the Commission should declare the whole German Government responsible for the atrocities committed by its subordinates.[40] This proposal was supported by the delegates of Australia, Belgium, China, India, Norway, Poland, and Yugoslavia. Although it was not decided to declare the Nazi Government a criminal group, this was implied in the decision taken by the Commission to collect evidence in respect of the Nazi Government and other 'arch-criminals'. The Sub-Committee appointed in December 1944 under the Chairmanship of Lord Wright was asked to advise on the question how far criminal responsibility for war crimes extended to 'subordinate members or officials of the guilty Government'.[41] The Sub-Committee dealt primarily with the question 'whether membership of enemy Governments may involve criminal responsibility for the criminal policy followed by such Governments'. It was concluded by the Czech representative:

membership of the German Government during a period in the course of which war crimes were either committed or prepared by members of the state apparatus, was a sufficient *prima facie* proof of their guilt and justified the decision to put them on the list of war criminals.[42]

This conclusion was approved by the Sub-Committee. Despite the fact that the German Government was never branded a criminal organization, this idea formed the basis of the trials against the major war criminals and lends credibility to the notion of governmental responsibility for state crimes. As the UN War Crimes Commission commented with reference to the Recommendation of 16 May 1945:

The recommendation did not go so far as to mention members of the Nazi Government in particular, or to proclaim the Nazi Government a criminal group as a whole. However the formula clearly included the Government and came very near to such a result.[43]

Oppenheim's *International Law* describes as acts which are directly imputable to the state its government's actions, or those of its officials or private individuals performed at the government's command or with its authorization.[44] One interpretation of the criminal responsibility of a state may therefore be to view the notion as equivalent to the criminal responsibility of

[39] P. N. Drost, *The Crime of State*, i. *Humanicide* (1959), 304.
[40] *History of the UNWCC*, 292.   [41] Ibid.   [42] Ibid. 293.   [43] Ibid. 297.
[44] R. Jennings and A. Watts (eds.), Oppenheim's *International Law*, i: *Peace*, 9th edn. (1992), 502, and see further Chapter 4 below, s. 4, on attribution to the state of the conduct of its agents.

the government. While the state may be an amoral entity, the government consists of identifiable individuals who have the power to do evil on a large scale, leaving the people suppressed or uninformed. There are countless situations where a split exists between the government apparatus and the majority of the people, the obvious example being apartheid. In accordance with the Nuremberg model, the members of the government could be held responsible individually before an international tribunal following a declaration that the government constituted a criminal organization. This would have the effect of condemning the state by holding that the existing government is no longer legitimate, while avoiding the risk of condemning an entire people, thereby allowing a fresh, legitimate government to begin a process of renewal. Sanctions could also be directed at the government itself as the entity representing the state.[45]

45 See further Chapter 4 below.

4

The Criminal Responsibility of Corporations

1. THE THEORY OF UNITY OF THE PATHS OF DEVELOPMENT OF NATIONAL LAW AND INTERNATIONAL LAW

It could be argued that the development of law represents a unified process in which national law and international law are merely at different stages. This may be described as the theory of unity of the paths of development of international law and national law.[1] Following the outbreak of the First World War, US jurists Root[2] and Peaslee[3] argued that international law ought to evolve in the same way as internal law and arrive at a distinction between two kinds of wrongs: those affecting only the directly injured state, and those affecting the entire international community. Thus, proponents of the concept of the criminal responsibility of a state might hold that, while until recently international law was unaware of such responsibility as it was still in a primitive form, it has since moved forward, and as a result, by analogy with national law, the criminal responsibility of states has emerged.

However, a mechanical transformation of the categories of national law into international law ignores the basic difference of structure between these two systems. As Judge Basdevant said in the *Phosphates in Morocco* case:

Quelle est la branche du droit interne qui présente de plus grandes différences avec le droit international que le droit pénal, le droit pénal qui est un droit d'autorité établi dans chaque Etat selon ses conceptions propres, le droit pénal que l'on rencontre dans tous les Etats, mais dont nous n'avons pas l'équivalent dans l'ordre juridique international? . . . Il est dangereux d'emprunter au droit pénal des concepts qu'on transporterait dans une matière où l'on ne mettrait plus en face l'un de l'autre un individu poursuivi au pénal et un Etat qui assure la régression, mais deux Etats. Le droit pénal, droit de hiérarchie et de subordination, peut difficilement inspirer le droit international, droit d'égalité et de coordination.[4]

Consequently, it would seem inadvisable to use national law indiscriminately as a reservoir from which international law can borrow new rules. National law relies on a vertical society, with the state in authority over its citizens. This structure conflicts with the principle of the equality of sovereign states.

Nevertheless, as Lord McNair remarked in the *International Status of South-West Africa* case, there has never been any question of importing

---

[1] See G. I. Tunkin, *Theory of International Law* (1974), 399.
[2] 'The Outlook for International Law', (1916) 10 *AJIL* 1, 8–9.
[3] 'The Sanction of International Law', (1916) 10 *AJIL* 328, 335.
[4] (1938) PCIJ, Series C, No. 85, 1060–1.

private law institutions 'lock, stock and barrel, ready-made and fully equipped with a set of rules'[5] into international law, and Waldock[6] comments that the question is one of finding in the private law institutions indications of legal policy and principles appropriate to the international problem at hand which may be useful general principles of international law. Brownlie has also remarked:

> the relations of states should not be equated to the relations of legal persons within domestic law, and . . . as a consequence, legal concepts should not be translated too readily from the realm of domestic law to the plane of international relations. At the same time there is no reason to refrain from subjecting international law and the sphere of international organization to analysis in terms of the values of national and, or, political systems.[7]

It is clearly necessary, taking into account the peculiarities of international law, to establish the basic features of a new phenomenon in international law, rather than trying to fit them into the maze of national law categories. For this task, certain aspects of national law may provide a framework for analysis and be useful as a guide.

One of the purposes of Article 38(1)(c) of the Statute of the ICJ is to allow international tribunals to apply the general principles of municipal jurisprudence to the extent that they are applicable in inter-state relations. In practice 'international tribunals have employed elements of legal reasoning and private law analogies in order to make the law of nations a viable system for application in a judicial process'.[8] Corporate criminal liability is now recognized in many national legal systems, and it may be helpful to draw certain analogies.

2. INDIVIDUALISM VERSUS HOLISM[9]

It has sometimes been said that criminal law deals necessarily with individuals because its premises bear on individual psychology and its sanctions are applicable to individuals alone. Phillimore was of this opinion:

> To speak of inflicting punishment upon a State is to mistake both the principles of criminal jurisprudence and the nature of the *legal* personality of a corporation. Criminal law is concerned with a *natural* person; a being of thought, feeling and will. A *legal* person is not, strictly speaking, a being of these attributes, though, through the mediums of representation and of government, the will of certain individuals is

5 (1950) ICJ Reports 128, 148.

6 'General Course on Public International Law', (1962–II) 106 Hague *Recueil* 5, 65.

7 'The Decisions of Political Organs of the United Nations and the Rule of Law', in R. St J. Macdonald (ed.), *Essays in Honour of Wang Tieya* (1993), 91, 91–2.

8 I. Brownlie, *Principles of Public International Law*, 4th edn. (1990), 16.

9 The phraseology is borrowed from B. Fisse and J. Braithwaite, *Corporations, Crime and Accountability* (1993), 20.

considered as the will of the corporation; but only for certain purposes. There must be *individual* will to found the jurisdiction of criminal law. Will by *representation* can not found that jurisdiction.[10]

The adage that 'guns don't kill people, people kill people' raises the same issue. It would be ridiculous to prosecute a tangible object such as a gun for manslaughter. Guns are controlled by human beings. The same is true of a state. Is it therefore equally absurd to talk of the criminality of an amorphous, fictional, intangible entity such as a state?

According to the philosophical position known as 'methodological individualism', corporate action is simply the sum of its individual parts and corporate crime is a fiction.[11] This view is embodied in the maxim *societas delinquere non potest*. In contrast, methodological holists such as Durkheim argue that individual will does not shape collective will. They focus on the institutional and social forces which shape individuals and before which individuals bow. Rejecting these extreme views, Fisse and Braithwaite aptly point out: 'We may readily agree with Durkheim that each kind of community is a thought world which penetrates and moulds the minds of its members, but that is not to deny the capacity of individuals to exercise their autonomy to resist and reshape thought worlds.'[12] Fisse and Braithwaite describe corporations as 'systems'[13] which reach decisions in unique ways but emit them in the same manner as individuals.[14] They go on to say that 'the moral responsibility of corporations for their actions relates essentially to social process and not to elusive attributes of personhood',[15] and argue that the appropriate attribution of responsibility and blame is more important than the 'attributes of moral personality'.[16] Corporate 'intentionality' is in their view expressed through corporate policy and strategy.[17] Emphasizing the relationship between law and culture, Fisse and Braithwaite conclude that it is not a legal fiction for the law to hold corporations responsible for their decisions,[18] and that corporate action is not merely the sum of individual actions.[19] In other words, the corporation as a legal entity may be blameworthy.

Despite the fact that some countries still adhere to the maxim *societas delinquere non potest*, indications are that the concept of corporate crime is increasingly being regarded as a necessary and legally defensible method of controlling and preventing wrongdoing by large organizations. Even France, which had resisted the idea of corporate criminal liability since the adoption of its *Code Pénal* in 1810, eventually succumbed to it in the *Nouveau Code Pénal* of 1992.[20]

---

[10] *Commentaries upon International Law*, 3rd edn. (1897), i. 5.
[11] See Fisse and Braithwaite, *Corporations, Crime and Accountability*, 17–18, and the works cited in nn. 1–8.   [12] Ibid. 21.
[13] Ibid.   [14] Ibid. 23.   [15] Ibid. 24.
[16] Ibid. 25, n. 34.   [17] Ibid. 26.   [18] Ibid. 28.
[19] Ibid. 135.   [20] Ss. 121–2.

3. THEORIES OF CORPORATE CRIMINAL RESPONSIBILITY

There are two major theories of corporate criminal liability: identification and imputation.[21] Under the identification theory, the basis for liability is that the acts of certain natural persons are actually the acts of the corporation. 'These people are seen not as the agents of the company but as its very person, and their guilt is the guilt of the company.'[22] Those who favour the identification rationale limit the scope of liability to those who represent the corporation. This would be equivalent to holding the government liable if this theory were transported into international law. Imputation is grounded in vicarious liability. According to this theory, the corporation is liable for the acts and intent of its employees, acting on behalf of the corporation, which are imputed to the entity. National courts began by adopting imputation of acts in cases of strict liability offences, and then gradually permitted imputation of specific intent of the employees to the corporation. In international law this would mean imputing the intent of the agents, acting on behalf of the state, to the state.

The imputation theory has been taken further in the form of the 'collective knowledge' concept. This approach imputes to the corporation the aggregate knowledge of several individuals, none of whom individually possesses sufficient information to satisfy the knowledge element of the offence. This theory has been found difficult to justify, as it stretches the criminal law principle of *mens rea*.

Alternative justifications for the criminal liability of corporations have been put forward. One theory in Italian law states that the corporation has a real and independent existence. This is based on an interpretation of the notion of a legal subject to mean any person whose interests or aims are defended by legal rules and who has an autonomous capacity to act. Certain objectives can only be achieved by means of a corporate structure, which, just like a physical person, has a will that is manifested by its individual organs. The difference between a physical person and a corporation is that in the case of the former goals and will coincide, whereas in the case of the latter the goals transcend the individual possessing the will and belong to many people.[23]

France, Germany, England and Wales, and Canada subscribe to the identification theory.[24] The French *Code Pénal* contains the most restrictive approach, in that a corporation can only be held criminally liable when one of

[21] See N. Parisi, 'Theories of Corporate Criminal Liability', in E. Hochstedler (ed.), *Corporations as Criminals* (1984), 41.

[22] J. Andrews, 'Reform in the Law of Corporate Liability', (1973) *Criminal Law Rev.* 91, 93.

[23] See C. E. Paliero, 'Criminal Liability of Corporations: Italy', in H. de Doelder and K. Tiedemann (eds.), *Criminal Liability of Corporations* (1996), 251, 256–7.

[24] See G. Stessens, 'Corporate Criminal Liability: A Comparative Perspective', (1994) 43 *ICLQ* 493, 506–10.

the legal representatives or organs of the corporation has acted.[25] In English law, 'Criminal liability of a corporation arises where an offence is committed in the course of the corporation's business by a person in control of its affairs to such a degree that it may fairly be said to think and act through him so that his actions and intent are the actions and intent of the corporation'.[26] In contrast to the French and German concept, the question whether a person is the 'directing mind and will' of a corporation does not depend on that person's formal title or position.

Dutch criminal law and US federal criminal law have adopted the imputation theory and the collective knowledge concept.[27] The American model is derived from the civil theory of *respondeat superior*, and there is no requirement that the wrongful acts be carried out by senior managers. South African criminal law adopts a wide theory of imputation resting upon the imputation to the corporation of the crimes of persons acting on its behalf, rather than on vicarious liability.[28]

4. ATTRIBUTION TO THE STATE OF THE CONDUCT OF ITS AGENTS

States, like corporations, can only function by means of natural persons, their agents. It has been demonstrated that criminal law principles do not preclude imputing the acts and intentions of individuals to the corporation, as if it were a natural person. The question is which wrongful acts and states of mind may be imputed to the state so as to make the state criminally liable. The doctrine of attribution deals with the allocation of responsibility to the state for the conduct of its organs and officials. In Part I, Chapter II, of the ILC's Draft Articles on State Responsibility entitled 'The Act of the State under International Law',[29] there are no separate provisions applicable to criminal acts and consequently no mention of fault or *mens rea*. The relevant Draft Articles[30] cover acts of state organs or entities exercising elements of the governmental authority, acts carried out by persons who were in fact acting under the direction or control of the state or exercising elements of the governmental authority, and also certain acts committed *ultra vires*. Caron states: 'Scholarly commentary on corporate crime strongly supports the view

---

[25] Ss. 121–2.

[26] *Halsbury's Laws*, xi (1): *Criminal Law, Evidence and Procedure*, para. 35; and see *Tesco Supermarkets Ltd v Nattrass* [1972] AC 153.

[27] See Stessens, 'Corporate Criminal Liability', 512, who refers to a Dutch case in which *mens rea* was aggregated.

[28] E. M. Burchell (ed.), *South African Criminal Law and Procedure, i: General Principles of Criminal Law* (1997), 299–301.

[29] Draft Articles provisionally adopted by the Drafting Committee, A/CN.4/L.569, 4 Aug. 1998.   [30] Draft Articles 5, 7–10, 15 and 15*bis*; see Appendix 3 below.

that if an organization gives specific instructions to its agents and a rogue individual nonetheless violates such instructions, then the organization should be free of at least criminal responsibility for the acts of the individual.'[31] This is the approach taken in the French *Code Pénal*.[32] It would seem appropriate in the early stages of development of the concept of state criminality to take a restrictive identification theory as a starting-point. One of the distinguishing features of a state crime is that the act is carried out as part of a state policy, and this feature must also be taken into account in determining whether a crime is attributable to the state.[33]

5. CUMULATIVE RESPONSIBILITY OF INDIVIDUALS AND CORPORATIONS

Another fact to be gleaned from national law relating to corporate criminal responsibility is that such responsibility is generally not exclusive or alternative, but cumulative with the responsibility of the individual criminals. For example, paragraph 51 of the Dutch Penal Code states that prosecution and punishment may be imposed on the corporation, and on those individuals who have initiated or guided the offence, simultaneously. The French *Code Pénal* provides that the criminal responsibility of *personnes morales* does not preclude the criminal responsibility of the individual perpetrators or accomplices for the same conduct.[34] Similarly, under Japanese law the so-called *Ryobatsu-kitei* regulation makes it possible to punish both individuals and the enterprise itself.[35] In English law, where in accordance with the identification principle a corporation is guilty of a crime, the person whose actions and intent are those of the corporation must also be criminally liable.[36]

Bassiouni[37] maintains that the individual responsibility of the corporate directors and officers seldom arises in the absence of the responsibility of the corporation. Unless the corporate directors or officers act on their own or as part of a conspiracy which is designed to benefit them personally and does not involve the corporation, the responsibility of such persons is almost invariably linked to that of the corporation of which they are custodians, agents, or operators acting on its behalf or for its benefit. Bassiouni goes on

---

[31] D. D. Caron, 'State Responsibility in a Multiactor World', (1998) 92 *American Society of International Law Proceedings*, 307, 311.

[32] See L. Orland and C. Cachera, 'Corporate Crime and Punishment in France: Criminal Responsibility of Legal Entities (Personnes Morales) under the New French Criminal Code (Nouveau Code Pénal)', (1995) 11 *Connecticut Journal of International Law*, 111, 124.

[33] This feature will be discussed in more detail in Chapter 8 below.   [34] Ss. 121–2.

[35] See N. Kyoto, 'Criminal Liability of Corporations: Japan', in de Doelder and Tiedemann, *Criminal Liability of Corporations*, 275.   [36] *Halsbury's Laws*, para. 35, n. 7.

[37] *Substantive Criminal Law* (1978), 151.

to say that even though a corporation can be held accountable for the criminal acts of its agents, it is nevertheless an abstract legal entity, and its responsibility would never be in question were it not for the conduct of the directors or officers.

6. CIVIL LIABILITY FOR CORPORATE CRIME?

The theoretical position on corporate criminality in Belgian law is that even though a corporation can commit a crime, it cannot be subject to criminal sanctions. *Societas delinquere, sed non puniri potest.*[38] The 'punishment' of corporations consequently consists in civil liability for criminal fines imposed on corporate officers or administrative sanctions. This technique is widespread in continental legal systems, and provides support for the notion that a state may commit a criminal act but be held responsible in primarily a civil sense. This seems to be the approach of the ICJ in the *Case Concerning the Application of the Genocide Convention*,[39] and has been the general attitude so far of the ILC towards state crimes.[40]

7. THE STATE AS A CORPORATION

A final question to consider is whether the state may be regarded as a corporation which is susceptible to punishment under national law. Under French law the state is excluded from the rules pertaining to corporations due to its special role as guardian of the public interest.[41] In Japan, on the other hand, both public corporations and the state itself may be criminally liable if there is no specific law excluding such liability, although there is no case in which a state has actually been punished.[42] In the Netherlands attempts have been made to penalize certain acts of public or state agencies.[43] In the *Limburg* case,[44] a district authority was responsible for chopping down part of a forest to increase the safety of aeroplanes flying into a military airbase. This act constituted a contravention of certain regulations and the district was prosecuted by the state prosecutor and convicted, although never punished. In February 1992 a large amount of kerosine was spilled on the Volkel airbase and due to the repetitive nature of the offence, the state was prosecuted. The defence argued that public bodies bore only political responsibility for

---

[38] See Stessens, 'Corporate Criminal Liability', 498.   [39] See further Chapter 17 below.
[40] See Chapter 8 below, s. 5.   [41] *Nouveau Code Pénal*, Ss. 121–2.
[42] See Kyoto 'Criminal Liability of Corporations', 283.
[43] See H. de Doelder, 'Criminal Liability of Corporations: Netherlands', in de Doelder and Tiedemann, *Criminal Liability of Corporations*, 289.
[44] HR 9 June 1992, NJ 1992, 794 (Streekgewest Oostelijk Zuid-Limburg-arrest), ibid. 297.

fulfilling public tasks and could not be prosecuted. The state was found guilty but no penalty was imposed.[45] These cases constitute a direct recognition of the state as a corporate entity which operates on a similar basis to any other corporation, although the modalities of punishment under national law do not seem to have been worked out.[46]

8. CONCLUSION

There does not appear to be any universally accepted concept of corporate criminality, and practice within a state sometimes lacks uniformity. States have tended to adapt doctrines already established in their own legal systems to fit the concept of corporate crime. For example, the English courts were inspired by the *alter ego* doctrine of the law of tort, while the Dutch courts turned to the criteria relating to 'intellectual perpetratorship'.[47]

Nevertheless, the notion of corporate crime would appear to be a relevant 'general principle of law' which may be used as a source of international law. The important point is that the duality of corporate and individual criminal liability under national law has been found to be of some value, and has been legally justified. The theories used to justify corporate criminal liability may also be applied to states if the state is viewed as a corporate structure with agents acting on its behalf, and a large population which may be likened to shareholders who are interested in and affected by the acts of the decision-makers.

[45] Rb Den Bosch, 1 Feb. 1993, NJ 1993, 257. See de Doelder 'Criminal Liability of Corporations: Netherlands', 298–9.

[46] See Chapters 13 and 14 below for a consideration of the modalities of punishment under international law.　　　　[47] See Stessens, 'Corporate Criminal Liability', 511.

Conclusion to Part II

The notion of the international criminal responsibility of states presents legal difficulties, but these difficulties do not, in principle, exclude such responsibility. The burden has been to show that the concept is not juridically impossible. A number of theories of responsibility have emerged both in national and international law which are designed to deal with specific instances of criminal behaviour. These theories assist in providing a legal justification for the novel concept of the criminal responsibility of states. Whether the criminal organization model or the corporate crime model is applicable in a given case will depend on the circumstances,[1] but both provide a legal rationale for holding states criminally responsible that is internally consistent, and in alignment with the elements of criminal law and with the uniqueness of international law. Both models also lead to the desired result of a duality of individual and state criminal responsibility, and allow the emphasis to be placed on the role of the government. The position may be summarized as follows:

1. In accordance with the criminal organization model, a declaration of criminality may be made against the state or its government, and individuals who knowingly and voluntarily took part in the criminal activities may face criminal proceedings.

2. In accordance with the corporate crime model, criminal sanctions may be directed against the state as a corporation, or against the government as the entity representing the state. The individual agents of the state may also face criminal proceedings.

---

[1] If there is no likelihood of bringing the members of the government before an international tribunal, then the corporate model may be more appropriate.

PART III

Candidate Criteria and Indicia
for Identifying State Crimes

Introduction to Part III

According to the traditional view, the international law of state responsibility was a single regime applicable to all state wrongs, and it is only quite recently that this conception has been brought into question, with much of the debate having been instigated by the work of the ILC. The ILC based its original decision to differentiate between state crimes and delicts upon three developments in international law: the establishment of a special category of rules known as *jus cogens*, the attachment by the UN Charter of special consequences to the breach of certain obligations, and the acceptance of the principle of individual criminal responsibility.[1]

These developments constitute some of the foundations of the concept of state criminality, but it is proposed here to delve deeper into an analysis of the common and specific underpinnings that justify the inclusion of a given wrongful state act in a special category of international crimes. This will involve an examination of eight candidate criteria and indicia that form a conceptual differentiation between crimes and delicts. The chosen approach is not an attempt to construct a definition of international crimes of state, as the density of satisfaction of the various criteria and indicia is likely to vary from crime to crime. A definition is designed to incorporate all the particular aspects of a concept and its value is measured by its precision. While murder and theft, for example, each have distinctive constituent elements in national law, both fall within the concept of crime. The aim here is to build a concept of state criminality which will not collapse if one or two elements are missing in a given case. The terms 'criteria' and 'indicia' differ in the sense that a criterion is an element which must be satisfied in order for an act to fall within the concept, while an indicium is merely an indicator which points towards the inclusion of the act in that group.

During the course of the proposed analysis it will be necessary to refer to 'pre-legal' or 'extra-legal' factors in recognition of the fact that the order and scale of importance of those obligations which are characterized as international crimes cannot necessarily be derived from within the system of positive international law. An examination of certain established and emerging concepts in international law will not be excluded, but equally the importance of more nebulous notions of public policy and morality cannot be ignored. As Verdross has pointed out, 'A truly realistic analysis of the law shows us that every positive order has its roots in the ethics of a certain community, that it cannot be understood apart from its moral basis',[2] the

---

[1] See (1976) *YrbkILC* 2, pt. 2, 95–122.
[2] A. Verdross, 'Forbidden Treaties in International Law', (1937) 31 *AJIL* 571, 576.

relevant community for current purposes being the international community of states.

The analysis will begin with a look at the theoretical notion of a hierarchy of international rules and the role of the international community in perpetuating such an idea. Certain intrinsic qualities of international crime will then be examined before considering the relationship between the different levels of international responsibility. It will also be necessary to determine which of the constitutive elements are criteria and which are indicia. The link between the different criteria and indicia is that together they form the foundations of the concept of state criminality. It is hoped to begin to establish a rationale for treating international crimes of state as a separate and justifiable category of rules in contemporary international law and to discover whether or not this category is grounded in principle.

5
Jus Cogens

1. A HIERARCHY OF INTERNATIONAL NORMS

The twin roots and functions of international law have been described as 'co-existence and common aims'.[1] It has been said that international law is designed, first, to enable heterogeneous and equal states to live side by side in a peaceful and orderly fashion, and second, to cater for the common interests which continue to surface over and above the diversity of states.[2] But certain common interests seem to have emerged as being more important for peaceful and orderly relations than others. This is reflected in the distinction between international crimes and international delicts and also by the *jus cogens* theory, both of which introduce 'a "normative differentiation" between two kinds of rules, and hence, of legal obligations'.[3] It may therefore be helpful to analyse the distinction between crimes and delicts, or in other words between essential and less essential obligations, in terms of its relationship to the distinction between peremptory and ordinary norms. On no account does this constitute an attempt to equate international crimes with *jus cogens*, and both the point at which the two notions converge and the point at which they diverge will be highlighted.

2. ORIGINS AND STATUS OF *JUS COGENS* IN INTERNATIONAL LAW

National legal systems are characterized by a deeply rooted hierarchy of norms, and many such systems make the distinction between *jus strictum* and *jus dispositivum*. A legal act which does not comply with the *jus strictum* is invalid, whereas rules of *jus dispositivum* may be ignored in contractual relationships. This distinction has also been framed in terms of public policy and public order, and the policies or prescriptions that are immune to private change vary from community to community. In Germany, for example, the provisions of public law are in principle peremptory because they reflect the general interest, and private law provisions are peremptory where it is necessary 'to safeguard the moral and economic basis of co-existence'.[4]

---

[1] See P. Weil, 'Towards Relative Normativity in International Law?', (1983) 77 *AJIL* 412, 418–19.   [2] Ibid.

[3] R. Ago, Fifth Report on State Responsibility, (1976) *YrbkILC* 2, pt. 1, 3, 32.

[4] Quoted in M. McDougal, H. Lasswell, and L. Chen (eds.), *Human Rights and World Public Order* (1980), 340.

Schwarzenberger has argued that peremptory norms in national law have two main aspects: they are public law in the strict sense because they remain unaffected by agreements to the contrary between private persons, and they are prohibitory rules.[5]

The index of Grotius in *De jure belli ac pacis* of 1758 has fifteen entries under *jus strictum*. In general, the great founders of international law distinguished between two kinds of law: first, the necessary law of nations embodying the law of nature, and second, the positive law created by agreement and custom, the former being *jus strictum*. The reasoning of Vattel went as follows:

Since therefore the necessary Law of Nations consists in the application of the law of nature to states,—which law is immutable as being founded on the nature of things, and particularly on the nature of man,— it follows, that the *Necessary* law of Nations is immutable.

Whence as this law is immutable, and the obligations that arise from it necessary and indispensable, nations can neither make any changes in it by their conventions, dispense with it in their own conduct, nor reciprocally release each other from the observance of it.[6]

Early in the twentieth century, Oppenheim[7] and Hall[8] made reference to 'fundamental' or 'universal' principles of international law whose peremptory effect was recognized by custom. In 1937 Verdross addressed the question whether 'international law contains rules which have the character of *jus cogens*'.[9] He argued that there exist higher interests in the world community corresponding to fundamental norms of international public policy that restrict the freedom and sovereignty of states, '[f]or it is the quintessence of norms of this character that they prescribe a certain, positive or negative behaviour unconditionally; norms of this character, therefore, cannot be derogated from by the will of the contracting parties'.[10] Advocates of natural law theory identify the concept of *jus cogens* with public policy and good morals, believing there are certain moral-ethical imperatives inherent in human beings.[11] Heffter regarded as impossible treaties which were 'contraire à l'ordre moral des choses et notamment aussi à la mission des Etats de contribuer au développement de la liberté humaine'.[12] Positivists regard any appeal to a higher law as utopian or at least meta-legal, and those of the nine-

---

[5] G. Schwarzenberger, 'International *Jus Cogens?*', (1965) 43 *Texas Law Rev.* 455, 456.

[6] E. de Vattel, *The Law of Nations or Principles of the Law of Nature* (1834), p. lviii.

[7] L. Oppenheim, *International Law*, i: *Peace* (1905), 528.

[8] W. E. Hall, *A Treatise on International Law*, 8th edn. (1924), 382–3.

[9] 'Forbidden Treaties in International Law'. See also '*Jus Dispositivum* and *Jus Cogens* in International Law', (1966) 60 *AJIL* 55.   [10] (1937) 31 *AJIL* 571–2.

[11] See also R. Quadri, 'Cours général de droit international public', (1964-III) Hague *Recueil* 237, 335–42.   [12] A. W. Heffter, *Le Droit international public de l'Europe* (1857), 174.

teenth and twentieth centuries have attached a peremptory character to basic principles and vitally important norms of international law, including purely moral categories, only if they are universally recognized by states.[13]

In his First Report on the Law of Treaties of 1953, Lauterpacht suggested that a treaty would be void if it were inconsistent with 'such overriding principles of international law which may be regarded as constituting principles of international public policy'.[14] These overriding principles 'may be expressive of rules of international morality so cogent that an international tribunal would consider them as forming part of [the] principles of law generally recognized by civilized nations'.[15] When Fitzmaurice succeeded Lauterpacht as Special Rapporteur he formally introduced the term *jus cogens* in his expository code on the Law of Treaties submitted to the ILC in 1958. He stressed that a feature common to most rules of *jus cogens* was that they involved not only legal rules but also considerations of morals and of international good order.[16]

It was argued by Waldock in his intervention at the Vienna Conference on the Law of Treaties in 1968 that the ILC based its approach to the question of *jus cogens* on positive law much more than on natural law. This was because it had been convinced that there existed at that time a number of principles of international law which were of a peremptory character.[17] This is borne out by Article 53 of the 1969 Vienna Convention on the Law of Treaties, which refers to acceptance and recognition of a rule as peremptory by the international community as a whole, rather than to natural law standing above the will of states. Article 53 states:

A treaty is void if, at the time of its conclusion, it conflicts with a peremptory norm of general international law. For the purposes of the present convention, a peremptory norm of general international law is a norm accepted and recognized by the international community of states as a whole as a norm from which no derogation is permitted and which can be modified only by a subsequent norm of general international law having the same character.

The principle of *jus cogens* is also accepted in the 1986 Vienna Convention on the Law of Treaties between States and International Organizations or between International Organizations.[18]

The limited case law on the subject of *jus cogens* seems to favour a positivist approach, although an exception is the case of Alfred Krupp et al. tried in 1947–8 by the US Military Tribunal in Nuremberg, where the Tribunal declared that any agreement with respect to the use of French

[13] See L. Alexidze, 'Legal Nature of *Jus Cogens* in Contemporary International Law', (1981-III) Hague *Recueil* 223.   [14] (1953) *YrbkILC*, vol. 2, 155.
[15] Ibid.   [16] (1958) *YrbkILC*, vol. 2, 41.
[17] UN Conference on the Law of Treaties, Summary Records of the Plenary Meetings and of the Meetings of the Committee of the Whole, Official Records, First Session, Vienna 26 Mar.–24 May 1968, (1969), 327–8.   [18] A/CONF.129/15, 20 March 1986; (1986) 25 *ILM* 543.

prisoners of war in German armament production would have been manifestly *contra bones mores* and therefore void.[19] In a decision of the German
Federal Constitutional Court in 1965[20] it was stated that certain elementary
legal commands had to be considered as rules of customary international law
from which no derogation is permitted. The quality of such peremptory
norms was said to be attributable only to those legal provisions which are
firmly rooted in the legal conviction of the community of states, which are
indispensable for the existence of international law as an international legal
order, and the observance of which can be demanded by all members of the
community of states. A US court has characterized the prohibition of torture
as a rule of general international law applicable under all circumstances.[21]
More recently, in the case of *Regina v Bow Street Magistrates Stipendiary
Magistrate, ex parte Pinochet Ugarte (Amnesty International Intervening)
(No 3)*,[22] the House of Lords accepted the *jus cogens* nature of the international crime of torture.[23]

The ICJ has made passing reference to *jus cogens* but has not so far felt
compelled to tackle the concept directly. In its Advisory Opinion in the
Reservations to the Genocide Convention case[24] the ICJ indicated that the policies embodied in the Genocide Convention were almost universally
demanded, and genocide could therefore be construed as a rule of *jus cogens*.
The Court declared that 'the principles underlying the Convention are principles which are recognized by civilized nations as binding on states, even
without any conventional obligation', and stressed 'the universal character
both of the condemnation of genocide and of the cooperation required "in
order to liberate mankind from such an odious scourge"'.[25] In the *Nicaragua*
case the ICJ referred to the principle of the prohibition of the use of force
expressed in Article 2(4) of the UN Charter as being a fundamental or cardinal principle of customary law, or a universal norm, and hence a rule of *jus
cogens*.[26] Finally, in its Advisory Opinion on the *Legality of the Threat or Use
of Nuclear Weapons*,[27] the Court spoke of certain fundamental rules of
humanitarian law applicable in armed conflict as being 'intransgressible
principles of international customary law',[28] but found there was no need to
pronounce on the issue of *jus cogens*.[29]

---

[19] Law Reports UNWCC, vol. 10, 69, 141.
[20] (1965) 18 Entscheidungen des Bundesverfassungsgerichts 449; (1966–7) 13 *Archiv des
Völkerrechts*, 122, 126.   [21] *Filartiga v. Pena-Irala*, (1984) 77 ILR 185.
[22] [1999] 2 All ER 97.
[23] Lord Browne-Wilkinson, ibid. 109; Lord Hope of Craighead, ibid. 152; Lord Hutton, ibid.
164. The Republic of Chile also accepted that the prohibition of torture was part of the *jus
cogens*.
[24] *Reservations to the Convention on the Prevention and Punishment of the Crime of Genocide*,
(1951) ICJ Reports 15.   [25] Ibid. 23.
[26] *Military and Paramilitary Activities in and against Nicaragua*, (1986) ICJ Reports 14, 100–1.
[27] (1996) ICJ Reports 226.   [28] Ibid. 257.   [29] Ibid. 258.

It can be said that the existence of *jus cogens* in public international law is recognized in state practice, by codified treaty law, by international and national tribunals, and in legal theory. Nevertheless there has been some reluctance to apply the concept until the international community of states has developed into a community with a higher degree of organization. In Sinclair's opinion:

> there is a place for the concept of *jus cogens* in international law. Its growth and development will parallel the growth and development of an international legal order expressive of the consensus of the international community as a whole. Such an international legal order is, at present, inchoate, unformed and only just discernible.[30]

3. RULES HAVING THE CHARACTER OF *JUS COGENS*

Article 53 of the Vienna Convention on the Law of Treaties leaves open the question of which rules are peremptory in character. The Article puts forward a test which does not define the substance of *jus cogens*. The ILC admitted that there was not yet any generally recognized criterion by which to identify a general rule of international law as having the character of *jus cogens*.[31] Waldock, who succeeded Fitzmaurice as Special Rapporteur, sought to specify the content of *jus cogens* by suggesting illustrative itemizations. His proposed draft stated:

> a treaty is contrary to international law and void if its object or execution involves: (a) the use or threat of force in contravention of the principles of the Charter of the UN; (b) any act or omission characterized by international law as an international crime; or (c) any act or omission in the suppression or punishment of which every state is required by international law to cooperate.[32]

Waldock's approach was rejected by the ILC for two reasons.[33] First, it was felt that the mention of some examples might lead to misunderstanding as to the position concerning others. Second, the ILC feared that it could be drawn into a prolonged study of matters which fell outside the scope of the articles on the law of treaties if it were to attempt to draw up a list of rules having the character of *jus cogens*. It seemed preferable to allow the precise content of *jus cogens* to be worked out in state practice and in the jurisprudence of international tribunals. Waldock's examples were nevertheless mentioned in the ILC's commentary to Article 53 (then Article 50), including others such as

---

[30] I. M. Sinclair, *The Vienna Convention on the Law of Treaties* (1973), 139. It has been suggested by C. de Visscher, *Théories et réalités en droit international public*, 4th edn. (1970), 295–6, that a proponent of a rule of *jus cogens* in relation to Article 53 of the Vienna Convention will have a considerable burden of proof.

[31] (1963) *YrbkILC*, vol. 2, 198 (Commentary to Article 37); (1966) *YrbkILC*, vol. 2, 247–8 (Commentary to Article 50).   [32] (1963) *YrbkILC*, vol. 2, 52 (Article 13).

[33] Ibid. 199; (1966) *YrbkILC*, vol. 2, 248.

treaties violating human rights, the equality of states, or the principle of self-determination.[34] The ILC added that it was not the form of a general rule of international law but the particular nature of the subject-matter with which it dealt that gave it the character of *jus cogens*.[35] The least controversial examples coincide with those acts characterized by the ILC as international crimes. However, even with regard to peremptory norms which are the subject of some agreement, such as the right to self-determination,[36] problems of application remain. For example, if force were used to assert this right there would be two competing rules of *jus cogens*.[37] So far the elucidation in state practice or by international tribunals which was anticipated by the ILC has not been forthcoming.

4. INTERNATIONAL CRIMES AND *JUS COGENS*: TWO SIDES OF THE SAME COIN?

The concept of state criminality and that of international rules having the special character of *jus cogens* converge to a considerable degree. On one side of the coin is the limitation placed upon the contractual freedom of states by the introduction into international law of a hierarchy of norms according to subject-matter, and the invalidity of international treaties which conflict with peremptory or essential norms. According to Article 71 of the Vienna Convention on the Law of Treaties, where a treaty is void under Article 53, states should eliminate as far as possible the consequences of acts performed in reliance on provisions which conflict with the peremptory norm and bring their mutual relations into conformity with that norm. This connects the concept of *jus cogens* to the field of state responsibility, because if a state is under an obligation to act in accordance with a peremptory norm, any breach of this norm entails the responsibility of that state. Arguably, the breach of a rule of higher normative value should entail more severe consequences than the breach of an ordinary norm. Thus, on the other side of the coin there exists the possibility of the application of a special regime of responsibility in the event of the breach of a peremptory or essential norm. Indeed, now that most states accept the notion of *jus cogens*, the possibility exists of bringing it more actively into the field of state responsibility.[38]

However, this image of a double-sided coin would appear to be a simplifica-

---

[34] (1966) *YrbkILC*, vol. 2, 248.   [35] Ibid.

[36] See I. Brownlie, *Principles of Public International Law*, 4th edn. (1990), 513.

[37] Ibid. 515.

[38] See First Report on State Responsibility by James Crawford, Special Rapporteur, A/CN.4/490/Add.2, para. 68, and A. Pellet, 'Can a State Commit a Crime? Definitely, Yes!', (1999) *EJIL*, vol. 10, no. 2, 425, 428, who states that 'nobody seriously doubts any more that norms of *jus cogens* have a real specificity among international law rules, and the past objections against the concept have proved unfounded'.

tion and is not conceptually acceptable. There is no automatic or necessary link between *jus cogens* and international crimes except to the extent that public policy and the protection of certain moral values and imperatives within the international community overlap with the concept of crime. The concept of *jus cogens* is potentially of far broader scope than that of international crimes, even though the two may coincide in certain instances. This was also the view taken initially by the ILC.[39] It may be that the degree of overlap has been exaggerated because the scope of neither concept has been fully delimited. In theory all basic values of the international legal order could give rise to rules of *jus cogens*. For example, the concept could embrace the UN Charter, many fundamental human rights prescriptions, principles of humanitarian law in armed conflict, and precepts which aim at cooperation among states such as the freedom of the seas or the peaceful uses of outer space. The law prohibiting international crimes, on the other hand, is a restricted category of rules which states do not, in reality, agree by treaty to break.

If a narrow view of *jus cogens* is taken, it may be said that although all international crimes do in fact also have the special character of *jus cogens*, the qualification is unhelpful if there is no treaty. In other words, while the concepts are conceptually close in terms of their role in protecting certain higher values, they belong to two separate areas of international law and serve different purposes. The approach adopted in the Vienna Convention, 'defining *jus cogens* rules not by the substantive cause or the *ratio legis* of attributing this character to them, but by the mere effect ... of this attribution, namely of their being non-derogable by agreement',[40] seems to support the narrow view.

On the other hand, the phrase 'non-derogable' in itself suggests that the concept of *jus cogens* has as much to do with the substance of rules as with conflicting treaties, and this broader view appears to be the modern view.[41] Abi-Saab draws a distinction between 'systemic' peremptory norms, which are inherent and necessary in order for a legal system to exist and operate, and 'substantive' peremptory norms, which are *d'ordre public* and whose violation entails an aggravated system of responsibility in international law.[42] He proposes that a concept of breaches of ' "substantive" (or some other such adjective) *jus cogens* norms or obligations'[43] could replace the concept of

---

[39] (1976) *YrbkILC*, vol. 2, pt. 2, 120. In the view of the ILC, 'the category of international obligations admitting of no derogation is much broader than the category of obligations whose breach is necessarily an international crime'. Cf. Pellet, who states that the ILC denied that a crime was a breach of a peremptory norm for prudential or political reasons, 'Can a State Commit a Crime?', 428.

[40] G. Abi-Saab, 'The Uses of Article 19', (1999) *EJIL*, vol. 10, no. 2, 339, 348.

[41] See e.g. M. Ragazzi, *The Concept of International Obligations* Erga Omnes (1997), 203, who states that the narrow view 'would be simplistic and would not take proper account of the expansion of the concept of *jus cogens* well beyond the law of treaties'.

[42] (1999) *EJIL*, vol. 10, no. 2, 349.   [43] Ibid.

state crimes. Pellet goes further in suggesting that 'it would be easier and more convenient to define an international crime as a breach of a norm of *jus cogens*'.[44] However, the question remains whether the concept of state crime is necessarily a distinct subcategory of 'substantive' *jus cogens* because of its intrinsic characteristics. If this is the case, the concept cannot be dismissed for the sake of convenience. Indeed, Pellet himself insists that the distinction between 'delicts' and 'crimes' answers an indisputable need,[45] and he does not explain fully how this need could be met if the concept of state crime were subsumed within that of *jus cogens*. Moreover, equating *jus cogens* with state crimes might restrict the development of both concepts.

It is submitted that an important point of divergence between *jus cogens* and state crimes is the fact that the former can be modified by subsequent rules having the same character (*jus cogens superveniens*). The ILC suggests that a subsequent rule of *jus cogens* modifying an earlier one can be established through practice and customary law that is in conflict with the earlier rule, or by a general multilateral treaty.[46] It is difficult to see how the rule prohibiting a state crime can be overturned in this way. In this sense it seems that the rationale underlying the concept of *jus cogens* is indeed the same as that underlying the concept of public policy, or international public order as described in the earlier literature. An existing head of public policy may be declared redundant if it no longer reflects the mores and fundamental assumptions of the community, and this may result in certain conduct being decriminalized. International crimes, on the other hand, are acts which the international community, on the basis of experience, found it necessary to outlaw once and for all, and such acts can never again become lawful. Just as it is inconceivable that murder and rape in domestic legal systems could be decriminalized, so is it inconceivable that genocide could be decriminalized in international law. Therefore, it can be said that international crimes are conceptually at the pinnacle of the hierarchy of norms.

---

[44] 'Can a State Commit a Crime?', 428.   [45] Ibid. 426–7.
[46] (1963) *YrbkILC*, vol. 2, 211 (Commentary to Article 45).

6

Obligations *Erga Omnes*

1. GENESIS OF THE CONCEPT OF OBLIGATIONS *ERGA OMNES*

The effect of a legal norm is to create obligations incumbent upon certain subjects of international law and rights for the benefit of others. In its Advisory Opinion in the *Reparation for Injuries Suffered in the Service of the UN* case, the ICJ affirmed the principle that 'only the party to whom an international obligation is due can bring a claim in respect of its breach'.[1] In other words, states do not possess a general right to the observance of international obligations in an absolute sense. Despite this, international law seems to be experiencing a trend in which the active and passive objects of international norms are becoming less specific. Shortly after the acceptance of the provisions of *jus cogens* in the Vienna Convention, the idea of a 'community interest' in the observance of international law received support by the ICJ.

In the 1970 *Barcelona Traction* case,[2] the ICJ pronounced, with reference to the obligations of a state concerning the treatment of aliens in its territory:

These obligations . . . are neither absolute nor unqualified. In particular, an essential distinction should be drawn between the obligations of a state towards the international community as a whole, and those arising vis-à-vis another state in the field of diplomatic protection. By their very nature the former are the concern of all states. In view of the importance of the rights involved, all states can be held to have a legal interest in their protection; they are obligations *erga omnes*.[3]

This passage is to be regarded as an *obiter dictum*, since on the facts of the case there was no suggestion that any obligations *erga omnes* had been violated. It was nonetheless a deliberate statement of principle which represented the considered opinion of twelve judges. The Court went on to clarify the essential distinction between obligations *erga omnes* and other obligations of international law:

Obligations the performance of which is the subject of diplomatic protection are not of the same category. It cannot be held, when one such obligation in particular is in question, in a specific case, that all states have a legal interest in its observance. In order to bring a claim in respect of the breach of such an obligation, a state must first establish its right to do so.[4]

The ILC interpreted these passages to mean that there were a small number of international obligations which, in view of the importance of their

---

[1] (1949) ICJ Reports 174, 181–2.   [2] (1970) ICJ Reports 3.
[3] Ibid. 32.   [4] Ibid.

subject-matter for the international community as a whole, were obligations in whose fulfilment all states possessed a legal interest.[5] It follows that:

the responsibility engaged by the breach of these obligations is engaged not only in regard to the state which was the direct victim of the breach: it is also engaged in regard to all the other members of the international community, so that, in the event of a breach of these obligations every state must be considered justified in invoking— probably through judicial channels—the responsibility of the state committing the internationally wrongful act.[6]

The precise implications in practice of the concept of obligations *erga omnes* have not yet been established, and the idea of an *actio popularis* in international law is not well accepted.[7] Still, an overemphasis on these difficulties runs the risk of neglecting the concept itself, and hence the focus here will be on conceptual issues. As Ragazzi has pointed out, 'the reason why special rights and remedies attach to these obligations is that these obligations are *erga omnes*, and not the other way around'.[8]

2. OBLIGATIONS GIVING RISE TO RESPONSIBILITY *ERGA OMNES*

The ICJ's method of defining obligations *erga omnes* by reference to their substance and supporting the definition with practical examples may be contrasted to Article 53 of the Vienna Convention which puts forward a test for the identification of peremptory norms. In the Barcelona Traction case the Court gave some indication as to which obligations 'by their very nature' qualified as obligations *erga omnes*:

Such obligations derive, for example, in contemporary international law, from the outlawing of acts of aggression, and of genocide, as also from the principles and rules concerning the basic rights of the human person, including protection from slavery and racial discrimination.[9]

It was added that 'some of the contemporary rights of protection have entered into the body of general international law; others are conferred by international instruments of a universal or quasi-universal character'.[10] Later in its judgment, the Court went on to say:

With regard more particularly to human rights . . . it should be noted that these also include protection against denial of justice. However, on the universal level, the instru-

---

[5] (1976) *YrbkILC*, vol. 2, pt. 2, 99.   [6] Ibid.

[7] See M. Lachs, 'General Course on Public International Law', (1980–IV) 169 Hague *Recueil* 13, 341, n. 796, who states: 'there is a long way from the dictum of the Court to *actio popularis*'; and see further Chapter 15 below, s. 3(b).

[8] M. Ragazzi, *The Concept of International Obligations* Erga Omnes (1997), 203.

[9] (1970) ICJ Reports 32.   [10] Ibid.

ments which embody human rights do not confer on states the capacity to protect the victim of infringements of such rights irrespective of their nationality.[11]

Consequently, rights of international protection may be divided into two categories: those which are conferred by 'international instruments of a universal or quasi-universal character' and those which have entered into the body of general international law. The Court seems to be saying that while the latter do confer on states the capacity to protect victims of infringement irrespective of their nationality, the former do not unless the specific instrument states otherwise. The Court fails to clarify the relationship between a right of protection conferred by a multilateral treaty and the principle that 'in view of the importance of the rights involved' all states have 'a legal interest in their protection'. There is no reason why a customary law right to invoke an *erga omnes* obligation could not complement the provisions of a universal or quasi-universal treaty.

Furthermore, the Court's pronouncements do not make clear whether 'basic rights of the human person' which give rise to obligations *erga omnes* are equivalent to human rights *tout court*, or are limited to those relating to the human person and human dignity. Meron has suggested that the Court may have intended to set apart 'basic' from ordinary human rights,[12] but it has been argued by Dinstein that such a distinction would be without foundation in the theory and practice of human rights.[13] A resolution adopted by the Institut de Droit International in 1989 on 'The protection of human rights and the principle of non-intervention in internal affairs of states' declares in Article 1 that the international obligation of states to ensure the observance of human rights 'as expressed by the ICJ is *erga omnes*; it is incumbent upon every state in relation to the international community as a whole, and every state has a legal interest in the protection of human rights'.[14] This encompasses all human rights recognized in the 1948 Universal Declaration of Human Rights. The notion of obligations *erga omnes* also seems relevant in environmental law as regards 'common property'. This refers to areas beyond national jurisdiction such as the high seas and superjacent airspace. A related notion is that of 'common concern' or 'common interest'. The UN General Assembly has declared that global climate change is the 'common concern of mankind'.[15] The implication is that all states share a common interest in suppressing any violations of international law relating to the protection of the global atmosphere.

[11] Ibid. 47.

[12] T. Meron, *Human Rights Law-Making in the United Nations* (1986), 185–6.

[13] Y. Dinstein, 'The *Erga Omnes* Applicability of Human Rights', (1992) 30 *Archiv des Völkerrechts*, 16, 17.

[14] *Annuaire de l'Institut de droit international*, Session de Saint-Jacques-de-Compostelle (1990), vol. 63(II), 339, 341.   [15] Resolution 43/53, 6 Dec. 1988.

Ragazzi has put forward five criteria for identifying obligations *erga omnes* based on the examples given in the *Barcelona Traction* case.[16] First, all four examples relate to narrowly defined obligations. Second, all the examples are essentially those of negative obligations. Third, all the examples are those of obligations or duties in the strict sense (i.e. what one ought or ought not to do). Fourth, all the examples are those of 'obligations deriving from rules of general international law belonging to *jus cogens* and codified by international treaties to which a high number of states have become parties'. Finally, all the examples are those of obligations 'instrumental to the main political objectives of the present time, namely, the preservation of peace and the promotion of fundamental human rights, which in turn reflect basic goods (or moral values), first and foremost life and human dignity'. Ragazzi describes this as a descriptive rather than a prescriptive list. He goes on to examine potential candidates for inclusion in the category of obligations *erga omnes* which would expand the concept so as to include general principles (in relation to human rights law), positive obligations (in relation to development law), and obligations attaching to optional rights (in relation to environmental law).[17]

3. THE RELATIONSHIP BETWEEN *JUS COGENS*, OBLIGATIONS *ERGA OMNES*, AND INTERNATIONAL CRIMES

It has been said that 'the intention behind the *erga omnes* theory . . . is to sound the death knell of narrow bilateralism and sanctified egoism for the sake of the universal protection of certain fundamental norms relating, in particular, to human rights. Like the *jus cogens* doctrine and the theory of international crimes, it is inspired by highly respectable ethical considerations.'[18] There are a number of similarities between these three concepts. All are designed to protect the common interests of states and basic moral values; the classic examples of acts falling within each concept largely coincide; and characteristic expressions such as the 'international community as a whole' appear in the commonly used description of each concept.[19] This raises the question whether the three forms of protection of common interests must be simultaneously granted in international law. It would seem to be an essential characteristic of the concept of state criminality that the commission of a crime would also be a violation of an obligation *erga omnes*.

---

[16] *The Concept of International Obligations* Erga Omnes, 132–4.   [17] Ibid. 132–63.

[18] P. Weil, 'Towards Relative Normativity in International Law', (1983) *AJIL* 77, 432.

[19] See Ragazzi, *The Concept of International Obligations* Erga Omnes, 72, describing the relationship between *jus cogens* and obligations *erga omnes*. Ragazzi concludes that the concept of obligations *erga omnes* is independent from that of *jus cogens*.

Equally, it would be contradictory if in the case of a breach of a rule so important to the entire international community that it is described as peremptory, there was only a relationship of responsibility between the state that committed the breach and the state that was directly injured.[20] But as Gaja has pointed out, 'the fact that responsibility is not established only in the relationship between the injuring state and the more directly affected state does not seem to be an element sufficient for asserting the existence of an international crime'.[21] At the Florence Conference on State Responsibility and the Concept of Crimes of States in 1984, Gaja put forward a theory of three circles, with obligations *erga omnes* constituting the widest circle. *Jus cogens* norms were also *erga omnes* but the reverse was not true, hence *jus cogens* norms formed a second, narrower circle.[22] The third circle of international crimes was narrower still.[23] Thus, the hierarchy of norms is perhaps best regarded as a set of overlapping discs.

Obligations *erga omnes* flow from a class of norms the performance of which is owed to the international community as a whole. Potentially, they constitute a very broad and useful category which may come into play even when an internationally prohibited act is committed by a state against its own citizens and there is no other directly affected state. The question whether the breach of an obligation *erga omnes* entails especially severe consequences has received less attention than the problem of the right of all states to bring an action in such a case. What is clear is that the concepts of *jus cogens* and international crimes invest some of these special obligations with particularly far-reaching legal effects, consisting of the invalidation of conflicting treaties and the imposition of severe consequences respectively. It may be that the notion of international crimes will only be able truly to take form once the practical implications of the notion of obligations *erga omnes* have been settled, which in turn depends on a more advanced institutionalization of the international community.[24] As Simma has warned,

If the gap between advances in substance and lack of institutional progress is allowed to widen, what we might witness in the future could likely be further developments

---

[20] See Fifth Report on State Responsibility by Roberto Ago, Special Rapporteur, A/CN.4/291/Adds. 1–2, (1976) *YrbkILC*, vol. 2, pt. 1, 3, 32.

[21] G. Gaja, '*Jus Cogens* Beyond the Vienna Convention', (1981–III) 172 Hague *Recueil* 273, 300.

[22] The ILC also takes the view that *jus cogens* is a narrower category than obligations *erga omnes*. See Report of the ILC on the Work of its Fiftieth Session, GAOR fifty-third session (1998), Suppl. no. 10 (A/53/10), 145.

[23] G. Gaja, 'Obligations *Erga Omnes*, International Crimes and *Jus Cogens*: A Tentative Analysis of Three Related Concepts', in J. H. H. Weiler, M. Spinedi, and A. Cassese (eds.), *International Crimes of States: A Critical Analysis of the ILC's Draft Article 19 on State Responsibility* (1989), 151, 160. See also G. Abi-Saab, 'The Uses of Article 19', (1999) *EJIL*, vol. 10, no. 2, 339, 348.

[24] See R. Ago, 'Obligations *Erga Omnes* and the International Community', in Weiler et al., *International Crimes of States*, 237–9 at 238, and see further Chapter 15 below.

moving away from bilateralism but merely passing (or by-passing) multilateralism and finally ending up in unilateralism.[25]

4. COMMENTS ON A HIERARCHY OF NORMS

It cannot be denied that hierarchical terms or quality labels serve a deterrent function by sending out a warning signal that the international community will not accept violations of certain 'higher' obligations. However, the hierarchy of international norms is still underdeveloped and the applications of the distinction between 'ordinary' and 'higher' obligations are unclear. It may be risky to resort to a category of superior obligations in the hope that no state will dare politically or morally to ignore them without the legal tools and institutional structure in place to ensure that they are respected as this could adversely affect the credibility of international law. Moreover, it has been questioned whether the shifting of the axis of international law away from states towards the international community will in fact lead to the 'victory of the ethical values common to all mankind over the centrifugal forces that [have] kept nations apart',[26] and the fear has been expressed that

By seeking to create today the law of tomorrow's international society, one runs the risk of cutting a key that will not fit the lock it will have to open. By projecting on today's international society the concepts appropriate to a different society, the present trends are indulging in the pleasures of anticipation in ways that, at best, are naively altruistic; at worst, amount to the hijacking of man's 'better feelings' for the ends of power or ideology.[27]

These sentiments echo Justice Pal's scepticism over very advanced notions in international law at the time of the Tokyo Trials.[28]

However, as Chinkin has pointed out, these fears are only justified if 'international law is to be confined within the parameters of the statist model' and not 'if it is to develop to regulate activities of States . . . with respect to a broader range of subject-matter, reflecting international community (not exclusively statist) concerns and morality'.[29] It is necessary to begin cutting a key in order to find out whether it will fit the lock it has to open. The risk of infinite gradations of international norms is perhaps exaggerated, and although the acts which may be committed by the subjects of international law are diverse, the boundaries between certain ineluctable gradations are beginning to be discernible. In his First Report on State

---

[25] B. Simma, 'Bilateralism and Community Interest in the Law of State Responsibility', in Dinstein Y, (ed.), *International Law at a Time of Perplexity: Essays in Honour of Shabtai Rosenne* (1989), 821, 844.

[26] Weil, 'Towards Relative Normativity in International Law', 441.   [27] Ibid. 442.

[28] See Chapter 1 below, s. 3(f).

[29] C. Chinkin, *Third Parties in International Law* (1993), 293.

Responsibility, Crawford admitted that 'within the field of general international law there is some hierarchy of norms, and the importance of at least a
few basic substantive norms is recognized as involving a difference not merely
of degree but of kind'.[30] International law is in a constant process of development, and the international community should be trusted to develop a system that corresponds to its needs. For this reason it is necessary to turn to a
more detailed examination of the single most important determining body
often referred to as 'the international community as a whole'.

---

[30] A/CN.4/490/Add.2, para. 71. Cf. C. Dominicé, 'The International Responsibility of States
for Breach of Multilateral Obligations', (1999) *EJIL*, vol. 10, no. 2, 353, 359: 'there is only one
type of breach. It is only that in certain cases the capacity to respond is, within precise limits,
also granted to other states than the one whose rights have been infringed.'

7

International Community Recognition

1. INTRODUCTION

The notions of *jus cogens*, obligations *erga omnes*, and international crimes seem to be more developed in theory than in practice. Yet in order for a differentiation between the quality of norms to have any practical utility it must be supported by states. Therefore an important element in distinguishing one form of internationally wrongful act from another is the recognition and acceptance by the international community of the act as being of a certain gravity. Indeed, this constitutes a major aspect of the definition of *jus cogens* in the Vienna Convention on the Law of Treaties and of the definition of international crimes developed by the ILC. It should be noted that international community 'recognition and acceptance' is both the result of an act belonging intrinsically to the category of international crimes, but also a necessary precondition for the inclusion of an act in that group.

2. ARTICLE 53 OF THE VIENNA CONVENTION ON THE LAW OF TREATIES AND THE BASIC CRITERION IN ARTICLE 19 OF THE DRAFT ARTICLES ON STATE RESPONSIBILITY

The original draft of Article 53 did not specify that a peremptory rule needed to be accepted and recognized as such by the international community as a whole.[1] But when it was agreed not to give specific examples of peremptory norms in the Vienna Convention, several amendments were put forward aimed at reducing the risk of states abusing the concept of peremptory norms to free themselves of valid treaty obligations. The US proposed that in order for a rule to have the character of *jus cogens* it should be 'recognized in common by the national and regional legal systems of the world'.[2] A joint amendment by Greece, Spain, and Finland proposed expanding the ILC's definition of *jus cogens* so that the article would read:

A treaty is void if it conflicts with a peremptory norm of general international law *recognized by the international community as a norm* from which no derogation is per-

---

[1] (1966) *YrbkILC*, vol. 2, 183 (Article 50).

[2] UN Doc.A/Conf.39/C.1/L.302. See Report of the Committee of the Whole on its Work at the First Session of the Conference, Doc.A/Conf.39/14, in UN Conference on the Law of Treaties, first and second sessions, Vienna, 26 Mar.–24 May 1968 and 9 Apr.–22 May 1969, Official Records, Documents of the Conference (1971), 95, 174.

mitted and which can be modified only by a subsequent norm of general international law having the same character.[3]

The word 'acceptance' was subsequently added to bring the draft in line with Article 38 of the Statute of the ICJ, which provides for the recognition of international conventions and general principles of law and the acceptance of international custom. The possibility of the emergence of *jus cogens* by way of custom was therefore covered. The final version was also intended to reject any allusion to natural law and to stress the consensual character of *jus cogens*.

The question of acceptance by the international community as a whole does not appear in the basic criterion of Article 19, although it is doubtful that the ILC was suggesting that an international crime could not arise by way of custom, particularly since this would be the most feasible method of achieving universality. The ILC pointed out that the analogous text of Article 53 of the Vienna Convention provided that in order for a norm of international law to be 'objectively' considered as peremptory, it must be 'subjectively' accepted and recognized as such by the international community as a whole, and:

> Similarly, paragraph 2 of the article under consideration provides that in order to be 'objectively' considered as an 'international crime' and as such liable to more severe legal consequences as a result of responsibility, an internationally wrongful act must be 'subjectively' recognized as a 'crime' by the international community as a whole.[4]

Hence, before it is possible to speak of the general acceptance of an act's criminal character as an objective fact, it is necessary to establish subjectively whether a specialized *opinio juris* exists.

3. DEFINITION OF THE INTERNATIONAL COMMUNITY AS A WHOLE

In its discussions on Draft Article 19 the ILC explained that the expression 'recognized by the international community as a whole'

> certainly does not mean the requirement of unanimous recognition by all the members of that community, which would give each state an inconceivable right of veto. What it is intended to ensure is that a given internationally wrongful act shall be recognized as an 'international crime', not only by some particular group of states, even if it constitutes a majority, but by all the essential components of the international community.[5]

---

[3] UN Doc.A/Conf.39/C.1/L.306 and Add. 1 and 2, in Report of the Committee of the Whole.
[4] (1976) *YrbkILC*, vol. 2, pt. 2, 119.   [5] Ibid.

It follows that it is only possible to speak of an international crime where Western states, developing states and all other relevant social and political groups have displayed the conviction that a certain act falls into this category. It is not enough if a large number of states from one group displays the conviction, even if it is a majority. Similarly, if the states from a given group opposed the designation of an act as an international crime it would not be considered as such. This condition comes close to a call for unanimity, but according to Special Rapporteur Ago this was a necessary guarantee because 'in the absence of such a safeguard, the introduction of the notions of a "peremptory norm" and an "international crime" would not be a genuine advance, but would tend to divide the international community'.[6] Such a guarantee could be regarded as excessive caution, but Ago 'thought it was a matter of common sense, since it was only in that way that the international community could progress towards greater cohesion and unity'.[7]

This reasoning confirmed that of the Drafting Committee at the Vienna Conference on the Law of Treaties where the Chairman, Mr Yasseen, explained with reference to the definition of *jus cogens* that

by inserting the words 'as a whole' in article 50 the Drafting Committee had wished to stress that there was no question of requiring a rule to be accepted and recognized as peremptory by all states. It would be enough if a very large majority did so; that would mean that, if one State in isolation refused to accept the peremptory character of the rule, or if that State was supported by a very small number of States, the acceptance and recognition of the peremptory character of the rule by the international community as a whole would not be affected.[8]

Thus, the best view is that peremptory norms accepted and recognized by an overwhelming majority of states, and including all major components of the international community, are binding on all states including a small minority of dissenting states. It would seem sensible to apply the same reasoning to international crimes.

4. COMMENTS ON THE NOTION OF 'RECOGNITION AND ACCEPTANCE BY THE INTERNATIONAL COMMUNITY AS A WHOLE'

Several comments may be made in relation to the determining body referred to as 'the international community as a whole'. Schwarzenberger[9] is of the opinion that the words 'as a whole' equate general international law with

---

[6] (1976) *YrbkILC*, vol. I, 251–2.   [7] Ibid.

[8] UN Conference on the Law of Treaties, first session, Vienna, 26 Mar.–24 May 1968, Official Records, Summary Records of the Plenary Meetings and of the Meetings of the Committee of the Whole, Doc.A/Conf.39/11 (1969), 472.

[9] G. Schwarzenberger, *International Law and Order* (1971), 52–3.

universal international law, and feels that it would be asking too much to expect positive evidence of acceptance by every state including the most recent and smallest states. He also suggests that a state's dissent during the formative stage of a rule is significant. This raises the question whether the 'persistent objector' principle is applicable in such instances.[10] It is difficult to see how a state could deny responsibility for an international crime on the basis that it persistently objected to the creation of the law prohibiting the act and so was not bound by it. A case in point is apartheid, as previously practised in South Africa, which attained the status of an international crime despite the fact that South Africa did not recognize its own regime as criminal.

Accordingly, there can be no persistent objectors to the law prohibiting an international crime as they are overridden by the specialized *opinio juris* of the international community as a whole. As Ragazzi has pointed out in relation to *jus cogens*: 'If the purpose of peremptory rules is to allow the common interests of states to prevail over the conflicting interest of a single state or a small number of states, this purpose would be frustrated if that state or small number of states were allowed to escape the application of a peremptory rule on the ground of persistent objection.'[11] However it is difficult to estimate how many objectors it would take to prevent the *opinio juris* of states which favoured a rule from rising to the level of acceptance and recognition by the international community as a whole. The test as laid down by the ILC may be almost impossible to satisfy if applied too literally.

A further difficulty with the words 'as a whole', and Ago's explanation of them, has been raised by Ragazzi.[12] He points out that the distinction between the Western and Eastern blocs is disappearing, and that the classification of developed or developing varies with the idea of development which is selected. The word development usually has economic connotations but may be interpreted more broadly to correspond to the integral development of human beings and society, which is arguably more in accordance with the moral considerations which underlie the concepts of *jus cogens* and international crimes.

Criticisms have also been levelled at the tendency to personify the international community.[13] In order for certain obligations to be owed to the international community of states, such a community must be identifiable, and similarly, in order for it to recognize that an international obligation is essential for the protection of its fundamental interests, the international community itself must possess such interests. In the opinion of the ICJ in the *Barcelona Traction* case, a state has obligations to the international

---

[10] See M. Ragazzi, *The Concept of International Obligations* Erga Omnes (1997), 67, who argues that the persistent objector principle is incompatible with the concept of *jus cogens*.
[11] Ibid.   [12] Ibid. 56–7.
[13] See P. Weil, 'Towards Relative Normativity in International Law?', (1983) 77 *AJIL* 412, 426.

community and can enter into commitments with it.[14] Referring to the Court's dictum in that case, Ago described the emergence of 'something which already exists to some extent today ... namely that the entity called the international community, distinct from its members who have rights and obligations, is able to enter into legal relationships with its members'.[15] In the case concerning *US Diplomatic and Consular Staff in Tehran,* Judge Lachs went so far as to speak of rules of law that are the 'common property of the international community' when 'confirmed in the interest of all'.[16] The problem is that the international community is 'un ordre en puissance dans l'esprit des hommes; dans les réalités de la vie internationale, elle en est encore à se chercher, elle ne correspond pas à un ordre effectivement établi.'[17] It is consequently difficult to identify the international community separately from its members, those members being states. A representative cross-section of these states then qualifies as the 'essential components of the international community', and because there is a danger that this might become an exclusive club of influential states, the test for 'international community recognition' must be stringent.

5. CONCLUSION

The requirement for the formation of a rule of customary international law is a uniform and general practice accepted by states as obligatory. It may be queried whether the idea of 'recognition and acceptance by the international community as a whole' is another way of describing the formation of custom in the field of international crimes. Given the fact that the generality of acceptance must verge on universality, that the persistent objector principle ought not to be applicable in this field, and that states must recognize a norm not just as obligatory but also as entailing criminal responsibility, is it perhaps a stricter variety of the formation of custom?[18] It would seem that the best approach is to regard the notion of 'recognition and acceptance by the international community as a whole' as a description of the formation of custom, albeit with a special form of *opinio juris.*[19]

---

[14] (1970) ICJ Reports 3, 32.

[15] 'Obligations *Erga Omnes* and the International Community', in J. H. H. Weiler, M. Spinedi, and A. Cassese (eds.), *International Crimes of States: A Critical Analysis of the ILC's Draft Article 19 on State Responsibility* (1989), 237, 238.

[16] Separate Opinion, (1980) ICJ Reports 3, 48.

[17] C. de Visscher, 'Positivisme et "jus cogens"', (1971) 75 *RGDIP* 5, 8.

[18] The question has been raised in relation to the definition of *jus cogens* by S. Sur, in a discussion statement in A. Cassese and J. H. H. Weiler (eds.), *Change and Stability in International Law-Making* (1988), 128.

[19] Gomez Robledo refers to 'le double consentement' required for the formation of peremptory norms. Such norms emerge in the first instance as rules of customary international law and those rules are then recognized and accepted as constituting peremptory norms, 'Le *Jus cogens* international: sa genèse, sa nature, ses fonctions', (1981–III) 172 Hague *Recueil* 9, 104–8.

'International community recognition' is clearly an important factor in differentiating international crimes and delicts owing to the consensual nature of international law, even though this is something of a contradiction given the element of compulsion inherent in criminal law. Nevertheless the 'international community as a whole' is moving towards existence as an autonomous entity in the sense that if enough states concur the community itself can act as legislator and determine its own social order. In simple terms, this is the way domestic criminal law operates by imposing the social order desired by the majority on the minority who offend.

The development of the concept of state criminality is inevitably a process of evolution which is dependent on the *opinio juris* of the international community as a whole. But this community must have some criteria of reference for deciding which of its interests are so essential that they should be protected by the concept. It is, after all, the subject-matter of a prohibition that makes it a candidate for promotion to the rank of an international crime. For this reason the remaining criteria and indicia address the question *why* the international community attaches, or has reason to attach, a special significance to certain acts and not others in an attempt to discern a pattern in the identification of acts which are intrinsically criminal from an international perspective.

8

The Seriousness Test

1. INTRODUCTION

Seriousness is a subjective concept which is not easy to quantify. Does one look at the nature of the act, the intention of the perpetrator, the consequences, or a combination of the three? What if Hitler's genocidal policy against the Jews and gypsies had not been effectively implemented, or if an accidental act of pollution wiped out an entire indigenous population?

In Draft Article 19, the ILC makes reference both to the 'essential importance' of the obligation and the 'seriousness' of the breach, but there is no suggestion that a two-stage test of seriousness was intended. The ILC has also identified 'seriousness' as the essential element of a crime against the peace and security of mankind entailing individual responsibility for the purposes of the Draft Code of Offences against the Peace and Security of Mankind.[1] In this context the ILC explained that seriousness was to be deduced either from the character of the act, i.e. its cruelty, monstrousness, and barbarity; the extent of its effects, i.e. its massiveness, in particular when the victims are peoples, populations, or ethnic groups; or the intention of the perpetrator.[2] These factors are equally relevant to an analysis of seriousness with regard to state crimes. In more general terms the ILC has stated that the seriousness of an act is to be 'gauged according to the public conscience . . . the disapproval it gives rise to, the shock it provokes, the degree of horror it arouses within the national or international community'.[3] These are relevant factors but insufficient indicators of seriousness in themselves, as they run the risk of facilitating the *ex post* and haphazard calling of names. The ILC has attempted to describe some of the objective factors that go into a definition of seriousness. Objectively, a serious offence is one that is directed against persons or property: 'In respect to persons, what is at stake is the life and physical well-being of individuals and groups. As to property, public or private property, a cultural heritage, historical interests etc., may be affected.'[4]

---

[1] See further Chapter 12 below.

[2] Fifth Report on the Draft Code of Offences against the Peace and Security of Mankind by D. Thiam, Special Rapporteur, A/CN.4/404; (1987) *YrbkILC*, vol. 2, pt. 1, 1, 2.

[3] Third Report on the Draft Code of Offences against the Peace and Security of Mankind by D. Thiam, Special Rapporteur, A/CN.4/387; (1985) *YrbkILC*, vol. 2, pt. 1, 63, 69.

[4] Ibid. 69.

2. NATURE OF THE ACT

The 1998 Rome Statute of the International Criminal Court[5] limits the Court's jurisdiction to 'the most serious crimes of concern to the international community as a whole', namely, genocide, crimes against humanity, war crimes, and aggression.[6] This constitutes a clear and up-to-date statement that these four crimes are by their very nature in a special category of seriousness.

In discussions on Article 19 in the ILC, Vallat argued that the pertinent factor was the nature of the particular obligation rather than the immensity of the breach.[7] This is confirmed in ILC discussions on the Draft Code in the 1980s, which relied to an appreciable extent on Article 19 as a guide:

The more important the subject-matter, the more serious the transgression. An offence against the peace and security of mankind covers transgressions arising from the breach of an obligation the subject-matter of which is of special importance to the international community. It is true that all international crimes are characterized by the breach of an international obligation that is essential for safeguarding the fundamental interests of mankind. But some interests should be placed at the top of the hierarchical list. These are international peace and security, the right of self-determination of peoples, the safeguarding of the human being, and the preservation of the human environment. Those are the four cardinal points round which the most essential concerns revolve, and these concerns constitute the summit of the pyramid on account of their primordial importance. It will be noted, moreover, that because of this primordial importance article 19 cites them as examples in subparagraphs (a) to (d) of paragraph 3.[8]

According to this interpretation, a minor breach of an essential obligation is an international crime, whereas a serious breach of a minor obligation is not. Thus it is the importance of the obligation, not the importance of the breach, which determines seriousness. This approach was perhaps adopted because it is possible to view the subject-matter of the obligation breached objectively. However, not all breaches of obligations having the same subject-matter are equally serious. For example, an isolated act of racial discrimination is not as serious as the establishment of a regime of apartheid, but both acts constitute a breach of an obligation safeguarding the human being. Because international crimes potentially form broad categories, it is necessary to have some regard to additional criteria of seriousness in order to create a useful test.

[5] A/CONF.183/9, 17 July 1998, (1998) 37 *ILM* 999.   [6] Article 5(1).
[7] (1976) *YrbkILC*, vol. 1, 69.   [8] Third Report . . . by D. Thiam, 70–1.

3. MASSIVENESS OF THE ACT

The question whether crimes against humanity implied the existence of a mass element arose in the decisions of the military tribunals established under Control Council Law No. 10 to try individuals after the Second World War. According to the Legal Committee of the UN War Crimes Commission, 'isolated offences did not fall within the notion of crimes against humanity'.[9] As a rule, systematic mass action, particularly if it was authoritative, was necessary to transform a common crime, punishable under municipal law, into a crime against humanity, which thus became also the concern of international law.[10] Only crimes which endangered the international community or shocked the conscience of mankind due to their magnitude and savagery, or by their large number, or by the fact that a similar pattern was applied at different times and places, warranted intervention by states other than the state on whose territory the crimes had been committed or whose subjects were the victims.[11]

More recently it has been argued that although the concept of crimes against humanity derived from an historical criminal phenomenon characterized by its mass nature (a great number of acts, a great number of agents, a great number of victims), this is no longer a constituent element of the offence, and that a crime against humanity may be committed against a single individual provided it is by reason of his race, nationality, religion, or political opinions.[12] However, while this may be sufficient to establish individual criminal responsibility under international law, it would be more difficult to establish state responsibility for a crime against an individual unless there is strong evidence of a systematic plan.

The Genocide Convention refers to the destruction 'in whole or in part' of a national, ethnical, racial, or religious group. This phrase was deleted by the UN *ad hoc* Committee on Genocide but then reinstated by the Sixth Committee. It is difficult to determine what proportion would constitute 'a part' for the purposes of the definition of genocide, but it is likely that the Convention is intended to deal with acts against a large number relative to the size of the victimized group. Again it could be argued that it is the intention which is decisive, and that a genocidal act committed against a single member of a group with the intention of destroying that group might constitute genocide. Nevertheless, the view that the crime must be of a mass nature prevails in Article 19, paragraph 3(c) and (d), which refers to genocide, slavery, apartheid, and acts of pollution committed 'on a widespread scale'. These

---

[9] UNWCC, *History of the United Nations War Crimes Commission and the Development of the Laws of War* (1948), 179.   [10] Ibid.
[11] Fourth Report on the Draft Code of Offences against the Peace and Security of Mankind, by D. Thiam, Special Rapporteur, A/CN.4/398; (1986) *YrbkILC*, vol. 2, pt. 1, 53.
[12] See discussion on crimes against humanity, ibid. 55–61.

words do not appear in sub-paragraphs (a) and (b), which implies that the effects of aggression or the denial of the right to self-determination need not be widespread in order for such acts to qualify as state crimes.

Despite the distinctions made by the ILC it is difficult to ignore the effects of any act when endeavouring to measure seriousness, although it should be remembered that acts such as attempts and conspiracy to commit international crimes may satisfy the seriousness test. Still, there is a natural tendency to measure seriousness in terms of the number of lives lost or threatened. As the Chief Prosecutor for the UK, Sir Hartley Shawcross, stated before the Nuremberg Tribunal: 'The mere number of victims is not the real criterion of the criminality of an act. The majesty of death, the compassion for the innocent, the horror and detestation of the ignominy inflicted upon man—man created in the image of God—these are not the subjects of mathematical calculation. None the less, somehow, numbers are relevant.'[13] A report by a Working Group set up by the ILC states that 'human life is the parameter against which gravity is measured'.[14] In a world where in ancient times human sacrifice to satisfy the appetite of the gods was widespread, an ethic has emerged which ennobles each individual human life. The right to life is the most fundamental human right as without it all other human rights become meaningless. The 1948 Universal Declaration of Human Rights states in Article 3: 'Everyone has the right to life, liberty and security of person.' Similarly, Article 2(1) of the 1950 European Convention on Human Rights provides: 'Everyone's right to life shall be protected by law.' In Article 4 of the 1981 African Charter on Human and Peoples' Rights it is proclaimed: 'Human beings are inviolable. Every human being shall be entitled to respect for his life and the integrity of his person. No one may be arbitrarily deprived of this right.' The extent to which these provisions are broken is some indication of seriousness. Be that as it may, the nature of an act and its effects cannot be evaluated in isolation from the motive and intention of the perpetrator.

4. MOTIVE AND INTENTION OF THE PERPETRATOR

The word 'motive' refers to the factors or circumstances which induce or impel a state or an individual to commit a criminal act. For example, the motive for aggression may be to seize territory, the motive for slavery tends to be economic greed, and the motive for terrorism is usually the furtherance

---

[13] *Trial of German Major War Criminals, Proceedings of the IMT*, 16–27 July 1946, pt. 19 (1949), 429.

[14] Report of the ILC on the Work of its Forty-Eighth Session, Draft Code of Crimes against the Peace and Security of Mankind, Crimes against the Environment prepared by Tomuschat, ILC(XLVIII)/DC/CRD.3, 27 Mar. 1996.

of a specific cause. While motive is not a relevant factor in determining criminality, it can be an indication of the seriousness of an act. Arguably a pathological motive is the most serious because it has no limit. In the Whitaker
Report on the Genocide Convention it is proposed that an interdisciplinary
investigation be undertaken 'into the psychological character and motivation
of individuals and groups who commit genocide or racism, or the psycho-
pathic dehumanizing of vulnerable minorities or scapegoats'.[15] Certain
current psychological and sociological theories emphasize the innate destruc-
tiveness in man and the instinct for self-preservation, and refer to modern
impersonal methods of killing at ever-increasing distances which remove the
natural mechanisms inhibiting the killing of members of one's own species.[16]

There is no clear evidence that genocide is a result of deep-rooted psychological traits, but the psychological theories are important in suggesting that
genocide is not a peculiar pathological phenomenon; rather, it may be close
to the nature of man. Periods of war and situations of change seem to
encourage or provide the opportunity for genocide, and there is never a short-
age of people who find themselves capable of carrying out genocidal
massacres. Unfortunately such people occasionally emerge as leaders.
Goldhagen, in his controversial book *Hitler's Willing Executioners*, focuses
on what he describes as the least well-understood cause of the Holocaust,
namely the crucial motivational element which moved ordinary Germans 'to
devote their bodies, souls, and ingenuity to the enterprise'.[17] In his opinion:

The Holocaust was a *sui generis* event that has a historically specific explanation. The
explanation specifies the enabling conditions created by the long-incubating, perva-
sive, virulent, racist, eliminationist antisemitism of German culture, which was mobi-
lized by a criminal regime beholden to an eliminationist, genocidal ideology, and
which was given shape and energized by a leader, Hitler, who was adored by the vast
majority of the German people, a leader who was known to be committed whole-
heartedly to the unfolding, brutal eliminationist program. During the Nazi period, the
eliminationist antisemitism provided the motivational source for the German leadership and for rank-and-file Germans to kill the Jews. It also was the motivational
source of the other non-killing actions of the perpetrators that were integral to the
Holocaust.[18]

There are a regrettable number of other occurrences which have been driven
by eliminationist motives, such as the massacre of Armenians in Turkey
between 1915 and 1917. The motive for genocide is on the face of it the most

---

[15] B. Whitaker, *Revised and Updated Report on the Question of the Prevention and Punishment of the Crime of Genocide* (1985), E/CN.4/Sub.2/1985/6, 41–2.

[16] See e.g. I. Charny, *How Can We Commit the Unthinkable? Genocide: The Human Cancer* (1982).

[17] D. J. Goldhagen, *Hitler's Willing Executioners: Ordinary Germans and the Holocaust* (1996), 416.   [18] Ibid. 419.

difficult to comprehend, and points towards the extreme seriousness of the crime.

Motive may be more significant in determining seriousness than intention, which is a technical legal term referring to the aim or objective of the actor in causing the consequences of the act. In some cases intention is a specific element and distinguishing feature of an offence. For example, genocide is different from mass murder in that by definition, the 'intent to destroy, in whole or in part, a national, ethnical, racial or religious group, as such' is required in order for the elements of the crime of genocide to be established. Intention to commit genocide is difficult to prove, as genocidal regimes may not be documented and perpetrators may attempt to evade the Genocide Convention by using the excuse that their actions are for political or economic reasons. The Defence Minister of Paraguay responded as follows to allegations of genocide against the Ache Indians: 'Although there are victims and victimizer, there is not the third element necessary to establish the crime of genocide—that is "intent". Therefore, as there is no "intent", one cannot speak of "genocide".'[19] Similarly, in its counter-claim in the *Case Concerning the Application of the Genocide Convention*, Yugoslavia argues that even if certain of the acts alleged by Bosnia-Herzegovina had been committed, 'there was absolutely no intention of committing genocide'.[20] Is it therefore less serious to kill people indiscriminately than to kill them with the intention of eliminating the group? The answer to this question possibly depends on how many people are killed.

It could be argued that a state makes its intention manifest by its actions, and that as regards intention *manifesta probatione non indigent*.[21] A state's actions are to a certain extent signposts which point in the direction of a particular intention. The UN Sixth Committee in fact turned down a proposition to replace the words 'committed with the intent to destroy' which appear in the Genocide Convention by 'aimed at physical destruction of a group'.[22] It has been suggested with regard to individual responsibility for genocide that a court should be able to infer the element of intent necessary for an act to be described as genocide from sufficient evidence, and this could include acts or omissions of such a degree of criminal negligence or recklessness that the defendant must reasonably be assumed to have been aware of the consequences of his conduct.[23] Intention is perhaps not the most useful indicator of seriousness, as it is so difficult to prove as an element in itself.

---

[19] Quoted in L. Kuper, *The Prevention of Genocide* (1985), 12.

[20] Counterclaims, Order of 17 Dec. 1997, http://www.icj-cij.org/idocket/ibhy/ibhyorders/ibhyorder971217.html.   [21] Things manifest do not require proof.

[22] Soviet amendment, AC.6/223; see Official Records of the Third Session of the General Assembly, Part I, Sixth Committee, Legal Questions, Summary Record of Meetings, (21 Sept.–10 Dec. 1948), 73rd Meeting, 97.   [23] Whitaker, *Revised and Updated Report*, 21.

5. THE ROLE OF THE STATE

A major feature which separates international crimes of states from the realm of international crimes of individuals, and places them in a special category of seriousness, is the involvement of the state bureaucratic apparatus in the perpetration of the crime. Large-scale criminal undertakings based on explicit or implicit state policy and executed by state bureaucracies and administrations and by enthusiastic subordinates are what the notion of state criminality is all about. In order for a crime to be attributable to the state,[24] it must be instigated or condoned by the state. In other words, the act must be systematic.

This element of system comes across clearly in cases of genocide. Hitler was able to persuade the mass of Germans that the Jews were a national menace. It seems that such

dehumanizing beliefs about people, or the attribution of extreme malevolence to them, are necessary and *can* be sufficient to induce others to take part in the genocidal slaughter of the dehumanized people, if they are given proper opportunity and coordination, typically by a state . . . Such beliefs constitute the enabling conditions necessary for a state to mobilize large groups of people to partake in genocidal slaughter.[25]

In 1935, the Nuremberg laws deprived Jews of German citizenship. Then, at the Wannsee Conference of 20 January 1942, plans were drawn up for the 'Final Solution' of the 'Jewish Problem'. It was envisaged that a total of 11,000,000 Jews would be liquidated. The routine efficiency of involvement in genocide in Nazi Germany is disturbing. Charny describes how the Nazis ran closed bids for the construction of the gas chambers:

1. A. Tops and Sons, Erfurt, manufacturers of heating equipment: 'We acknowledge receipt of your order for five triple furnaces, including two electric elevators for raising the corpses . . .'
2. Vidier Works, Berlin: 'For putting the bodies into the furnace, we suggest simply a metal fork moving on cylinders . . .'
3. C.H. Kori: 'We guarantee the effectiveness of the cremation ovens, as well as their durability, the use of the best material and our faultless workmanship.'[26]

In his so-called Political Testament, written just before he died, Hitler tried to pass on the torch of anti-semitism to those whom he was leaving behind. 'Above all,' he wrote, 'I enjoin the Government and the people to uphold the racial laws to the limit and to resist mercilessly the poisoner of all nations, international Jewry.'[27]

---

[24] See further Chapter 4 above, s. 4.   [25] Goldhagen, *Hitler's Willing Executioners*, 418.
[26] Charny, *How Can We Commit the Unthinkable?*, 185.
[27] Quoted in Lord Russell of Liverpool, *The Trial of Adolph Eichmann* (1962), 20.

The genocide of the Second World War is perhaps the most indisputable example of a crime organized, endorsed, and perpetrated by the state. Another example is apartheid in South Africa, where racial discrimination was legally endorsed in a carefully constructed system based on racial separation. This was rooted in a state policy to carve up the country into a series of states within a state under the overall control of the white minority. Such a policy demanded the cooperation of the white South Africans in the suppression of the black South Africans.

It is generally not difficult to detect the extent to which the state itself is involved in the commission of a crime. For example, the decision to engage in a war of aggression or to suppress the right of a group to self-determination must emanate from the highest decision-making powers. In more ambiguous cases, such as in acts of terrorism, a state may reveal the extent of its involvement in the criminal act by its reluctance to extradite the responsible individuals or to try them in its domestic courts.

6. DISTINGUISHING BETWEEN THE CATEGORIES OF INTERNATIONAL CRIMES ON THE BASIS OF SERIOUSNESS

In developing Draft Article 19, all members of the ILC agreed on mentioning first the area of obligations relating to the maintenance of international peace and security. Some members even wanted this area to be put in a separate category altogether, which indicates that in the ILC's opinion breaches of obligations relating to the maintenance of international peace and security represent the most serious crimes in the legal consciousness of states. This was the approach adopted in the preliminary Draft Articles submitted to the Commission by the Special Rapporteur.[28] Castaneda and El-Erian stated that they would have liked the ILC to adopt this approach.[29] The proposal to segregate the categories of crimes was not adopted, but it was specified in the commentary that the regime of responsibility in Part II of the Draft Articles might vary in accordance with the crime.[30]

It was decided to refer solely to aggression as an example of a breach of the ban on the threat or use of force as this was 'the most indisputable example, the supreme international crime'.[31] However, this did not mean that other breaches could not be regarded as international crimes, which raises the question whether all aggressive acts are of the same seriousness. The General Assembly 1974 consensus definition of aggression describes only a 'war' of aggression as a crime.[32] A 'war' of aggression is different from other types of aggression in that it comprises a series of acts and implies a sustained intent.

---

[28] (1976) *YrbkILC*, vol. 2, pt. 1, 54.   [29] Ibid. vol. 1, 242–3.
[30] Ibid. vol. 2, pt. 2, 109, 117–18.   [31] Ibid. 121.   [32] See also Chapter 16 below, s. 2.

But the ILC has never made such distinctions. The 1996 Draft Code refers to 'an individual who as leader or organizer, actively participates in or orders the planning, preparation, initiation, or waging of aggression committed by a state'.[33] In terms of the nature of the act it would seem that all aggressive acts including threats of aggression are equally serious; however, the motive and intention of the perpetrator and the consequences of the act are likely to differ in each case. For this reason seriousness must to some extent be judged on a case by case basis.

The ILC chose to refer next to the breach of obligations aimed at safeguarding the right of self-determination of peoples, and pointed to the maintenance by force of colonial domination as an example. Acts falling within this category often involve the use of force and can result in civil war, which is perhaps why this category appears directly below that of acts against international peace and security. It would be difficult to argue, however, that this is a more serious category than the ones following in paragraph 3(c), which refers to breaches of obligations safeguarding the human being, such as slavery, genocide, and apartheid.

The fourth area of obligations is that aimed at the safeguard and preservation of the human environment. Some members of the ILC would have preferred to speak of a broader category, that of the conservation and the free enjoyment for everyone of a resource common to all mankind,[34] but it was felt that this wording was rather vague. Many would argue that this is a far less serious category of acts than those preceding it, and that its inclusion in Article 19 creates a danger of trivialization. It is perhaps felt that the nature of the act is not comparable to aggression or genocide. Even so, the consequences of environmental damage can be immense, and this could be one of the more important categories for the future. It is consequently difficult to distinguish between the categories of crimes in paragraph 3(a)–(d) in terms of seriousness, although it seems that obligations relating to the maintenance of international peace and security were treated by the ILC as being in a league of their own. The categories appear to be listed according to how well established the rules are, and as the subject of environmental crimes in international law is relatively new, this category appears last.

7. CONCLUSION

The difficulty of laying down a strict test for measuring seriousness is readily apparent, and human suffering as a result of state crimes cannot be cali-

---

[33] Article 16; see A/CN.4/L.532, 8 July 1996.
[34] Castaneda, (1976) *YrbkILC*, vol. 1, 243; El-Erian, ibid. 244; Njenga, ibid. 246–7.

brated. Seriousness is a relative rather than an absolute notion, and perhaps the most that can be said is that when several factors coincide the elusive boundary between the serious and the non-serious is crossed. Motives may be innocent or pathological, acts may be accidental or intentional, consequences may be non-existent or massive, and an act may be a one-off by an individual or it may be systematic. Even aggression can occur as a result of genuine error, as in the accidental outbreak of hostilities, for instance, where borders are unstable.

It is important to recognize that even though a wrongful act may fall within the broad category of seriousness as identified in the ILC's description of international crimes, this is no guarantee that it comes within the *concept* of state criminality. The nature of the act is clearly a key factor and the initial indicator of seriousness, but an evaluation based on this factor alone would be artificial and risks widening the concept of state crimes beyond its proper domain. Some of the acts which are potentially included in subparagraphs (c) and (d) of Article 19, paragraph 3, are more appropriately dealt with by developments in the fields of human rights and the environment, and also by the *erga omnes* concept.[35]

The difficulties faced here are not exclusive to international law. In criminology many attempts have been made to assess criminal harm on a scale of seriousness, and the issue is relevant both at the law-creating and at the sentencing stage in national law systems.[36] Von Hirsch and Jareborg[37] have attempted to gauge criminal harm by using a 'living-standard analysis'. They argue that criminal acts can be ranked by a scale of 'degrees of intrusion' on a number of legally protected interests such as physical integrity; material support and amenity; freedom from humiliation; privacy and autonomy. Cohen[38] likens these 'interests' to human rights, and suggests that the argument should be taken further to include crimes committed by a state against its citizens: 'In fact, there are good *moral* reasons why any grading of seriousness should take this into account—in particular, the fact that the very agent responsible for upholding law is actually responsible for the crime.'[39] The concept of state criminality is slowly making its way into criminology in recognition

---

[35] See further Chapter 6 above.

[36] In English law, offence seriousness is the sole criterion for determining whether a community sentence may be imposed and the primary criterion for a custodial sentence, see sections 6(1) and 1(2)(a) of the Criminal Justice Act (CJA) 1991. In addition, offence seriousness is the main factor in determining the length of a custodial sentence (section 2(2)(a) CJA 1991).

[37] A. Von Hirsch and N. Jareborg, 'Gauging Criminal Harm: A Living Standard Analysis', (1991) *Oxford Journal of Legal Studies* II(1), 1–38.

[38] S. Cohen, 'Human Rights and Crimes of the State: The Culture of Denial', in J. Muncie, E. McLaughlin, and M. Langan, (eds.), *Criminological Perspectives: A Reader* (1996), 489–507.

[39] Ibid. 493.

of the fact that the consequences of such acts are more widespread and destructive than traditional crime, and because this would be a logical extension of the white-collar crime debate.[40] This movement is still only in its formative stages.[41]

---

[40] See e.g. G. Barak (ed.), *Crimes by the Capitalist State: An Introduction to State Criminality* (1991); J. I. Ross (ed.), *Controlling State Crime: An Introduction* (1995); D. O. Friedrichs (ed.), *State Crime,* i: *Defining, Delineating and Explaining State Crime* and ii: *Exposing, Sanctioning and Preventing State Crime* (1998).

[41] Cf. Tunkin, *Theory of International Law* (1974), 402, who suggests that the debate on state criminality in international law was sparked off by the work of criminologists.

9

The Conscience of Mankind

1. INTRODUCTION

There was a time when the binding power of social imperatives derived from a divine source, and the sanctions for violation were applied in the name of heaven. Legal prohibitions, moral rules, and religious commandments were all part of the same sphere. As society progressed, this sphere separated into interrelated domains. To take the Ten Commandments as an example, 'thou shalt not kill' is now classified as a legal prohibition to be enforced by the institutions of the state. To honour one's father and mother is classified as a moral rule which derives its binding power from a social consensus. The ban on taking the name of God in vain is classified as a religious commandment to be enforced, according to believers, by divine sanctions.[1]

Nevertheless, there is still a substantial overlap between the three domains in a certain area, namely the hard core of the criminal law; the *mala per se* which includes, in particular, crimes against humanity. Such crimes are prohibited in all modern societies despite differences in the basic religion and morality because they are offences against what might be described as the conscience of mankind. This conscience, deemed to be universal, comes into play when law, morality, and religion coincide.

The 'Martens Clause', which was first included in the Hague Convention II with Respect to the Laws and Customs of War on Land of 1899, appears in its modern version in Additional Protocol I of 1977:

In cases not covered by this Protocol or by other international agreements, civilians and combatants remain under the protection and authority of the principles of international law derived from established custom, from the *principles of humanity* and from the *dictates of the public conscience*.[2]

Thus it was believed even before the First World War that the public conscience could be a protective and balancing force, and the Martens Clause has remained central to international humanitarian law.

---

[1] See A. Rubinstein, 'The Enforcement of Morals in a Secular Society', (1972) *Israel Yearbook on Human Rights,* vol. 2, 57.   [2] Article 1, para. 2 (emphasis added).

2. THE NUREMBERG TRIALS

In the aftermath of the Second World War it was felt that the conscience of
mankind could only be satisfied by the holding of war crimes trials:

The *common sense of mankind* demands that law shall not stop with the punishment
of petty crimes by little people. It must also reach men who possess themselves of
great power and make deliberate and concerted use of it to set in motion evils which
leave no home in the world untouched.[3]

At the opening of the Nuremberg Trials, Francois de Menthon, the French
Chief Prosecutor, declared:

The *conscience of the peoples*, who only yesterday were enslaved and tortured both in
soul and body, calls upon you to judge and to condemn the most monstrous attempt
at domination and barbarism of all times, both in the persons of some of those who
bear the chief responsibility, and in the collective groups and organizations which
were the essential instruments of their crimes.[4]

Justice needed to be done and seen to be done in order for mankind to look
to the future and put aside sentiments of vengeance and guilt. It was felt that
the trials would also strengthen and revive the conscience of mankind and act
as a deterrent. The conduct of the Nazi leaders would be 'exposed in all its
naked wickedness . . . in the hope that the *conscience and good sense of all the
world* will see the consequences of such conduct and the end to which it must
inevitably lead'.[5]

3. CRIMES AGAINST HUMANITY

One of the major innovations among the charges at Nuremberg was the category of crimes against humanity. Certain of the crimes committed during
the Second World War were so heinous that they were considered to be international crimes against the very foundations of civilization. This idea can be
found in Gentili's *De Iure Belli Libri Tres*. Gentili regarded the 'general violation of the common law of humanity and a wrong done to mankind'[6] as a
justification for war. In *Ivanhoe*, Sir Walter Scott describes the 'excesses contrary not only to the laws of England, but to those of nature and humanity'
of the Norman barons.[7] The term 'crimes against humanity' was used for the
first time in a non-technical sense in a Declaration by the Governments of

---

[3] Opening Speech of Justice Robert H. Jackson before the Nuremberg Tribunal, *The Trial of
German Major War Criminals: Opening Speeches of the Chief Prosecutors* (1946), 3 (emphasis
added).   [4] Ibid. 89 (emphasis added).
[5] HM Attorney-General Sir Hartley Shawcross, ibid. 88 (emphasis added).
[6] Vol. ii, J. B. Scott ed., translation of edn. of 1612 (1933), 124.
[7] First published 1819, Penguin Popular Classics (1994), 242.

France, the UK, and Russia on 28 May 1915 concerning the massacre of the Armenian population in Turkey. The atrocities were denounced as 'crimes against humanity and civilization'[8] for which all members of the Turkish Government were to be held responsible. In the opinion of the UN War Crimes Commission the category of crimes against humanity was intended to cover precisely that sort of situation, namely, inhumane acts committed by a government against its own citizens.[9] Crimes against humanity as defined in the Nuremberg Charter,[10] in Law No. 10 of the Allied Control Council,[11] and in the Charter of the International Military Tribunal for the Far East[12] were linked to the state of belligerency, and it has to be admitted that war and crimes against humanity often go hand in hand.[13] However, the relative autonomy of crimes against humanity has become absolute, and such crimes can now be committed both during the course of armed conflict and independently.

The term 'humanity' in this context is ambiguous, but essentially a crime against humanity consists of cruelty directed against human existence, the degradation of human dignity, and the destruction of human culture. The prime examples of crimes against humanity are genocide and apartheid. In its Resolution of 11 December 1946, the General Assembly declared that genocide is a denial of the right of existence of entire human groups which 'shocks the conscience of mankind' and is 'contrary to moral law'. These words were quoted in the Order on Provisional Measures in the *Case Concerning the Application of the Genocide Convention*.[14] Similar language appears in the many resolutions and declarations concerning apartheid. In 1970 the General Assembly announced: 'We strongly condemn the civil policy of apartheid, which is a *crime against the conscience and dignity of mankind* and, like nazism, is contrary to the principles of the Charter.'[15] This was affirmed in the Lagos Declaration for Action against Apartheid of 1977.[16] In its 1989 Declaration on Apartheid and its Destructive Consequences in Southern Africa, the General Assembly explained:

apartheid, characterized as a crime against the conscience and dignity of mankind, is responsible for the death of countless numbers of people in South Africa, has sought

---

[8] See UNWCC, *History of the United Nations War Crimes Commission and the Development of the Laws of War* (1948), 35. [9] Ibid. 189.
  [10] Article 6(c).   [11] Article 11(1)(c).   [12] Article 5(c).
  [13] For a discussion of the differences between these two concepts, see B. B. Jia, 'The Differing Concepts of War Crimes and Crimes Against Humanity in International Criminal Law', in G. S. Goodwin-Gill and S. Talmon, (eds.), *The Reality of International Law: Essays in Honour of Ian Brownlie* (1999), 243.   [14] (1993) ICJ Reports 325, 348.
  [15] UNGA Declaration on the Occasion of the Twenty-Fifth Anniversary of the UN, Resolution 2627(XXV), 24 Oct. 1970 (emphasis added).
  [16] 22–6 Aug. 1977, S/12426, 28 Oct. 1977, in United Nations, *The United Nations and Apartheid 1948–1994*, Blue Books Series, vol. 1, Document 87, 344; endorsed by GA Resolution 32/105B, 14 Dec. 1977.

to dehumanize entire peoples and has imposed a brutal war on the region of Southern Africa, which has resulted in untold loss of life, destruction of property and massive displacement of innocent men, women and children and which is a *scourge and
affront to humanity* that must be fought and eradicated in its totality.[17]

In the *South-West Africa* cases it was argued in the Pleadings that

the norm of non-discrimination and non-separation involves the promotion of common interests and collective interests of states, and of the organized international
community taken as a whole. These are, moreover, common interests which rest upon
a widely shared and deeply felt and often eloquently expressed humanitarian conviction. *In this respect apartheid corresponds to genocide, and the nature of the law-
creating process in response to both has been remarkably similar: one in which the
collective will of the international community has been shocked into virtual unanimity,
and in which the moral basis of law is most visible.* It is precisely because there is an
offender that there has been a drive to create a norm. If the offender is allowed to
avoid the legal condemnation of his action by stating a protest, then international law
is rendered impotent in the face of a grave challenge to the values underlying the international social order.[18]

The Preamble to the Universal Declaration of Human Rights links the most
grave human rights abuses with crimes against humanity: 'disregard and contempt for human rights have resulted in barbarous acts which have *outraged
the conscience of mankind.*' Finally, the Preamble to the Rome Statute of the
International Criminal Court states 'that during this century millions of children, women and men have been victims of unimaginable atrocities that
deeply shock the conscience of humanity'.[19] The examples demonstrate that
the conscience of mankind is a source of positive morality in international
law and has played a significant role in developing the law relating to crimes
against humanity.

4. DURKHEIM AND THE *CONSCIENCE COLLECTIVE*

The idea of a conscience of mankind is reminiscent of Durkheim's *conscience
collective*. Durkheim's overriding concern is with the nature and source of
social cohesion or integration. According to him, crime consists in acts that
'shock . . . sentiments which for a given social system are found in all healthy
consciences',[20] or in other words, crime is an act which violates the *conscience
collective*. Furthermore, morality is equivalent to everything which is a source

---

[17] GA Resolution S-16/1, 14 Dec. 1989, in UN, *The United Nations and Apartheid 1948–1994*,
Document 135, 419 (emphasis added).
[18] Statement by Gross in ICJ Pleadings, Oral Arguments, Documents, *South-West Africa*
cases (1966), vol. 9, 351 (emphasis added).
[19] A/CONF.183/9, 17 July 1998, (1998) 37 *ILM* 999 (emphasis added).
[20] E. Durkheim, *The Division of Labour in Society* (1964), 73.

of solidarity. A central tenet of Durkheim's *The Division of Labour in Society* is that society is held together by certain shared sentiments and beliefs. The solidarity and cohesion of society is threatened by a breach of these common sentiments, which consequently necessitates a collective response against the offender in order to repair and reinforce the injured conscience. Durkheim is of the opinion that healthy societies need crime and punishment in order to promote social integration through a reaffirmation of collective beliefs and thus social solidarity. These basic aspects of Durkheim's much broader theory help to explain the functioning of positive morality in the international society of states. When incidents occur which shock the conscience of mankind there is a natural tendency to embody the sentiment in the criminal law, which can then be invoked to restore social cohesion whenever it is threatened.

5. EVALUATION

The phrase 'conscience of mankind' might be dismissed by some as mere rhetoric, and indeed the phrase does not appear in more recent UN declarations and resolutions.[21] The focus seems to have shifted from the perceived evil of certain acts to the degree to which those acts threaten international peace and security.[22] Perhaps the human conscience is becoming impervious to the images of human beings destroying each other which appear daily on television news broadcasts.

Nevertheless, it does seem that the international community feels compelled to take concerted action in certain instances and not in others. For example, the Western world was shocked when pictures from the Omarska detention camp in north-western Bosnia were broadcast. These pictures were a sinister evocation of Europe's last war, and government officials feared that the West was once again becoming complicit in crimes against humanity by its silence. In such situations there are no innocent bystanders, and it was felt that war crimes trials would expunge the guilt both of the perpetrators of atrocities and of those who had turned a blind eye. When faced with these realities it cannot be denied that the human conscience is troubled by emotions of shock, fear, and shame.

In an address delivered to a joint session of Congress on 2 April 1917, President Woodrow Wilson observed in relation to humanitarian law: 'By

---

[21] But states sometimes use the phrase. For example, Democratic Yemen and India felt that the 'conscience of humanity' had been shaken by the 1982 massacre of Palestinians in the Sabra and Shatila camps in Lebanon, see (1982) *YrbkUN*, 486.

[22] The Preamble to the Rome Statute of the International Criminal Court (n. 19 above) suggests that 'atrocities that deeply shock the conscience of humanity' also threaten 'the peace, security and well-being of the world'. See further Chapter 9 above.

painful stage after stage that law has been built up, with meager enough results, indeed . . . but always with a clear view, at least, of what the heart and conscience of mankind demanded.'[23] O'Connell has referred to the 'habits, sentiments and interests of humanity which lie at the basis of the legal conscience'.[24] In his opinion it is deference to this common conscience which crystallizes even an ordinary customary rule whereby a state 'admits its subjection to a rule not exclusively of its own manufacture'.[25] In the *South-West Africa* cases, Judge Tanaka described in his Dissenting Opinion the law that was deeply rooted in the conscience of mankind and of any reasonable man in terms of natural law.[26]

There is probably no 'universal' conscience of mankind, just as there is no 'universal' international law. Nevertheless, there are certain breaches of international law which affect us more deeply and pervasively than others for which compensation is an adequate remedy. So it can be said that with regard to their effect on the human conscience, all state actions are not equal. The question is whether the solidarity of the human race is strong enough at this stage to stand up against states which commit international crimes. In the words of President Nelson Mandela:

Our common humanity transcends the oceans and all national boundaries. It binds us together in a common cause against tyranny, to act together in defence of our very humanity. Let it never be asked of any one of us—what did we do when we knew that another was repressed?[27]

Spiritual cohesion has traditionally been weak in the international community, and the development of an international conscience and morality through acceptance of the concept of state criminality might help to strengthen international solidarity.[28]

---

[23] Address of the President of the United States at a Joint Session of the Two Houses of Congress, 2 Apr. 1917, repr. in (1917) 11 *AJIL Suppl.* 143, 144.

[24] *International Law*, i, 2nd edn. (1970), 16.   [25] Ibid.

[26] *South-West Africa*, Second Phase, Judgment, (1966) ICJ Reports 5, 298.

[27] On receiving a special Carter-Menil Human Rights Award from Mrs Dominique de Menil and President Jimmy Carter at the Rothko Chapel in Houston, Tex. (1992).

[28] During the discussions on state crimes in the ILC, 'the duty of non-recognition and of cooperation in expunging the consequences of a crime were described as reflecting a growing spirit of solidarity among members of the international community and an attempt to act as a community according to a notion of international public order, which was a positive development in the obligation of solidarity among States. It was suggested that the concept of community based on solidarity was slowly gaining ground and must be taken into account in elaborating the legal provisions that would regulate relations among states': Report of the ILC on the Work of its Fiftieth Session, GAOR, Fifty-Third session (1998), Suppl. No. 10, (A/53/10), para. 301.

10

Elementary Considerations of Humanity

1. INTRODUCTION

Like the 'conscience of mankind', the notion of 'elementary considerations of humanity' is linked to crimes against humanity and the plight of the ordinary citizen. International law has never completely ignored the fate of individuals within a state, although until the 1800s a state's internal affairs were shielded by the character and values of the state system. The notion of 'principles of humanity' began to seep into the international system with the Enlightenment and the belief that humanity would make great progress with the spread of reason and knowledge. French Enlightenment philosophers fought actively for the natural rights of the citizen both in matters of freedom of thought and speech and regarding more profound issues of religion, morals, and politics. The principle of the inviolability of the individual culminated in the Declaration of the Rights of Man and Citizen adopted by the French National Assembly in 1789. The Declaration referred to 'natural rights'; those to which everyone was entitled simply by being born.

In the nineteenth century Europe and America took steps to abolish slavery and agreements were later pursued to make war less inhumane. Meanwhile, international law was developing a doctrine concerning the legitimacy of humanitarian intervention in cases where a state committed atrocities against its own subjects which shocked the conscience of mankind. Such a doctrine was invoked against the Ottoman Empire in 1827 on behalf of the Greeks, in 1860–1 by France in Syria, and again in 1876, when thousands of Christians were massacred by irregular Ottoman troops in what is today Bulgaria. Following the First World War the League of Nations developed programmes which reflected concern for individuals such as the treaties dealing with minority groups. The establishment of the International Labour Office (now Organization) represented another milestone in international concern for individual welfare.

It is possible to take a cynical view of these developments. If states wished to reduce the horrors of war for their own people, it was necessary in exchange to reduce them for others. Minorities treaties may have been promoted by powerful states because they feared that maltreatment of minorities with which other states identified threatened their security. Finally, the conventions of the ILO could be regarded as capitalism's defence against the spread of socialism. Thus, these developments may have had political-economic rather than humanitarian motivations. On the other hand this view ignores the fact that principles of humanity were considered to be inherent and did not begin to exist merely at the point when they were acknowledged to exist. Naturally it took time for states to fit these notions into their traditional modes of behaviour, but later instruments such as the Universal Declaration of Human Rights demonstrated a commitment to the protection of human rights as an end in itself.

2. REFERENCE TO ELEMENTARY CONSIDERATIONS OF HUMANITY IN STATE PRACTICE AND INTERNATIONAL JURISPRUDENCE

Following the First World War, the so-called Commission of Fifteen Members of the Preliminary Peace Conference drafted a report which contemplated the prosecution of those guilty of offences against the laws and customs of war or the laws of humanity.[1] The implication was that the laws and customs of war was a separate category from the laws of humanity. The two American members of the Commission, Lansing and Brown, opposed this suggestion and objected that the laws and principles of humanity are not certain, 'varying with time, place and circumstance'.[2] Writing in 1946, Wright disagreed:

> They said there was no fixed and universal standard of humanity, but that it varied with time, place and circumstance, and, it may be, the conscience of the individual judge. They referred to the place of equity in the Anglo-American legal system and to John Selden's definition of equity as a roguish thing. But, if I may also take the parallel from Anglo-American law, equity has established itself as a regular branch of that legal system.[3]

In 1919 opinions differed as to how vague the idea of laws of humanity actually was, and the Recommendation by the majority of the Commission did not appear in the final Peace Treaty. Reference was, however, made to the laws of humanity in the Leipzig Trials.[4]

In 1937, an International Agreement for Collective Measures against Piratical Attacks in the Mediterranean by Submarines was signed at Nyon and supplemented three days later by an agreement signed at Geneva in respect of similar acts by surface vessels and aircraft. The Agreement states that acts committed during the Spanish conflict against merchant ships not belonging to the warring parties 'constitute acts contrary to the most *elementary dictates of humanity*, which should be justly treated as acts of piracy'.[5]

---

[1] Commission on the Responsibility of the Authors of the War and on Enforcement of Penalties, Report presented to the Preliminary Peace Conference; see UNWCC, *History of the United Nations War Crimes Commission and the Development of the Laws of War* (1948), 33.

[2] Memorandum of Reservations Presented by the Representatives of the US to the Report of the Commission on Responsibilities, ibid., 36–7.

[3] Q. Wright, 'War Crimes Under International Law', (1946) 62 *LQR* 40, 48.

[4] See C. Mullins, *The Leipzig Trials* (1921), 218.

[5] 181 *LNTS* 135, 137 (emphasis added).

Principles of humanity were referred to without further comment or query in the High Command Trial[6] which took place after the Second World War. The Tribunal declared that the responsibility of commanders of occupied territories is 'fixed according to the customs of war, international agreements, *fundamental principles of humanity*, and the authority of the commander which has been delegated to him by his own government'.[7] It was subsequently confirmed that certain 'principles of humanity' were considered to be part of international law and the notion of 'inherent criminality' was stressed:

From an international standpoint, criminality may arise by reason that the act is forbidden by international agreements or is *inherently criminal and contrary to accepted principles of humanity as recognized and accepted by civilized nations*. In the case of violations of international agreements, the criminality arises from violations of the agreement itself—in other cases, by the inherent nature of the act.[8]

These ideas were taken up in the *Corfu Channel* case,[9] in which the ICJ held that Albania had violated its obligations under international law by its failure to notify British ships of mines in its territorial waters. This finding was supported by rules of customary law which were expressly invoked, but in addition the Court made reference 'first and foremost'[10] to 'elementary considerations of humanity, even more exacting in peace than in war',[11] as a possible basis of legal obligations. Such considerations were included among the 'general and well-recognized principles'[12] upon which the Court based its judgment. The statement of the ICJ in the *Corfu Channel* case was given additional force when it was quoted in the *Nicaragua* case[13] many years later.

3. SOURCE, SCOPE AND EFFECT OF ELEMENTARY CONSIDERATIONS OF HUMANITY

In his initial comment on the topic, Fitzmaurice[14] regarded 'elementary considerations of humanity' as an extension of the 'good neighbour principle' which proclaims that it is 'every state's obligation not to allow knowingly its territory to be used for acts contrary to the rights of other states'.[15] In his opinion both notions formed the 'source of obligations that have neither

---

[6] Law Reports UNWCC, vol. 12, 1.   [7] Ibid. 75.   [8] Ibid.
[9] (1949) ICJ Reports 4.
[10] G. Fitzmaurice, 'Judicial Innovation: Its Uses and Its Perils', in *Cambridge Essays in International Law: Essays in Honour of Lord McNair* (1965), 24, 29.
[11] (1949) ICJ Reports 22.   [12] Ibid.
[13] *Case Concerning Military and Paramilitary Activities in and against Nicaragua*, (1986) ICJ Reports 14, 112.
[14] G. G. Fitzmaurice, 'The Law and Procedure of the ICJ: General Principles and Substantive Law', (1950) 27 *BYIL* 1, 4.   [15] *Corfu Channel* case, (1949) ICJ Reports 4, 22.

been expressly assumed nor arise from any specific rule of international law'.[16] This means that even if a state is not a party to a particular convention containing an express obligation, it is not relieved of responsibility for a breach of a similar obligation on other grounds. In the *Corfu Channel* case the Court denied that a state's obligation to notify other states of the existence of a minefield in its territorial waters arose from Hague Convention VIII of 1907 which was applicable in time of war. The humanitarian provisions underlying the Hague Conventions were 'special applications of a much more general principle of universal applicability which, for understandable reasons, had been "spelt-out" in detail only for the particular conditions of warfare, but which remained equally valid under analogous peacetime conditions'.[17] Fitzmaurice seems subsequently to have adopted the view that principles of humanity are not a separate source of law but derive from conventional or customary international law.[18] He refers to the 'antecedent, if implicit, general principle of customary international law'[19] which had originally been expressed only in conventional form in the Hague Conventions, but had subsequently become a received rule of customary international law.

While recognizing that considerations of humanity have been powerful creative agencies assisting in the formation of important rules of international customary and treaty law, Schwarzenberger[20] argues that they are neither a law-creating process nor operative rules of customary law, and do not easily fall into the category of general principles of law recognized by civilized nations. He points to the network of treaties which seemed necessary to bring an end to the slave trade to support his argument. He does not entirely exclude considerations of equity, humanity, or other values which are inseparable from civilized life from the scope of international law, but believes that they can only be taken into account by international courts and tribunals after they have passed through a law-creating process. For example, where the parties to a treaty confer on an international institution an equitable discretion it may legitimately supplement treaty law by 'general principles of justice',[21] thereby allowing the reception of international morality into international law via the law-creating process of treaties.

Wright is sceptical of the ICJ's reliance in the *Corfu Channel* case upon broad principles of law which are deemed to be self-evident and stated without citation of precedent or authority.[22] He notes that these principles refer

---

[16] Fitzmaurice, 'The Law and Procedure of the ICJ', 4.
[17] Fitzmaurice, 'Judicial Innovation', 29.
[18] Ibid. See also H. Thirlway, 'The Law and Procedure of the ICJ, 1960–1989', (1990) 61 *BYIL* 1, 6.   [19] Fitzmaurice, 'Judicial Innovation', 29–30.
[20] G. Schwarzenberger, *International Law as Applied by International Courts and Tribunals*, i, 3rd edn. (1957), 51.   [21] See *Norwegian Shipowners' Claims*, (1922) 1 *RIAA* 307, 331.
[22] 'The Corfu Channel Case', (1949) 43 *AJIL* 491, 494.

to rights of humanity and obligations not to resort to force which are emphasized in certain general conventions. Brownlie relates considerations of humanity more specifically to human values which are already protected by positive legal principles, and describes the notion in terms of public policy.[23] He also sees a connection between considerations of humanity, general principles of law, and equity, all of which have had a firmer basis since the UN Charter and its provisions concerning the protection of human rights and fundamental freedoms. Shaw has suggested that elementary principles of humanity may lie at the base of certain norms of international law and 'perform a valuable role in endowing such norms with an additional force within the system'.[24]

In the 1966 *South-West Africa* cases[25] the ICJ addressed the question of the relationship between principles of a humanitarian character and rules of law, and concluded that humanitarian considerations were insufficient in themselves to generate legal rights and obligations:

Humanitarian considerations may constitute the inspirational basis for rules of law, just as, for instance, the preambular parts of the United Nations Charter constitute the moral and political basis for the specific legal provisions thereafter set out. Such considerations do not, however, in themselves amount to rules of law. All states are interested—have an interest—in such matters. But the existence of an 'interest' does not of itself entail that this interest is specifically juridical in character.[26]

The Court felt that it could take account of moral principles only in so far as these were given sufficient expression in legal form. In contrast, the Court's choice of words in the *Nicaragua* case seems to confirm Fitzmaurice's early view of considerations of humanity as a source of law. In this case mines had been laid close to Nicaraguan ports with no prior warning or notification to Nicaragua or to international shipping. The Court referred to this act as a 'breach of the principles of humanitarian law *underlying* the specific provisions of Convention No. VIII of 1907'.[27] The Court went on in the operative clause of its judgment to describe America's failure to make known the existence and location of the mines laid by it as a 'breach of its obligations under customary international law',[28] although no reference was made to state practice in this context. Humanitarian law was again referred to in relation to the 1949 Geneva Conventions. In the Court's view:

the conduct of the United States may be judged according to the fundamental general principles of humanitarian law ... the Geneva Conventions are in some respects a development, and in other respects no more than the expression, of such principles.[29]

---

[23] I. Brownlie, *Principles of Public International Law*, 4th edn. (1990), 28.
[24] M. N. Shaw, *International Law* (1997), 85.
[25] *South-West Africa*, Second Phase, Judgment, (1966) ICJ Reports 6.   [26] Ibid. 34.
[27] (1986) ICJ Reports 112 (emphasis added).   [28] Ibid. 147–8.   [29] Ibid. 113.

Common Article 3 was said to embody rules which reflected so-called 'elementary considerations of humanity'.[30] Moreover, it was found that the US was under an obligation not to encourage breaches of the laws of war which derived 'from the general principles of humanitarian law to which the Conventions merely give specific expression'.[31] Thus, the Court seems to have had in mind principles which are so fundamental that they do not require translation into customary law in order to be applicable. Consequently, these principles of humanitarian law must either be a source of obligations or one of the general principles of law in the sense of Article 38, paragraph 1(c) of the ICJ's Statute. In its Advisory Opinion on the *Legality of the Threat or Use of Nuclear Weapons*, the ICJ avoided the issue by arguing that 'the most universally recognized humanitarian principles'[32] already constituted 'intransgressible principles of international customary law'.[33]

4. CONCLUSION

It seems that there is a certain amount of disagreement concerning the source, scope, and effect of 'elementary considerations of humanity'. Is it a separate category of obligations in international law or is it merely an aspect of public policy, *jus cogens*, morality, or humanitarian law generally? Furthermore, is it a category of obligations that exists independently of the usual law-creating process? It is probably true that the concept contains elements of a variety of similar concepts, but like related concepts it can boast its own process of development and is therefore unique. Ragazzi is of the opinion that the notion of elementary considerations of humanity, by its absolute value, is functionally equivalent to that of obligations *erga omnes* and raises the possibility that the former concept has evolved into the latter.[34] However, it would seem a pity to merge the two ideas in this way, as it is not yet clear if they are following the same path of development, and obligations *erga omnes* have failed to receive favourable treatment by the ICJ since the *Barcelona Traction* case.[35]

Judge Tanaka has warned that 'there must be no legal vacuum in the protection of human rights',[36] and has explained that a certain amount of natural law is inherent in the notion of general principles of law as stated in Article 38(1)(c) of the Statute of the ICJ, which 'extends the concept of the source of international law beyond the limit of legal positivism according to which, the states being bound only by their own will, international law is

---

[30] (1986) ICJ Reports 114.   [31] Ibid.
[32] (1996) ICJ Reports 4, 258.   [33] Ibid. 257.
[34] M. Ragazzi, *The Concept of Obligations* Erga Omnes (1997), 85–6.
[35] See Chapter 15 below, s. 3(b).
[36] Dissenting Opinion, *South-West Africa* cases, (1966) ICJ Reports 298.

nothing but the law of the consent and auto-limitation of the state'.[37] This is probably the pretext upon which the ICJ first recognized elementary considerations of humanity, although it was never stated so expressly. Gradually such considerations have been protected and promoted by positive law as the driving force behind certain treaties and custom. In its Advisory Opinion in the *Reservations to the Genocide Convention* case, the ICJ stated that the object of the Convention was on the one hand 'to safeguard the very existence of certain human groups and on the other to *confirm* and *endorse* the most elementary considerations of humanity'.[38]

In the High Command Trial the Tribunal spoke of acts which were inherently criminal *and* contrary to accepted principles of humanity, and it was suggested that criminal responsibility arose from the inherent nature of the act. This notion of 'inherent criminality' implies that 'absolute', 'inherent', 'inalienable', 'sacred', 'eternal', and 'inviolate' rights possess a 'super-constitutional' significance. Almost invariably it is these rights which are at issue when an international crime is committed. In the *Nicaragua* case the Court made repeated reference to certain fundamental principles of humanity seemingly as an alternative basis for responsibility in case it could be argued that customary or treaty law did not support the Court's submissions. The message appears to be that there is a fixed and universal standard of humanity which is making its way into the corpus of international law via the traditional law-creating channels, but which nevertheless stands alone and is sufficient to be applied in areas where the law is unclear or under-developed.

Judge Alvarez stated in his Separate Opinion in the *Corfu Channel* case that the 'characteristics of an international delinquency are that it is an act contrary to the sentiments of humanity'.[39] This is certainly true of international crimes. All acts which are inherently criminal are also contrary to elementary considerations of humanity, and the latter concept is therefore another building block in the development of the former. This is already evident in the field of individual responsibility for war crimes and crimes against humanity, but is also relevant to state responsibility. The link between criminal responsibility and elementary considerations of humanity was recently confirmed in the case of *Prosecutor v Tadic* (Jurisdiction) before the Appeals Chamber of the International Criminal Tribunal for the Former Yugoslavia. The Tribunal's justification for its assertion that certain acts entailed individual criminal responsibility regardless of whether they were committed in internal or international armed conflict was that 'Principles and rules of humanitarian law reflect "elementary considerations of humanity" widely recognized as the mandatory minimum for conduct in armed conflicts of any kind'.[40] The

---

[37] Ibid.   [38] (1951) ICJ Reports 15, 23 (emphasis added).
[39] (1949) ICJ Reports 45.   [40] (1996) 35 *ILM* 32, 70.

encouragement by a state of breaches of the laws of war could be described as a state crime having reference to the criteria and indicia outlined so far, and on the basis of the ICJ's characterization of such an act as unlawful because it violated general principles of humanitarian law.

In his Dissenting Opinion in the *South-West Africa* cases, Judge Tanaka stated:

> The historical development of law demonstrates the continual process of the cultural enrichment of the legal order by taking into consideration values or interests which had previously been excluded from the sphere of law. In particular, the extension of the object of rights to cultural, and therefore intangible, matters and the legalization of social justice and of humanitarian ideas which cannot be separated from the gradual realization of world peace, are worthy of our attention . . .

> As outstanding examples of the recognition of the legal interests of states in general humanitarian causes, the international efforts to suppress the slave trade, the minorities treaties, the Genocide Convention and the Constitution of the International Labour Organization are cited.

> We consider that in these treaties and organizations common and humanitarian interests are incorporated.[41]

The significance of the notion of elementary considerations of humanity as a criterion or indicium in differentiating crimes and delicts is that it bears meta-juridical values which are threatened by the commission of acts amounting to international crimes but tend not to be threatened by lesser evils. When these values come into play the international community feels compelled to act, and considerations of humanity therefore enter the law-creating process and ought to override those elements of positivism which allow the continuation of criminal regimes. The notion underlies human rights and humanitarian law, and is particularly relevant to crimes committed within states where intervention by other states is not always so easily justifiable.

[41] (1966) ICJ Reports 252.

11

Peace and Security

1. INTRODUCTION

In order for an act to be considered an international crime it must be both criminal and international in character. While it may seem self-evident that the commission of a crime by a state is a matter of international concern, many cases of civil war and crimes against humanity which occur within a state are not so obviously international. This chapter deals with the element of 'internationality'. There has been a tendency to construe the word narrowly in terms of the collective security interests of the international community. This tendency results both from the work of the ILC in creating a Draft Code of Crimes against the Peace and Security of Mankind dealing with international crimes committed by individuals and from the increased role of the UN in maintaining or restoring international peace and security. It should be recalled in this context that in the opinion of the ILC in 1976, the institution under the UN Charter of a special regime of sanctions following the breach of certain international obligations provided evidence of the existence of state responsibility for international crimes.[1]

2. THE CONCEPT OF CRIMES AGAINST THE PEACE AND SECURITY OF MANKIND

In the ILC, Graven chose to distinguish between the two values which were protected by the term 'offence against the peace and security of mankind'. He argued that offences against peace were ones which were likely to, or did in fact, lead to aggression or hostilities within the meaning of international law, whereas offences against security were those which were likely to, or in fact, led to disorders or disturbances and impaired public tranquillity, peace of mind, and confidence on the part of an individual, a community, or a state.[2] However, it is difficult to specify in advance whether certain acts will produce a particular effect, and it therefore seems logical to consider Graven's values together. This was the general approach taken by the ILC in its elaboration of a Draft Code, most members agreeing that the two words 'peace' and 'security' had a certain unity and linked the various offences within the

---

[1] (1976) *YrbkILC*, vol. 2, pt. 2, 102 (para. 16).
[2] Third Report on the Draft Code of Offences against the Peace and Security of Mankind by D. Thiam, Special Rapporteur, A/CN.4/387; (1985) *YrbkILC*, vol. 2, pt, 1, 63, 68.

Code, despite the fact that each offence had its own special characteristics.[3] This particular debate has not since been reopened.

A more difficult task was to *define* the concept of an offence against the peace and security of mankind. In his initial report on the topic of a Draft Code in 1950, Spiropoulos suggested that the main characteristic of the offences in question was their highly political nature. They were offences which, on account of their specific characteristics, would normally affect international relations in a way which was dangerous for the maintenance of peace.[4] In formulating the 1991 Draft Code, it was decided to define the concept using the framework of Article 19 of the ILC's Draft on State Responsibility in an effort to achieve a certain unity of approach and a single guiding theme in the ILC's work. Thus it was agreed that a crime against the peace and security of mankind resulted from: a serious breach of an international obligation of essential importance for the maintenance of international peace and security; a serious breach of an international obligation of essential importance for safeguarding the right of self-determination of peoples; a serious breach on a widespread scale of an obligation of essential importance for safeguarding the human being; and a serious breach on a widespread scale of an obligation of essential importance for the safeguarding and preservation of the human environment.[5] In the ILC's Commentary to Article 19 it is stated:

The rules of international law which are now of greater importance than others for safeguarding the fundamental interests of the international community are to a large extent those which give rise to the obligations comprised within the four main categories mentioned.[6]

3. THE CONCEPT OF A THREAT TO INTERNATIONAL PEACE AND SECURITY

In its work on the Draft Code the ILC raised an important distinction between the two concepts of 'international peace and security' and 'peace and security of mankind'. In the opinion of the ILC, the former is synonymous with non-belligerence and refers to peaceful relations between states, while the latter encompasses a wider terrain and covers not only acts committed by one state against another but also acts committed against peoples.[7] The expression 'international peace and security' which appears in Chapter

[3] (1985) *YrbkILC*, vol. 2, pt, 1, 67.
[4] A/CN.4/19 and Add. 1 and 2; (1950) *YrbkILC*, vol. 2, 249, 259.
[5] Third Report on the Draft Code of Offences against the Peace and Security of Mankind by D. Thiam, 71.   [6] (1976) *YrbkILC*, vol. 2, pt. 2, 121.
[7] Third Report on the Draft Code of Offences against the Peace and Security of Mankind by D. Thiam, 71.

VII of the UN Charter may therefore be viewed as a correlative of the term 'peace and security of mankind' against which the crimes listed in the ILC's Draft Code are directed, although it is of a narrower scope. This raises the question whether UN resolutions and declarations which classify acts as threats to, or breaches of, international peace and security can be a valuable guide in determining which acts are international crimes. In formulating the rules on state responsibility in the ILC, Vallat was of the opinion that the idea of a threat to international peace and security lay at the root of the categorization of acts as international crimes.[8] The UN seems to use this phrase broadly in a sense which is perhaps synonymous with the phrase 'peace and security of mankind'. Many of the acts listed as examples of crimes in Article 19, besides the obvious case of aggression, have repeatedly been considered by the UN to affect international peace and security.

In Resolution 1514(XV) of 14 December 1960, the General Assembly unanimously declared that 'the subjection of peoples to alien subjugation, domination and exploitation . . . is an impediment to the promotion of world peace and cooperation'. Indeed, the struggle for self-determination often results in the direct use of force. In Resolution 2270(XXII) of 17 November 1967 the General Assembly condemned the war being waged by the Government of Portugal against the peaceful peoples of the territories under its domination, which it believed constituted a grave threat to international peace and security.

The Genocide Convention establishes the principle that genocide, even if perpetrated by a state within its own territory, is not an internal matter but a matter of international concern. Recent possible cases of genocide include Iraqi action against the Kurds before and during the Gulf War of 1991, acts committed by various sides in the recent conflict in the former Yugoslavia, and the massacre of Tutsi by Hutu in Rwanda in 1994. In 1991 the Security Council spoke of 'the repression of the Iraqi civilian population in many parts of Iraq, including most recently in Kurdish populated areas, which led to a massive flow of refugees towards and across international frontiers and to cross-border incursions which threaten international peace and security in the region'.[9] The Security Council went on to demand that Iraq, as a contribution to removing the threat to international peace and security in the region, immediately end this repression. The conflict in the former Yugoslavia has repeatedly been described as a threat to international peace and security.[10] In 1992 the General Assembly, deploring the situation in Bosnia-Herzegovina, which constituted a grave threat to international peace and security, condemned the practice of ethnic cleansing, believed to be a concerted effort by the Serbs of Bosnia-Herzegovina, with the acquiescence of

---

[8] (1976) *YrbkILC*, vol. 1, 69.   [9] Resolution 688, 5 Apr. 1991.
[10] See e.g. SC Resolutions 713, 25 Sept. 1991; 721, 27 Nov. 1991; 770, 15 Aug. 1992.

and some support from the Yugoslav National Army, to create 'ethnically pure' regions.[11] In 1993 the Security Council established the International Criminal Tribunal to try those accused of serious violations of international humanitarian law, including genocide, in the former Yugoslavia since 1991.[12] The Security Council was convinced that the establishment of such a tribunal would contribute to the restoration and maintenance of peace and its lifespan was limited to the achievement of this purpose. A similar tribunal was subsequently established on the same basis to try those responsible for the Rwandan massacres.[13]

In 1960 the Security Council adopted a resolution recognizing that the regime of apartheid in South Africa led to international friction and potentially endangered international peace and security.[14] From 1965 onwards the General Assembly regularly drew the attention of the Security Council to the fact that the situation in South Africa constituted a threat, or even a grave threat, to international peace and security and that economic and other measures of the kind envisaged in Chapter VII of the Charter were essential in order to solve the problem of apartheid.[15]

Terrorism has also been held to have implications for international peace and security.[16] In 1992 the Security Council was 'deeply disturbed by the world-wide persistence of acts of international terrorism in all its forms, including those in which states are directly or indirectly involved, which endanger or take innocent lives, have a deleterious effect on international relations and jeopardize the security of states'.[17] Later the same year the Security Council was 'convinced that the suppression of acts of international terrorism, including those in which states are directly or indirectly involved, is essential for the maintenance of international peace and security'.[18]

It is more difficult to establish how slavery and environmental damage affect international peace, although arguably they threaten international security in the sense used by Graven and qualify as offences against the peace and security of mankind as understood by the ILC. Slavery in its modern manifestations (debt bondage, serfdom, exploitation of women and children, persecution of tribal minorities, forced labour, political and penal slavery) is kept relatively quiet, and those who are enslaved are usually powerless to rise up against their enslavement. The threat to international security perhaps lies in the fact that the fear of enslavement still exists for some. Environmental damage may occur during the course of armed conflict, in which case it aggravates an existing breach of international peace and security. Other

---

[11] Resolution 46/242, 25 Aug. 1992.   [12] Resolution 808, 22 Feb. 1993.
[13] SC Resolution 955, 8 Nov. 1994.   [14] SC Resolution 134, 1 Apr. 1960.
[15] See GA Resolution 2054(XX), 15 Dec. 1965; 2202(XXI), 16 Dec. 1966; 2307(XXII), 13 Dec. 1967; 2506A(XXIV), 21 Nov. 1969; 2671F(XXV), 8 Dec. 1970; 3151G(XXVIII), 14 Dec. 1973; 3411G(XXX), 10 Dec. 1975.   [16] SC Resolution 635, 14 June 1989.
[17] SC Resolution 731, 21 Jan. 1992.   [18] SC Resolution 748, 31 Mar. 1992.

forms of environmental damage could be said to threaten international security in the sense that acid rain, radioactivity, and ozone depletion, for
instance, cause international concern and jeopardize the survival of future
generations.

The difficulty with using UN resolutions as a guide to determining which
acts threaten international peace and security is that the pronouncements
made by the General Assembly and the Security Council have a political
basis and consistency is often lacking. The Security Council does not seem to
apply specific criteria to determine whether a situation poses a threat to the
peace, but uses this classification as a trigger to bring the desired UN procedures into motion. Some of the dangers in placing too much emphasis on
Security Council classifications are revealed by the problems relating to civil
wars.

4. THE PROBLEM OF CIVIL WAR

Since 1990, the UN has demonstrated a willingness to take action in respect
of internal conflicts which are deemed to pose a threat to international peace
and security, even where the state concerned has not requested such action.
Examples are Somalia, Haiti, Liberia, and Rwanda. A conflict within a state
may cause a direct threat to international peace and security by spreading
across borders or by causing an unmanageable refugee displacement. In other
cases, where the cross-border element is less evident, the UN has justified
intervention on the basis that the plight of individuals within the country
itself constitutes a threat to international peace and security. The preamble to
the resolution authorizing US intervention in Somalia explained that 'the
magnitude of the human tragedy caused by the conflict in Somalia, further
exacerbated by the obstacles being created to the distribution of humanitarian assistance, constitutes a threat to international peace and security'.[19]

According to Article 2(7) of the UN Charter:

Nothing contained in the present Charter shall authorize the UN to intervene in
matters which are essentially within the domestic jurisdiction of any state or shall
require the Members to submit such matters to settlement under the present Charter;
but this principle shall not prejudice the application of enforcement measures under
Chapter VII.

Article 2(7) does not specify who is to determine the sphere of the 'domestic'.
The domestic nature of the recent Chechen crisis, for example, was vigorously
supported by the Government of Russia. But if the Security Council determines at a certain point that there exists a threat to the peace, breach of the

---

[19] SC Resolution 794, 3 Dec. 1992.

peace, or act of aggression, then non-military enforcement measures under Article 41 and military measures under Article 42 may be employed to restore international peace and security. The difficulty is to establish when this point arises. In the opinion of the UN Secretary-General there are three kinds of internal conflict which disturb international peace and security: 'First, when conflict within a state threatens to cross borders. Second, when conflict within a state creates a grave humanitarian emergency. Third, when conflict challenges fundamental principles of international order.'[20] It is still difficult to discover the threshold after which a situation ceases to be a matter essentially within the domestic jurisdiction of a state and to explain why the Security Council instigates a wholesale intrusion in some cases, but only recommendations or nothing at all in others. The initial response to the conflict in the former Yugoslavia indicates that states were reluctant to set a precedent for intervention in the 'internal affairs' of one of their 'exclusive club'. Even when the situation clearly became a threat to international peace and security and was classified as such by the Security Council,[21] some states felt it was premature to use the language of Chapter VII and that a 'country's internal affairs should be handled by the people in that country themselves'.[22]

In the Decision of the Appeals Chamber of the International Criminal Tribunal for the Former Yugoslavia in the case of *Prosecutor v Dusko Tadic*, of 2 October 1995,[23] concerning the legality of the establishment of the Tribunal, the power of the Security Council to invoke Chapter VII was clarified. The Tribunal spoke of the constitutional limitations on the broad powers of the Security Council, and declared that the determination that there exists a threat to the peace was not a totally unfettered discretion, as it had to remain within the limits of the purposes and principles of the Charter.[24] The Tribunal went on to say that if the series of armed conflicts taking place in the former Yugoslavia were considered to be international in character, they would fall within the literal sense of the words 'breach of the peace':

But even if it were considered merely as an 'internal armed conflict', it would still constitute a 'threat to the peace' according to the settled practice of the Security Council and the common understanding of the UN membership in general. Indeed, the practice of the Security Council is rich with cases of civil war or internal strife which it classified as a 'threat to the peace' and dealt with under Chapter VII, with the encouragement or even at the behest of the General Assembly, such as the Congo crisis at the beginning of the 1960s and, more recently, Liberia and Somalia. It can thus be said that there is a common understanding manifested by the 'subsequent practice' of

---

[20] 'Secretary-General Says Outlook in Somalia Remains Uncertain Despite Tremendous Progress', in UN Press Release, SG/SM/5153, 9 Nov. 1993.
[21] Resolution 713, 25 Sept. 1991.   [22] Statement of China, S/PV.3009, 25 Sept. 1991, 50.
[23] Decision on the Defence Motion for Interlocutory Appeal on Jurisdiction, (1996) 35 *ILM* 32.   [24] Ibid. 43.

the membership of the UN at large, that the 'threat to the peace' of Article 39 may include, as one of its species, internal armed conflicts.[25]

This raises the question why the large-scale invasion of the little breakaway republic of Chechnya by Russian troops in 1994 was not internationalized. Both the decision-makers and public opinion were fully informed about the tragedy, and there was a risk that the situation could trigger declarations of independence and provoke civil war across a vast area. Moreover, it could be argued that the Russian action in Chechnya in 1994–6 and 1999–2000 was a blatant denial of the right of a people to self-determination. Chechnya first proclaimed its independence on 27 November 1990, and declared its independence on 1 November 1991, prior to the break-up of the former USSR and international recognition of Russia as its successor state. In December 1994 the Russian Government declared that the Chechen Republic was part of the territory of the Russian Federation and that constitutional order should be restored. In the meantime Chechnya had been enjoying the status of a *de facto* independent state, confirming it by not participating in federal referenda and elections, by not sending any representative to the Russian parliament, and by not paying any taxes to the federal budget. In addition, Russian Army regiments were completely withdrawn from Chechnya prior to their withdrawal from Estonia, Lithuania, and Azerbaijan.

The violations of human rights and the right to self-determination that have occurred in Chechnya, and the bringing of the region to the brink of war by Russia, would appear to be the legitimate concern of the international community. However, during a visit to Moscow in May 1995 the US President was informed by Russia that the 'internal disturbance' in Chechnya was not 'serious enough' to be called an armed conflict,[26] and Russia has maintained this position in the face of allegations of crimes against humanity in the international press.[27]

5. CONCLUSION

It is difficult to see how the situation in Chechnya poses less of a threat to peace than the recent conflicts in Rwanda or Somalia, but it is important to draw a distinction between conscious and purposeful decision-making by UN organs and an act or omission which is not the result of a deliberate decision. If the Security Council refrains from stating that a particular act constitutes a threat to international peace and security, this is not necessarily

---

[25] Ibid.
[26] See Z. Tskhovrebov, 'An Unfolding Case of Genocide: Chechnya, World Order and the "Right to be Left Alone"', (1995) 64 *Nordic Journal of International Law*, 501, 520, n. 55.
[27] See e.g. *International Herald Tribune*, 19 Nov. 1999 and 9 Dec. 1999.

equivalent to a statement that it does not constitute such a threat. The UN's failure to take appropriate action in the case of Chechnya, therefore, does not mean that the legal quality of any wrongful act committed in that case is considered to be different from acts committed in similar cases. Thus, if the distinction between crimes and delicts is one of principle, then the fact that the UN does not classify some clear cases of crimes as threats to, or breaches of, the peace does not make those cases less criminal.[28] Despite this, the UN ought to act in all such cases to avoid allegations of double standards and selectivity.

In contrast to the Draft Code, the element of peace and security does not feature in paragraph 2 of Draft Article 19,[29] but indications are that this concern is also inherent in the concept of state criminality. The UN has not hesitated to classify acts falling within most of the categories of international crime in Article 19 as threats to, or breaches of, international peace and security, and peace and security is a central tenet of the ILC's work on international crimes generally, probably because it also points towards the seriousness of the offence.

If international crimes, by their nature, tend to affect peace and security, then Security Council classifications should provide circumstantial evidence of the existence of an international crime. Such classifications have some legal significance and serve as an indication of collective state practice. However, it is doubtful if the political organs of the UN go so far as to base their determinations upon a concept of crime. This means that the element of 'peace and security' may be unreliable as a criterion or indicium for differentiating crimes and delicts because of its definite interaction with the concept of 'peace and security' as employed by the Security Council. Even so, Security Council classifications will inform any decisions of a court or other independent body facing the task of determining whether a crime has been committed.

---

[28] Following the 1982 Israeli invasion of Lebanon, an International Commission was set up under the Chairmanship of Seán MacBride to enquire into reported violations of international law by Israel. The Commission concluded that Israel had been guilty of aggression against Lebanon and had breached the obligation to safeguard the right to self-determination of the Palestinians, and that such violations of international law were international crimes under the terms of the ILC's Draft Article 19. It was stated: 'These crimes of state give rise to criminal liability as far as the State of Israel is concerned': see S. MacBride, *Israel in Lebanon* (1983), 187. The Security Council condemned the invasion and called repeatedly for remedial action to be taken, but failed to classify Israel's actions as a breach of the peace, see (1982) *Yrbk UN*, 428 ff.

[29] But cf. paragraph 2 of Ago's original proposal, p. 49 above.

12

Individual Criminal Responsibility
under International Law

1. INTRODUCTION

The notion that individuals may be criminally responsible for certain acts which constitute crimes under international law, regardless of the law of their state, is an accepted and recognized aspect of international law. However, it should be remembered that at the turn of the twentieth century this was a radical notion which was concretized as recently as the Nuremberg Trials.[1] Prior to this the only active subjects of international law were states, but the idea of states being criminally responsible for acts that violated international law had always been viewed with suspicion. In the work of the ILC relating to the codification of the Nuremberg principles, the creation of a Draft Code of Crimes against the Peace and Security of Mankind, and the drawing up of a statute for an International Criminal Court,[2] the notion of individual responsibility for international crimes has consistently prevailed as politically and practically the best way to proceed. The same is true of international conventions such as the Genocide and Apartheid Conventions. But the inclusion of the concept of international crimes of state in Article 19 of the Draft Articles on State Responsibility reopened the debate as to whether the exclusion of state responsibility from the Draft Code in particular could still be maintained.

There is a definite link between state criminal responsibility and individual criminal responsibility in terms of certain of the criteria used to determine which acts are criminal. Indeed, it could be argued that all acts which constitute international crimes may in principle entail individual or state responsibility, or both, depending on the nature and circumstances of the breach, and that the two notions can complement each other.[3] As Jennings and Watts have pointed out, although the Draft Code is related to the international criminal responsibility of individuals rather than of states, 'a number of the particular acts giving rise to such international criminal responsibility are likely by their nature to be as much, if not more, state acts as acts committed by individuals in their private capacity'.[4] At this stage it

[1] See Chapter 1 above. [2] See Ibid. s. 3(h), and Chapter 2 above, s. 4.
[3] See also Chapter 4 above on corporate crime.
[4] Oppenheim's *International Law*, i: *Peace*, 9th edn. (1992), 535.

is proposed to examine individual criminal responsibility under international law as a criterion or indicium which may assist in differentiating state crimes and delicts, as it endorses the exceptional importance of certain international obligations. In a report prepared for the ILC by Tomuschat it is stated:

the parallelism of Article 19 of part one of the Draft Articles on State Responsibility and the Draft Code of Crimes Against the Peace and Security of Mankind constitutes a logical inference from a common premise. Under the Draft Articles, states as juridical entities may incur responsibility if they breach fundamental rules of conduct securing a civilized state of affairs in international relations. Additionally, for the same acts, those who hold leadership positions in the governmental machinery of such states may be made accountable in their individual capacity . . . There is no denying the fact that rules imposing obligations upon states must be framed differently from rules that address individuals. Notwithstanding this technical difference the substantive background is the same. In both instances, the foundations of the international community are at stake.[5]

2. THE QUESTION OF STATE RESPONSIBILITY IN THE INTERNATIONAL LAW COMMISSION'S WORK ON A DRAFT CODE OF CRIMES AGAINST THE PEACE AND SECURITY OF MANKIND

By its Resolution 36/106 of 10 December 1981, the General Assembly referred to the ILC the question of the codification of crimes against the peace and security of mankind which had lain dormant pending agreement on a definition of aggression. The ILC appointed Doudou Thiam as Special Rapporteur, who, in his initial, exploratory report,[6] considered the question of the subjects of law to which international criminal responsibility could be attributed. In its earlier drafts the ILC had confined its field of inquiry to acts by individuals and excluded other legal entities such as states. Thiam concluded that the ILC ought to harmonize its positions by bringing the 1954 Draft Code in line with Article 19 of the Draft Articles on State Responsibility.

In a subsequent analytical paper on the topic of a Draft Code,[7] most of the representatives, while emphasizing the principle of individual criminal responsibility, felt that the question of state responsibility should not be over-

---

[5] Report of the ILC on the Work of its Forty-Eighth Session, Draft Code of Crimes against the Peace and Security of Mankind, 'Crimes against the Environment', ILC(XLVIII)/DC/CRD.3, 27 Mar. 1996.

[6] First Report on the Draft Code of Offences against the Peace and Security of Mankind, A/CN.4/364; (1983) *YrbkILC*, vol. 2, pt 1, 137, 144–6.

[7] Report of the ILC on the Work of its Thirty-Fifth Session, Draft Code of Offences against the Peace and Security of Mankind, Analytical paper prepared pursuant to the request contained in paragraph 256 of the Report of the Commission on the Work of its Thirty-Fourth Session, A/CN.4/365, 25 Mar. 1983.

looked. The Polish representative,[8] for example, felt that international practice had already established a link between state responsibility and the criminal responsibility of individuals, and the Cuban representative[9] objected to considering individual responsibility as a question completely isolated from any responsibility that might arise for states as a result of the actions of individuals. The German representative shared the view that states should and could be held responsible for their actions even though individuals guilty of such actions must also be liable to criminal proceedings, adding that 'holding individuals responsible should not replace the responsibility under international law of a state which organized, committed or supported such crimes'.[10] The German Government went on to suggest in its written comments that an express provision should be included in the Code to the effect that the assertion of individual criminal responsibility would not preclude state responsibility for these crimes.[11]

The representative of Congo[12] felt that the 'possibility of taking measures not only against individuals but also against abstract entities such as states and governments should not be discounted', and the representative of Trinidad and Tobago[13] similarly stated that 'responsibility for offences against the peace and security of mankind should not be confined to public officials . . . it should also be attributed directly to states, irrespective of the criminal responsibility of the person or persons having committed the offences'. The representative of Syria,[14] heedful of recent events in Lebanon, felt that the Code should envisage state responsibility. Meanwhile, the Jordanian representative[15] emphasized that the principle according to which the state as such was responsible for its criminal acts had gained acceptance and lay at the heart of the Draft Articles on State Responsibility. Despite these utterances, no representative specifically referred to the criminal responsibility of the state as distinct from ordinary state responsibility.

The resulting Draft Code of 1991[16] made no reference to state responsibility except in Article 5, entitled 'Responsibility of States', which provided that 'Prosecution of an individual for a crime against the peace and security of mankind does not relieve a state of any responsibility under international law for an act or omission attributable to it'. This provision implies that the prosecution of an individual for a crime does not preclude prosecution of a state for the same crime. However, it effectively leaves the nature of state responsibility completely open, which corresponds to the ILC's aim of setting out as clearly as possible the criminal responsibility of individuals without prejudice

---

[8] A/C.6/36/SR.62, para. 40.   [9] Ibid. para. 35, and A/C.6/37/SR.53, para. 18.
[10] A/C.6/36/SR.60, para. 26, and A/37/325, 9, paras 13–15.   [11] A/37/325, 9, para. 13.
[12] A/C.6/37/SR.54, para. 47.   [13] Ibid. para. 25.   [14] A/C.6/37/SR.53, para. 25.
[15] A/C.6/36/SR.62, para. 68.
[16] Report of the ILC on the Work of its Forty-Third Session; (1991) *YrbkILC*, vol. 2, pt. 2, 79, 94–7 (text of articles).

to any subsequent consideration of the possible application to states of the notion of international criminal responsibility.

In the comments and observations of governments on the 1991 Draft Code,[17] it was hoped by Belarus[18] that in future the ILC would try to make the provisions in the Code applicable to all perpetrators including states. Belarus argued that the objections raised in this connection, which concerned the fact that perpetrators would have to be subjected to different regimes from the standpoint of penalties and procedural rules, essentially related to procedural law and did not have to be taken into account at the substantive stage. The procedure for implementing the substantive provisions would subsequently need to be worked out in stages, starting with individual responsibility, then taking into account acts involving the participation of states, and ending with state responsibility for international crimes.

In contrast, the UK[19] did not approve of any link between state responsibility and individual responsibility for international crimes, and condemned the reliance placed on Article 19 in identifying crimes against peace and security.[20] In the UK's opinion such reliance was misplaced, as it failed to acknowledge the fundamental distinction between state responsibility and individual responsibility. The UK found three fundamental weaknesses in the ILC's approach. First, it was not guided by a concept of crimes against the peace and security of mankind in selecting offences for inclusion in the draft. As a result the offences listed could not be regarded as a logically defensible or coherent catalogue of crimes against the peace and security of mankind. Second, the draft articles failed to maintain a distinction between international crimes in general and crimes against the peace and security of mankind, and between crimes committed by an individual and those which may be attributable to the state. Third, many of the definitions of crimes contained in the draft were derived from General Assembly resolutions and international conventions which had not in every case garnered widespread support and which, in any case, needed much closer examination to ensure that the language used was appropriate for a criminal code. It was added that if there were a crime of aggression it would be more suited to state responsibility than individual responsibility.

With regard to the first argument, it is true that it is difficult to regard acts such as environmental damage as a threat to international peace and security. In the course of its work the ILC has abandoned the distinction between crimes against peace, war crimes, and crimes against humanity which began with the Nuremberg and Tokyo Charters and was maintained in earlier ver-

---

[17] Report of the ILC on the Work of its Forty-Fifth Session, Comments and Observations of Governments on the Draft Code of Crimes against the Peace and Security of Mankind Adopted on First Reading by the ILC at its Forty-Third Session, A/CN.4/448, 1 Mar. 1993.
[18] Ibid. 28.   [19] Ibid. 84.   [20] See further p. 132 above.

sions of the Draft Code.[21] The categories of crimes have now been expanded and subsumed under the heading 'crimes against the peace and security of mankind'. On the one hand this limits the number and type of crimes which may be included in the Code, but on the other hand the common understanding of what constitutes a crime against peace and security has been stretched.

Regarding the UK's second argument, it may be that the ILC failed to maintain a clear distinction between individual crimes and state crimes because such a distinction is artificial. An act of genocide, for example, requires the participation of the state at the organizational level, but the killings themselves are carried out by individuals. There is no reason why responsibility cannot be incurred at each level.

In its third argument the UK points out that certain acts appearing in the Draft Code are derived from UN resolutions which are normally directed at states and do not make reference to individual criminal responsibility. The UK also recognizes that certain acts, such as threats of aggression, are more amenable to state responsibility than individual responsibility. Nonetheless, it is difficult to say that an act, by its nature, invariably gives rise to a specific form of responsibility which is why segregating international crimes on this basis is such an arduous task.

In the Twelfth Report on the Draft Code[22] it was again stressed, this time by Belgium,[23] that there ought to be an article in the Code dealing with the question of the international responsibility of states. In Belgium's opinion:

The state as such is inevitably involved in any crime against the peace and security of mankind, either directly as the active and, in some cases, the sole agent, or indirectly because of its failure to act or its own improvidence. It therefore seems unusual that state responsibility should not have been dealt with in the Code. It should also be noted that the inclusion of state responsibility in the Code would make it possible to provide a sound juridical basis for the granting of compensation to the victims of crimes and other eligible parties. Moreover, holding the state responsible for crimes, independently of the responsibility of the Government and agents of the state, would make the nation feel affected by the act in question, thereby making it difficult for the nation to lay all the blame on the Government, on which it has conferred political power.[24]

The ILC's only response to these arguments was radically to reduce the number of offences contained in the Draft Code from twelve to six in 1995.[25]

---

[21] See s. 3(a) below.
[22] Report of the ILC on the Work of its Forty-Sixth Session, Twelfth Report on the Draft Code of Crimes against the Peace and Security of Mankind by D. Thiam, Special Rapporteur, A/CN.4/460, 15 Apr. 1994.   [23] Ibid. 11.
[24] Ibid.
[25] See Report of the ILC on the Work of its Forty-Seventh Session, Thirteenth Report on the Draft Code of Crimes against the Peace and Security of Mankind by D. Thiam, Special Rapporteur, A/CN.4/466, 24 Mar. 1995.

At its Forty-Eighth Session in 1996, the ILC adopted a revised text of the Draft Code.[26] The issue of state responsibility is now dealt with in Article 4:

The fact that the present Code provides for the responsibility of individuals for crimes against the peace and security of mankind is without prejudice to any question of the responsibility of states under international law.

Despite the slightly different and more qualified wording, Article 4 throws no more light on the topic than the earlier Article 5.

3. CRIMES ENTAILING INDIVIDUAL CRIMINAL RESPONSIBILITY UNDER INTERNATIONAL LAW

(a) The 1954 Draft Code[27]

In the original Draft Code which was finalized in 1954, the ILC listed eleven crimes and attempted to establish a distinction between crimes which could only be committed by the authorities of a state and crimes which could be committed by any individual. The first seven crimes fall into the Nuremberg category of 'crimes against peace'. These include:

(1) The employment or threat of employment, by the authorities of a state, of armed force against another state for any purpose other than national or collective self-defence or execution of a decision by a competent organ of the UN;
(2) The planning of or preparation for the employment, by the authorities of a state, of armed force against another state for any purpose other than national or collective self-defence or execution of a decision by a competent organ of the UN;
(3) The incursion into the territory of a state by armed bands coming from the territory of another state and acting for a political purpose;
(4) The undertaking, encouragement or toleration by the authorities of a state of organized activities calculated to foment civil strife in the territory of another state;
(5) The undertaking, encouragement or toleration by the authorities of a state of organized activities intended or calculated to create a state of terror in the minds of particular persons or a group of persons or the general public in another state;
(6) Acts by the authorities of a state in violation of international treaty obligations designed to ensure international peace and security, including but not limited to treaty obligations concerning: (i) The character or strength or location of armed forces or armaments; (ii) The training for service in armed forces; (iii) The maintenance of fortifications;

---

[26] Report of the ILC on the Work of its Forty-Eighth Session, Titles and texts of articles on the Draft Code of Crimes against the Peace and Security of Mankind adopted by the ILC at its forty-eighth session (1996), A/CN.4/L.532, 8 July 1996.
[27] Text of Draft in (1951) *YrbkILC*, vol. 2, 58.

(7) Acts by authorities of a state resulting in or directed toward the forcible annexation of territory belonging to another state, or of territory under an international regime.

With the exception of crime (3) it is stated in the ILC commentaries to all of these crimes that by their nature such crimes can only be committed by the authorities of a state. However, the penal responsibility of private individuals may result through the application of crime (11) dealing with conspiracy, incitement, attempt, and complicity. With regard to crime (3) it is stated:

While in the case of crime No. 1 the simple soldier would not be criminally responsible under international law, in case of invasion by armed bands of the territory of another state, any member of the band would be responsible. This difference of treatment is justified because, in the case of state action, it would go beyond any logic to consider a mere soldier as criminally responsible for an action which has been decided and directed by the authorities of a state while in the case of armed bands the participation in them will result from the free decision of the individual members of the band.[28]

The distinction here is based on the extent of the individual's knowledge of, and voluntary participation in, the criminal activities of the state, and there is a persistent recognition that certain acts are in fact committed by the entities of the state itself. Such acts could validly be described as state crimes, even though the Draft Code does not deal with state responsibility.

Crime (8) deals with genocide and crime (9) corresponds to the 'crime against humanity' of the Nuremberg Charter. The commentary states that both these crimes can be committed either by the authorities of the state or by private individuals, and in effect in many cases such acts would be attributable both to the state and to private individuals. Finally, crime (10) concerns acts committed in violation of the laws or customs of war. Notably, the commentary states that such crimes do not, in reality, affect the peace and security of mankind, but are included simply because they figure among the crimes enumerated in the Nuremberg Charter.[29] If war crimes are a borderline category for inclusion in the Draft Code, this raises the question of how the catalogue of crimes could be expanded in 1991 to include acts such as colonialism and crimes against the environment.

(b) The 1991 Draft Code[30]

The 1954 Draft Code remained faithful to the Nuremberg Charter and included only the most heinous crimes equally deserving the harshest punishment. The tendency in 1991 was to include all acts which provoked moral indignation regardless of whether or not the relevant rules of international

---

[28] Ibid.   [29] Ibid. 59.   [30] See n. 16 above.

law were well established. The 1991 Draft Code lists twelve crimes, starting with aggression (Article 15), which is defined as 'the use of armed force by a state against the sovereignty, territorial integrity or political independence of another state, or in any other manner inconsistent with the charter of the UN'. The Article goes on to list acts of aggression entailing individual responsibility, and closely tracks the 1974 General Assembly consensus Resolution on a definition of aggression but without making any reference to it. The stated reason for this was that the General Assembly Resolution is addressed to the Security Council, which has a very different function from a court, to which the Code is addressed.[31] It was felt that it would be inappropriate for a penal code to refer to an instrument intended to serve as a guide for a political organ, which begs the question why the General Assembly definition appears in the Draft Code in disguise. It is neither a sound basis for individual responsibility nor an uncontroversial guide to state responsibility.

Article 16 deals with a threat of aggression, which is defined as 'declarations, communications, demonstrations of force or any other measures which would give good reason to the Government of a state to believe that aggression is being seriously contemplated against that state'. Paragraph 1 envisages the responsibility of an individual who as leader or organizer commits or orders the commission of a threat of aggression. This article is highly ambiguous. In particular it is not clear whether the existence of a threat of aggression is dependent solely upon the subjective belief of the apprehending state or whether there is an objective test for a court to apply. An added problem is that threats of aggression are not unanimously considered to constitute international crimes, although they are illegal acts for which the state can at least be held responsible under the ordinary rules of state responsibility. It would seem that, like aggression, threats of aggression are more amenable to state responsibility, as the actions listed have a collective flavour which is inappropriate to the creation of individual responsibility. Charging individuals for threats of aggression could even be counterproductive, as it might generate tensions among nations by encouraging criminal charges for statements or conduct that could better be addressed through constructive diplomatic dialogue.

Article 17 covers intervention in the internal or external affairs of a state which consists of 'fomenting [armed] subversive or terrorist activities or by organizing, assisting or financing such activities, or supplying arms for the purpose of such activities, thereby [seriously] undermining the free exercise by that state of its sovereign rights'. Yet it is doubtful if intervention constitutes a separate crime under international law. Article 17 is based on the 1970 Declaration on Principles of International Law concerning Friendly Relations and Co-operation among States which was never intended to be the

---

[31] See (1988) *YrbkILC*, vol. 2, pt. 2, 72.

legal basis for imposing criminal liability on individuals. Moreover, the criminalization of the non-intervention principle is divorced from the practical relationships between states.

Article 18 deals with colonial domination, and again it is difficult to describe such acts in terms of individual responsibility aside from the fact that colonialism no longer occurs in its traditional and historic form. In addition to colonial domination itself, Article 18 refers rather vaguely to 'any other form of alien domination contrary to the right of peoples to self-determination'.

Articles 19 and 20 refer less controversially to genocide and apartheid respectively, for the commission of which individual responsibility is provided in the relevant Conventions. However, Article 20 refers only to the responsibility of the leaders and organizers of apartheid, while the Convention casts a wider net. Article 21 refers more generally to systematic or mass violations of human rights.

Exceptionally serious war crimes are covered in Article 22, and are defined as serious violations of principles or rules of international law applicable in an armed conflict. The use of 'serious' and 'exceptionally serious' is confusing here, as all crimes must fulfil a criterion of seriousness in order to be included in the Code in the first place.[32] Article 23 deals with individuals who as agents or representatives of a state commit or order the commission of any of the following acts: 'recruitment, use, financing or training of mercenaries for activities directed against another state or for the purpose of opposing the legitimate exercise of the inalienable right of peoples to self-determination as recognized under international law'. Article 23 adopts a narrow approach to responsibility by referring exclusively to 'agents or representatives of a state'. This is also the approach adopted in Article 24, which defines international terrorism as 'undertaking, organizing, assisting, financing, encouraging or tolerating acts against another state directed at persons or property and of such a nature as to create a state of terror in the minds of public figures, groups of persons or the general public' when committed or ordered by an individual as agent or representative of a state.

Article 25 criminalizes illicit traffic in narcotic drugs, whether carried out by agents of a state or by individuals acting on their own behalf. It is noteworthy that it was concern by a Trinidadian-led coalition of Latin American and Caribbean states about international drug-trafficking which put the establishment of an International Criminal Court back on the agenda of the UN in 1989.[33] Finally, Article 26 criminalizes, somewhat controversially, 'wilful and severe damage to the environment', and is inspired by Article 19 of

---

[32] See also Chapter 8 above.
[33] Request for the inclusion of a supplementary item in the agenda of the forty-fourth session, UN Doc A/44/195 (1989).

the ILC's Draft Articles on State Responsibility. Thus, the 1991 Draft Code is a confusing blend of acts which may be more suitable for state responsibility, acts which can be committed only by leaders, organizers, agents, or representatives of the state, acts which are genuine crimes against the peace and security of mankind committed by individuals in any capacity, and acts which do not perhaps belong in a code of crimes at all.

(c) The 1995 Draft Code and the Statutes of the International Criminal Tribunals

In 1995 it was decided to reduce dramatically the list of crimes in the Draft Code to those whose characterization as crimes against the peace and security of mankind was hard to challenge.[34] Acts were to be included in the Code on the basis of two criteria: extreme seriousness and international community recognition. The resulting list included aggression, genocide, crimes against humanity, war crimes, international terrorism, and illicit traffic in narcotic drugs. This signified a shift back to the Nuremberg categories and an attempt to include only those acts which are well established and well recognized. The ILC was influenced by the Statute of the International Criminal Tribunal for the former Yugoslavia,[35] which goes some way towards affirming certain major components of international humanitarian law as customary law. In the opinion of the Secretary-General, the principle *nullum crimen sine lege* required that 'the international tribunal should apply rules of international humanitarian law which are beyond any doubt part of customary law so that the problem of adherence of some but not all states to specific conventions does not arise'.[36] Those rules were stated to include the law of armed conflict embodied in the 1949 Geneva Conventions for the Protection of War Victims, the 1907 Hague Convention (No. IV) Respecting the Laws and Customs of War on Land and Annexed Regulations, the 1948 Genocide Convention, and the Charter of the Nuremberg Tribunal. The Statute treats the ensemble of conflicts in the former Yugoslavia as international in character, and includes grave breaches of the 1949 Geneva Conventions, violations of the laws or customs of war, genocide, and crimes against humanity 'when committed in armed conflict, whether internal or international in character, and directed against any civilian population'. In contrast, the Statute for the International Criminal Tribunal for Rwanda[37] is based on an internal conflict, and includes genocide, crimes against humanity 'when committed as part of a widespread or systematic attack against any civilian population on

[34] See n. 25 above.

[35] Report of the Secretary-General pursuant to paragraph 2 of SC Resolution 808, 22 Feb. 1993, S/25704 and Annex, (3 May 1993); repr. in (1993) 32 *ILM* 1159, 1203.

[36] Ibid. para. 34; (1993) 32 *ILM* 1170.

[37] SC Resolution 955, 8 Nov. 1994, Annex; repr. in (1994) 33 *ILM* 1598.

national, political, ethnic, racial or religious grounds', and violations of Article 3 common to the Geneva Conventions and of Additional Protocol II.

Several observations may be made in relation to these Statutes. First, crimes against humanity have never been defined by treaty and are therefore seldom viewed in an identical fashion. The Statute of the Tribunal for the former Yugoslavia requires a connection between crimes against humanity and armed conflict which marks only a modest advance over the Nuremberg Charter, which linked crimes against humanity with the other crimes within the jurisdiction of the Tribunal. The Statute of the Tribunal for Rwanda restricts this category in a different way by adding the requirement of establishing the large-scale, systematic nature of attacks against a civilian population. The word 'systematic' implies the involvement of the state, and 'large-scale' indicates that a crime against humanity could not be committed against a few individuals.[38] The 1991 Draft Code referred to 'systematic' or 'mass' violations of human rights, but the 1995 Code, in contrast, merely refers to an individual who commits or orders the commission of any of a number of specified human rights violations. Second, Article 4 of the Rwanda Statute provides an innovative safety net by allowing the Tribunal to prosecute persons who have violated common Article 3 of the Geneva Conventions and Additional Protocol II. No proof of deliberate planning is required to satisfy the elements of these crimes. Until recently, common Article 3 and Protocol II have provided an uncertain basis for individual criminal responsibility, and were specifically excluded by the ILC in its 1994 Draft Statute for an International Criminal Court along with other treaties 'which merely regulate conduct, or which prohibit conduct but only on an interstate basis'.[39]

(d) The 1994 Draft Statute for an International Criminal Court

The 1994 Draft Statute for an International Criminal Court (ICC) includes as crimes under general international law falling within the Court's jurisdiction genocide, aggression, serious violations of the laws and customs applicable in armed conflict, and crimes against humanity.[40] The ILC's criteria for including 'treaty crimes' in the Statute were first, that the crimes were themselves defined by treaty so that an international criminal court could apply that treaty as law in relation to the crime, subject to the *nullum crimen* guarantee contained in Article 39, and second, that the treaty created either a system of universal jurisdiction based on the principle *aut dedere aut judicare* or the possibility for an international criminal court to try the crime, or both,

---

[38] See also Chapter 8 above, s. 3.
[39] Report of the ILC on the Work of its Forty-Sixth Session, GAOR, 49th Session, Suppl. no. 10, UN Doc A/49/10 (1994), 142; (1994) *YrbkILC*, vol. 2, pt. 2, 68.
[40] Article 20, (1994) *YrbkILC*, vol. 2, pt. 2, 38.

thus recognizing clearly the principle of international concern.[41] Using these criteria the ILC drew up a list of crimes which bore no relationship to the Draft Code, although it seemed to be accepted that the Court would have jurisdiction over the crimes listed in the Draft Code, were such a Code to be accepted by states. Draft Article 20(e) of the Statute includes grave breaches of the 1949 Geneva Conventions and additional Protocol I; unlawful seizure of aircraft as defined by Article 1 of the 1970 Convention for the Suppression of Unlawful Seizure of Aircraft; crimes defined by Article 1 of the 1971 Convention for the Suppression of Unlawful Acts against the Safety of Civil Aviation; crimes defined in the Apartheid Convention; crimes defined by Article 2 of the 1973 Convention on the Prevention and Punishment of Crimes Against Internationally Protected Persons, including Diplomatic Agents; hostage-taking and related crimes as defined by Article 1 of the 1979 International Convention against the Taking of Hostages; the crime of torture made punishable pursuant to article 4 of the 1984 Convention against Torture and Other Cruel, Inhuman or Degrading Treatment or Punishment; crimes defined by Article 3 of the Convention for the Suppression of Unlawful Acts against the Safety of Maritime Navigation and by Article 2 of the Protocol for the Suppression of Unlawful Acts against the Safety of Fixed Platforms located on the Continental Shelf, both of 1988; and certain crimes involving illicit traffic in narcotic drugs as envisaged in the 1988 UN Convention against Illicit Traffic in Narcotic Drugs and Psychotropic Substances.

The Draft Statute clearly adopted a broader interpretation of crime than the Draft Code, and was not limited to crimes against peace and security. It appeared to include those areas where it was believed that an ICC would be both useful and used, without having regard to the relative seriousness of the acts listed. It is stated in the ILC commentary that the inclusion of specific crimes in the Statute was 'without prejudice to the identification and application of the concept of crimes under general international law for other purposes'.[42]

(e) The 1996 Draft Code

The revised Draft Code of 1996 deals with aggression, genocide, and crimes against humanity, and there is an extensive article on war crimes 'when committed in a systematic manner or on a large scale'.[43] Crimes against humanity are once again defined differently as any of a number of acts 'when committed in a systematic manner or on a large scale and instigated or directed by a government or by any organization or group'.[44] There is also a new article dealing with crimes against UN and Associated Personnel, a topic

---

[41] (1994) *YrbkILC*, vol. 2, pt. 2, 41 and 67 (Annex listing crimes pursuant to treaties).
[42] Ibid. 38.   [43] Article 20.   [44] Article 18.

which had not been considered previously. The Code has therefore become much more exclusive in the interest of making it less controversial.[45]

(f) The 1998 Rome Statute of the International Criminal Court[46]

The jurisdiction of the International Criminal Court extends to the crime of genocide, crimes against humanity defined as any of a number of acts when committed as part of, and with knowledge of, a widespread or systematic attack directed against any civilian population, war crimes 'in particular when committed as a part of a plan or policy or as part of a large-scale commission of such crimes', and the crime of aggression.[47] The Preparatory Committee[48] had considered including in the Court's Statute crimes of terrorism, crimes against UN and associated personnel, crimes involving the illicit traffic in narcotic drugs and psychotropic substances, and other treaty-based crimes, but for practical reasons it was decided to limit the Court's jurisdiction to the core crimes under general international law.[49]

4. THE RELATIONSHIP BETWEEN STATE AND INDIVIDUAL RESPONSIBILITY FOR INTERNATIONAL CRIMES

The 1996 Draft Code puts forward several possible solutions for identifying the persons to whom responsibility for each of the crimes listed in the Code could be ascribed, based on the nature of the crime concerned.[50] For certain crimes, such as aggression (and previously threat of aggression, intervention, colonial domination, and apartheid), the circle of potential perpetrators is restricted to leaders or organizers, as these crimes, in the opinion of the ILC, are always committed by, or on orders from, individuals occupying the highest decision-making positions in the political or military apparatus of the state or in its financial or economic life. In relation to such crimes it ought to be legitimate to talk in terms of state criminal responsibility without

---

[45] It should be recalled in this context that the original vision was to create a Draft Code that would 'perpetuate the vital principle that war of aggression is the supreme international crime': see p. 43 above. This goal has proved difficult to achieve in practice and seems to have become obscured. [46] A/CONF.183/9, 17 July 1998, (1998) 37 *ILM* 999.

[47] Article 5(1). The Court will only be able to exercise its jurisdiction over the crime of aggression once a provision is adopted in accordance with Articles 121 and 123 of the Statute defining the crime and setting out the conditions for the exercise of jurisdiction (Article 5(2)).

[48] See Report of the Preparatory Committee on the Establishment of an International Criminal Court, Draft Statute and Final Act (A/CONF.183/2/Add.1, 1998), in M. C. Bassiouni, *The Statute of the International Criminal Court: A Documentary History* (1998), 119, 129.

[49] The elements of the crimes over which the Court has jurisdiction are currently being defined by the Preparatory Committee. See PCNICC/1999/L.5/Rev. 1/Add. 2, 22 Dec. 1999, Annex II: Elements of Crimes; Annex III: Rules of Procedure and Evidence.

[50] (1991) *YrbkILC*, vol. 1, 198.

excluding the individual responsibility of the leaders and organizers. Another group of crimes including genocide, war crimes, and crimes against humanity (and previously illicit traffic in narcotic drugs and severe damage to the environment) would be punishable under the Code by whomever they are committed. Such crimes may therefore be state crimes or individual crimes or both, depending on the circumstances of the breach. The remaining crimes which appeared in the 1991 Draft Code, including the recruitment, use, financing, and training of mercenaries and international terrorism would fall in between and would come under the Code whenever therein agents or representatives of a state were involved. There is consequently a hierarchy of criminal involvement by the state going from 'undertaking' through 'assisting', 'financing', and 'encouraging' down to 'tolerating'.

Through these stages we pass from the case in which criminal acts are committed directly by one state against another to the case in which the state's involvement is very limited or non-existent. The ILC added in its commentary to the 1991 Draft Code that the order in which the crimes were listed did not imply any value judgement as to the degree of seriousness of these crimes. However, 'Article 15, like the next three articles, defined a crime which presupposed decisions taken at the policy-making level and in which large segments of the population of a state might be regarded as being directly or indirectly involved'.[51] Throughout, the ILC has recognized that the state as such is behind many criminal acts, and has placed such acts in a special category of seriousness, but has found it expedient to target the individual agents of the state rather than the entity itself. But if certain acts are criminal under international law when committed by individuals, must they not also be criminal when committed by the state?

The Nuremberg Charter and the Draft Code expressly allow for the punishment of individuals for acts of state, which means 'acts committed on behalf of the state or in their capacity as members of the government, state administration or high command of the armed forces'.[52] The act of the individual derived its unlawful character from the unlawfulness of the state act. Would it not then have followed that in order for an act to entail criminal responsibility when committed by an individual, the same act must also have entailed criminal responsibility when committed by the state? Following the Second World War, McNair[53] utilized this logic to reach the conclusion that individuals could not be held criminally liable for aggressive war because the state as such could not be the subject of criminal liability. This view is obviously outdated (and McNair himself favoured the criminalization of aggressive war for the future), but logic

---

[51] (1991) *YrbkILC*, vol. 1, 199.

[52] I. Brownlie, *International Law and the Use of Force by States* (1963), 165–6.

[53] UNWCC, *History of the United Nations War Crimes Commission and the Development of the Laws of War* (1948), 181–2.

suggests that the responsibility of states and individuals for international crimes should potentially be of the same nature.[54] Brownlie argues that the illogicality is only apparent, as it is the individual and not the state which has the *mens rea*, and there is no juridical reason why the legal quality of the acts of the agent must be identical with that of the acts of the state.[55] While this may be true, the argument here is that there is no juridical reason why the legal quality of the acts of the state *should not* be identical with that of the acts of the agent.[56]

The discussion on individual criminal responsibility so far suggests that certain acts are criminal under international law irrespective of the degree of state involvement. The difficulty, rather, is to describe the consequences of individual and state crimes in equivalent legal terms.[57] States cannot be punished in the same manner as individuals. But recent developments suggest that a state can be held responsible, albeit in primarily a civil sense, for what is recognized to be a criminal act.[58] In the *Case Concerning the Application of the Genocide Convention* the criminal character of genocide is not disputed even though it is the state's responsibility for genocide that is under examination.[59] On the other hand it could be argued that the legal quality of an act is conditioned by the anticipated response to it, and that if states can only be held responsible in a civil sense, they cannot commit crimes. But this argument finds the essence of the criminal law in a feature of its structure, rather than in its function and intrinsic nature.[60]

A preliminary picture of the operation of international criminal responsibility on different levels may be sketched at this stage.[61] First, apart from any action taken by UN agencies designed to halt the criminal act and to prevent future similar acts, there would be the option of civil action against the state responsible for the criminal act to compensate the victim state, involving the possible imposition of punitive damages.[62] An analogy may be drawn here with domestic legal systems, where, in addition to the criminal conviction of an offender, a civil case may be brought to compensate the victim in pecuniary terms. Next, individual perpetrators would be brought to justice either in national courts or by an international criminal court. This would to some extent provide a continuum of responsibility, even if it is acknowledged that the legal institutions are not yet in place for ensuring that the response to a

---

[54] See also D. H. N. Johnson, 'The Draft Code of Offences Against the Peace and Security of Mankind', (1955) 4 *ICLQ* 461–2.

[55] *International Law and the Use of Force by States*, 166.   [56] See also Part II above.

[57] See further Chapters 13 and 14 below.   [58] See also Chapter 4 above, s. 6.

[59] See Chapter 17 below for a more complete discussion of the *Genocide* case.

[60] See M. S. Moore, *Placing Blame: A Theory of Criminal Law* (1997), 23.

[61] A more complete picture will be painted in Part IV below.

[62] See Chapter 14 below.

criminal act is of an identical quality whether the act is committed by a state or an individual.[63]

5. MAINTAINING THE DISTINCTION BETWEEN STATE AND INDIVIDUAL RESPONSIBILITY FOR INTERNATIONAL CRIMES

It has been demonstrated that certain acts which are generally recognized as entailing individual criminal responsibility under international law are often committed by agents of the state ranging from heads of state to those at the bottom of the chain of command. The question may be raised as to whether the punishment of such individuals is a form of punishment of the state itself. Oppenheim's *International Law* indicates that this could be the case at least with regard to war crimes:

The universal recognition as part of international law of rules penalizing war crimes by individuals responsible for violations of the laws of war affords another instance of the recognition of criminal responsibility of states, for war criminals are, as a rule, guilty of acts committed not in pursuance of private purposes but on behalf of and as organs of the state.[64]

The same could be said of many other international crimes which have traditionally entailed individual responsibility. It is an established rule of international law that responsibility is borne by a state for acts of its government or officials or those of private individuals performed at the government's command or with its authorization, which are imputable to the state.[65] Therefore if a state's agents commit criminal acts and are made punishable under the principle of universal jurisdiction or by an international criminal tribunal, could this not be viewed as a form of punishment of the state?

This argument has special force when the persons held responsible are heads of state. The attempt to bring Kaiser Wilhelm II to trial after the First World War reflected a desire to punish Germany for all it stood for at the time.[66] The International Criminal Tribunal for the Former Yugoslavia has indicted Radovan Karadzic, President of the Bosnian Serb administration in Pale, for genocide, crimes against humanity, and war crimes, which could be viewed as a condemnation of the whole administration. On 27 May 1999, the Tribunal set a new precedent by indicting an existing head of state, namely Slobodan Milosevic, President of the Federal Republic of Yugoslavia (FRY),

---

[63] See further Chapter 15 below on the possible institutional framework and procedures for imposing criminal responsibility on states.

[64] R. Jennings and A. Watts (eds.), Oppenheim's *International Law*, i: *Peace*, 9th edn. (1992), 536.   [65] See further Chapter 4 above, s. 4.

[66] See Chapter 1 above.

for crimes against humanity and a violation of the laws or customs of war.[67] Also indicted for the same crimes were the President of Serbia, the Deputy Prime Minister of the FRY, the Chief of Staff of the Yugoslav Army, and the Minister of Internal Affairs of Serbia. With the exception of the Deputy Prime Minister of the FRY, all of the accused were charged with 'superior' criminal responsibility under Article 7(3) of the Tribunal's Statute by virtue of their high positions of power.

Nevertheless, these arguments seem to put the cart before the horse. The criminal responsibility of states ought not to depend on whether trials of individuals are called for. There is a clear division in international law between the concept of the criminal responsibility of the state *qua* state, which implies something more than the traditional forms of state responsibility, and individual criminal responsibility of those who commit crimes under international law when acting as organs of the state. This is manifest in the articles relating to the question of superior orders and the responsibility of heads of state which appear in most conventions dealing with individual responsibility and in the statutes of international criminal tribunals since the Nuremberg Charter. For instance, the Statute of the International Criminal Tribunal for the Former Yugoslavia states in Article 7:

(2) The official position of any accused person, whether as Head of State or Government or as a responsible Government official, shall not relieve such person of criminal responsibility nor mitigate punishment.
(3) The fact that any of the acts referred to in articles 2 to 5 of the present statute was committed by a subordinate does not relieve his superior of criminal responsibility if he knew or had reason to know that the subordinate was about to commit such acts or had done so and the superior failed to take the necessary and reasonable measures to prevent such acts or to punish the perpetrators thereof.
(4) The fact that an accused person acted pursuant to an order of a Government or of a superior shall not relieve him of criminal responsibility, but may be considered in mitigation of punishment if the International Tribunal determines that justice so requires.

Just as individuals are unable to hide their guilt behind the state, the state should not be permitted to hide its guilt behind the punishment of individuals.

The rule relating to superior orders is the subject of controversy. The general rule is that obedience to superior orders is no defence except in cases of duress or mistake of law.[68] It is often the case that superior orders can be traced upwards to the state itself, and allowing such a defence would mean

---

[67] International Criminal Tribunal for the Former Yugoslavia, Press Release, 27 May 1999, http://www.un.org/icty/.
[68] The Rome Statute adds some further qualifications to the general rule in Article 33 which states that superior orders may be a defence if (a) the person was under a legal obligation to obey the order; (b) the person did not know that the order was unlawful; and (c) the order was not manifestly unlawful, A/CONF.183/9, 17 July 1998.

that in certain cases individual responsibility would be eliminated. Passing on the burden in this manner would lead to absurd results, and arguably the rule merely requires individuals to act as humans rather than as heroes. Despite this, the first and second editions of Oppenheim's *International Law*[69] stated that members of the armed forces who commit breaches of the law in conformity with the orders of their superiors are exempt from liability, Aristotle taught that a slave who murders under orders does not act unjustly, being his master's instrument, and Grotius wrote that a 'community, or its rulers, may be held responsible for the crime of a subject if they know of it and do not prevent it when they could and should prevent it'.[70] But later editions of Oppenheim adhere to the stated rule, soldiers are not slaves, and Grotius does not exclude the responsibility of individual subjects. Perhaps the most useful aspect of the notion of superior orders is precisely that it enables responsibility to be traced to different levels in the structure of state actors thereby ensuring that the attribution of responsibility is a flexible system which can be adapted to a particular situation. For example, the International Criminal Tribunal for the Former Yugoslavia is employing the notion of 'command responsibility' in order to cast as wide a net as possible. This involves tracing the chain of command upwards from the executor of the crime to the head of state if this is where it leads. Responsibility is borne by the individual perpetrators of the act, by those who command, condone, or permit it, and by those who develop the policy that guides it. The Rwanda Tribunal, on the other hand, is directing its investigations towards the top figures who authorized the 1994 massacres.

Rosenne appears to be in favour of such an elastic system.[71] He sees Article 19 of the ILC's Draft Articles on State Responsibility as engendering state responsibility on different levels, and argues that paragraph 3, sub-paragraphs (a) and (b), are on a different footing from (c) and (d). In his opinion the first two relate to acts by or directly attributable to the state, while sub-paragraph (c) relates in equal measure to an act of state and to an individual's acts and includes war crimes, and sub-paragraph (d) usually relates to acts of an individual whether he is acting in the name of a state or not. This implies that state responsibility in the last two instances could take the form of punishment of the guilty individual. Rosenne is sceptical of the utility of a firm distinction between crimes and delicts, and suggests an alternative point of departure: 'namely that *any* internationally wrongful act attributable to *any* subject of international law involves international responsibility'.[72] This involves shifting the attention 'from the qualification of the act in abstract jurisprudential terms to determination of its consequences in terms

---

[69] 1st edn. 1906, 2nd edn. 1912.

[70] *De Jure Belli ac Pacis Libri Tres* (1625), vol. ii, trans. F. W. Kelsey (1925), bk. 2, 523.

[71] S. Rosenne, 'War Crimes and State Responsibility', (1994) 24 *Israel Yearbook on Human Rights*, 63. [72] Ibid. 99.

of appropriate reparative action by or on account of the offending subject of international law, be it a state or any other subject of the law, in favour of another state or entity, or even of the international community at large (*erga omnes*)'.[73] The question is therefore whether the prosecution of the individual criminal, whatever the outcome of that prosecution, can be adequate reparative action for the victim state. Rosenne argues that if the accused is found guilty, his punishment will at least be a relevant factor. In the *Case Concerning the Application of the Genocide Convention* the ICJ has so far not drawn any direct conclusions from the establishment of the International Criminal Tribunal for the Former Yugoslavia, although in its second Order on Provisional Measures it noted the Security Council's decision.[74] It may be that the existence and activities of the Tribunal will become a relevant factor when the Court assesses state responsibility in this case. The Tribunal's importance in this respect may depend on the extent to which it deals with major as opposed to relatively petty criminals.

6. CONCLUDING REMARKS ON THE SIGNIFICANCE OF INDIVIDUAL CRIMINAL RESPONSIBILITY UNDER INTERNATIONAL LAW AS A CRITERION OR INDICIUM IN DIFFERENTIATING CRIMES AND DELICTS

The development of a system of individual criminal responsibility under international law raises three main points that are relevant to state responsibility. First, there is some agreement over a list of which acts are criminal according to international law. Second, an examination of the debate relating to the creation of a Draft Code of Crimes reveals that a state's possible involvement in a number of these crimes is generally recognized. Third, the criminal character of an act remains constant regardless of whether the state or an individual is the main actor. This creates a presumption that if an act is recognized as entailing individual criminal responsibility, the same act, in the right context, might also constitute a state crime. However, reference must also be made to the remaining criteria and indicia to test if this is in fact the case.

The notion of international crime is potentially broad and adaptable to different circumstances, as demonstrated by the various definitions of crimes against humanity, and individual criminal responsibility under international law is still developing. Despite the logical link between individual crimes and state crimes, there is no guarantee that the two notions will develop along an

---

[73] Ibid.
[74] (1993) ICJ Reports 325, 348. See Chapter 17 below for a more complete discussion of the case.

identical route. The concept of state criminality is much more exclusive, and it is therefore important to maintain the distinction between the two forms of responsibility.

It is perhaps a pity that the ILC was not mandated to create a comprehensive criminal code dealing with all levels of responsibility. Some sort of connection between the Draft Code and Article 19 of the Draft Articles on State Responsibility would seem desirable in order to preserve the essence of the concept of crime in international law regardless of which actor is responsible. The provisions of Article 19 and the corresponding consequences could have been incorporated into the Draft Code, which is perhaps where they belong. This would have enabled a complete system of international criminal responsibility to be created without contaminating the Draft Articles on State Responsibility with notions of criminality. As it stands, Article 19 is somewhat out on a limb and may inhibit the acceptance by states of the draft generally. It is likely that the ILC will attempt to deal with this problem by eliminating the word 'crime' from the realm of state responsibility.[75]

Finally, it is worth noticing that individuals who commit crimes are no longer well protected by the doctrines of act of state and superior orders. Equally, it would not make sense for states to be protected by the notion of individual criminal responsibility. Acts of state may be imputed to individuals, and individual acts may be imputed to states. The result enables responsibility to be invoked at whichever point in the chain of command is appropriate in a given situation.

---

[75] See further Chapter 2 above, s. 6(d).

Conclusion to Part III

The aim of this Part has been to delve deeper into an analysis of the concept of state criminality while offering a guide to the identification of state crimes. This analysis does not proclaim to be exhaustive but has attempted to portray the concept as one which is not alien to international law but rooted in existing concepts, categories, and modes of behaviour. Certain of the criteria and indicia which have been discussed may be regarded as intrinsic or inductive, while others are deductive. For example, the seriousness test is designed to measure the inherent criminality of an act, whereas the recognition and acceptance of an act as criminal by the international community is a process by which the nature of an act may be deduced. In addition, the 'criminal' element and the 'international' element of an international crime are emphasized differently by the various criteria and indicia. For instance, when an act threatens international peace and security, this is primarily an international effect, but it also points towards the criminality of the act. When the conscience of mankind is considered, the important factor is the criminality of the act, but a universal conscience is one which transcends boundaries.

The concept of international crimes of state can be seen to emerge out of the different criteria and indicia. However, it remains to be determined which of the constituent elements of the concept are criteria and which are indicia, or in other words, it is necessary to assess the relative importance of the different criteria and indicia. While it is likely that an international crime also belongs to the category of *jus cogens*, this need not necessarily be the case as the two concepts differ in subtle but significant respects, and this factor is therefore an indicium. Referring to the parallel between the basic criterion in Article 19 of the Draft Articles on State Responsibility and Article 53 of the Vienna Convention on the Law of Treaties, the ILC commented in 1976:

Care must be taken not to carry this parallel further than it really goes. It would be wrong simply to conclude that any breach of an obligation deriving from a peremptory norm of international law is an international crime and that only the breach of an obligation having this origin can constitute such a crime. It can be accepted that obligations whose breach is a crime will 'normally' be those deriving from rules of *jus cogens*, though this conclusion cannot be absolute.[1]

Such caution may be less necessary now that the concept of *jus cogens* is well accepted, but it would nevertheless be inappropriate to make the development of one concept, designed to meet a specific need of the international community, conditional upon the development of another concept, designed

---

[1] (1976) *YrbkILC*, vol. 2, pt. 2, 119–20.

to meet a different need. On the other hand, an international crime must apply *erga omnes* as the enlargement of the number of subjects entitled to invoke responsibility is an essential element of the concept.

It would seem that international community recognition and acceptance is a criterion because it is the nature of international law that an act can only rise to the level of an international crime, and be treated as such, with the international community's consent. It could be argued that this criterion renders all the other criteria and indicia irrelevant but it is only by investigating all the features of the concept of state criminality that it can be understood and the need for it recognized. Norms may be international crimes by their nature before they are regarded as such and judged according to their effect, and the seriousness test is therefore clearly a criterion, however difficult it may be to measure seriousness. Indeed, this has been the exclusive criterion invoked by the ILC in determining which acts should be included in the Draft Code despite its vague and subjective nature.[2] The key distinguishing feature of state crimes within the seriousness test is the element of system. A crime can only be attributable to the state if it is committed by state organs or agents in furtherance of a definite state policy. The Deputy Chief Prosecutor for France before the Nuremberg Tribunal, Charles Dobost, described the 'Atrocity of the State-committed Crime'[3] in the following manner:

> We have already shown that the crime committed by these men is not a simple crime. The common criminal knows his victim; he sees him with his own eyes. He himself strikes and knows the effect of his blow. Even if he is only an accomplice, he is never sufficiently dissociated, morally and psychologically speaking, from the chief perpetrator, not to share to a certain extent his apprehensions and reactions when the blow is delivered and the victim falls.
>
> Genocide, murder or any other crime becomes anonymous when it is committed by the State. Nobody bears the chief responsibility. Everybody shares it: those who by their presence maintain and support the administration, those who conceived the crime and those who ordained it, as well as he who issued the order. As for the executioner, he says to himself: 'Befehl ist Befehl': 'An order is an order,' and carries out his hangman's task.[4]

The remaining criteria and indicia can to a large extent be viewed as indicators of seriousness. The effect of an act on international peace and security is clearly such an indicator and is best described as an indicium in order to avoid placing too much emphasis on Security Council classifications. Furthermore, although an international crime must possess an international element, this need not be supplied in a literal sense. The two ideas of the conscience of mankind and elementary considerations of humanity inject the

---

[2] Third Report on the Draft Code of Offences against the Peace and Security of Mankind by D. Thiam, Special Rapporteur, A/CN.4/387; (1985) *YrbkILC*, vol. 2, pt. 1, 63, 69.
[3] *Trial of German Major War Criminals, Proceedings of the IMT*, 29 July–8 Aug. 1946, pt. 20, (1949), 23.   [4] Ibid.

description of the concept of state criminality with a psychological element. These special psychological effects are perhaps more important than the extent to which a wrongful act crosses borders as they are more fundamental. Therefore, it is suggested that an act must affect the conscience of mankind and offend against elementary considerations of humanity in order to be considered a state crime. Finally, it is submitted that the discussion of individual criminal responsibility in Chapter 12 revealed the need for a concept of state criminality which would come into play in respect of the most serious systematic wrongful acts and complement the existing rules relating to individuals. However, it is not certain at this stage that the two regimes will follow the same path of development, and it would therefore be unwise to view individual criminal responsibility as a criterion, however logical it might be so to do.

The position may be summarized as follows:

Candidate criteria for differentiating crimes and delicts
1. Crimes are a sub-set of the broader category of obligations *erga omnes*.
2. Crimes must be recognized and accepted as such by the international community as a whole.
3. Crimes must pass the 'seriousness test' in order to be considered as such.
4. Crimes have a special effect on the conscience of mankind.
5. Crimes offend against elementary considerations of humanity.

Candidate indicia for differentiating crimes and delicts
1. Crimes are likely to overlap with *jus cogens*.
2. Crimes will normally affect international peace and security.
3. State crimes generally also entail individual criminal responsibility under international law.

A further question which may be raised is whether the criteria and indicia point towards the existence of two regimes of state responsibility or many such regimes. In other words, are international crimes a clear-cut category of acts, or does the degree of fulfilment of the various criteria and indicia blur the distinction between crimes and delicts? It is submitted that the concept of international crimes of state is distinct even though the consequences will inevitably vary depending on the circumstances of a given case. Murder and theft both fall within the concept of domestic crime even though murder leads to more severe consequences. Moreover, the difficulty in fulfilling the different criteria and indicia ensures that the category of international crimes will remain restricted. International crimes are an exception, and the purpose is not to relegate delicts to an inferior status.

One of the aims of this part was to investigate whether the concept of state criminality was grounded in principle. Article 38(1)(c) of the Statute of the ICJ describes 'the general principles of law recognized by civilized nations' as a source of international law which is listed below those sources depending more immediately on the consent of states but is nevertheless not categorized as a subsidiary means in paragraph (d). Schwarzenberger has stated that the draftsmen of the Statute of the Permanent Court of International Justice, in incorporating general principles, achieved seven purposes, one of which was to 'thr[o]w out a challenge to the Doctrine of International Law to sail into new and uncharted seas'.[5]

Fitzmaurice has suggested that '[a] rule answers the question "what": a principle answers the question "why"'.[6] In attempting to answer the question *why* international crimes and international delicts are two qualitatively different concepts, it seems that a general principle of international law has begun to emerge. This general principle has its roots in the aspects of international law that have been discussed in the preceding chapters and also in municipal law analogies, in particular in relation to corporate crime.[7] It is nevertheless unlikely that the general principle will come of age until it completes its emergence as custom or is applied through judicial reasoning.[8]

An analysis in terms of principle helps to establish the outline of a new legal development, and if a principle is sound, and attractive enough, this is soon reflected in practice. Indications are that the general principle embodying the concept of state criminality is already crossing the threshold between *lex ferenda* and *lex lata*. The degree to which the principle is sound, attractive, and ready to meet the challenges beyond the threshold will continue to emerge in the remaining chapters.

---

[5] Foreword to B. Cheng, *General Principles of Law as Applied by International Courts and Tribunals* (1953).

[6] G. G. Fitzmaurice, 'The General Principles of International Law Seen from the Standpoint of the Rule of Law', (1957–II) 92 Hague *Recueil* 1, 7.   [7] See Chapter 4 above.

[8] See Part V and Conclusion to Part IV below.

PART IV

Practical Feasibility of the Concept of State Criminality

Introduction to Part IV

One is entitled to test the soundness of a principle by the consequences which would flow from its application.[1]

Perhaps the most difficult aspect of the concept of state criminality is the question of its practical implications. This question has many facets which rest in the first instance on the juridical soundness of the concept.[2] In Chapters 13 and 14 the possible consequences of state crimes, ranging from punishment to the milder regime of responsibility promoted by the ILC,[3] will be considered. Then in Chapter 15 the question of who decides that a crime has been committed and the difficulties associated with finding a suitable institutional framework for imposing criminal responsibility upon states will be addressed.

The current part raises two separate but connected themes. The first is the problem of giving legal substance to the concept of state criminality in the form of a system of consequences and a structure for their implementation. The second is the potential moral dilemma and clash with rule of law principles which may flow from an application of the concept of state criminality. In other words, are there consequences that give substance to the concept and do these consequences confirm the soundness of the principle? If these questions can be answered in the affirmative, then additional force is given to the argument that the concept is an emergent general principle of international law.

---

[1] Judge Jessup, Separate Opinion, *Barcelona Traction, Light and Power Company, Limited,* (1970) ICJ Reports 3, 220.   [2] This facet was considered in Part II above.

[3] The ILC has persistently tried to avoid the penal implications of the word 'crime' and is likely to dispense with Article 19 and develop a new regime for breaches of obligations *erga omnes*. See above Chapter 2, s. 6(d) and Chapter 13, s. 5, and see also First Report on State Responsibility by James Crawford, Special Rapporteur, A/CN.4/490/Add.3, 11 May 1998, paras. 97–101.

13

The Problems and Modalities of Punishing a State

1. INTRODUCTION: TRADITIONAL REMEDIES AND TERMINOLOGY

The *modus operandi* for imposing criminal responsibility upon states must be examined if the state is to be regarded as a corporate entity or organization susceptible to punishment. The remedies currently available to a state injured by an internationally wrongful act committed by another state include declaratory judgments, satisfaction, restitution, and compensation. A preliminary question is whether these remedies, which presuppose collective responsibility in the sense that they are directed against the wrongdoing state as such, can have the character of punishment. Declaratory judgments, for instance, contain a certain condemnatory element which can cause embarrassment to states in the same way that a domestic criminal conviction can cause embarrassment to individuals.[1] Pecuniary compensation is perhaps the most interesting from this point of view, and will be treated separately in the next chapter.

The remedies which are available under the general law of state responsibility are to be distinguished from 'sanctions', 'countermeasures', or 'measures' which may be diplomatic, political, economic, or military, and are applied by the political bodies of the UN, or by states collectively or unilaterally. These are acts which are designed to stop the wrongful conduct or to demonstrate disapproval, although they may also provide relief. However, the question here is not whether the possible responses to international crimes have a strictly legal or primarily a political basis, but whether they may be regarded as containing a punitive element. Thus it is the effect of a response which is the focus and not its name, and it seems futile to argue in this context that penalties cannot be preventative while measures can be, or that punishment can only be applied after the event. The point is that the legal methods whereby justice can be obtained in the face of an international crime are bound to differ between cases, and:

The basic principle must be that actions which are clearly and incontestably criminal . . . and which are really without question deliberately committed by *the state as such* . . . *cannot be above the law or immune from its penalties.*[2]

---

[1] Declarations also form the basis of the criminal organization model.

[2] J. Graven, Reply to the questionnaire of the International Association for Penal Law and International Bar Association, quoted in *Memorandum Concerning a Draft Code of Offences Against the Peace and Security of Mankind*, prepared by V. V. Pella, (1950), A/CN.4/39, 105.

Ultimately it is desirable for a response to have multiple effects, in particular for it to be both preventive and corrective.

2. THE NOTION OF COLLECTIVE PUNISHMENT

The notion of collective punishment tends to conjure up images of 'the seizure and shooting of hostages, the burning of towns and villages, the destruction of private houses, the deportation of the civil population, the commercial isolation of refractory towns, the interdiction of public charitable relief to the unemployed, the confinement of the inhabitants within doors for certain periods, and the like'.[3] In fact, a belligerent occupant possesses certain rights under international law to impose collective punishments upon occupied districts under specific conditions. The restrictions are laid down in Article 50 of the 1907 Hague Convention Respecting the Laws and Customs of War on Land, which declares that 'no general penalty, pecuniary or otherwise, shall be inflicted upon the population on account of the acts of individuals for which they can not be regarded as jointly and severally responsible'. Thus, a community may be held responsible if, either actively or passively, it is a party to the offence.[4] This theory of collective responsibility is, however, open to abuse, and was abused extensively by the Germans in the Franco-German War of 1870–1 and in the First World War.[5]

Following the First World War, the separation of the Saar from Germany under a League of Nations mandate, against the will of its ethnically German inhabitants, and the refusal to allow the inhabitants to register their opinion in the matter for fifteen years thereafter has a flavour of collective punishment. Those 65,000 or so inhabitants suffered considerable French interference and were denied democratic participation in their own Government as a means of punishing Germany for having been insufficiently democratic before 1918. This contradicted Wilson's principle that 'peoples and provinces are not to be bartered about from sovereignty to sovereignty as if they were mere chattels and pawns in a game'.[6]

Collective punishment implies collective guilt, and Grotius maintained that participation in punishment arose from participation in guilt. In cases where a whole community was at fault as a result of a crime committed by the majority representing the personality of the community, the loss of political

---

[3] J. W. Garner, 'Community Fines and Collective Responsibility', (1917) 2 *AJIL* 511.

[4] Cf. Common Article 3 of the 1949 Geneva Conventions and Article 4(2) of the 1977 Additional Protocol II Relating to the Protection of Victims of Non-International Armed Conflicts, which provide that collective punishments against persons who are not taking a direct part in hostilities are prohibited.

[5] See Garner, 'Community Fines and Collective Responsibility'.

[6] H. W. V. Temperley (ed.), *A History of the Peace Conference of Paris*, i (1920), 439; and see A. Osiander, *The States System of Europe 1640–1990* (1994), 286–7.

liberty, fortifications, and other privileges which followed would also be felt by individuals who were innocent 'but only in respect to such things as belonged to them not directly but through the community'.[7] He likened the death penalty to the dissolution of the state. Pufendorf argued along similar lines in relation to the equity of reprisals:

That just as a result of the union into a civil body is that an injury done to one of its members by foreigners is regarded as affecting the entire state, so it does not appear unjust that individual subjects should be obligated to contribute to the debt of the state, since, after all, what they contribute on that score has to be made up to them by their state. But if one or another citizen suffer some loss thereby, he should count it among those inconveniences which almost necessarily attend states, and which, in any event, are but a small part of those which they could have expected outside the shelter of a state.[8]

In his *Criminalité collective des états et le droit pénal de l'avenir* of 1925, Pella argued on the basis of theories relating to collective psychology and collective will which suggest that every human group has feelings, reflexes, and a will distinct from those of its members, that the nation has a collective will expressed through its constitutional organs. He rejected Napoleon's maxim that nobody is answerable for collective crimes, and contended that establishing the criminal responsibility of states should expose each individual to the threat of measures that would serve as a deterrent against international crime. In his *Memorandum on a Draft Code of Offences against the Peace and Security of Mankind*, Pella suggests that '[t]he active element in international crime can be reached by punishing the natural persons who decided upon and ordered the commission of the crimes. The passive element of the population can be reached by imposing suitable penalties on the State.'[9]

Kelsen defines punishment as 'the forcible deprivation of life, freedom or property for the purpose of retribution or prevention'.[10] He maintains that the sanctions of reprisals and war are directed against the state as such, which includes those individuals who have not committed the act or who have not had the ability to prevent it. In other words, 'the statement that according to international law the state is responsible for its acts means that the subjects of the state are collectively responsible for the acts of the organs of the state'.[11] In a later work Kelsen denies that reprisals and war have the specific character of punishment.[12]

Adopting a seemingly different approach, Gentili wrote: 'The punishment

---

[7] *De Jure Belli ac Pacis Libri Tres*, ii, trans. F. W. Kelsey (1925), bk. 2, 538.

[8] S. Pufendorf, *De Jure Naturae et Gentium Libri Octo*, ii, translation of the edn. of 1688 by C. H. Oldfather and W. A. Oldfather (1934), bk 8, 1305.   [9] See n. 2 above, 96.

[10] H Kelsen, *Peace Through Law* (1944), 72.   [11] Ibid. 73.

[12] H. Kelsen, *Principles of International Law* (1966), 196.

ought to fall upon the one by whom the crime is committed. It ought to affect none save the authors of the fault.'[13] Drost[14] argues in favour of the collective civil liability of the nationals of a state for the wrongful acts committed by governmental authorities and public officials acting in the name of the state. Such responsibility, he submits, is acceptable on political, economic, and social grounds and also from the point of view of ethical considerations of justice and fairness vis-à-vis the injured parties. He refers to Grotius, who wrote that subjects should not be punished for the guilt of rulers but that they were nevertheless liable for the debts of rulers.[15] In Drost's opinion, collective punishment, when inflicted upon individuals who are morally innocent of the criminal deed, neither constitutes personal justice nor serves any social preventative purpose. This raises the question to what extent the active or passive support of a population for a criminal act instigated by its government is a relevant factor. Should a population which is browbeaten into submission by an autocratic regime suffer along with the principals and accessories directly responsible? In other words, should the entire population be regarded as an accessory?

In national legal systems corporate responsibility results in the placing of an economic sanction on the owners of a company who may not have had any role in, or knowledge of, the violation. Thus, shareholders are collectively punished for acts committed by their managers and representatives. Bassiouni[16] asserts that the policy underlying such a model of responsibility is to compel shareholders to scrutinize the operation of their corporation or to be vigilant in the election and control of corporate directors. The suffering of innocent shareholders is commonly justified on the basis that they were unjustly enriched as a result of the crimes of the corporation. But even if, in a general sense, citizens in a state may be likened to shareholders in a corporation, the analogy only goes so far, as most citizens are not in a real sense 'shareholders' in the state and may not be able to leave the state without difficulty.[17] Furthermore, a state can commit a crime against its own citizens, whereas it is unusual for a corporation to commit a crime against itself. If the state is then punished, the citizens are twice the victims.

The controversy surrounding the question of collective punishment arose with respect to measures, including a twenty-two-hour curfew, which were imposed by British forces on civilians of Tanjong Malim in Malaya during an internal conflict there in 1952. In the House of Commons question period of 30 April 1952,[18] the Secretary of State for the Colonies, Mr Lyttelton, was asked:

---

[13] *De Iure Belli Libri Tres*, ii, translation of the edn. of 1612 by C. J. Rolfe (1933), 295.
[14] P. N. Drost, *The Crime of State*, i: *Humanicide* (1959), 292.
[15] *De Jure Belli ac Pacis Libri Tres*, ii, bk. 3, 624.
[16] M. C. Bassiouni, *Substantive Criminal Law* (1978), 151.
[17] See D. D. Caron, 'State Crimes in the ILC Draft Articles on State Responsibility: Insights from Municipal Experience with Corporate Crimes', (1998) 92 *ASIL Proceedings* 307, 311.
[18] 499 Parliamentary Debates (Hansard), 5th ser., cols. 1454–5 (30 Apr. 1952).

will the right honourable Gentleman not agree that it is desirable . . . that General Templer should proceed with the utmost caution in enforcing collective punishment, which may not be at all efficacious?

Lyttelton replied:

The right honourable Gentleman must be aware that these measures are not primarily punitive. They are in the main in order to prevent rice being passed through the wire to the bandits and also to control movement in these black spots . . .

During a later question period[19] Lyttelton was asked:

whether, when imposing collective punishments or when restricting rations in Malaya in order to deny resources to terrorists, he will ensure that such punishments or restrictions do not fall upon children.

Answering on Lyttelton's behalf, Mr Hopkinson stated:

Curfew orders apply to children as well as adults. One reason is that the terrorists do not scruple to force children to fetch supplies or bear information. It is similarly not possible to exempt children from rationing restrictions, but care was taken to ensure that the supply of food was adequate to maintain health in places where these restrictions have had to be imposed.

In 1997, it was argued by the Palestinians that the Israeli Government's ban on economic activity and travel in Palestinian areas constituted collective punishment of the Palestinian people. Mr Arafat alleged that these restrictions on the movement of people and goods between Israel and the Palestinian territories were costing Palestinians £4.2 million a day.[20] The term 'collective punishment' is also current regarding Rwanda because it is feared that the Hutu may be condemned as a group for the massacre of mostly Tutsi in 1994. Garner has remarked, in relation to the theory of collective punishment during wartime occupation, that 'even when applied in its mildest form [it] necessarily involves the punishment of innocent persons, and for this reason . . . ought never be resorted to when other more just measures would accomplish the same end, and in no case unless an active or passive responsibility can really be imputed to the mass of the population'.[21]

Nevertheless, the implications of the term 'collective punishment' ought not, perhaps, to be exaggerated. As Pella has remarked:

Some have gone so far as to assert that to impose penalties on a state would be to punish all the individuals composing it, who are frequently in no way guilty of any international crimes committed. In reply to this argument it may be pointed out that even at present an entire nation—of which the state in merely the juridical embodiment—

---

[19] 501 Parliamentary Debates (Hansard), 5th ser., cols. 1345–6 (28 May 1952).
[20] *The Times*, 3 Feb. 1997.
[21] Garner, 'Community Fines and Collective Responsibility', 535.

may suffer the consequences of measures taken against the state for offences committed by state agencies.[22]

In a democratic system it is not necessarily unfair for the population to
endure some degree of vicarious responsibility for the acts of its elected
government, and the same is true of popular dictatorships such as Nazi
Germany. More tricky is the situation of a dictatorship that oppresses its own
people, but an application of the criminal organization model[23] in such cases
should ensure that the innocent escape punishment. The UN repeatedly
imposes economic sanctions on states which tend to affect the entire population, particularly the poor. There is clearly a moral dilemma here, but state
practice points in favour of collective sanctions which often have the aim of
encouraging a state to improve the treatment of its own citizens. As Lord
Owen has pointed out, sanctions often hit the innocent harder than the
guilty, but in his opinion they are the only peaceful weapon the international
community has.[24] Those sanctions that are designed to deter or to provide
retribution have the effect of collective punishment even if politically the
phrase is controversial.

3. THE USE OF FORCE, UNITED NATIONS MEASURES, AND REPRISALS AS FORMS OF PUNISHMENT

Grotius demonstrated, and 'histories everywhere teach, that wars are usually
begun for the purpose of exacting punishment'.[25] However, Grotius asserted:
'War should not be undertaken for every sort of crime.'[26] Article 41 of the
UN Charter contains an enumeration of compulsory measures not involving
the use of force which includes complete or partial interruption of economic
relations and of rail, sea, air, postal, telegraphic, radio, and other means of
communication, and the severance of diplomatic relations. If these measures
prove or are likely to prove inadequate, then the Security Council can take
such action by air, sea, or land forces as is necessary to maintain or restore
international peace and security. Under Chapter VII of the UN Charter, the
right and duty of the Security Council to have recourse to compulsory measures depend upon its prior determination that a 'threat to the peace, breach
of the peace, or act of aggression' has occurred. Force is vital to law, although
it normally plays a less obvious part than in international law. In national law
a criminal is induced by force or the fear of force to come before a court and
submit to punishment. This threat of force also promotes obedience to the
law.

---

[22] See n. 2 above, 92–3.   [23] See Chapter 3 above.
[24] News Summary, 12–18 Nov. 1992, UN Information Centre, 19 Nov. 1992.
[25] *De Jure Belli ac Pacis Libri Tres*, 502.   [26] Ibid.

With respect to compulsive means of dispute settlement by the UN, Hersch Lauterpacht wrote:

Although compulsive measures may be purely remedial, *i.e.*, limited to the restoration of the status *quo ante*, they need not be so. They may be in the nature of a penal sanction. Thus conceived they give expression to the correct view that certain manifestations of unlawful conduct on the part of sovereign states are liable both to repression and to punishment by the collective efforts of the general international organization. That principle rejects the opinion that individuals ought to be able to escape the consequences of their conduct in so far as they act as States, or that the admittedly great difficulties of repression when directed against collective units must result in an immunity destructive alike of justice and of the possibility of an effective international order.[27]

Therefore, these measures that are part of the UN machinery for the enforcement of peace may sometimes result in the punishment of a state, even though their primary purpose is not to impose criminal responsibility. Jennings and Watts state that the 'sanctions of Chapter VII of the Charter of the United Nations are, in part, of a penal character in relation to what may properly be described as the crime of war'.[28] Kunz has suggested that these sanctions are old-fashioned because 'they are directed against states, are based on collective responsibility, and do not distinguish between criminal and civil sanctions'.[29]

Reprisals are a form of self-help which have traditionally been of a punitive nature. As Bowett confirms, 'reprisals are punitive in character: they seek to impose reparation for the harm done, or to compel a satisfactory settlement of the dispute created by the initial illegal act, or to compel the delinquent state to abide by the law in the future'.[30] Armed reprisals are expressly prohibited in paragraph 6 of the Section on the Principle of the Use of Force in the 1970 Declaration on Principles of International Law, but they are frequently resorted to by states despite their probable illegality. States clearly desire to inflict punishment on other states in certain situations, and indications are that reprisals are resorted to when more legitimate means of invoking responsibility are seen as inadequate. Unilateral action in the form of reprisals leads to a weakening of the international public order, and therefore, while the philosophy behind reprisals is relevant, the pressure is on existing institutions to make their use redundant.

---

[27] Oppenheim's *International Law*, ii, 7th edn. (1952), 160.
[28] R. Y. Jennings and A. Watts (eds.), Oppenheim's *International Law*, i: *Peace*, 536.
[29] J. L. Kunz, 'Sanctions in International Law', (1960) 54 *AJIL* 324, 329.
[30] D. Bowett, 'Reprisals Involving Recourse to Armed Force', (1972) 66 *AJIL* 1, 2.

4. ALTERNATIVE POSSIBILITIES OF PUNISHMENT

Donnedieu de Vabres put forward some suggestions for imposing a penalty upon a state in his report to the first international congress on penal law in 1925.[31] Depending on which material, territorial, and intellectual assets and privileges were held by the state, he proposed measures ranging from the severance of diplomatic relations to the sequestration of property, the destruction of installations and the demolition of factories, blockades, boycotts, embargoes, heavy fines, levies and seizure of assets, enforced disarmament, and military occupation.

In *La Guerre-crime et les criminels de guerre*,[32] Pella appends a 'Plan d'un code répressif mondial' in which he puts forward a variety of possible criminal sanctions including diplomatic sanctions such as warnings and the breaking off of diplomatic relations; legal sanctions such as the sequestration of the property of a state's nationals; economic sanctions such as economic blockades, boycotts, and embargoes; and other sanctions such as censure, deprivation for a certain time of representation in international organizations, deprivation of a mandate to administer a trust territory, complete or partial occupation of the territory of a state, and deprivation of independence. The Plan also provides for security measures that might be undertaken with respect to a state which has committed a crime, including the destruction of strategic railways and fortifications, prohibiting military production, the confiscation of armaments, the limitation of the size of armed forces, complete disarmament, the formation of demilitarized zones on the territory of the state and the establishment of control over them, and the distribution of military units at various points of a state's territory for the purposes of control.

In corporate crime theory, it is now an outdated view that corporations can only be punished by means of a fine or monetary penalty, such punishment being ineffective as it tends to be treated as one of the costs of doing business. Other methods of punishing a corporation include adverse publicity, community service, and corporate probation consisting of a specified period of judicial monitoring of the activities of the convicted corporation. A more severe option is the punitive injunction, which provides a way of requiring the corporation to 'revamp its internal controls . . . in some punitively demanding way',[33] and corporate capital punishment in the form of a company's liquidation has also been envisaged.

There are numerous possible means of punishing a state, and whether an act amounts to a 'measure' or a 'penalty' is sometimes a matter of interpretation. Having exposed the punitive element within many possible responses

---

[31] See Pella's *Memorandum* (n. 2 above), 106.   [32] (1964), 145, 153–5.
[33] B. Fisse and J. Braithwaite, *Corporations, Crime and Accountability* (1993), 43.

to acts amounting to international crimes, it seems unnecessary to devise entirely new responses which fulfil all the criteria of a penalty. Alternative penalties which could be applied against a state include the payment of a fine into a special fund which could be used as aid to developing countries, to finance health projects, or to assist in areas hit by natural disasters or drought, or the removal of aid programmes.[34] States could also be placed under surveillance and in extreme cases, if it is politically feasible, a change of leadership could be brought about.

5. CONSEQUENCES OF STATE CRIMES ENVISAGED BY THE INTERNATIONAL LAW COMMISSION

(a) Preliminary Work on Part II of the Draft Articles on State Responsibility

The ILC completed its first reading of Part I of the Draft Articles on State Responsibility in 1980, and then began work on Part II, devoted to the content, forms, and degrees of international responsibility. Mr Riphagen, who was appointed Special Rapporteur for the topic in 1979, submitted seven reports to the ILC between 1980 and 1986. By this time the ILC had many new members, and the method of approaching the question of the consequences of international crimes had therefore altered somewhat since the adoption of Draft Article 19. This meant that the two parts were not well coordinated in their consideration of the topic, and there was no reconsideration of the substance of Article 19 until 1998.

Riphagen construed the notion of international responsibility broadly to mean all the forms of new legal relationships that may be established in international law by a state's wrongful act. In his opinion, the 'primary' rules which impose obligations, the 'secondary' rules relating to the determination of an internationally wrongful act, and the 'tertiary' rules concerning the implementation of responsibility were inseparable. These three types of rule, taken together, formed a 'subsystem' of international law for each particular field of international relations. 'A particular case of the shift from one

---

[34] 'Conditionality' in modern aid terminology refers to a set of strategies that the donor can employ to induce economic and political change in the recipient country. Conditionality is essentially a coercive approach, and conditions often include the promotion and fulfilment of democratic and human rights objectives. Conditionality can be applied *ex post* and can amount to a form of punishment which is referred to as 'negative conditionality'. This means that the donor terminates, suspends, or reduces aid flow or threatens so to do. Withholding payments and suspending debt relief are the most common forms of sanction where 'negative conditionality' is applied, as these are believed to hurt the government more directly than the withdrawal of project support. 'The latter would present the donor with the so-called "double penalty" dilemma, which means that also "innocent" recipients would be adversely affected.' See H. Selbervik, *Aid and Conditionality*, Draft Final Report, Chr. Michelsens Institute, Development Studies and Human Rights, Apr. 1999, 4–5.

subsystem to another is . . . the qualification of an internationally wrongful act as an "international crime".'[35] As Riphagen discovered, there is currently in international law 'an abundance of primary rules of conduct but a relative scarcity of secondary rules and a virtual absence of tertiary rules'.[36] The notion of international crime implied that the wrongful act thus qualified could not be made good by any substitute performance, and that an injury was suffered by all states. Thus, Riphagen envisaged some form of international enforcement by the international community as a whole.

In 1982 Riphagen submitted to the ILC Draft Article 6 on the consequences of international crimes, worded as follows:

1. An internationally wrongful act of a state, which constitutes an international crime, entails an obligation for every other state:
(a) not to recognize as legal the situation created by such an act; and
(b) not to render aid or assistance to the author state in maintaining the situation created by such act;
(c) to join other states in affording mutual assistance in carrying out the obligations under (a) and (b).
2. Unless otherwise provided for by an applicable rule of international law, the performance of the obligations mentioned in paragraph 1 is subject *mutatis mutandis* to the procedures embodied in the UN Charter with respect to the maintenance of international peace and security.
3. Subject to Article 103 of the UN Charter, in the event of a conflict between the obligations of a state under any other rule of international law, the obligations under the present article shall prevail.[37]

This was not felt by the ILC to be an exhaustive list of the consequences of international crimes, and in 1984 Riphagen submitted a set of sixteen draft articles designed to replace all earlier articles proposed by him and to constitute Part II of the Draft Articles on State Responsibility.[38]

The new Draft Article 5 provided that:

For the purposes of the present articles 'injured state' means:
(3) if the internationally wrongful act constitutes an international crime, all other states.

Draft Article 14 followed the format of the earlier Draft Article 6, except that paragraph 1 refers to 'such rights and obligations as are determined by the

---

[35] Third Report on the content, forms and degrees of international responsibility (part II of the draft articles) by W. Riphagen, Special Rapporteur, A/CN.4/354 and Add. 1 and 2; (1982) *YrbkILC*, vol. 2, part 1, 22, 44.

[36] Fourth Report on the content, forms and degrees of international responsibility (part II of the draft articles) by W. Riphagen, Special Rapporteur, A/CN.4/366 and Add. 1; (1983) *YrbkILC*, vol. 2, part 1, 3, 8.

[37] Third Report . . . by Riphagen; (1982) *YrbkILC*, vol. 2, pt. 1, 48.

[38] Fifth Report on the content, forms and degrees of international responsibility (part II of the draft articles), A/CN.4/380; (1984) *YrbkILC*, vol. 2, pt. 1, 1, 2–4.

applicable rules accepted by the international community as a whole'. Draft Article 15 added: 'An act of aggression entails all the legal consequences of an international crime and, in addition, such rights and obligations as are provided for in or by virtue of the UN Charter.' A question which troubled the ILC was whether it was necessary to deal with the sanctions provided for by the UN Charter in the codification of state responsibility. In Riphagen's opinion, the specific consequences of aggression dealt with in the Charter would prevail over the rules contained in the Draft Articles, and it was not necessary to set them out in detail.

Riphagen's approach was to try to ascertain the 'elements of special legal consequences common to all international crimes'[39] and to distinguish in general the regime of crimes from that of delicts, despite his earlier recognition of the fact that the international crimes listed in Article 19, paragraph 3, could not each entail the same new legal relationships.[40] In other words, the aim was to discover the 'common minimum' whereby it would be appropriate to 'aggravate' the consequences of crimes as opposed to delicts. Riphagen failed to elaborate this minimum threshold beyond the obligations of 'non-recognition' and 'solidarity' that would be incumbent on all states in the case of an international crime, and widespread dissatisfaction was expressed in the Sixth Committee with the idea of reducing the essence of crimes to such minimalist requirements.[41]

A point of contention in relation to Riphagen's proposals was that he did not differentiate very precisely between the position of states which are indirectly injured by an international crime and that of the principal victim of the breach. His focus was more on the former than the latter. This led to the implication that, in the case of a crime, all states possessed exactly the same rights as the directly injured state, which would make every state entitled to receive pecuniary compensation and to adopt all available countermeasures. However, Riphagen argued that the 'active' rights of indirectly injured states would depend on the type of injury sustained, material or otherwise, and that a 'state which is considered to be an injured state only by virtue of article 5, sub-paragraph (e), enjoys this status as a member of the international community as a whole and should exercise its new rights and perform its new obligations within the framework of the organized community of States'.[42] Arguably, this puts too much discretion in the hands of what is barely an 'organized' community, although Riphagen suggested that in the absence of,

---

[39] Fourth Report . . . by Riphagen; (1983) *YrbkILC*, vol. 2, pt. 1, 11.

[40] Preliminary Report on the content, forms and degrees of international responsibility (part II of the draft articles), A/CN.4/330; (1980) *YrbkILC*, vol. 2, pt. 1, 129.

[41] See Fifth Report on State Responsibility by G. Arangio-Ruiz, Special Rapporteur, A/CN.4/453/Add. 2, 21.

[42] Sixth Report on the content, forms and degrees of international responsibility (part 2 of the draft articles); and 'Implementation' (*mise en œuvre*) of international responsibility and the settlement of disputes (part 3 of the draft articles), A/CN.4/389; (1985) *YrbkILC*, vol. 2, pt. 1, 3, 14.

and prior to, a collective decision, presumably on the part of the UN, a state injured solely within the meaning of Article 5(e) could resort, *uti singulis*, only to the measures provided for in Article 14.

It is also notable that Riphagen seemed inclined to banish from the concept of international responsibility for crimes any punitive aspect, in particular with regard to the aims legitimately pursuable through countermeasures, although it is not clear whether the same was considered to be true of collective sanctions applied by competent international bodies.

At its Thirty-Ninth Session in 1987, the ILC appointed Arangio-Ruiz Special Rapporteur for the topic of State Responsibility.[43] There was no further direct discussion of international crimes until 1993, when Arangio-Ruiz presented his Fifth Report, which dealt in Chapter II with 'The consequences of the so-called international crimes of states (article 19 of part I of the draft)'.[44]

(b) The Special Regime of State Responsibility for International Crimes Drafted in 1996

In his Fifth Report, Arangio-Ruiz presented a thorough review of the potential hindrances to the creation of a special regime of state responsibility for international crimes. His starting-point was the recognition of the two lines along which the theme of state responsibility for crimes had developed. The first concerned the imposition upon a state which had committed an international crime of more severe consequences than would be applicable in the case of an international delict. The second related to the broadening of the category of subjects of international law entitled to invoke the responsibility of the state in the case of an international crime. Two further features of the new regime of 'aggravated responsibility' were also highlighted, namely that the regime would vary according to the crime, and that it could not in any way derogate from the provisions of the UN Charter.

Arangio-Ruiz's approach was to raise an objective and a subjective question in the light of which the specific problems posed by the consequences of international crimes could be presented. From an objective viewpoint the question was whether, and in what way, the seriousness of the breach aggravated the content, and reduced the limits of the consequences, that characterize *erga omnes* breaches in general. From a subjective viewpoint the question was whether or not the fundamental importance of the violated rule resulted in any changes in the otherwise disorganized multilateral relations that normally arose in the presence of a breach of an *erga omnes* obligation under general law, either between the wrongdoing state and all other states or among the injured states themselves.

---

[43] Report of the ILC on the Work of its Thirty-Ninth Session, 4 May–17 July 1987; (1987) *YrbkILC*, vol. 2, pt. 2, 1.   [44] Fifth Report . . . by Arangio-Ruiz.

Arangio-Ruiz addressed first the substantive consequences of international crimes, namely cessation and reparation (including *restitutio*, compensation, satisfaction, and guarantees of non-repetition). Cessation did not require special elaboration in the case of crimes because it was not susceptible of aggravation, attenuation, or modification, and was incumbent on the responsible state even in the absence of any demand on the part of other states. With regard to reparation *lato sensu*, Arangio-Ruiz pointed out that in the case of delicts, some of the forms of reparation, in particular restitution in kind and satisfaction, were subject to certain limits, for instance in relation to proportionality and the preservation of the dignity of the state, such as the prohibition of punitive damages or of humiliating demands. Therefore the question was whether, and to what extent, these limits would be subject to derogation in the case of an international crime. A related question, given that crimes were to be treated as breaches *erga omnes*, was whether indirectly injured states would be entitled to the same remedies as the principal victim, and if so, whether these states could demand remedies *uti singulus* or only on the basis of coordinated, insitutionalized procedures.

In his Seventh Report on State Responsibility[45] Arangio-Ruiz formulated a set of draft articles dealing with the substantive and instrumental consequences of international crimes.[46] The 1995 proposals met with a wide measure of support by the ILC while at the same time giving rise to serious reservations. It was evident in the comments of governments that the problem was as much the concept of state crimes itself as the precise nature of the special regime of consequences. In his Eighth Report on State Responsibility[47] it was Arangio-Ruiz's aim to prepare the project for its first reading. A revised draft of Parts II and III was provisionally adopted by the Drafting Committee on first reading at the Forty-Eighth Session of the ILC in 1996,[48] which included a new Chapter IV entitled 'International Crimes':

Article 51
Consequences of International Crimes
An international crime entails all the legal consequences of any other internationally wrongful act and, in addition, such further consequences as are set out in articles 52 and 53.

Article 52
Specific Consequences
Where an internationally wrongful act of a state is an international crime:
(a) an injured state's entitlement to obtain restitution in kind is not subject to the limitations set out in subparagraphs (c) and (d) of article 43;[49]

---

[45] A/CN.4/469, and see A/CN.4/469/Add.1 for draft articles.   [46] See Appendix 2 below.
[47] A/CN.4/476.   [48] A/CN.4/L.524.
[49] Article 43 relates to the injured state's entitlement to obtain restitution in kind provided this: (c) would not involve a burden out of all proportion to the benefit which the injured state

(b) an injured state's entitlement to obtain satisfaction is not subject to the restriction in paragraph 3 of article 45.[50]

Article 53
Obligations for all States

An international crime committed by a state entails an obligation for every other state:

(a) not to recognize as lawful the situation created by the crime;

(b) not to render aid or assistance to the state which has committed the crime in maintaining the situation so created;

(c) to cooperate with other states in carrying out the obligations under subparagraphs (a) and (b); and

(d) to cooperate with other states in the application of measures designed to eliminate the consequences of the crime.

Draft Article 37 is also of some relevance with respect to international crimes. It states that the provisions of Part II are not applicable if the legal consequences of an internationally wrongful act of a state have been determined by other rules of international law forming self-contained regimes relating specifically to that act. This gives some scope for the separate development of the concept of state criminality if it is excluded from the final Draft on State Responsibility.

(c) Analysis of the ILC's Work on the Consequences of International Crimes of State

The central theme of the ILC's stance on the consequences of international crimes in 1996 is not difficult to grasp. The commission of an international crime should cause certain remedial rights to vest in every state. The difficulty is to determine which rights vest in which states under which circumstances. The ILC recognized that not all international crimes are equal and that not all states are equally affected by them, but nevertheless tended to assume a unitary notion of international crimes apart from aggression, and a uniform idea of an injured state. Following Arangio-Ruiz's detailed consideration of the topic, it is significant that only three short articles on international crimes remained in the 1996 Draft. These provisions do not place a heavy or distinct burden on states, and add little to what is expected of them under the rules of general international law relating to state responsibility for wrongful acts. In essence, when an international crime is committed, it is thought necessary

would gain from obtaining restitution in kind instead of compensation; or (d) would not seriously jeopardize the political independence or economic stability of the state which has committed the internationally wrongful act, whereas the injured state would not be similarly affected if it did not obtain restitution in kind.

[50] This paragraph states: 'The right of the injured state to obtain satisfaction does not justify demands which would impair the dignity of the state which has committed the internationally wrongful act.'

to provide for the mobilization of the international community as a whole in order to ensure that breaches of certain fundamental rules are suppressed.[51] The basic rights which all states possess are the right to demand that the violation cease and the right to take countermeasures to persuade the wrongdoing state to fulfil its international obligations. These rights belong to each state as a result of its individual interest as a member of the international community in maintaining the order of that society, and they ought to remain unaffected if the state which is the main victim fails to take action or even waives the crime.

The first point which may be raised relates to the failure of the ILC to explain how the regime of responsibility for international crimes would vary according to the crime. This is presumably due in part to the uncertainties surrounding the question of which acts actually constitute state crimes. However, it is not clear whether an act of genocide, for example, will always entail more severe consequences than an act of massive pollution, or whether the consequences will depend on the particular circumstances of the case. It seems that a considerable amount of discretion is left to whichever body, whether legal or political, sits in judgement.

A related question is whether all states apart from the directly injured state are injured in the same manner by an international crime. Article 5(e) (subsequently Article 40, paragraph 3) does not explain what exactly constitutes an 'injury' in this context. Article 40 formulated the law relating to standing, but one of its weaknesses was that it appeared to tie the notion of obligations *erga omnes* to that of crimes, and could be said to cause the eclipse of the former notion. There may be borderline cases in which it is difficult to establish whether a wrongful act crosses the boundaries between bilateral relations, *erga omnes* breaches, and international crimes. Arangio-Ruiz made reference to 'general' *erga omnes* breaches which are not international crimes as if this were a settled category in international law from which special consequences flow.

The potential problems inherent in a lack of clear distinctions are demonstrated by the hostage-taking of American diplomatic and consular staff in Tehran in December 1979 and their subsequent detention until January 1981. The act led to widespread condemnation and the issue came before the General Assembly and Security Council. The US subsequently instituted judicial proceedings against Iran in the ICJ which described the act as contrary to international law and considered it 'to be its duty to draw the attention of the entire international community . . . to the irreparable harm that may be caused by events of the kind . . . before the Court'.[52] No mention was

---

[51] See Roukounas, (1985) *YrbkILC*, vol. 1, 140.
[52] *Case Concerning United States Diplomatic and Consular Staff in Tehran*, (1980) ICJ Reports 3, 43.

made either of international crimes or *erga omnes* violations. The US was clearly the directly injured state in this case, and urged its allies to join it in adopting sanctions against Iran. However, on 10 January 1980 the Soviet Union vetoed a Security Council draft resolution on collective sanctions against Iran by reference to the bilateral nature of the dispute.[53] Nevertheless, the nine member states of the EC decided independently that the continuance of the situation was likely to endanger international peace and security and adopted measures in conformity with the draft Security Council resolution.[54]

It was never decided whether the Iranian action had been a mere delict, or an *erga omnes* breach, or an international crime. The situation seemed to be treated at least as an *erga omnes* breach, although it would appear that certain states (particularly Western states) felt that they had suffered a greater injury than others. It is also unclear whether the indirectly injured states were acting on their own behalf, or whether they were assisting the directly injured state in enforcing its rights. In the Report of the ILC on the Work of its Forty-Eighth Session[55] it was suggested that the concept of 'injured state' should differentiate between directly and indirectly affected states, which would have different entitlements regarding the substantive and instrumental consequences of a crime.

A further difficulty which can also be illustrated by the Tehran hostage-taking relates to the *a contrario* implications of Draft Article 53. If it is assumed that the taking of hostages in this instance was not a crime, could other states have recognized the act as lawful? If the provisions of Article 53 are equally applicable to delicts, then they do not belong in a separate section on the consequences of international crimes.

Another problem is to determine the nature of the 'injury' to third states in cases of international crimes committed by a state within its own territory and against its own people. In the ILC Mr McCaffrey was of the opinion that an injury to the 'collectivity of humanity' was caused by such crimes.[56] The ILC failed to specify whether different consequences would be applicable in the situation where there is no directly injured state. Arguably, collective responses on the part of the international community in these instances would be vital. This raises the question whether resort to force unilaterally or collectively in order to obtain cessation of large-scale violations of human rights or to curb oppressive regimes committing grave violations of the principle of self-determination would be admissible. Arangio-Ruiz raised these issues in his Fifth Report,[57] but no express provisions appear in the 1996 Draft. In his Seventh Report he pointed out the danger of states' diverse per-

---

[53] (1980) *YrbkUN*, 309–11.

[54] See (1980) *Bulletin of the European Communities*, vol. 13, no. 4, 20–6.

[55] Topical summary of the discussion held in the Sixth Committee of the General Assembly during its fifty-first session prepared by the Secretariat, A/CN.4/479/Add.1, 1 May 1997, 11.

[56] (1985) *YrbkILC*, vol. 1, 97.   [57] A/CN.4/453/Add. 3, 7.

ceptions of an injury.[58] Certain states with highly developed systems for the protection of human rights and public opinion which is sensitive to violations by other states may be outraged by acts which other states consider to be minor or non-existent.

A final comment may be made in relation to the 'mild, non-penalistic character of the proposals'[59] put forward by the ILC. The ILC has so far avoided any punitive element when drawing up the consequences of international crimes. In fact, the 1996 Draft adds as a footnote to Article 40, paragraph 3:

The term 'crime' is used for consistency with article 19 of Part I of the articles. It was, however, noted that alternative phrases such as 'an international wrongful act of a serious nature' or 'an exceptionally serious wrongful act' could be substituted for the term 'crime', thus, *inter alia, avoiding the penal implication of the term.*[60]

The consequences of international crimes envisaged by the ILC amount neither to punishment nor to ordinary state responsibility but to something in between. Reference is made generally to 'remedial rights' and even punitive damages[61] barely receive a mention. The ILC has clearly found it problematic to agree on modalities for giving legal substance to the concept of state responsibility for international crimes, and its task has been made more onerous by the lukewarm response of many states to Draft Article 19.[62]

The problem faced by the ILC is that of dealing with an element of criminality within the remit of a draft on ordinary state responsibility. It is clearly difficult to give effect to the concept of state criminality within these boundaries, as the special regime which needs to be established does not fit easily into the structure of ordinary state responsibility. It seems that what is required is a real regime of criminal responsibility as advocated by Arangio-Ruiz if Article 19 is to be retained. Alternatively, the Draft Articles could reserve the possibility that such a regime will be established in the future. While on the one hand this approach could be criticized for evading the issue, it does have the advantage of allowing the concept of state criminality to evolve before a regime which may prove unsuitable is cast in stone. The option contained in the footnote to Draft Article 40 of drawing a new distinction between more and less serious wrongful acts would seem to be an attempt to bring crimes into the international arena via the back door and might result in analytical chaos. The option recommended by the current Special Rapporteur of deleting Articles 19 and 51 to 53 and reverting to a unitary regime of responsibility while elaborating upon the effects of violating *jus cogens* norms and obligations *erga omnes* is likely to have a similar

---

[58] A/CN.4/469, 20. [59] See Fifth Report . . . by Arangio-Ruiz, A/CN.4/453/Add. 2, 20.
[60] A/CN.4/L.524, 14 (emphasis added). [61] See further Chapter 14 below.
[62] See further Chapter 16 below, s. 5.

result and will necessarily reintroduce a binary regime.[63] As Abi-Saab has pointed out: 'By setting aside the "aggravated regime", the articulation of the unitary regime would thus take place in the absence of (or without taking into consideration) an important parameter, with the risk of developing a backward tilt.'[64]

6. THE LIMITATIONS OF PUNISHMENT

A number of the proposals by Donnedieu de Vabres and Pella for punishing a state are no longer feasible, as they collide with other principles of international law such as those embodied in the 1970 Friendly Relations Declaration,[65] unless the wrongdoing state is occupied following a situation of war. In formulating Part II of the Draft Articles on State Responsibility the ILC was conscious of the fact that the consequences of international crimes could not extend beyond prescribed limits. In Draft Article 16, presented in Special Rapporteur Arangio-Ruiz's Seventh Report on State Responsibility,[66] all consequences of international crimes were made subject to the preservation of a state's 'existence as an independent member of the international community and to the safeguarding of its territorial integrity and the vital needs of its people'. Clearly the punishment must be applied in accordance with international law, otherwise it will itself be an offence against international law, hence the importance of a centralized system for determining the existence and consequences of international crimes.[67] In other words, state responsibility for international crimes must comply with rule of law principles such as an insistence on equal subjection to the law, and the exercise of the law in accordance with certain standards of substantial and procedural justice especially when applied by political bodies.

7. CONCLUSION: PUNISHMENT, DETERRENCE, AND REINTEGRATION

The difficulties surrounding the question of punishment is one of the main sources of objection to the concept of state criminality. The tendency to overemphasize and dramatize this aspect has led to a lack of focus on the preventative side of the concept and its value in the realm of public opinion. In national law, when conduct is stigmatized as criminal, attitudes towards it

[63] First Report on State Responsibility by J. Crawford, Special Rapporteur, A/CN.4/490/Add.3, paras 100–1.
[64] G. Abi-Saab, 'The Uses of Article 19', (1999) *EJIL*, vol. 10, no. 2, 339, 351.
[65] GA Resolution 2625(XXV), 24 Oct. 1970.
[66] A/CN.4/469 and Add. 1; see Appendix 2 below.   [67] See further Chapter 15 below.

change, and equally, public opinion provides the drive to make certain acts criminal as we feel better protected when a criminal law is in place. The purpose of the concept of state criminality is to make it more difficult for states to engage in criminal conduct and still maintain credibility with their own populations or with other states. Many of the possible responses to acts qualifying as international crimes are essentially preventative in the sense that they are designed to halt the criminal act and prevent future similar acts. Where punishment is called for after the event, declaratory judgments and punitive damages,[68] combined with the prosecution of guilty individuals, would be appropriate, although alternative methods of punishing a state can also be envisaged.

If a state is accused of committing a 'crime', there is considerably more stigma attached than if it is accused of committing a 'very serious internationally wrongful act', and it cannot be denied that the word 'crime' has a certain symbolic, psychological value. As Weiler has remarked in relation to Draft Article 19: 'Try and imagine the reaction to a Draft Article which said something like: "Particularly serious wrongs affecting the international community as a whole may produce a different regime of responsibility".'[69] Ago also emphasized: 'When aggressive war and certain other violations of international law are called crimes, one only wishes to emphasize thereby, with regard to the state, the especially dangerous character of the delinquency.'[70] On this plane the question becomes purely terminological. However, it is unwise to be lax with terms like 'crime', and the penological issues raised by the use of the term cannot be ignored, even if the deterrent aspect is initially more significant than the retributive aspect.[71]

Roxburgh has suggested that a form of intervention which does not involve recourse to the use of force is 'by pressure of moral disapprobation'.[72] He argues that the 'adverse judgment of the family of nations does, in some cases and to a certain extent, deter or punish; but it is impossible to assess the strength of this elusive form of sanction'.[73] In his *Crime, Shame and Reintegration*,[74] Braithwaite describes a theory of 'reintegrative shaming' which he developed initially in relation to corporate crime. It is his contention that the nature of man is undermined by repressive social control with its stigmatic undertones which amplifies deviance by progressively casting the offender out. Braithwaite believes that the feeling of shame makes criminal behaviour unthinkable to most people, and he appeals for criminal justice

---

[68] See further Chapter 14 below.

[69] J. H. H. Weiler, 'On Prophets and Judges, Some Personal Reflections on State Responsibility and Crimes of State', in J. H. H. Weiler, A. Casesse, and M. Spinedi, (eds.), *International Crimes of State: A Critical Analysis of the ILC's Draft Article 19 on State Responsibility* (1989), 319, 323.   [70] (1971) *YrbkILC*, vol. 2, 184.

[71] See also the discussion of hierarchical terms in Chapter 6 above, s. 4.

[72] 'The Sanction of International Law', (1920) 14 *AJIL* 26, 31.   [73] Ibid.

[74] (1989).

practices which requalify guilty individuals as citizens, thereby paving the way for freely chosen compliance with legal rules. The theory is relevant to international law given the relative ease with which a state can become a pariah and the difficulty of subsequent reintegration into the international community. This is part of the legacy of the idealist school of international relations which inspired the League Covenant and distinguished 'civilized' international society from a class of renegades or outcasts.[75] An act must be recognized as criminal, and the actor must be stigmatized, in order for reintegrative shaming to occur, but forgiveness of, and repentance by, the actor is also essential in order to avoid disintegrative shaming and the furtherance of a threat to international stability. It is of course difficult to apply criminal theories to international relations, but it is important to recognize and interpret criminal responsibility as a reintegrative, rather than a disintegrative, concept.

[75] See Osiander, *The States System of Europe*, 293.

14
Punitive Damages in International Law

1. INTRODUCTION

The main legal consequence of state responsibility for a breach of international law is reparation for the material and moral harm caused. The principle of complete reparation was established in the *Chorzow Factory (Indemnity)* case:

reparation must, as far as possible, wipe out all the consequences of the illegal act and re-establish the situation which would, in all probability, have existed if that act had not been committed. Restitution in kind, or, if this is not possible, payment of a sum corresponding to the value which a restitution in kind would bear; the award, if need be, of damages for loss sustained which would not be covered by restitution in kind or payment in place of it—such are the principles which should serve to determine the amount of compensation due for an act contrary to international law.[1]

The question may be raised whether deviations from this premise are known to international law. In the ninth edition of Oppenheim's *International Law*, Jennings and Watts assert that the view according to which state responsibility for international wrongs is limited to such reparation as does not exceed the limits of restitution 'hardly accords either with principle or with practice'.[2] It is proposed to test this assertion with reference to the categories of damages known as 'moral', 'aggravated', 'exemplary', 'vindictive', and 'punitive' or 'penal'.

The term 'moral damage' refers to non-pecuniary losses which are often vague and difficult to quantify, and can result in the award of a very substantial sum of damages. These damages are normally included in the concept of complete reparation and sometimes overlap with aggravated damages. Aggravated damages are also compensatory in nature, as the emphasis is on the aggravated injury to the plaintiff caused by some aspect of the defendant's behaviour. The distinction between aggravated damages and exemplary damages, designed to punish a defendant, is not always clear. When the interests affected are incapable of precise monetary valuation it is not easy to identify at which point punishment of the defendant begins. The terms 'vindictive', 'punitive', and 'penal' damages are generally used interchangeably with 'exemplary' damages. All of these categories may involve awards of damages which appear to surpass the ceiling of compensation.

---

[1] (1928) PCIJ, Series A, No. 17, 47.

[2] R. Y. Jennings and A. Watts (eds.), Oppenheim's *International Law*, i: *Peace*, 9th edn. (1992), 533.

Although non-compensatory damages are not necessarily punitive in nature, the emphasis here will be on the possible punitive function of damages and on the question whether punitive damages are a distinct category. This punitive function is not only relevant to criminal acts, but the existing or potential link between punitive damages and international crimes will be explored in an attempt to demonstrate the usefulness of such a category of damages as a possible consequence of state crimes.

2. EARLY INTERNATIONAL CASE LAW

One of the earliest cases cited in support of punitive damages in international law is *Moke*, in which an award of $500 was made against Mexico 'to condemn the practice of forcing loans by the military'.[3] The tribunal claimed: 'If larger sums in damages, in such cases, were needed to vindicate the right of individuals to be exempt from such abuses, we would undoubtedly feel required to give them.'[4] *Janes'* case[5] has sometimes been put forward as an example of an award of punitive damages,[6] and represents a category of cases in which the state has failed to prevent or punish crimes against aliens under domestic law. In this case the US was awarded $12,000 on account of the failure by the Mexican authorities to apprehend the murderer of Janes. The tribunal cited a number of arbitral awards which, in allowing damages for the failure by a state to punish crimes, made reasonable and substantial redress for the mistrust and insecurity resulting from the state's attitude in these circumstances.

This aspect of the case indicates that the international claim had a wider bearing than damages for the wounded feelings of Janes' relatives. Borchard[7] refers to the 'inarticulate purpose' of the damages awarded, which Brierly[8] articulates as being 'penal'. Freeman[9] agrees that the award in *Janes'* case is unwarranted on the basis of an assessment of damages for personal loss, and that a sounder justification must be sought for it. He believes it is justifiable as a 'punishment for the maintenance of an inadequate governmental system and an admonition that the delinquent state had better mend its ways lest it be subjected to similar future demands'.[10] However, the tribunal in *Janes'* case did not consider itself to be advancing a doctrine of punitive damages

---

[3] J. B. Moore, *History and Digest of the International Arbitrations to which the United States has been a Party* (1898), iv. 3411.   [4] Ibid.

[5] (1925–1926) 3 *Annual Digest*, 256; (1927) 21 *AJIL* 362.

[6] See Jennings and Watts, Oppenheim's *International Law*, i: *Peace*, 533, n. 3.

[7] E. M. Borchard, 'Important Decisions of the Mixed Claims Commission: United States and Mexico', (1927) 21 *AJIL* 516, 518.

[8] J. L. Brierly, 'The Theory of Implied State Complicity in International Claims', (1928) 9 *BYIL* 49.

[9] A. V. Freeeman, *The International Responsibility of States for Denial of Justice* (1938), 613–15.   [10] Ibid. 613.

and the punitive nature of awards in cases such as this can only be inferred. In the opinion of the majority in *Janes'* case the theory of implied state complicity in the act of the individual criminal was rejected, and an attempt was made to separate in principle the individual's crime from the state's delinquency. The state was responsible only for the damage caused as a result of its failure to punish the murderer, and not for the murder itself. The tribunal anticipated the objection that if in a case of non-punishment a state was not liable for the crime itself, it ought only to be held liable 'in a punitive way'[11] to another state rather than to an individual claimant.

Thus, three different types of damage were under consideration. First, the damage caused by the delinquent state to the relatives of the victim; second, the damage caused by the killing itself; and finally, the damage caused to the national honour and feeling of the state of which the victim was a national. In the result the whole award was stated to be 'satisfaction for the personal damage caused the claimants by the non-apprehension and non-punishment of the murderer of Janes'.[12] The fact that the claimants had in reality suffered no substantial damage from the state's delinquency as such seems to be the main justification for regarding the award as punitive,[13] although the distinctions drawn by the tribunal are somewhat artificial, as it is likely that the gravity of the original offence was an influential factor in determining the sum payable.

The award recommended in the *I'm Alone* case[14] is another instance of pecuniary redress unrelated to the damage caused which has been regarded as punitive.[15] In addition to apologizing to the Canadian Government, the US was obliged to pay $25,000 as a 'material amend'[16] in respect of the unlawful sinking of a Canadian ship. [17] The compensation was related to the indignity suffered by Canada and not to the value of the ship or its cargo. Shawcross states that the decision of the Joint Commission in this case supports the idea that a state can be bound to pay what are in effect penal demands.[18] Nonetheless, the award could also be regarded as pecuniary satisfaction for the political and moral harm caused.

There are a number of cases in which international tribunals have held that punitive damages cannot be awarded against states, but it is noteworthy that

---

[11] (1927) 21 *AJIL* 362, 369.   [12] Ibid. 370.
[13] See H. Lauterpacht, 'Règles générales du droit de la paix', (1937-IV) 62 Hague *Recueil* 99, 356.
[14] (1933–4) 7 *Annual Digest*, 203.
[15] See Jennings and Watts, Oppenheim's *International Law*, i: *Peace*, 533; C. Parry, 'Some Considerations Upon the Protection of Individuals in International Law', (1956-II) 90 Hague *Recueil* 653, 694.   [16] (1933–4) 7 *Annual Digest*, 206.
[17] See C. C. Hyde, 'The Adjustment of the I'm Alone Case', (1935) 29 *AJIL* 296, 300, for possible reasons why this case is not a precedent for the award of punitive damages against a state.
[18] See *Trial of German Major War Criminals: Opening Speeches of the Chief Prosecutors* (1946), 57; also referred to in Q. Wright, 'The Law of the Nuremberg Trial', (1947) 41 *AJIL* 38, 64–5, n. 108.

in most of these decisions the tribunals were guided in the matter by the terms of an arbitration agreement. The most famous of these is the *Lusitania* case,[19] in which the tribunal claimed: 'The words "exemplary", "vindictive" or "punitive" as applied to damages were misnomers. The fundamental concept of "damages" is satisfaction, reparation for a loss suffered; a judicially ascertained compensation for a wrong.' The tribunal went on to say that apart from the absence of precedent[20] it lacked the power to award such damages under the terms of its Charter—the Treaty of Berlin. Moreover, Umpire Parker argued that 'as between sovereign nations the question of the right and power to impose penalties, unlimited in amount, is political rather than legal in its nature'. These words imply that he did not rule out the possibility of applying a penalty against a state altogether, but that this was a political rather than a legal question. In the *Naulilaa* case, in which Portugal claimed punitive damages for 'violations of Portuguese sovereignty and offences against international law' committed by Germany, it was held that the contracting parties, in charging the Tribunal with fixing the amount of damages, did not intend to endow it with the right to inflict punishment, and that this was borne out by the part of the Versailles Treaty under which the Tribunal was acting.[21] Lack of competence was probably also the reason for not allowing punitive damages in the *Miliani*,[22] *Stevenson*,[23] and *Carthage*[24] cases. A consideration of these cases caused Eagleton to conclude:

While it is true that few arbitral tribunals have avowedly awarded punitive damages, it is to be observed that, on the one hand, none of them go as far as to deny the right, under international law, to award such damages. Where they have explicitly rejected damages of this type it has been for reasons other than their illegality.[25]

Cheng takes the view that even though international tribunals have not suggested that punitive damages can never be allowed, their lack of jurisdiction to award them 'proceeds directly from the premise that the question of punitive damages is not a justiciable issue' and 'does not fall within the legal notion of responsibility'.[26] If punitive damages can only be awarded where they are expressly permitted by the *compromis*, then they will not be an issue in most cases.

The reluctance to impose punitive damages seems to have been less apparent in diplomatic practice contemporaneous with the cases just cited. An example is the case of Lt. Cooper, who was killed while capturing a slave ship off Zanzibar, and two of his seamen, who were wounded in the operation.

[19] (1923–4) 2 *Annual Digest*, 209.
[20] *Moke's* case was rejected as a precedent by Judge Parker even though the average award in similar cases was $100. See C. Eagleton, 'Measure of Damages in International Law', (1929–30) 39 *Yale Law Journal* 52, 62, n. 26.   [21] (1929–30) 5 *Annual Digest*, 200, 202.
[22] *RIAA*, vol. 10, 591.   [23] Ibid. vol. 9, 506.   [24] Ibid. vol. 11, 460–1.
[25] Eagleton 'Measure of Damages in International Law', 61–2.
[26] B. Cheng, *General Principles of Law as Applied by International Courts and Tribunals* (1953, repr. 1993), 235.

The victims were British subjects. The Sultan of Zanzibar was unsuccessful in securing the arrest of the assailants who had fled first to Pemba and then to the mainland, whereupon the British Government requested the Sultan to collect a 'fine' of $10,000 from the Arabs of Pemba, who allegedly assisted the assailants in their escape.[27] The fine was solely punitive in nature, as no mention appeared to be made of any dependants of the deceased nor of what was to be done with the money. The punishment appeared to be directed against the Arabs of Pemba collectively, although it was the Sultan's duty to ensure that the fine was paid, which he duly did. Following an incident of a US missionary who was murdered by a mob in Canton province, an extra indemnity of 50,000 taels was asked for the relatives of the deceased as 'exemplary damages to which China, by the failure of her officials to prevent this outrage, has made herself liable'.[28] The killing in 1923 of General Tellini, an Italian officer commissioned by the Conference of Ambassadors to assist in the delimitation of the frontier between Greece and Albania, resulted in the demand for the payment of L50,000,000 by Greece to the Italian Government.[29] These cases may be indicative of the attitude of stronger states towards weaker ones, but there does seem to be a serious intention to exact a penalty.[30] In this context, mention may also be made of the decision of the Council of the League of Nations of 14 December 1925 awarding 10,000,000 levas to Bulgaria as reparation for material and moral damage caused by Greece, in addition to compensation for damage to moveable property.[31]

The early cases and practice supportive of punitive damages are relevant for three principal reasons. First, they are still quoted in the ninth edition of Oppenheim's *International Law* in support of the editors' thesis, and no subsequent cases are mentioned. Second, they provide some evidence that there are various degrees of state delinquency which are possibly to be taken into account in arriving at a sum of damages.[32] As Whiteman has commented:

At times, the excess in the amount of damages awarded over the actual loss or injury may . . . be accounted for in part by the fact that the . . . persons making the award were influenced by the seriousness of the part taken by the respondent state in the incident out of which the claim arose. Such damages might well be considered punitive in their nature, although they are not so denominated.[33]

---

[27] (1888–9) 81 *British and Foreign State Papers*, 170, 175, 177 and 178; see also M. M. Whiteman, *Damages in International Law* (1937), i. 724.

[28] (1906) *Foreign Relations of the United States*, 319; see also Whiteman, *Damages in International Law*, 729.

[29] Referred to in Second Report on State Responsibility by G. Arangio-Ruiz, Special Rapporteur, (1989) *YrbkILC*, vol. 2, pt. 1, 37–8.

[30] For further examples of this type see Whiteman, *Damages in International Law*, 722–33.

[31] (1926) 7 *LNOJ* 172.   [32] See Freeman, *International Responsibility*, 615.

[33] Whiteman, *Damages in International Law*, 628.

Third, the early cases highlighted the debate over whether compensation contained, or could contain, an element of punishment which was useful for its retributory and deterrent value. Brierly asserts that any attempt to exclude this notion 'would either be instinctively defeated by the action of arbitral tribunals, and in that case would only introduce an unreality into the theory of the law, or it would defeat its own purpose by denying a legitimate satisfaction to complainant states, and thus discouraging the submission of claims to arbitral settlement'.[34]

3. PUNITIVE DAMAGES IN CASES OF INTERNATIONAL CRIMES AND HUMAN RIGHTS VIOLATIONS

The examples given so far have not concerned the most serious internationally wrongful acts and have related largely to domestic crimes against foreigners. If punitive damages are an issue in these cases, then it is to be expected that they have a significant role to play, for example, with respect to international crimes and human rights violations generally. However, international jurisprudence fails to substantiate this claim. The *Corfu Channel* case[35] dealt with the question of compensation for unlawful killings for which Albania was responsible. In the Security Council, Sir Alexander Cadogan described Albania's mining of the Corfu Channel as an 'international crime'.[36] The Australian representative characterized the act as an 'international crime of the most serious sort', and as amounting 'in substance to something very much of the character of mass murder'.[37] On 25 March 1947, seven members of the Security Council voted in favour of a British draft resolution which declared that the laying of mines in peacetime without notification was 'unjustified and an offence against humanity'.[38] The Australian member argued that when there had been a crime against humanity the Security Council should make a recommendation so that the crime would be punished.[39] The resolution was vetoed by the Soviet Union and the dispute was subsequently referred to the ICJ. In the UK Memorial, the Albanian action was described as an 'international delinquency' and an 'offence against humanity which most seriously *aggravates* the breach of international law and the international delinquency committed by that state'.[40] When the case came before the Court, it was found that Albania was liable for the consequences, which included unlawful killings, of the laying of mines in its territorial waters, and for failing to warn of the danger:

These grave omissions involve the international responsibility of Albania. The Court therefore reaches the conclusion that Albania is responsible under international law

---

[34] 'Implied State Complicity', 49.   [35] (1949) ICJ Reports 4.   [36] 18 Feb. 1947.
[37] 24 Feb. 1947.   [38] (1946–7) *Yrbk UN*, 393.   [39] Ibid.
[40] ICJ Pleadings, Oral Arguments, Documents, (1949), UK Memorial, 19, 40 (emphasis added).

for the explosions which occurred ... and for the damage and loss of human life which resulted from them, and that there is a duty upon Albania to pay compensation to the United Kingdom.[41]

Despite the references to an 'aggravated breach' of international law, in this case it seems that the 'crime against humanity' was treated like any other wrongful act by the ICJ. There was no attempt to link the award of damages with responsibility for the commission of an international crime, even though the jurisdiction of the Court extends to determining 'the nature or extent of the reparation to be made for the breach of an international obligation'.[42]

The *Velasquez Rodriguez* case involved extremely serious violations of human rights, and yet the Inter-American Court of Human Rights refused to award punitive damages against Honduras, claiming that such a principle was not applicable in international law at the time of the decision in 1989.[43] Although the reference here is to international law, the general approach of the Inter-American Court is based on its interpretation of Article 63(1) of its Statute, which refers to the award of 'fair compensation'. In the Court's view this implies that damages should be compensatory. It should nevertheless be noted that the Inter-American Commission on Human Rights has invited the Court to consider granting punitive damages.[44] The approach of the Inter-American Court was followed in the case of *Re Letelier and Moffit* concerning the murder of a former Foreign Minister of Chile and another person in Washington, allegedly at the hands of Chilean agents. In this case the Government of Chile did not admit responsibility but agreed to make an *ex gratia* payment equal to the amount due if liability were established. The award of the Chile–US International Commission was not punitive, perhaps in part because it took account of Chile's efforts to remedy human rights problems and its willingness to compensate the families of victims. In his Separate Concurring Opinion, Commissioner Orrego Vicuña

reiterated that international law has not accepted as one of its principles the concept of punitive damages. While this type of damage has not been claimed in the instance, the issue is whether a claim of an excessive or disproportionate amount of compensation can result in a similar effect, that is in the punishment or repression of the defendant state. The Commissioner undersigned is of the opinion that this would be very much the case irrespectively of the claim being labelled punitive or not. It follows that a claim involving this result would be entirely unwarranted and contrary to the principles of international law.[45]

---

[41] (1949) ICJ Reports 4, 23.

[42] Article 36(2)(d), Statute of the International Court of Justice. See Eagleton, 'Measures of Damages', 64, who argues that the same provision in the Statute of the Permanent Court of International Justice empowers the Court to assess penal damages.

[43] (1989) 95 ILR 233, 315.

[44] See S. Davidson, *The Inter-American Human Rights System* (1997), 217.

[45] (1992) 88 ILR 727, 741.

A US court had initially awarded \$2,000,000 in punitive damages against Chile[46] in an action brought by members of the Letelier and Moffit families, and while this occurred under domestic law the court mentioned that the 'tortious actions' proven were 'in violation of international law'.[47] This judgment was not satisfied, but it is evidence of the seriousness of the violations of international law under consideration and of the desire to punish the responsible state. In the determination under international law any notion of punishment was seemingly excluded, although it was not done so expressly in the judgment of the Commission. The award amounted to a settlement of all outstanding claims against Chile.

In *Filartiga v Pena-Irala*[48] a US court considered a case between two Paraguayan citizens concerning the international crime of torture. Despite the fact that this was a domestic case, involving the responsibility of an individual, the court considered the question of punitive damages in international law, and cited a number of cases which provided 'some precedent for the award of punitive damages in tort even against a national government'.[49] The court argued that 'the objective of the international law making torture punishable as a crime can only be vindicated by imposing punitive damages',[50] and felt that it was completely justified in imposing them where the defendant was an individual as there were no obstacles posed by diplomatic considerations. In assessing the quantum of punitive damages the court felt that the nature of the act was important, which in this case consisted of 'the ultimate in human cruelty and barbarity'.[51] In addition, the fact that the act was not a 'local tort' but an international wrong was a chief consideration. The court decided to award punitive damages of \$5,000,000 to each plaintiff 'to reflect adherence to the world community's proscription of torture and to attempt to deter its practice'.[52] It was not necessary to determine whether punitive damages could have been awarded if the defendant had been Paraguay itself, but the court seemed open to the possibility in its conclusion that 'it is essential and proper to grant the remedy of punitive damages in order to give effect to the manifest objectives of the international prohibition against torture'.[53]

In diplomatic practice large amounts of damages have sometimes been awarded in situations involving the commission of international crimes, but there is no pattern which suggests that these awards are punitive in nature.

---

[46] (1992) 88 ILR 747–8.
[47] *De Letelier v Republic of Chile*, 502 F. Supp. 259 (DDC 1980), 266.
[48] (1984) 77 ILR 185.   [49] Ibid. 189.   [50] Ibid. 188.
[51] Ibid. 190.   [52] Ibid. 191.
[53] Ibid. 189. However, the Foreign Sovereign Immunities Act excludes punitive damages against a state, although it allows them against an agency or instrumentality of the foreign state. See *Restatement of the Law Third: The Foreign Relations Law of the United States*, ii (1987), § 901, 345.

The *Rainbow Warrior* affair[54] of 1985, in which France was required to pay a sum of $7,000,000 in compensation to New Zealand for the 'criminal outrage'[55] committed on its territory, is perhaps the best example.[56]

In cases of aggression, which is considered to be the gravest of international offences, the Security Council has played a role in attempting to secure compensation payments, but it is difficult to discern any punitive intention. The first such demand by the Security Council occurred in 1964 as part of its condemnation of Vietnam's invasion of Cambodia.[57] When Israel bombed an Iraqi nuclear reactor in 1981, the Security Council felt that Iraq was entitled to appropriate redress.[58] The Compensation Commission[59] established after the 1991 Gulf crisis allowed claims to be made for moral damage. Given the nature of the wrongful acts under consideration, the sums awarded in respect of moral damage could potentially be very high, but claims expressly for punitive damages do not seem to have been made. Although the overall result may have involved the punishment of Iraq, it is probable that the individual claims have been of a compensatory and not a punitive character, and reflect the fact that out of a limited fund, compensation must come first. The demands for compensation following the Gulf crisis can be compared to the requirement after the Second World War that Germany pay billions of German marks to Israel by way of atonement for the Nazi persecution of Jews, which is more obviously a punitive demand.

4. PUNITIVE DAMAGES IN THE EUROPEAN COURT OF JUSTICE AND THE EUROPEAN COURT OF HUMAN RIGHTS

The issue of punitive damages does not appear to have been considered in the European Court of Justice, but there is a possibility that member states could be required to allow such damages in their national courts in order to ensure the effective implementation of certain directives. This possibility arises from the *Von Colson* case[60] in which the European Court was asked whether Article 6 of the equal treatment directive required member states to lay down special sanctions or other legal consequences in cases of discrimination which breached the directive. The case concerned two female social workers who applied for posts in a male prison and were rejected because of the problems and risks said to be associated with the appointment of female candidates. The positions were filled by less qualified male candidates.

The national court accepted that sex discrimination had occurred but was

---

[54] 74 ILR 241.

[55] Letter of 8 Aug. 1985 from the President of France to the Prime Minister of New Zealand, ibid. 263.   [56] See further Chapter 16 below, s. 4(a).

[57] (1964) *Yrbk UN*, 145.   [58] Resolution 487, 19 June 1981.

[59] See further Chapter 16 below, s. 2.   [60] Case 14/83, [1984] ECR 1891.

of the opinion that under German law only nominal damages were available. The European Court, on the other hand, emphasized that an appropriate system of sanctions was necessary to ensure equal opportunities for men and women. The directive did not stipulate which particular type of sanction should be adopted but the Court insisted that the chosen sanction should exert a real deterrent effect on employers. Thus, if a member state chose to 'penalize'[61] breaches of the principle of equal treatment by an award of compensation, any such award had to represent adequate recompense for the injury suffered 'in order to ensure that it is effective and that it has a deterrent effect'.[62] It was therefore recognized by the Court that where it was chosen to provide a sanction for a breach of a fundamental principle of the Treaty of the European Union by an award of damages, the damages must have a broader deterrent and regulatory function. The purpose of the damages would be to seek to alter behaviour rather than to compensate for past misconduct.

This future-oriented approach is consistent with the notion of punitive damages, although the damages are to be awarded by the national court as part of its effective implementation of the directive rather than by the European Court itself. It was stressed by the Court that the establishment of an employment relationship was of such pivotal importance to an individual that it required employers to treat applicants with great care. The *Arbeitsgericht*, Hamm, finally awarded the plaintiffs damages of six gross monthly salary payments amounting to a sum of DM 21,000.[63]

In European competition law it is generally accepted that the huge fines imposed on companies for violating competition law are penal in nature, and it has been argued that their imposition should be accompanied by the procedural guarantees of Article 6 of the 1950 European Convention for the Protection of Human Rights and Fundamental Freedoms.[64] Stessen predicts that the European Commission will in the future extend the application of these administrative fines to other areas of European law.[65]

European human rights law is surprisingly silent on the question of punitive damages, even though the European Convention on Human Rights prohibits acts such as slavery, forced labour, torture, unlawful detention, and discrimination which often amount to criminal acts deserving of punishment. Article 50 of the Convention provides that if the European Court of Human Rights

---

[61] Case 14/83, [1984] ECR 1892.   [62] Ibid.

[63] Cf. *Marshall v Southampton & South West Area Health Authority*, where the emphasis was on the 'adequacy' of financial compensation in the sense that 'it must enable the loss and damage actually sustained as a result of the discriminatory dismissal to be made good in full in accordance with the applicable national rules': [1993] 3 CMLR 293, 324.

[64] See G. Stessens, 'Corporate Criminal Liability: A Comparative Perspective', (1994) 43 *ICLQ* 493, 505–6 and the materials cited in n. 55.   [65] Ibid. 506.

finds that a decision or a measure taken by a legal authority or any other authority of a High Contracting Party is completely or partially in conflict with the obligations arising from the . . . Convention, and if the internal law of the said Party allows only partial reparation to be made for the consequences of this decision or measure, the decision of the Court shall, if necessary, afford just satisfaction to the injured party.

The question whether Article 50 allows punitive damages to be awarded has not been addressed directly. In the case of *B v United Kingdom*,[66] the applicant claimed exemplary and aggravated, but unquantified, damages[67] under Article 50 for violations of Articles 6(1) and 8 of the Convention concerning the right to respect for family life, which resulted in the loss of her child by adoption, and mental anguish. The European Court of Human Rights awarded £12,000 for non-pecuniary damage in respect of lost opportunities and distress. The issue of exemplary damages was not raised and an assessment was made on an equitable basis. The sum awarded was somewhat higher than the £5000 which the UK argued should be the upper limit but this is not, perhaps, significant. In *Zander v Sweden*[68] the applicants claimed kr250,000 for non-pecuniary damage with respect to distress caused as a result of drinking polluted water. The Court awarded them kr30,000 each, which, it has been argued,[69] is a lot more than had been awarded in similar cases, but again, this provides very equivocal support for the notion of punitive damages. The European Court of Human Rights has awarded varying amounts of damages for non-pecuniary loss, making its assessment on an equitable basis, but it is difficult to discern a pattern which suggests any punitive intention.

5. PUNITIVE DAMAGES IN NATIONAL LAW

Common law systems have a tradition of allowing exemplary or punitive damages which constitute a penal surcharge upon compensatory damages. Their primary function is to punish the wrongdoer, but they may also be used to draw off the profits of the tort. Punitive damages may only be awarded in the context of humiliating or outrageous circumstances surrounding the tort inflicted upon the victim. This prerequisite is most obviously satisfied if the wrongdoer acted with malice or intent in disregarding the victim's rights. An award of punitive damages is not limited to specific injuries but is more likely where the victim suffers a grievous affront, as in cases of personal attack,

---

[66] European Court of Human Rights (1988), Series A, No. 136D, 29.

[67] In the case of *W v UK*, (1988) 92 ILR 212, which related to similar facts, the applicant claimed damages of at least £100,000.

[68] European Court of Human Rights (1994), Series A, No. 279B, 41–2.

[69] See D. J. Harris, M. O'Boyle, and C. Warbrick, *Law of the European Convention on Human Rights* (1995), 687, n. 6.

false imprisonment, or defamation. The sum awarded generally reflects the gravity of the wrongful act, and punitive damages are most easily justified where the wrongful act constitutes a crime which might be ignored by the criminal justice system. In the US, punitive damages are frequently awarded in cases of personal injury caused deliberately or by conscious recklessness. In the Philippines, exemplary damages have received a statutory formulation in the 1949 Civil Code, and may be awarded as a consequence of civil liability generally for all criminal offences if the act was committed under 'one or more aggravating circumstances'.[70]

Whereas the institution of punitive damages is prevalent in the US, in England it has been curtailed. In the case of *Rookes v Barnard*[71] the House of Lords held that exemplary damages should be awarded exclusively in cases of arbitrary excess of state authority or in cases involving a wrongdoer's willingness to assume the risk of liability in view of the prospect of benefits exceeding the loss. It added that the remedy of exemplary damages should be invoked only if the award of compensatory damages would not provide an adequate sanction for the wrongful act. This decision has been criticized for putting exemplary damages 'in a straitjacket',[72] and has not been followed in Australia,[73] New Zealand,[74] or Canada.[75] In Singapore and Malaysia the English principles of aggravated and exemplary or punitive damages are applicable.[76]

A survey of personal injury awards in EU and EFTA countries has shown that damages which punish the defendant for his actions rather than compensating the injured party for his actual loss are rarely awarded in the civil courts of those countries.[77] The rule in France is: 'Les dommages-intérêts doivent être à la mesure des préjudices réellement subis, sans en surajouter pour punir le responsable fautif: il faut strictement limiter le rôle punitif aux amendes pénales.'[78] Nonetheless, there is some evidence outside the common law of a preparedness to give higher awards of damages where the defendant has inflicted the harm intentionally or recklessly, although this can generally be explained as moral damages. The policy in Norway is that damages for pain and suffering are not permitted in personal injury cases except where the tortfeasor has acted intentionally or recklessly, and the approach in the

---

[70] Article 2230. See H. Stoll, 'Consequences of Liability: Remedies', *Int. Enc. Comp. L* (1986), vol. XI/2, *Torts*, ch. 8, s. 113, 106.   [71] [1964] AC 1129.

[72] *Broome v Cassell & Co. Ltd.*, [1971] 2 WLR 853, 876, *per* Salmon LJ.

[73] See *Uren v John Fairfax and Sons Pty. Ltd.*, (1966) 117 CLR 118.

[74] See *Fogg v McKnight*, [1968] NZLR 330.

[75] See *McElroy v Cowper-Smith and Woodman*, (1967) 62 DLR (2d) 65.

[76] See M. F. Rutter, *Handbook on Damages for Personal Injuries and Death in Singapore and Malaysia* (1988), 40.

[77] D. McIntosh and M. Holmes (eds.), *Personal Injury Awards in EU and EFTA Countries: An Industry Report*, 2nd edn. (1994), 97.

[78] Y. Lambert-Faivre, *Droit du dommage corporel: systèmes d'indemnisation*, 3rd edn. (1996), 161.

Netherlands is similar.[79] In contrast, awards for moral damage in personal injury cases in Sweden are generally unaffected by the intention of the tortfeasor.[80] Italy seems to have taken steps towards basing compensation for 'dommage moral' or non-pecuniary loss upon a criterion of punishment, and in Switzerland there are numerous decisions in which the award for non-pecuniary loss explicitly reflects the degree of fault of the tortfeasor.[81] The German approach is essentially the same.[82] In 1955 the Grosse Zivilsenat des Bundesgerichtshofs established that damages for the non-pecuniary loss of a physically injured person were intended to perform two distinct functions. One of these was the *Genugtuungsfunktion*, which sought to give the victim the sense of satisfaction that the wrongdoer had been made to pay for his misdeeds, and was only compensation in the sense that a person may suffer less if he knows that the person responsible for his loss has paid for it. In assessing the part played by this function in an award, the foremost consideration was the extent of the 'injury to life' and a relevant factor was the degree of the tortfeasor's fault.

The Italian interest in the idea of imposing the obligation to pay damages on a tortfeasor as a form of punishment has been influential in South America,[83] and in South Africa the English principles of aggravated and exemplary damages have had a considerable influence.[84] In Senegal, moral damages may serve a punitive, rather than a strictly compensatory, function:

il n'est pas sûr que l'indemnisation du préjudice moral soit une véritable réparation. Il s'agit bien plutôt d'une sanction de la faute de l'auteur du dommage—sanction dont le montant pourra parfois être symbolique . . . ou, dans d'autre cas, proportionné au profit que l'auteur du dommage en a retiré . . . On est ici dans un des ces cas où la responsabilité civile n'est pas si éloignée de la reponsabilité pénale, où elle tend moins à réparer qu'à sanctionner par le moyen d'une peine privée. . . .[85]

In Japanese law relating to product liability, a manufacturer who is at serious fault may be liable for punitive damages up to a maximum of twice the amount of ordinary damages.[86] Damages which serve a punitive function have consequently received some recognition even outside the common law, and such damages may come into play when the combination of a significant degree of fault on the part of the wrongdoer and great damage caused to the victim aggravates the ordinary tort.

It does not seem that the notion of punitive damages has so far been regarded as a general principle of law which has a role to play in interstate

---

[79] See H. McGregor, 'Personal Injury and Death', *Int. Enc. Comp. L* (1986), vol. XI/2, *Torts*, ch. 9, s. 11, 6.   [80] Ibid. n. 24.

[81] Ibid. ss. 11–12, 7.   [82] Ibid. s. 13, 8.   [83] Ibid. s. 11, 7.

[84] See P. J. Visser, and J. M. Potgieter, *Law of Damages* (1993), 156.

[85] J.-P. Tosi, *Le Droit des obligations au Sénégal* (1981), 221.

[86] See H. Oda, *Japanese Law* (1992), 231.

relations.[87] In national law, damages which either explicitly or implicitly serve a punitive function are occasionally used to fill in a gap by ensuring that those who are deserving of punishment, because of some feature which aggravates the seriousness of their torts, do not escape punishment. In international law, where states are not subject to a criminal justice system, and where there is consequently a larger gap to be filled than in domestic law, acceptance of the principle of punitive damages could serve a useful function in giving international tribunals another tool with which to attempt to do justice. The suggestion of Jennings and Watts that the rejection of punitive damages does not accord with principle perhaps derives from national law analogies which are no longer overshadowed in international law by the doctrine of sovereignty.

6. THE DIFFICULTY IN DRAWING DISTINCTIONS BETWEEN PUNITIVE AND COMPENSATORY DAMAGES

In English law the distinction between aggravated damages considered to be compensatory and exemplary damages is not always clear. As Lord Devlin observed in *Rookes v Barnard*,[88] it is possible to

take into account the motives and conduct of the defendant where they aggravate the injury caused to the plaintiff . . . Indeed, when one examines the cases in which large damages have been awarded for conduct of this sort, it is not at all easy to say whether the idea of compensation or the idea of punishment has prevailed.[89]

Lord Atkin had previously remarked: 'The punitive element is not something which is or can be added to some known factor which is not punitive.'[90] In the US, in contrast, punitive damages are usually awarded as a discrete sum.

Many of the early cases which caused debate over punitive damages in international law concerned the responsibility of a state to pay damages to another member of the international community for its failure effectively to apprehend, prosecute, and punish criminals who had victimized foreign nationals. Despite the fact that none of the tribunals in these cases spoke of punitive damages, most commentators at the time agreed that the idea of punishment could be part of the concept of

---

[87] However, it has been pointed out that 'The expansion of the scope of arbitral claims has generated marked debate in the international community over the question of whether arbitral tribunals should have the authority to award punitive damages': J. Y. Gotanda, 'Awarding Punitive Damages in International Commercial Arbitrations in the Wake of *Mastrobuono v Shearson Lehman Hutton, Inc*', (1997) *Harvard International Law Journal*, vol. 38, no. 1, 59, 60. In *Mastrobuono v Shearson Lehman Hutton, Inc*, 115 S Ct 1212 (1995), the United States Supreme Court held that an arbitrator could award punitive damages if the arbitration clause gave explicit or implicit authorization or was ambiguous.   [88] [1964] AC 1129.

[89] Ibid. 1221.   [90] *Ley v Hamilton*, (1935) 153 LT 384, 386 (HL).

damages.[91] These cases related to a public interest in the repression of crime in general, in addition to a private interest, and it was probably hoped that large awards of damages would have a deterrent effect and result in an eventual improvement in the security of aliens, which is in the interests of the international community generally. However, it should be stressed that this purpose can only be inferred, as there was never an express attempt to separate punishment from restitution, and although the principle seemed to be that the state's delinquency was a separate issue from the individual's crime, the award of damages often corresponded to the seriousness of the original offence.

In more recent cases the question of punitive damages has arisen in the context of human rights and a state's involvement in unlawful killings. The tribunals in these instances have recognized that punitive damages should be considered separately from compensation as generally understood, but have not felt they have the authority under international law to award them. This is tantamount to saying that if international law did allow punitive damages they might be willing to award them in cases such as these as no other reason for disallowing them is supplied, which raises the question of which elements are in reality taken into account in assessing damages. It is often difficult to draw a line between damages designed to punish the wrongdoing state, and purely compensatory damages which nevertheless reflect the state's degree of misconduct. In this regard, a certain quantum of the damages or the entire sum awarded in a given case may be designed to cater for various forms of non-pecuniary loss or moral damage, but the purpose is still compensatory. A large award of damages in a situation involving an international crime could be justified simply on the basis that it takes more to remedy the consequences of such an act. In the *Roberts* case[92] Mexico was required to pay $8000 to the US for the illegal imprisonment of Roberts for a period of seven months. A considerable part of the damages awarded related to the subjection of Roberts to cruel and degrading treatment during the period of imprisonment. These elements in an award of damages were raised in the *Lusitania* case, where the Tribunal confirmed:

That one injured is, under the rules of international law, entitled to be compensated for an injury inflicted resulting in mental suffering, injury to his feelings, humiliation, shame, degradation, loss of social position or injury to his credit or to his reputation, there can be no doubt . . . Such damages are very real, and the mere fact that they are difficult to measure or estimate by money standards makes them none the less real and affords no reason why the injured person should not be compensated therefor as compensatory damages, but not as a penalty.[93]

---

[91] See e.g. Brierly, 'Implied State Complicity', and F. S. Dunn, *The Protection of Nationals* (1932), 186, who argues that 'the fixing of damages in such cases seems at bottom to be largely prophylactic in nature'. [92] (1926) 4 *RIAA* 77.

[93] (1923–4) 2 *Annual Digest*, 209.

Hersch Lauterpacht states that 'la réparation morale contient un élément distinct de châtiment',[94] and there is evidence to support the contention that there is sometimes an overlap between moral damages and punitive damages. But the fact that an award of damages often involves a considerable discretionary element does not mean that this is primarily of a punitive character. Whether an award is 90 per cent remedial and 10 per cent punitive may be irrelevant so long as the victim receives reasonable reparation for the injuries and losses suffered. If the temptation to extract the punitive element from such awards is resistible, then perhaps the term 'punitive damages' is redundant. However, Commissioner Vicuña in *Re Letelier and Moffit* warned that an award of a disproportionate amount of compensation will result in the punishment of the defendant state regardless of whether or not it is labelled punitive. It may be questioned how it is possible to 'wipe out the consequences' of a particularly serious act, especially if it constitutes a crime, while awarding neither a substantial sum of moral damages, which could involve some punitive element, nor a discrete sum of punitive damages.

7. DOCTRINE

In the first four editions of Oppenheim's *International Law* the doctrine of sovereignty is raised as the main objection against the imposition of punitive damages:

The nature of the Law of Nations as a law between, not above, sovereign states, excludes the possibility of punishing a state for an international delinquency and of considering the latter in the light of a crime . . . The only legal consequences of an international delinquency that are possible under existing circumstances are such as create reparation of the moral and material harm done.[95]

Lauterpacht abandoned this view in the sixth edition, although Cheng[96] objected that the new approach could not be sustained. Nonetheless, Jennings and Watts go further in linking the notion of punitive damages with that of the international criminal responsibility of states. The attitude of most other writers is cautious.

Schwarzenberger is openly opposed to the idea of punitive damages because, he argues, international tribunals have denied any jurisdiction to exercise 'quasi-penal powers'.[97] In contrast Briggs finds it 'undeniable . . . that many awards contain also a strong punitive element',[98] while admitting that this element is usually covert. Whiteman asserts:

---

[94] 'Règles générales du droit de la paix', (1937-IV) 62 Hague *Recueil* 355.
[95] 4th edn. (1928), § 156.　　　[96] *General Principles of Law*, 237–8.
[97] G. Schwarzenberger, *International Law*, i: *International Law as Applied by International Courts and Tribunals*, 3rd edn. (1957), 673.
[98] H. W. Briggs (ed.), *The Law of Nations: Cases, Documents and Notes*, 2nd edn. (1953), 754.

it is plain that international tribunals have hesitated . . . to pass judgment upon the actions of states in the form of punishment. Where a state is held responsible in damages by an international tribunal or through diplomatic channels, the wrong is not denominated a crime, but merely an international delinquency which gives rise to the payment of compensatory damages.[99]

Brownlie has proposed that 'the award of punitive damages is probably permitted in international law',[100] although he qualifies this in a later work, where he argues that in cases where punitive damages have seemingly been awarded it is really a question of quantification.[101] Gray[102] regards punitive damages as a possible exception to the general rule of full compensation assessed in accordance with the nature of the injury suffered, but does not favour the notion. However, she does link punitive damages with the wider debate over the possibility or desirability of the international criminal responsibility of states.

The American Restatement of Foreign Relations Law asserts simply: 'If a violation is not merely a delict but an international crime . . . punitive damages may be awarded.'[103] The Restatement goes on to maintain that some international tribunals have taken into account the seriousness of the offence and included an element of punishment in the award. The *I'm Alone* case is cited in support of this contention, but no further comment is made.

8. PUNITIVE DAMAGES IN THE INTERNATIONAL LAW COMMISSION

Jennings and Watts fail to elaborate upon the connection between punitive damages and the criminal responsibility of states and admit:

> The legal consequences of state conduct being categorized as criminal in international law and giving rise to a special regime of international responsibility different from that applying to other situations involving state responsibility, and in particular the nature of the sanctions which may be taken against such conduct, are not clear.[104]

The ILC has been dealing with this question since the adoption of Draft Article 19. The early case law considered to support punitive damages may have provided some justification for drawing the distinction between crimes and delicts, but the ILC has not subsequently paid significant attention to this form of reparation.

---

[99] M. M. Whiteman, *Damages in International Law* (1937), i. 717.
[100] I. Brownlie, *International Law and the Use of Force by States* (1963), 148, n. 7.
[101] I. Brownlie, *Principles of Public International Law*, 4th edn. (1990), 464–5.
[102] C. D. Gray, *Judicial Remedies in International Law* (1987), 26–8.
[103] *Restatement of the Law Third*, § 901, 344.
[104] Jennings and Watts, Oppenheim's *International Law*, i: *Peace*, 535.

The notion of punitive damages appeared in the early work of the ILC on the topic of state responsibility. In his First Report on State Responsibility of 1956 the Special Rapporteur, Garcia-Amador, wrote as a basis for discussion: 'The purpose of reparation is not necessarily solely restitution or compensation for material damage. "Reparation" measures may also have a punitive function. In such cases the measures in question should be regarded as a penalty, applicable to the party guilty of the act giving rise to responsibility.'[105] Further, 'The character and measure of reparation should be determined by reference to the extent of the damage caused and to the seriousness of the act giving rise to responsibility, and also by reference to the purpose which the reparation is to serve.'[106] In response, Whiteman commented:

While it may be that certain persons or tribunals have in their zeal or general unfamiliarity with the field of damages, or as an aftermath of war in which hatreds were still glowing, presumed to assess damages intended to be punitive, it is the function of the International Law Commission, and of the Governments which will consider any draft produced by the Commission, to consider carefully whether the law on responsibility of States, and reparation or damages therefor, should include, or encourage, the engrafting therein of punitive damages.[107]

Garcia-Amador later abandoned his provision on punitive damages, and the Special Rapporteurs Ago and Riphagen did not resurrect the idea.

In his Second Report on State Responsibility of 1989, Special Rapporteur Arangio-Ruiz considered the notion of punitive damages in depth, particularly in relation to the remedy of satisfaction. Satisfaction is generally understood to be applicable where the state has suffered a moral injury (sometimes called a political injury) which consists in the infringement of the state's rights *per se*, and in the injury to its honour, dignity, and prestige. Arangio-Ruiz argued that this type of moral damage is separate from the material damage suffered by the state and any moral damage caused to individuals belonging to the offended state, the appropriate remedy for both of which would be compensation. Opinion is divided as to whether satisfaction is punitive or compensatory in nature,[108] but in the opinion of the Special Rapporteur, the payment of a sum of money not in proportion to the size of the material loss is equivalent to punitive damages. Arangio-Ruiz does not treat satisfaction as a remedy specific to crimes in his decision to include it in the Draft Articles as a distinct form of reparation, he merely states:

To confine the consequences of any international delict (let alone an international

---

[105] (1956) *YrbkILC*, vol. 2, 220.   [106] Ibid.

[107] Memorandum prepared by M. M. Whiteman, Assistant Legal Advisor, Department of State, 'Comments on Report on "International Responsibility" by Dr. Garcia-Amador, Special Rapporteur, International Law Commission (A/CN.4/96, 20 January 1956)', 18 Dec. 1956, MS. Department of State, 27–9; in M. M. Whiteman, *Digest of International Law*, viii (1968), 1215.

[108] See (1989) *YrbkILC*, vol. 2, pt. 1, 32–3, nn. 257–67, for some of the arguments.

crime) to restitution in kind and pecuniary compensation would mean to overlook the necessity of providing some specific remedy—having a preventive as well as a punitive function—for the moral, political and juridical wrong suffered by the offended state or states in addition to, or instead of, any amount of material damage.[109]

He goes on to stress that 'it is precisely by resorting to one or more of the various forms of satisfaction (as qualitatively distinct from purely compensatory remedies) that the consequences of the offending state's wrongful conduct can be adapted to the gravity of the wrongful act'.[110]

In his Fifth Report on State Responsibility,[111] Arangio-Ruiz raised the question of punitive damages as a possible derogation, in cases of crimes, from the limits of reparation in cases of delicts. But Part II of the ILC's Draft Articles on State Responsibility[112] concerning the content, forms, and degrees of international responsibility, as adopted on first reading, did not refer to punitive damages. Article 44 entitled 'compensation' provides in section 1:

The injured state is entitled to obtain from the state which has committed an internationally wrongful act compensation for the damage caused by that act, if and to the extent that the damage is not made good by restitution in kind.

It is extraordinary that no exception is made in Articles 51–3 dealing specifically with international crimes.[113] Article 45 entitles the injured state to obtain satisfaction for moral damage to the extent necessary to provide full reparation, and in cases of international crimes this right is not restricted to demands which do not impair the dignity of the wrongdoing state. Having regard to Arangio-Ruiz's interpretation of satisfaction, this would appear to leave open the possibility of punitive damages in relation to both crimes and delicts so long as in the latter case the demands are not excessive or humiliating.[114]

9. THE POSSIBLE APPLICATION OF PUNITIVE DAMAGES IN CASES OF INTERNATIONAL CRIMES

The idea that acceptance of punitive damages is linked to the concept of state criminality is logical, but there is little state practice to support this assertion and the ILC does not pay significant attention to the link. The idea is logical because the notion of punitive damages could help to reduce the gap in international society caused by the absence of institutions of criminal justice having jurisdiction over states. As Hersch Lauterpacht has pointed out:

---

[109] Ibid. 41.   [110] Ibid. 42.   [111] A/CN.4/453/Add.3, 24 June 1993.
[112] A/CN.4/L.524, 21 June 1996.   [113] See Chapter 13 above, s. 5.
[114] M. N. Shaw, *International Law* (1997), 557, interprets Article 45(2)(c), which states that 'in cases of gross infringement of the rights of the injured State, damages reflecting the gravity of the infringement' may be awarded, as providing for punitive damages.

la violation du droit international peut être telle qu'elle nécessite, dans l'intérêt de la justice, une expression de désapprobation dépassant la réparation matérielle. Limiter la responsabilité à l'intérieur de l'Etat à la *restitutio in integrum* serait abolir le droit criminel et une partie importante de la loi en matière de 'tort'. Abolir ces aspects de la responsabilité entre les Etats serait adopter, du fait de leur souveraineté, un principe qui répugne à la justice et qui porte en lui-même un encouragement à l'illégalité.[115]

Punitive damages could be made payable into a fund which would be used to compensate victims of state crimes or put towards another good cause. This approach has been adopted in Poland, where, in order not to overcompensate the victim through an award of punitive damages, the intentional tortfeasor may be required to pay over a suitable sum of money to the Polish Red Cross.[116] A similar system operates in Ethiopia.[117]

Gray has made the point that it is difficult to imagine the International Court of Justice being prepared to award punitive damages.[118] But the Court has entered into new territory in the *Case Concerning the Application of the Genocide Convention*.[119] Bosnia-Herzegovina has contended that Yugoslavia has an obligation to pay reparations for damage to persons and property as well as to the Bosnian economy and environment caused by genocide and other violations of international law committed by Yugoslavia. It is possible that the ICJ could decide to hold Yugoslavia responsible for genocide and order it to pay compensation to Bosnia-Herzegovina. If this proves to be the case, given the magnitude of the offences which have been committed, the sum involved is likely to be large, and it will be difficult to resist the conclusion that the award of compensation contains an element of punishment for the crime of genocide.

10. CONCLUSION

Under current international law it seems that punitive damages may only be awarded covertly so that they are indistinguishable from compensation in its true sense, although the degree of wrongfulness of the act in question is likely to be a relevant factor in determining the quantum of damages. The question may be raised, as it was to a limited extent in *Filartiga v Pena-Irala*, how it is hoped to meet the objectives of international law in making certain acts criminal, even when committed by the state, if the possibility of damages which not only have the purpose of erasing the past but also attempt to encourage change for the future is excluded. All that can be said with certainty is that the future of punitive damages in international law is unsettled. The early

---

[115] 'Règles générales du droit de la paix', (1937-IV) 62 Hague *Recueil* 94, 350.
[116] See McGregor, 'Personal Injury and Death', s. 11, 6.   [117] Ibid. n. 23.
[118] *Judicial Remedies*, 28.   [119] See Chapter 17 below.

case law is unreliable, the more recent case law is inconclusive and the doctrine is divided. Some weight must be accorded to the statement in Oppenheim's *International Law*:

international tribunals have in numerous cases awarded damages which must, upon analysis, be regarded as penal, particularly in relation to the failure of states to apprehend or effectively to punish persons guilty of criminal acts against aliens. The practice of states and tribunals shows other instances of reparation, indistinguishable from punishment, in the form of pecuniary redress unrelated to the damage actually inflicted. Acceptance of the possibility of penal damages against states is linked to the developing concept of the criminal responsibility of states.[120]

Even though this statement does not seem to be a wholly accurate description of past practice, it arguably reflects the direction in which practice is moving. The US cases, on the other hand, should not be given too much weight due to the general prevalence there of punitive and multiple damages on a scale unknown elsewhere. It is lamentable that the European human rights cases have failed to address the issue and offer guidelines for the application of punitive damages, given that European human rights law is a sophisticated and institutionalized system where there can be consistency of application.

Before 1930 the trend in international law appeared to be to expand the concept of damages so as to include within it punitive elements. More recently, the trend has been to treat punitive damages as an independent notion, which may be a step forward. It is, however, still difficult to find support for the argument that damages having a punitive character are accepted as something separate from, and independent of, compensation in its broad sense, and therefore international practice cannot currently be said to embrace the concept of punitive damages. But the idea that pecuniary reparation can exceed the limits of restitution, and in some instances go beyond even moral damages and amount to punishment, would seem to be a general principle of law, and it could be that practice is simply lagging behind principle. The emergent general principle of the international criminal responsibility of states may provide a fitting arena in which to begin to bring practice in line with principle.

[120] Jennings and Watts, Oppenheim's *International Law*, i: *Peace*, 533.

15

The Institutional Framework and Procedures for Imposing Criminal Responsibility on States

1. INTRODUCTION

The previous two chapters raised some of the difficult questions involved in finding suitable modalities for imposing criminal responsibility on states. Although it cannot be said that under current international law there is a specific system for punishing states, it does seem that states may be amenable to punishment and that stigmatization by the international community can be a potent deterrent. These factors lend further credibility to the emergent general principle. However, the question remains as to which international body is in a position to determine whether or not a crime has been committed. In other words, there must be some sort of institutional framework within which state responsibility for criminal acts can be imposed, and the relationship between this framework and the substance of the concept is pivotal.[1] It was shown in Chapters 13 and 14 that the punishment itself need not be something radically divorced from ideas already known to international law, but if the concept of state criminality is to have any meaning, the application of a punishment must depend on a prior determination that a crime has in fact been committed. The institutional framework should also act to regulate the response to state crimes and ensure abidance by rule of law principles.

2. AVAILABLE FRAMEWORKS AND PROCEDURES FOR IMPOSING CRIMINAL RESPONSIBILITY ON STATES

(a) The Role of the International Court of Justice

The first stage is to ensure that the decision as to whether a criminal act has been committed is made objectively by a credible international institution. Under existing international law, this requires reliance on UN organs. The main judicial body which would be qualified to make the determination and adjudicate in cases of state crimes is the ICJ, and the *Case Concerning the Application of the Genocide Convention* may be indicative of the Court's potential role in this sphere.[2] In its favour, it is the function of the Court to

---

[1] Article IX of the Genocide Convention may be construed as an attempt to achieve such a relationship in relation to genocide; see Chapter 2 above, s. 3(b) and Chapter 17 below.

[2] See further Chapter 12 below.

'make a decision in accordance with international law'[3] and its pronouncements possess 'binding force between the parties' to the dispute.[4] The Court would also have the option of establishing a special Chamber under Article 26 of its Statute[5] to consider allegations of criminal behaviour by a state.

On the negative side is, in the first instance, the voluntary nature of a state's subjection to the exercise of the Court's functions. In order for the ICJ to have competence to exercise its jurisdiction in respect of a crime there would need to be a prior acceptance by the alleged wrongdoer of its jurisdiction in such terms as to allow one or more injured states, including indirectly injured states, to summon unilaterally the alleged wrongdoer before the Court. This would be possible if all states had accepted the 'Optional Clause' of Article 36(2) of the Court's Statute[6] or if the declarations of the state bringing the action and the defendant state matched up; if the injured state or states and the wrongdoer happened to be bound by bilateral agreements envisaging the possibility of unilateral application; and if an action could be brought under a clause of a treaty binding the relevant states, such as Article IX of the Genocide Convention. The second set of difficulties relates to the Court's capacity for the careful fact-finding required in cases involving allegations of criminal conduct and for interviewing witnesses. These factors could greatly increase the cost of hearings, and it is not certain that the judges will consider themselves to have the relevant experience. Moreover, it would be difficult for the Court to apply a policy of procedural economy in criminal cases. The Court already faces these problems in the *Case Concerning the Application of the Genocide Convention (Bosnia and Herzegovina v Yugoslavia)* and they have not so far proved insurmountable, even with the addition of a counterclaim and a similar case brought by Croatia against Yugoslavia,[7] which

[3] ICJ Statute, Article 38(1).   [4] ICJ Statute, Article 59.
[5] Article 26 states: 'The Court may from time to time form one or more chambers . . . for dealing with particular categories of cases' (Article 26(1)), or 'for dealing with a particular case' (Article 26(2)). The establishment of a Chamber depends on the consent of the parties.
[6] Article 36(2) provides: 'The states parties to the present Statute may at any time declare that they recognize as compulsory *ipso facto* and without special agreement, in relation to any other state accepting the same obligation, the jurisdiction of the Court in all legal disputes concerning:

(a) the interpretation of a treaty;
(b) any question of international law;
(c) the existence of any fact which, if established, would constitute a breach of an international obligation;
(d) the nature or extent of the reparation to be made for the breach of an international obligation.'

But an illustration of the manner in which some states regard the justiciability of the question of responsibility for acts potentially constituting crimes is provided by France and the US, which terminated their declarations under the 'Optional Clause' of the ICJ's Statute in 1974 and 1985 respectively, following the *Nuclear Tests* cases and the *Nicaragua* case.
[7] See ICJ Press Communiqué 9/38, 2 July 1999 and ICJ web site: http://www.icj-cij.org.

means that there are in effect three separate genocide cases for the Court to consider.

While the possibilities for bringing a case involving the alleged commission of a crime before the ICJ are somewhat restricted, the *Genocide* case demonstrates that the Court may, in the right circumstances, be called upon to consider criminal cases. If the Court is satisfied that any wrongful act under consideration constitutes a crime for which the state is responsible, it places itself in a position to make a declaratory judgment to this effect and/or award punitive damages.[8] It is also conceivable that the Court will find itself involved in questions relating to criminal conduct even where these issues do not form the basis of the cause of action.[9] With regard to the implementation of the Court's judgment, Article 94(2) of the UN Charter, which states that if 'any party to a case fails to perform the obligations incumbent upon it under a judgment rendered by the Court, the other party may have recourse to the Security Council, which may, if it deems necessary, make recommendations or decide upon measures to be taken to give effect to the judgment', could have a role to play. It should be noted that the bringing of proceedings before the ICJ on points of law does not prevent the bringing of other connected questions before the Security Council or the General Assembly.[10]

In his Seventh Report on State Responsibility, Arangio-Ruiz proposed that the ICJ should play a central role in the imposition of criminal responsibility on states.[11] According to his proposed Article 19 of Part II of the Draft Articles,[12] any state could bring the possible commission of an international crime to the attention of the General Assembly or the Security Council under Chapter VI of the UN Charter. If either of these organs resolved that the allegation was sufficiently substantiated so as 'to justify the grave concern of the international community', any state could bring the matter to the attention of the ICJ by unilateral application. If the ICJ found

---

[8] See Chapter 14 above.

[9] The *Lockerbie* and *Nicaragua* cases provide some support for this argument. In the *Nicaragua* case the Court decided that jurisdiction existed by virtue of the 1956 Treaty of Friendship, Commerce, and Navigation between the US and Nicaragua, as well as on the basis of Article 36(2) of the Court's Statute, (1984) ICJ Reports 392. The Court considered *inter alia* the extent to which the US had encouraged breaches of the laws of war by individuals, but the crimes that had been committed were not held to be imputable to the US, (1986) ICJ Reports 14, para. 9 of the operative part of the Court's judgment. In the *Lockerbie* case the Court based its jurisdiction on Article 14(1) of the 1971 Montreal Convention for the Suppression of Unlawful Acts against the Safety of Civil Aviation, (1998) ICJ Reports. It is not yet clear whether the Court will restrict itself to a narrow interpretation of the Convention or whether it will consider evidence in relation to the alleged acts of terrorism and address broader questions such as the relationship between state and individual responsibility for terrorism in the context of the Convention; see further Chapter 16 below, s. 4(b).

[10] See generally S. Torres Bernardez, 'Problems and Issues Raised by Crimes of States: An Overview,' in J. H. H. Weiler, A. Cassese, and M. Spinedi (eds.), *International Crimes of States: A Critical Analysis of the ILC's Draft Article 19 on State Responsibility* (1989), 271, 278–9.

[11] A/CN.4/469/Add. 1, 4.   [12] See Appendix 2 below.

that an international crime had been or was being committed, the legal consequences envisaged in Part II of the Draft Articles would come into operation. This procedure would involve some development of the existing methods of bringing a case before the Court. Despite the fact that Arangio-Ruiz's proposal would appear to have some merit, it has not been favoured by the ILC.

In his Eighth Report on State Responsibility, Arangio-Ruiz discussed the comments that had been made in relation to his proposed Article 19.[13] First, an objection had been raised as to the possible risk of conflict between the General Assembly and the Security Council, but Arangio-Ruiz felt that this risk was exaggerated given that the Security Council's functions relating to the maintenance of international peace and security would be safeguarded by means of Article 20.[14] The second group of objections related to the slow and cumbersome nature of the scheme. In response, Arangio-Ruiz argued that strict collective or community control over the severe consequences of an international crime was necessary and would not preclude urgent interim measures. Moreover, the alternative might be unilateral action or exclusively political action.

The involvement of a large number of states in reaction to a crime is a likely source of differences, controversies, and dispute. Judicial settlement before the ICJ would be the preferred mode of resolving disputes. If a dispute arose out of any action taken by the UN or by states collectively or unilaterally in response to a crime, it may be that the states concerned would agree to refer the dispute to the ICJ. In his Seventh Report, Arangio-Ruiz envisaged a compulsory procedure which would be initiated by unilateral application by any one of the parties to the dispute, including the state accused of committing the crime. The parties would, however, be at liberty to opt for arbitration.[15] The proposed provision does not appear in the 1996 Draft, which limits the procedure for the settlement of disputes to conciliation and arbitration, without explaining whether these procedures could be adapted to deal with disputes relating to international crimes.

(b) The Role of the Political Organs

The role of the General Assembly and the Security Council in imposing criminal responsibility on states must be considered from two perspectives. The first of these is the rule of law perspective. The key elements constituting the rule of law that need to be taken into account for current purposes are conformity of the law to certain standards of justice, both substantial and procedural, and equal subjection to the law. The second perspective is that of

[13] A/CN.4/476, 8–11.   [14] See Appendix 2 below.
[15] See Draft Article 7 of Part III, A/CN.4/469/Add. 2, 3.

UN constitutional law. Articles 7(2), 22, and 29 of the UN Charter empower the General Assembly and the Security Council to establish '[s]uch subsidiary organs as may be found necessary' for the performance of their functions. In principle, when a political body requires a legal task to be performed, it establishes a subsidiary organ to serve a judicial function.[16] Furthermore, when a subsidiary body is established to exercise powers and functions that cannot be exercised by the principal organ, it acts independently and the latter organ is bound by the decisions of the former.[17]

The body which is most representative of the interstate system is the General Assembly. The General Assembly could in principle establish a judicial organ to determine issues of state responsibility for criminal acts.[18] Such action would be appropriate from the perspective of UN constitutional law, and would to a considerable extent ensure abidance by rule of law principles, given that the General Assembly is reasonably democratic. However, the nature of most international crimes means that the primary involvement of the Security Council is likely,[19] although the Assembly may have a role to play with regard to human rights violations and environmental matters. Pierre-Marie Dupuy has proposed a mechanism whereby the General Assembly, on the basis of a qualified majority, would request the Security Council to take action to determine the sanction for a crime. A dispute settlement procedure involving the ICJ would be indispensable, and Dupuy suggests that Article IX of the Genocide Convention or Article XII of the Apartheid Convention could be taken as a basis.[20]

The Security Council seems best disposed to take coercive action under Chapter VII of the Charter to bring the commission of an international crime to a halt. On the one hand, the view has been held that the notion of a 'threat to the peace' in Article 39 of the UN Charter could be interpreted broadly so as to cover all acts constituting international crimes. In Graefrath's opinion, Chapter VII leaves 'sufficient margin and discretionary power to cover the whole area of international crimes'.[21] On the other hand,

---

[16] See the *Administrative Tribunal* case, (1954) ICJ Reports 47, in which the ICJ found that the General Assembly had the competence to establish a judicial body; and consider the establishment of International Criminal Tribunals for the Former Yugoslavia and Rwanda by Security Council Resolutions 808 and 955 respectively. See also D. Sarooshi, 'The Legal Framework Governing United Nations Subsidiary Organs', (1996) *BYIL* 413.   [17] See ibid. 453.

[18] In Resolution 37/123D, 16 Dec. 1982, the General Assembly resolved that the massacre of Palestinian civilians in the Sabra and Shatila refugee camps 'was an act of genocide'. The Assembly took no further steps after this verbal condemnation, and the case demonstrates the need for careful handling of precise legal concepts such as genocide. Canada and Denmark (on behalf of the EC) rightly questioned the General Assembly's competence to make such a determination (see (1982) *YrbkUN*, 486) and it would seem that a better approach would have been to establish a judicial organ to consider the question.   [19] See Chapter 11 above.

[20] 'Implications of the Institutionalization of International Crimes of States', in Weiler et al., *International Crimes of States*, 170, 182–3.

[21] 'International Crimes: A Specific Regime of International Responsibility of States and Its Legal Consequences', in Weiler et al., *International Crimes of States*, 161, 164.

it has been suggested that the category of state crimes should be limited to those which constitute a breach of or threat to the peace in order to fit the notion of international crimes into existing mechanisms, which would place it on a firmer legal footing without broadening the scope of the UN security system.[22] Quigley argues that the ILC should have stated explicitly that the acts in Article 19 of Part I of the Draft Articles on State Responsibility constituted threats to the peace and consequently triggered Chapter VII procedures.[23] But this confers on the Security Council the exclusive power to determine whether or not a crime has been committed, and to apply the necessary consequences.[24] Moreover, the determination is unlikely to be express, and this approach is consequently unacceptable having regard to the two perspectives outlined at the beginning of this section. It must nevertheless be acknowledged that in practice there is a certain grey area, described by Elihu Lauterpacht as 'quasi-judicial activity',[25] in which the political organs have in fact made findings of responsibility.[26]

The problems with reliance on the Security Council are manifold. This organ lacks the means to determine the existence or attribute the consequences of an international crime on a strict legal basis, and can provide only economic, political, or military measures against a state. As a political body the Security Council tends to act selectively, need not base its decisions in comparable situations on uniform criteria, and is not bound to motivate its choices from the viewpoint of international law. There is no verification of the legitimacy of actual choices, and no comparison between such choices is possible. These disadvantages must nevertheless be balanced against the necessity for a timely reaction in many instances where objective assessments of guilt and liability may need to be pushed aside in order to safeguard the peace and maintain order. Such considerations are not necessarily applicable only in cases of aggression, but may also be relevant, for instance, in situations of massive human rights violations.

As the ILC points out, the Security Council's competence has evolved since the end of the Cold War, and recent practice has signified a move towards providing an organized reaction to certain cases of serious wrongful acts.[27] Examples include Resolution 687 (1991), which imposed upon Iraq the

---

[22] See V. Starace, 'La Responsabilité résultant de la violation des obligations à l'égard de la communauté internationale', (1976–V) Hague *Recueil* 267, 294 ff.

[23] J. Quigley, 'The International Law Commission's Crime-Delict Distinction: A Toothless Tiger?', (1988) 66 *Revue de Droit International de Sciences Diplomatiques et Politiques*, 117, 134.

[24] See also the concerns raised in Chapter 11 above.

[25] *Aspects of the Administration of International Justice* (1991), 37.

[26] See ibid. 37–48; I. Brownlie, *System of the Law of Nations, pt. i: State Responsibility* (1983), 123–31; D. W. Bowett, 'Crimes of State and the 1996 Report of the International Law Commission on State Responsibility', (1998) 9 *EJIL* 163, 165–6, 169–70. See also the discussion in Chapter 16 below of the Security Council's response to the 1990–1 Gulf crisis and the Lockerbie incident, and cf. Chapter 11 above.   [27] A/CN.4/453/Add. 3, 14.

obligation to pay reparations for 'war damage' and stipulated the modalities of assessment and payment,[28] and Resolution 748 (1992), in which Article 39 was understood so broadly as to allow the taking of measures against Libya for its failure to extradite the terrorists allegedly responsible for the Lockerbie bombing.[29] However, the Security Council has drawn the line at expressly determining criminal responsibility and recognized that it needed to set up tribunals as subsidiary organs to determine criminal responsibility in the cases of the Former Yugoslavia and Rwanda. Thus, even the Security Council acknowledges that liability for international crimes should be determined by a judicial, rather than a political process.

There are certain basic requirements of criminal justice, such as impartiality and the regular conduct of a trial, which the Security Council cannot meet itself. Thus, it is not wholly inconceivable that the Security Council would establish an ad hoc international criminal tribunal specifically to determine state responsibility, as opposed to individual responsibility, in appropriate circumstances.[30] Alternatively, it has been suggested in the Sixth Committee that an independent commission of jurists could be appointed by the General Assembly or Security Council for this purpose.[31] Nevertheless, the relationship between the Security Council and its subsidiary organ, or even an organ such as the proposed International Criminal Court, is likely to be intimate. Article 23 of the 1994 Draft Statute for an ICC[32] gave the Council significant powers to control the operation of the Court. In particular, with regard to the crime of aggression, the Court was to be precluded from functioning unless the Council had determined that the relevant state had committed the act of aggression under consideration. It would seem that it should be part of the Court's function to make this determination. Article 23 was criticized and a proposal to reformulate it was presented to the Preparatory Committee.[33] Article 16 of the Rome Statute now states that 'No investigation or prosecution may be commenced or proceeded with under this Statute for a period of 12 months after the Security Council, in a resolution adopted under Chapter VII of the Charter of the United Nations, has requested the Court to that effect'.[34] Achieving the correct balance between the role of the political

---

[28] See Chapter 16 below, s. 2.   [29] See ibid. s. 4(b).

[30] In *Prosecutor v Blaskic (Objection to the Issue of* Subpoena Duces Tecum), the Appeals Chamber of the International Criminal Tribunal for the Former Yugoslavia stated: 'the international Tribunal does not possess any power to take enforcement measures against States. Had the drafters of the Statute intended to vest the International Tribunal with such a power, they would have expressly provided for it. In the case of an international judicial body, this is not a power that can be regarded as inherent in its functions.' Judgment of 29 Oct. 1997, para. 25; 110 ILR 608, 697–8.

[31] Report of the ILC on the Work of its Forty-Seventh Session, A/C.6/50/SR.25, 1 Dec. 1995, GAOR 50th session, Mr Ayewah—Nigeria.   [32] See section 3(a) below.

[33] This was known as the 'Singapore Proposal' and was supported by the UK. See also S. Yee, 'A Proposal to Reformulate Article 23 of the ILC Draft Statute for an International Criminal Court', (1996) *Hastings International and Comparative Law Rev*, vol. 19, no. 3, 529.

[34] A/CONF.183/9, 17 July 1998, (1998) 37 *ILM* 999.

organs and judicial independence is clearly a key consideration in establishing an institutional framework for imposing criminal responsibility on states.

(c) The Role of Third States and the International Community

The role of third states[35] in a situation involving the commission of a state crime would be limited to assisting in the enforcement of any decisions made by the determining body.[36] It would be unacceptable for third states to make unilateral assessments of whether a crime has been committed and to engage in acts of armed intervention or reprisal, and the concept of state criminality must not be interpreted to create new justifications for such action.[37] Third states are, however, entitled to take limited, non-forcible countermeasures unilaterally.[38] Chinkin has examined 'third party collective responses to international State crime'[39] in relation to aggression, but her analysis is necessarily tied to the UN collective security system and may not be equally applicable to all state crimes.

A possible duty of states to take measures against the author of an international crime must be distinguished from their *faculté* so to do. There should be no neutrality in the face of an international crime,[40] and in order for state responsibility to be implemented effectively, it is imperative that states do not interfere with the response to a crime on the part of the authoritative body representing the international community, and that any decisions made by this body are duly carried out. In this manner the 'third party' is 'replaced by the ideal of the international community'.[41]

3. POSSIBLE ALTERNATIVE FRAMEWORKS AND PROCEDURES FOR IMPOSING CRIMINAL RESPONSIBILITY ON STATES: SOME PROPOSALS

(a) The Establishment of an International Criminal Court

In Resolution 46/54 of 9 December 1991, the General Assembly invited the ILC to consider the question of the establishment of an International

---

[35] See also section 3(b) below.

[36] Cf. Articles 48 and 49 of the UN Charter, and see also Article 35(1) according to which any member state may bring a situation to the attention of the Security Council or General Assembly.

[37] Cf. C. Chinkin, *Third Parties in International Law* (1993), 337, 'In respect of international crimes, where the concept of obligations *erga omnes* is all important, it seems that third parties should have the right to resort to forcible reprisals against an aggressor, but there should be a preference for collective rather than individual response.' However, she recognizes that 'the preferred approach is towards developing authoritative, institutional responses': ibid. 344.

[38] See generally O. Y. Elagab, *The Legality of Non-Forcible Counter-Measures in International Law* (1988).   [39] *Third Parties*, 291–342.

[40] See ibid. 292.   [41] Ibid. 355.

Criminal Court (ICC) within the framework of the Draft Code. Following consideration of the Tenth Report by the Special Rapporteur, Doudou Thiam,[42] the ILC set up a Working Group on the topic in 1992. The Working Group proposed the establishment of an ICC by statute in the form of a treaty agreed to by states parties, which, at least in the first phase of its operations, should exercise jurisdiction over private persons and not states.[43] In 1994 a working group was re-established, and the ILC adopted a revised Draft Statute for an ICC.[44] A Preparatory Committee on the Establishment of an ICC was later set up in accordance with General Assembly Resolution 50/46 of 11 December 1995. The Rome Statute of the International Criminal Court was adopted by the United Nations Diplomatic Conference of Plenipotentiaries in July 1998.[45]

There was no mention of state responsibility in the ILC's revised Draft Statute for an ICC which reflected the trend set by the ad hoc International Criminal Tribunals for the Former Yugoslavia and Rwanda. In 1995 and 1996, a Committee of Experts on the Establishment of a Permanent International Criminal Court met at the International Institute of Higher Studies in Criminal Sciences in Siracusa to discuss possible modifications to the 1994 Draft Statute of the proposed ICC, which were to be transmitted to the Preparatory Committee. Article 33–3 of the 1996 'Updated Siracusa Draft',[46] entitled 'Individual and State Responsibility', amended Article 33 of the ILC Draft and provided in paragraph 4 that '[c]riminal responsibility for persons under this Statute shall not prejudice [affect] the responsibility of States under international law'. It was also noted that the question of the criminal liability of corporations or other legal persons may need to be considered. There was little feedback on these questions by the Committee of Experts, but it is significant that the issues were raised. The substance of Article 33–3 appears in the document *General Principles of Criminal Law* which provided a basis for discussion in the Preparatory Committee.[47] The Rome Statute states in Article 25(4): 'No provision in this Statute relating to individual criminal responsibility shall affect the responsibility of States under international law.'

It seems reasonable to consider the extension of the jurisdiction of the ICC to include states for the future. A number of international bodies advocated the establishment of an international criminal court with jurisdiction over states in the inter-war period; the notion was favoured by François and oth-

---

[42] See Report of the ILC on the Work of its Forty-Fourth Session, A/CN.4/442; (1992) *YrbkILC*, vol. 2, pt. 2, 8.

[43] Report of the working group on the question of an international criminal jurisdiction, (1992) *YrbkILC*, vol. 2, pt. 2, 58.

[44] Report of the ILC on the Work of its Forty-Sixth Session, (1994) *YrbkILC*, vol. 2, pt. 2, 18.

[45] See n. 34 above.   [46] 15 Mar. 1996.

[47] A/AC.249/CRP. 9, 4 Apr. 1996. For documents and information on the proposed ICC see http://www.igc.apc.org/icc.

ers in the *Institut de Droit International* following the Second World War; and the idea was discussed in relation to the establishment of an international criminal tribunal to try those accused of apartheid.[48] It is also worth mentioning in this context that the NGO 'Avocats sans Frontiers' favoured expanding the jurisdiction of the Rwanda Tribunal to include states given that 'the assertion of state prerogatives in the face of universally-recognized norms is increasingly dubious',[49] and believing that the opportunity should be taken to 'consider anew the possibility of state criminal liability'.[50]

An international criminal court would be the ideal venue for determining the responsibility of states accused of crimes, and would be the most effective way to achieve the desired connection between the substantive issues of the concept of state criminality and its procedural and institutional aspects. However, it remains to be seen to what extent states would be willing to commit themselves to this idea by signing a convention to establish such a court and accepting its compulsory jurisdiction. For the time being it is conceivable that the ICJ and other international tribunals will consider awarding punitive damages against states in appropriate circumstances, and perhaps once an international criminal court with jurisdiction over individuals has been up and running for some time, its jurisdiction could be extended to include states.[51]

(b) Application of the Principle of Obligations *Erga Omnes*

If international crimes are a subset of the category of obligations *erga omnes*, and obligations *erga omnes* are owed to the international community as a whole, 'one would expect that community to be in possession of a corresponding right to demand the performance of those obligations and to be in possession of a legal interest if such obligations are breached'.[52] The future development of the notion of obligations *erga omnes* could theoretically, therefore, provide a means of bringing cases concerning the alleged commission of an international crime before the ICJ by third parties. This would have particular relevance where a state is accused of committing a crime against its own citizens and there is no directly injured state, and could result

[48] See Chapter 2 above, s. 5.
[49] Open Letter Regarding the Need to Expand the Jurisdiction of the International Tribunal for Rwanda, 18 May 1995, http://www.asf.be/asf/letter/letterlong.html, 2.   [50] Ibid.
[51] In an appendix (Appendix I) to the 1994 Draft Statute it is stated that provision will be made for amendment and review of the Statute, probably at the request of a specified number of states after it has been in force for at least five years. See also Article 21 of the Draft Statute drawn up in 1993, Revised Report of the Working Group on the Draft Statute for an ICC, A/CN.4/L.490, 20. Article 123(1) of the Rome Statute (n. 34 above) provides that 'Seven years after the entry into force of this Statute the Secretary-General of the UN shall convene a Review Conference to consider any amendments to this Statute'.
[52] A. J. De Hoogh, *Obligations Erga Omnes and International Crimes: A Theoretical Inquiry into the Implementation and Enforcement of the International Responsibility of States* (1996), 70.

in an order by the Court that the state must compensate its own citizens. It is not proposed to discuss the relevant case law in detail here, but merely to give an indication of the direction in which the law in this sphere is moving.

In the *Barcelona Traction* case[53] the Court did not find it necessary to elaborate upon the practical application of the notion of obligations *erga omnes*. Some enlightenment can be gained, however, from an examination of the earlier *South-West Africa* cases.[54] These cases related to Article 7 of the 1920 Mandate for South-West Africa[55] whereby South Africa, the Mandatory, agreed that 'any dispute whatever' between it and another member of the League of Nations relating to the interpretation or application of the provisions of the Mandate should either be settled by negotiation or submitted to the Permanent Court of International Justice.

In its 1962 Judgment (Preliminary Objections) the Court dismissed South Africa's contention that it was not involved in a 'dispute' with Ethiopia and Liberia, as envisaged in Article 7, concerning its alleged failure to observe the requirements of the Mandate regarding its treatment of the native inhabitants and administration of the Territory, because no material interests of these countries or of their nationals were involved or affected.

the manifest scope and purport of the provisions of [Article 7] indicate that the members of the League were understood to have a legal right or interest in the observance by the Mandatory of its obligations both towards the inhabitants of the Mandated Territory, and towards the League of Nations and its Members.[56]

The Court thereby concluded by a majority vote that it had jurisdiction to adjudicate upon the merits of the dispute.

Several judges filed dissenting opinions. Judges Fitzmaurice and Spender were of the view that Article 7 should be understood as referring to a dispute between the actual parties before the Court representing themselves and their own interests rather than some other entity or interests.[57] President Winiarski felt that the institution under the old Roman penal law known as *actio popularis* seemed alien to the modern legal systems of 1919–20 and to international law, and he did not believe that the framers of the Mandate could have had such notions in mind.[58]

In its 1966 Judgment (Second Phase) the ICJ rejected the contention that the question whether the applicants had a legal right or interest in the subject-matter of the proceedings had been settled by the 1962 judgment, and tackled the question afresh. The Court began by dividing the substantive provisions of the Mandate into two main categories: 'conduct provisions', relating to the carrying out of the Mandate as such, and 'special interests'

[53] (1970) ICJ Reports 3.
[54] *South-West Africa* cases (*Ethiopia v South Africa*; *Liberia v South Africa*), Preliminary Objections, (1962) ICJ Reports 319; *South-West Africa* cases, Second Phase, (1966) ICJ Reports 6.   [55] (1962) ICJ Reports 335.
[56] Ibid. 343.   [57] Joint Dissenting Opinion, ibid. 558–9.   [58] Ibid. 452.

provisions, which directly conferred certain rights in respect of the Mandated territory upon the members of the League or in favour of their nationals. The Court went on to say that members of the League had *locus standi* only in regard to the 'special interests' provisions, which in this case meant only in regard to the rights of missionaries who were their nationals. It was argued that the suggestion that judicial control of the 'conduct' obligations was a 'necessary' part of the Mandate system and could only be secured by reading Article 7 in a wide sense as conferring individual enforcement rights on the members of the League:

amounts to a plea that the Court should allow the equivalent of an *'actio popularis'*, or right resident in any member of a community to take legal action in vindication of a public interest. But although a right of this kind may be known to certain municipal systems of law, it is not known to international law as it stands at present: nor is the Court able to regard it as imported by the 'general principles of law' referred to in Article 38, paragraph 1(c), of its statute.[59]

It should be noted that the applicants never in fact claimed that their alleged right of enforcement was exercisable by any state whatever. The relevant 'community' in this case was therefore clearly that of the members of the League of Nations rather than the international community as a whole. Nevertheless, the Court specifically based its finding on contemporary international law, and it could be argued that a wider contention was being addressed which had not been specifically advanced, namely that certain 'conduct' obligations were enforceable by a true *actio popularis*, in other words, that they were obligations *erga omnes*. If this were the case, the contention was rejected.

This aspect of the Court's decision may be challenged, and the dictum in the *Barcelona Traction* judgment with its specific reference to 'protection from racial discrimination' may be interpreted as a refutation of the 1966 judgment. In the words of Judge Jessup, in his Separate Opinion in the 1962 judgment, '[i]nternational law has long recognized that states may have legal interests in matters which do not affect their financial, economic, or other "material", or, say, "physical" or "tangible" interests'.[60] This is evident in various Conventions which have been created since the First World War.[61] In particular, the European Convention on Human Rights of 1950 provides in Article 24 that any contracting party may refer to the European Commission on Human Rights any alleged breach of the provisions of the Convention by another contracting party. This applies 'regardless of whether the victims of the alleged breach are nationals of the applicant State or whether the

---

[59] (1966) ICJ Reports 47.   [60] (1962) ICJ Reports 425.
[61] See e.g. the Constitution of the 1919 International Labour Organization and Article VIII of the 1948 Genocide Convention.

alleged breach otherwise particularly [a]ffects the interests of the applicant State'.[62]

The European Commission has also stated 'that the obligations undertaken by the High Contracting Parties in the Convention are essentially of an objective character, being designed rather to protect the fundamental rights of individual human beings from infringements by any of the High Contracting Parties than to create subjective and reciprocal rights for the High Contracting Parties themselves'.[63] Further, 'a High Contracting Party, when it refers an alleged breach of the Convention to the Commission under Article 24, is not to be regarded as exercising a right of action for the purpose of enforcing its own rights, but rather as bringing before the Commission an *alleged violation of the public order of Europe*'.[64] An obligation which is owed, for example, to all members of the EU, is not an obligation *erga omnes*, but it has one thing in common with obligations *erga omnes* in that it is owed to states which do not necessarily have a direct interest in its fulfilment. There are grounds for arguing that 'the equivalent of an *actio popularis*' was known to international law at the time of the *South-West Africa* cases and is known to contemporary international law. Nevertheless, despite its dicta in the *Barcelona Traction* case, the ICJ has not established a general right to secure the observance of certain international obligations in subsequent cases.

In its Judgment in the *Nuclear Tests* case (*Australia v France*)[65] the ICJ analysed certain unilateral statements made by France concerning its intention to end nuclear testing as having been made *erga omnes*: 'The objects of these statements are clear and they were addressed to the international community as a whole, and the Court holds that they constitute an undertaking possessing legal effect.'[66] The Applicants contended that the right 'to inherit a world in which nuclear testing in the atmosphere does not take place'[67] and the right 'to the preservation of the environment from unjustified artificial radio-active contamination'[68] were of the same kind as the basic rights of the human person and derived from obligations *erga omnes*. They did not seek reparation for proven damage, but simply a judgment that there should be no further nuclear testing, no deposit of nuclear fallout in breach of their territorial sovereignty, and no more interference with high seas freedoms. However, the Court was unsympathetic to the notion of an *actio popularis* allowing such rights to be upheld.

The notion of obligations *erga omnes* received some mention in the *Case Concerning Military and Paramilitary Activities in and against Nicaragua.*[69] In

---

[62] *Austria v Italy*, [1961] *Yrbk European Convention on Human Rights*, 116, 140.
[63] Ibid.   [64] Ibid.   [65] (1974) ICJ Reports 253.
[66] Ibid. 269.
[67] Quoted in Joint Dissenting Opinion of Judges Onyeama, Dillard, Jiménez de Aréchaga, and Waldock, ibid. 514.   [68] Ibid.
[69] (1986) ICJ Reports 14.

its judgment the ICJ noted that Nicaragua was being accused of violating human rights as partial justification for the US Government's actions against the Government of Nicaragua. In the *Barcelona Traction* case, obligations *erga omnes* included those deriving from 'principles and rules concerning the basic rights of the human person'. The Court, perhaps thinking in these terms, felt:

This particular point requires to be studied independently of the question of the existence of a 'legal commitment' by Nicaragua towards the Organization of American States to respect these rights; the absence of such a commitment would not mean that Nicaragua could with impunity violate human rights.[70]

This may be interpreted as implying that Nicaragua and all other states were subject to a customary obligation *erga omnes* to respect human rights; however, the Court then proceeded to deny any suggestion of a customary law right of action in the human rights field.

In his Dissenting Opinion in relation to the Court's decision on Nicaragua's request for interim measures, Judge Schwebel went so far as to suggest that the holding in the 1966 *South-West Africa* judgment was 'rapidly and decisively displaced'[71] by the Court's dictum in the *Barcelona Traction* case. Arguably he goes too far, and even Ago admitted in the ILC that 'the position taken in the judgment on the *Barcelona Traction* case is perhaps still too isolated to permit the conclusion that a definite new trend in international judicial decisions has emerged'.[72]

The *East Timor* case[73] concerned a dispute between Portugal and Australia over a treaty between Australia and Indonesia concluded in 1989 dealing with the use of the continental shelf of the 'Timor Gap'. East Timor was occupied by Indonesia in 1975, and the UN repeatedly condemned this action in 1975 and 1976 while recognizing Portugal as the 'administrating Power'. Portugal claimed that Australia, by negotiating, concluding, and initiating the performance of the Timor Gap Treaty, had infringed the right of the people of East Timor to self-determination and to permanent sovereignty over natural resources, infringed the rights of Portugal as the administering power, and contravened Security Council Resolutions 384 (1975) and 389 (1976). The action was brought against Australia rather than Indonesia because the latter did not accept the compulsory jurisdiction of the ICJ. Australia's principal objection was that Portugal's Application would require the Court to determine the rights and obligations of Indonesia in the absence of that state's consent. The Court upheld this objection and dismissed Portugal's argument that Australia's behaviour could be separated from that of Indonesia, because in the Court's opinion Australia's actions could not be assessed

---

[70] Ibid. 134.   [71] (1984) ICJ Reports 169, 197.   [72] (1976) *YrbkILC*, vol. 2, pt. 1, 29.
[73] (1995) ICJ Reports 90.

without addressing the question why Indonesia could not lawfully have concluded the 1989 Treaty. Portugal argued further that 'the rights which Australia allegedly breached were rights *erga omnes* and that accordingly Portugal could require it, individually, to respect them regardless of whether or not another state had conducted itself in a similarly unlawful manner'.[74] The Court responded:

In the Court's view, Portugal's assertion that the right of peoples to self-determination, as it evolved from the Charter and from the United Nations practice, has an *erga omnes* character, is irreproachable. The principle of self-determination of peoples has been recognized by the United Nations Charter and in the jurisprudence of the Court ... it is one of the essential principles of contemporary international law. However, the Court considers that the *erga omnes* character of a norm and the rule of consent to jurisdiction are two different things. Whatever the nature of the obligations invoked, the Court could not rule on the lawfulness of the conduct of a state when its judgment would imply an evaluation of the lawfulness of the conduct of another state which is not a party to the case. Where this is so, the Court cannot act, even if the right in question is a right *erga omnes*.[75]

The conflict between an obligation *erga omnes* and the rule that the ICJ may not exercise jurisdiction over a party to a dispute without the consent of that state, which was central to the *East Timor* case, was not dealt with satisfactorily by the Court. In his Dissenting Opinion Judge ad hoc Skubiszewski observed:

There is yet another reason why the presence of Indonesia, a country which has an interest in the case ... is not a precondition of adjudication. If the contrary were true, the Court would practically be barred from deciding whenever the application of the *erga omnes* rule or rules and the opposability of the legal situation so created were at stake.[76]

The broader community interest was ignored by the Court, and the suggestion is that for the future, obligations *erga omnes* will not trump existing obstacles to the Court's jurisdiction; rather, they will make the acceptance of jurisdiction on this basis virtually impossible as by definition they involve the interests of all states. In his Dissenting Opinion, Judge Weeramantry refers to the ICJ's 'jurisdictional reach in the wide range of third party-related disputes which are increasingly brought before it in a more closely interrelated world'.[77] He warns:

The *erga omnes* concept has been at the door of this Court for many years. A disregard of *erga omnes* obligations makes a serious tear in the web of international obligations, and the current state of international law requires that violations of the concept be followed through to their logical and legal conclusion.[78]

The theory of obligations *erga omnes* is that all states should have *locus*

---

[74] (1995) ICJ Reports 102.   [75] Ibid.   [76] Ibid. 248.
[77] Ibid. 142.   [78] Ibid. 216.

standi to protect certain rights which by their nature are vested in the entire international community. In practice, courts have been reluctant to allow third parties to enforce such rights. It is therefore unlikely for the time being that the notion of obligations *erga omnes* will assist in bringing cases involving international crimes before the ICJ, but the possibility of increased judicial support for the rapidly developing hierarchy of international norms should not be ruled out for the future.

Acts committed by individuals which may be the cause for prosecution by any state are those which the community of nations believes to be of universal concern and as subject to universal condemnation. This idea of a universal interest is also the foundation of obligations *erga omnes*.[79] Universal jurisdiction is provided in a number of treaties on matters of general international concern including drug-trafficking, hijacking and sabotage of aircraft, hostage-taking, apartheid, torture, and attacks upon diplomats, and it is generally accepted that breaches of the laws of war, in particular the Hague Convention (IV) of 1907 and the Geneva Conventions of 1949, may be punished by any state obtaining custody over the accused persons. It is also widely accepted that crimes against humanity and genocide (despite the absence of a provision on universal jurisdiction in the Genocide Convention)[80] fall into this category.

In the *Eichmann Case*[81] it was proclaimed:

> The state of Israel's 'right to punish' the accused derives . . . from . . . a universal source (pertaining to the whole of mankind), which vests the right to prosecute and punish crimes of this order in every state within the society of nations. . . .[82]

According to the theory of obligations *erga omnes*, crimes of this order should, when committed by a state, be actionable by any other state; therefore an analogy with the notion of universal jurisdiction may be drawn. It seems that the idea of an *actio popularis* in relation to state crimes parallels the system of universal jurisdiction in relation to certain individual crimes, except that the latter system is more advanced than the former.

(c) The Current and Potential Role of National Courts in Determining Responsibility for State Crimes

Sovereign immunity refers to the right of a state and its organs not to have proceedings brought against them for their actions in front of the judicial organs of other states. The issue of sovereign immunity is most relevant to cases of state acts constituting torts which violate the domestic law of a foreign state, but can be extended to questions of human rights abuses and

---

[79] See further Chapter 6 above.   [80] See p. 35 above.
[81] *Attorney-General of the Government of Israel v Eichmann*, District Court of Jerusalem, 12 Dec. 1961, (1961) 36 ILR 5.   [82] Ibid. 50.

international crimes. The current trend is towards a restrictive view of immunity where the tort occurs in the forum state, particularly in cases of torts resulting in death or personal injury, or damage to or loss of property, but a state is generally immune from criminal proceedings in another state.[83] Regrettably, the International Law Association's draft proposal for an international convention on state immunity essentially excludes punitive damages against a state. Article VI entitled 'Extent of Liability' states:

As to any claim with respect to which a foreign State is not entitled to immunity under this Convention, the foreign State shall be liable as to amount to the same extent as a private individual under like circumstances; but a foreign state shall not be liable for punitive damages. If, however, in any case wherein death or other loss has occurred, the law of the place where the action or omission occurred provides, or has been construed to provide for damages only punitive in nature, the foreign State shall be liable for actual or compensatory damages measured by the primary loss incurred by the persons for whose benefit the suit was brought.[84]

In the *Al-Adsani* case[85] a British national claimed damages against, *inter alia*, the Government of Kuwait for alleged torture inflicted upon him in Kuwait. The Court of Appeal granted leave for service of a writ on the basis that the plaintiff had shown a good arguable case that under the State Immunity Act 1978, there was no immunity for a state in respect of alleged acts of torture. In the Court's opinion the Act was to be interpreted in accordance with the rules of customary international law, and the fact that section 134 of the Criminal Justice Act 1988 recognized the extraterritorial character of conduct such as torture supported the submissions that torture was unlawful under public international law. Thus, the Court based its decision in part on evidence that 'there is at the very least a reluctance under public international law to give any legal status to acts of torture such as are here alleged'.[86] This decision was reached at a very preliminary stage of the proceedings, and international law does not entitle third states to give remedies in their national courts against offending states in cases of torture or other human rights violations. But Bröhmer has raised the apt question why national courts should be considered ill-equipped to apply international law rules aimed at the protection of human beings,[87] and Cassese has commented that

---

[83] Cassese has pointed out: 'It is no accident that domestic courts rarely decide on the *criminal* implications of the alleged unlawful acts of foreign states. Should this occur, the "interference" of the courts would be more far-reaching and the outcome more unpredictable': A. Cassese, *Violence and Law in the Modern Age* (1986), 170.

[84] See ILA, *Report of the Sixtieth Conference*, Montreal, 29 Aug.–4 Sept. 1982, (1983), 5–10 and 325–48; *Report of the Sixty-Sixth Conference*, Buenos Aires, 14–20 Aug. 1994, (1994), 492.

[85] *Al-Adsani v Government of Kuwait*, Judgment of the Supreme Court of Judicature, Court of Appeal (Civil Division) on appeal from the High Court of Justice, 21 Jan. 1994, 100 ILR 465.

[86] Ibid. 471.

[87] J. Bröhmer, *State Immunity and the Violation of Human Rights* (1997), 95. See also the *Letelier* case, 63 ILR 378, in which the 1976 US Foreign Sovereign Immunities Act was given a very broad interpretation.

'judges feel less and less bound to avoid international issues traditionally considered the exclusive preserve of the executive'.[88]

The question of the immunity of a former head of state from criminal proceedings in the national courts of another state recently arose in the case of *R v Bow Street Metropolitan Stipendiary Magistrate, ex parte Pinochet Ugarte (Amnesty International interveneing) (No 3)*.[89] General Pinochet was arrested in a London hospital on the execution of two provisional warrants dated 16 and 22 October 1998 issued by the magistrate at Bow Street Magistrates Court in London at the instigation of a Spanish judge. Pinochet was accused of torture, hostage-taking, and conspiracy to commit these offences and murder. In an application for judicial review in respect of the two warrants, the Divisional Court[90] held that Pinochet was entitled to state immunity as a former head of state in respect of the acts with which he was charged, and as a result he could not be extradited to Spain to stand trial. The Divisional Court granted leave to appeal to the House of Lords on the grounds that a point of law of general public importance had arisen, namely, 'the proper interpretation and scope of the immunity enjoyed by a former Head of State from arrest and extradition proceedings in the UK in respect of acts committed while he was Head of State'.[91]

The House of Lords ruled by a majority on 25 November 1998 that a former head of state had no immunity in relation to acts of official torture made crimes in the UK by section 134(1) of the Criminal Justice Act 1988 or of acts of hostage-taking made criminal by the Taking of Hostages Act 1982.[92] The judgment was subsequently set aside because the Judicial Committee had not been properly constituted, and a rehearing began on 18 January 1999. Before the first hearing of the appeal the Spanish Government had submitted a formal Request for Extradition with an expanded list of crimes which included genocide. The charge of genocide was deleted by the Home Secretary in the exercise of his statutory power allowing extradition to proceed following the first appeal hearing. At the rehearing all the Law Lords interpreted the 'double criminality' rule embodied in the 1989 Extradition Act to mean that the alleged conduct must be criminal under English law at the conduct date rather than at the date of the request for extradition. This meant that out of thirty-two charges, only three qualified as valid extradition crimes, having

---

[88] *Violence and Law*, 169.

[89] [1999] 2 All ER 97. See F. Webber, 'The Pinochet Case: The Struggle for the Realization of Human Rights', (1999) *Journal of Law and Society*, vol. 26, no. 4, 523, for a summary of the background to the case. A similar case has been brought in Senegal against the exiled former dictator of Chad, Hissene Habre. See *International Herald Tribune*, 12–13 Feb. 2000.

[90] Lord Bingham CJ sitting with Collins and Richards JJ. Lord Bingham deleted the charge of murder as not within the requested UK extraterritorial jurisdiction. [1998] All ER (D) 629, 28 Oct. 1998.   [91] [1998] 4 All ER 897, 899.

[92] [1998] 4 All ER 897. See also H. Fox, 'The First Pinochet Case: Immunity of a Former Head of State', (1999) 48 *ICLQ*, 207.

been committed after 28 September 1988 which was the date of entry into force of the Criminal Justice Act 1988 implementing the 1984 UN Torture Convention.

There were two basic approaches to the core issue in relation to the question of immunity, all their Lordships in both appeals agreeing that a former head of state was immune from criminal proceedings in the UK with respect to official acts performed in the exercise of his functions as head of state. The first approach was that immunity was absolute, and although a line should be drawn between public and private acts, it was impossible to draw lines between different degrees of criminality. The second and majority approach was that the immunity from criminal proceedings in the courts of another state which was afforded to a former head of state in respect of the exercise of official functions did not extend to international crimes committed while in office. Article 1 of the Torture Convention confines the definition of torture to acts committed by public officials or other persons acting in an official capacity, which, according to their Lordships, includes heads of state. Distinguishing immunity *ratione materiae* (conduct immunity) from immunity *ratione personae* (status immunity), the majority held that Pinochet was not protected by immunity *ratione materiae*. The argument of Lords Hutton[93] and Phillips[94] was that torture as defined in the Convention was not within the official functions of a head of state, while the others in the majority focused on the inconsistency between the obligation in the Convention to try or extradite offenders including heads of state and the retention of immunity *ratione materiae*.[95] The Law Lords in the majority (apart from Lord Hope) adopted 8 December 1988, the date on which the UK ratified the Torture Convention, as the date on which Pinochet lost his immunity.

The effect of the House of Lords Judgment is to remove the immunity of former heads of state with respect to the international crime of torture while preserving the absolute immunity of the state itself and its serving head. Lady Fox[96] has raised the question whether such an approach ignores the peculiar role of the head of state. She draws an analogy with the identification theory of corporate crime,[97] and suggests that head of state immunity is subsumed within the immunity of the state.[98] Despite the fact that leave to intervene was given to the Republic of Chile on the basis that any immunity

---

[93] [1999] 2 All ER 97, 165.   [94] Ibid. 192.

[95] Lord Browne-Wilkinson, ibid. 114; Lord Millett, ibid. 169; Lord Hope, ibid. 152.

[96] 'The Pinochet Case No. 3', (1999) 48 *ICLQ*, 687, 694.

[97] Ibid. See also Chapter 4 above.

[98] Cf. J. Craig Barker, 'The Future of Head of State Immunity after Ex Parte Pinochet', (1999) 48 *ICLQ*, 937, 939, who states that head of state immunity would seem to import elements of both diplomatic and state immunity. 'In that respect, it is possible to draw a distinction between the immunity *ratione personae* of the head of state which is analogous to the immunity of the diplomatic agent, and the head of state's immunity *rationae materiae* which exists alongside the doctrine of state immunity but is not identical to it.'

precluding criminal charges against Pinochet was the immunity of Chile rather than Pinochet himself,[99] the Law Lords seemed to limit their analysis to a former head of state's individual immunity. Lady Fox argues that the immunity attaching to an individual's conduct of official business of the state is that of the state and not the individual. Against this background, she describes the Lords' ruling as recognizing the 'novel proposition that a State's municipal criminal jurisdiction extends to international State crimes committed by former public officials'.[100] She goes on to say:

> On this basis one might advance a new criminal law exception to State immunity on the basis that an international State crime contrary to *jus cogens* incorporated into the municipal criminal code constitutes a municipal crime subject to the forum State's jurisdiction. But unlike the adjudication stage of civil proceedings, criminal proceedings if they are not to be nugatory immediately move to the enforcement stage of jurisdiction by way of arrest and punishment of a State. To allow enforcement, however, would make such 'inroads' into the rationale of the restrictive doctrine, that it is likely to spell the abandonment of State immunity as a general bar to local proceedings.[101]

Denza has also suggested that one consequence of the Law Lords' finding was that 'the State of Chile may now in effect be subjected to criminal proceedings in the domestic courts of another State' although this does not appear to have been their Lordships' intention.[102] Thus it would seem that the citadel of state immunity in respect of criminal acts has at least to some extent been broken down by the *Pinochet* case.

The treatment, or indeed lack of treatment, by the Law Lords of the interplay between state and individual responsibility for international crimes does, however, have further implications. If torture is an international crime when committed by a public official acting in an official capacity but cannot constitute an official function of a head of state for the purposes of immunity *rationae materiae*, it could be argued that it is not imputable to the state for the purposes of state responsibility. This argument may be overcome by the rules of attribution, which allow certain *ultra vires* acts to be imputed to the state,

---

[99] *Per* Lord Browne-Wilkinson, [1999] 2 All ER 103.

[100] Fox, 'The First Pinochet Case', 700.

[101] Ibid. 700–1. Cf. C. Dominicé, 'Quelques observations sur l'immunité de juridiction pénale de l'ancien chef d'état', (1999) 103 *RGDIP* 297, 306, who draws a clear distinction between state responsibility and individual responsibility in this context: 'Dès l'apparition de la notion de crime de guerre—qui est le fait d'un individu-organe—il a été bien clair qu'un même acte engendre deux responsabilités internationales: celle de l'Etat dont l'individu est l'organe, de nature essentiellement compensatoire, et celle, pénale, de l'individu-organe.' See also M. Cosnard, 'Quelques observations sur les décisions de la chambre des Lords du 25 novembre 1998 et du 24 mars 1999 dans l'affaire Pinochet': ibid. 309, 320–3.

[102] 'Ex Parte Pinochet: Lacuna or Leap?', (1999) 48 *ICLQ* 949, 953. Denza points to the controversial nature of the concept of the criminal responsibility of states and remarks: 'Even if it were to be accepted in principle, it would be unlikely to extend to trial of one State in the domestic courts of another': ibid. 954.

although it is doubtful whether this could involve the criminal responsibility of the state.[103] A connected question is whether acceptance of responsibility by the state in these circumstances would preclude any trial of the individual.

The question has also been raised whether the Law Lords' approach should be construed as relevant to all international crimes or merely to the crime of torture.[104] The majority in the first Appellate Committee seemed to refer to international crimes generally, while the majority in the second Committee confined their analysis to acts of torture. Since the Torture Convention defines torture in terms of official or governmental action, it is possible that 'the plea of immunity *ratione materiae* could only be defeated by those crimes of international law which presuppose or require state action'.[105] Even though the problem of state immunity can be circumvented by bringing criminal proceedings against state officials, any trial of a former head of state would be likely to require extensive investigation of state policies and actions.[106]

It is difficult at this stage to assess the full impact of the House of Lords Judgment in the *Pinochet* case, but if it is to be interpreted broadly, it highlights the need for a treaty or customary rule which states expressly that there is no immunity from the jurisdiction of national courts for the commission of international crimes generally, or for those which presuppose state action. In the absence of such a rule there is unlikely to be any uniformity of practice in the national courts of different states.

In April 1997, a Berlin court delivered a verdict that directly implicated senior Iranian Government officials in the murder of exiled Kurdish leaders in a Berlin restaurant in 1992. Although Judge Kubsch pointed out that the 'Iranian Government was not in the dock',[107] Iran's Supreme Security Council was identified as the planning centre for assassinations abroad and President Rafsanjani, the supreme spiritual leader Ayatollah Khamenei, the Intelligence Minister, and the head of foreign policy were found to be involved. In response to the court verdict, the German Foreign Minister accused Iran of a 'flagrant violation of international law'.[108] The EU recalled diplomats from Tehran and suspended its so-called critical dialogue with Iran, declaring that 'no progress can be possible while Iran flouts international norms and indulges in acts of terrorism'.[109] The Iranian Foreign Minister, Dr Ali Akbar Velayeti, complained in a press release of the politically motivated allegations against Iran and accused Germany of violating the

---

[103] See Article 10 of the International Law Commission's Draft Articles on State Responsibility, Appendix III, and see also Chapter 4 above, s. 4.

[104] A. Bianchi, 'Immunity versus Human Rights: The Pinochet Case', (1999) *EJIL*, vol. 10, no. 2, 237, 249.   [105] Ibid.

[106] As Lord Nicholls pointed out: 'since torture is a crime of universal jurisdiction defined by reference to the perpetrator's official position, every torture trial involves scrutiny of "official acts"', [1998] 3 WLR 1456.   [107] *The Times*, 11 Apr. 1997.

[108] *International Herald Tribune*, 11 Apr. 1997.   [109] Ibid.

principle of state immunity. He warned that such behaviour would be detrimental to international peace and security.

The German court case perhaps illustrates why domestic courts may be inappropriate venues for dealing with state crimes due to the politically sensitive nature of many such cases.[110] The difficulty is to ensure the objectivity of a domestic court in dealing with allegations against a state with a poor human rights record. The situation is different when the national court of a state considers charges against members of that state's previous government or regime. In December 1994, trials began in Ethiopia of up to several thousand former members of the dictatorial regime under Lieutenant-Colonel Mengistu Haile Mariam. Mengistu, who fled to Zimbabwe in 1991, was one of seventy-three defendants to be formally accused of genocide.[111] Clearly the development of domestic court involvement in cases of state crimes is worth following closely, and it has been pointed out that the frequent reference in the *Pinochet* case 'to such notions as *jus cogens*, obligations *erga omnes* and crimes of international law attests to the fact that the emerging notion of an international public order based on the primacy of certain values and common interests is making its way into the legal culture and common practice of municipal courts'.[112] It may be noted in this context that a decision of the District Court of Tokyo in 1963 provides the only explicit statement that the dropping of atomic bombs on Hiroshima and Nagasaki by the US was contrary to certain fundamental precepts of international law.[113]

4. CONCLUSION

The international community has not yet established any authoritative and exclusive institutional framework for imposing criminal responsibility on states, and it may be particularly in this respect that the concept of state criminality has yet to reach its final stage of development. But indications are that it has already come a long way towards completing its journey. There is no need to create entirely new institutions to cater for the concept, although certain refinements to existing institutions may be necessary, and, ideally, a determination of state criminality should be a judicial one. It is possible, or even likely, that one day the proposed ICC will be endowed with jurisdiction over states, especially since this idea has repeatedly been debated and reserved for future consideration. It should be recalled in this context that consideration was once given to the creation of a criminal division of the Permanent

---

[110] See also *Tel-Oren v Libyan Arab Republic*, 77 ILR 193.
[111] *The Times*, 13 Dec. 1994; *International Herald Tribune*, 15 Dec. 1994.
[112] Bianchi, 'Immunity versus Human Rights', 248.
[113] (1964) *The Japanese Annual of International Law*, no. 8, 212 ff.

Court of International Justice,[114] and another possibility for the future would be to create such a division in the ICJ.[115]

It must be emphasized that there is not necessarily a conflict between the goal of guaranteeing that immediate steps are taken to bring about the cessation of an international crime and restore the pre-existing situation, and the goal of ensuring that the concept of state responsibility for international crimes operates within an institutional framework governed by rule of law principles. The UN can and does take action to maintain or restore peace without a prior assessment of the type of wrongful act in issue, and this may involve the application of measures that contain an element of punishment and may also involve some determination of responsibility. But when the UN responds to an act of aggression, for example, it generally does so not because it determines that aggression is an international crime, but because aggression disturbs the peace. Although the concept of state criminality may be linked to UN structures,[116] it can operate separately, and the assessment as to whether a crime has been committed may come into play at a later stage, for instance when the question of compensation is considered, or, if there has been a situation of war, it could form the basis of the conditions of peace. However, unless existing procedures are developed and enhanced, or new ones are created, it is unlikely that the general principle embodying the concept of state criminality will emerge fully.

In order to keep the issues and difficulties raised in this chapter in perspective, a further parallel may be drawn between the concept of state criminality and that of obligations *erga omnes*.[117] Obligations *erga omnes* are referred to widely in the literature, and it is difficult to question their existence as part of customary international law. However, this law has not yet been translated into specific procedural abilities.[118] By analogy, it is possible for the concept of state criminality to become established in an initial stage of development, and this could provide the impetus for the creation of a suitable institutional framework.

[114] See Chapter 2 above, s. 2(a).

[115] This idea was considered by the ILC as a means of establishing a permanent international criminal court having jurisdiction over individuals (see e.g. Report by Sandstrøm, A/CN.4/20, 20), but it was rejected because it would have involved amending the UN Charter. See also V. V. Pella's 'Projet de statut pour la création d'une chambre criminelle au sein de la cour permanente de justice internationale' in *La Guerre crime et les criminels de guerre* (1964), 129–44.   [116] See also Chapter 11 above.

[117] See also Chapter 6 above.

[118] See O. Schachter, *International Law in Theory and Practice* (1991), 211–12, who argues that although the general concept of obligations *erga omnes* has become part of customary international law, it is not yet clear whether states will use the concept 'to lodge bilateral diplomatic claims, counter-measures, or judicial (or quasi-judicial) proceedings'.

Conclusion to Part IV

The conclusions reached on the basis of the material discussed in Part IV support the proposition that the concept of state criminality is an emergent general principle of international law. The concept has been shown to be juridically sound and it can be transported into the practical sphere. Obstacles remain to be overcome in this sphere of practical application, but they are not such as to destroy the viability of the concept. It should be recalled that the methods of enforcing most aspects of international law are as yet imperfect. Punitive damages, in such situations where they can be awarded, are perhaps the most appropriate and least objectionable response to a state crime, as they are usually applied as a result of a judicial process, do not extend too far a state's well-established duty to make pecuniary reparation to an amount equivalent to restitution in kind, and are useful in that the money obtained can be put towards some international purpose.

In his Opening Speech before the Nuremberg Tribunal, Sir Hartley Shawcross spoke of the refusal 'to reduce justice to impotence by subscribing to the outworn doctrines that a sovereign state can commit no crime and that no crime can be committed on behalf of the sovereign state by individuals acting in its behalf'.[1] If this were an innovation, he described it as one that was desirable and beneficent, and fully consistent with justice, common sense, and the abiding purposes of the Law of Nations. But, he queried, was this indeed an innovation, or was it merely the logical development of the law?

Shawcross's remarks raise the question of a more flexible 'common law' approach to an analysis of the concept of state criminality. There is a possibility that authoritative decision-makers will consider themselves justified in applying the concept even in the absence of any relevant UN resolution, convention, or ILC draft. This is an aspect of international law which could be a prime target for judicial legislation. Oppenheim's *International Law* states: 'It is probable that in view of the difficulties surrounding the codification of international law, international tribunals will in the future fulfil, inconspicuously but efficiently, a large part of the task of developing international law.'[2] Anand subscribes to this view, and argues that 'when the chances of large-scale codification are dim and growth by custom is slow and uncertain, this method of law-making is of special importance and ought to be encouraged'.[3] Jimenez de Aréchaga has observed that general principles of law 'should not be underestimated as to their influence on the minds and the

---

[1] *Trial of German Major War Criminals, Opening Speeches of the Chief Prosecutors* (1946), 57.
[2] R. Y. Jennings and A. Watts (eds.), Oppenheim's *International Law*, i: *Peace* (1992), 41.
[3] *Studies in International Adjudication* (1969), 189.

intellectual processes of judges', and he quotes a statement by Cardozo to this effect.[4]

Certain of the notions that have been relied upon in the antecedent chapters are essentially the product of judicial 'innovation'.[5] This is true in particular of elementary considerations of humanity and of the very idea of emergent principles of international law. An example of judicial legislation is the decision of the ICJ in the *North Sea Continental Shelf* cases,[6] which does not appear to reflect pre-existing principles or a pattern of state practice[7] and is based primarily upon 'certain basic legal notions'.[8] The concept of state criminality could be described as a 'basic legal notion' which has its basis in principle.[9] In a similar manner to the ICJ in the *North Sea* cases, a court might declare that an act constitutes a state crime and consider itself simply to be discovering a 'basic legal notion' which in reality already exists, but its existence has not so far been acknowledged. It is noteworthy that few lawyers have sought to challenge the general approach of the ICJ in the *North Sea* cases. This demonstrates the creativity with which decision-makers may make law or influence legal developments.

The development and application of the concept of state criminality calls for some imagination and consequently the 'common law' evolution of the concept may provide the force necessary to propel it across the threshold between *lex ferenda* and *lex lata*. In Brownlie's opinion, the Court in the *North Sea* cases 'affirmed by implication that a concept . . . may crystallize in a first stage, even although the basic elements thus recognized need a consequential apparatus of rules dealing with related problems'.[10] It is entirely possible for the concept of state criminality to crystallize 'in a first stage' before the 'related problems' are completely worked out. The potential significance of the *Case Concerning the Application of the Genocide Convention*[11] can be stressed in this context. This is not to say, of course, that the ICJ does not act with caution. It is also imaginable that national courts will take the concept into account and assist in its development even if the doctrine of sovereign immunity currently restricts their competence to make a judgment directly against a state.

It is submitted that the international community has already come too far

---

[4] Comment in A. Cassese and J. H. H. Weiler (eds.), *Change and Stability in International Law-Making* (1988), 50.

[5] See G. Fitzmaurice, 'Judicial Innovation: Its Uses and Its Perils', in *Cambridge Essays in International Law: Essays in Honour of Lord McNair* (1965), 24–47; H. Lauterpacht, *The Development of International Law by the International Court* (1958), 155–223.

[6] (1969) ICJ Reports 4.

[7] See I. Brownlie, 'General Course on Public International Law', (1995) 215 Hague *Recueil* 9, 45–9.   [8] (1969) ICJ Reports 46–7.

[9] The extent to which it is also an emerging category of custom will be examined in Chapter 16 below.   [10] Brownlie, 'General Course', 47.

[11] See Chapter 17 below.

to abandon the concept of state criminality. The road has been built, and if some states are unhappy about this development[12] the most they can do is to fail to maintain this road. However, it has been demonstrated that there are many sources from which the maintenance can derive. Moreover, the logical development and evolution of the law suggest that the concept will continue to emerge from its post-Second World War 'back seat' position and appear as a workable category of positive law.

[12] See Chapter 16 below, s. 5, for the views of some states.

PART V

Status of the Concept of State Criminality in Contemporary International Law

16

State Practice since the Second World War

1. INTRODUCTION

Writing at the time of the First World War, Peaslee predicted 'that international law will ultimately provide for some method of central control over acts of nations of a quasi-criminal nature'.[1] It would seem that this point was reached some time ago, and the question is whether the logical development of the law is leading to the emergence of full-blown state criminal responsibility. In other words, to what extent has the threshold between *lex ferenda* and *lex lata* already been crossed?

The discussion in this chapter of state practice since the Second World War will be limited to a few examples of cases which are permissive of useful analysis. As examples of international *in*action in the face of criminal behaviour by a state, it may be sufficient to mention Stalinist Russia, the Cambodian genocide, and the aggression which sparked off the 1980–88 Iran–Iraq war. Inconsistency on the part of the international community could be interpreted as pointing towards the non-existence of the concept of state criminal responsibility. However, the argument here is that such inconsistency points towards the need for a fully developed concept. It is submitted that the post-Cold War international community may now be ready and willing to accommodate the emergent general principle and encourage its development.

2. THE CRIME OF AGGRESSION

Between the two world wars, states repeatedly affirmed the principle prohibiting recourse to war as a means of settling international disputes and a number of international instruments defined a war of aggression as an international crime.[2] Even though the rules of state responsibility which would be applicable in cases of aggression were never described, it is arguable that states could not have unhesitatingly qualified such an act as a crime and then expect the consequences to be no different from those which normally followed from much less serious internationally wrongful acts.

The UN Charter instituted a special regime of responsibility for the breach of certain international obligations. The purposes of the UN, as stated in Article 1 of the Charter are to 'maintain international peace and security, and

---

[1] A. J. Peaslee, 'The Sanction of International Law', (1916) 10 *AJIL* 328, 335.
[2] See Chapter 1 above.

to that end: to take effective collective measures for the prevention and removal of threats to the peace, and for the suppression of acts of aggression or other breaches of the peace', to ensure 'respect for the principle of equal rights and self-determination of peoples', and to encourage 'respect for human rights and for fundamental freedoms for all'. Article 2(4) provides that:

All members shall refrain in their international relations from the threat or use of force against the territorial integrity or political independence of any state, or in any other manner inconsistent with the purposes of the United Nations.

This provision stipulates a general prohibition of the unilateral use of force by states, and has for practical purposes superseded the Kellogg–Briand Pact.[3] In order to ensure that states respect Article 2(4), Chapter VII of the Charter provides for the possibility of 'preventative measures' against a threatened breach of the peace or 'enforcement action' to restore international peace and security where a breach has been committed. The procedure for restoring peace, following a determination by the Security Council that a breach of the peace has taken place, includes both sanctions not involving the use of armed force specified in Article 41 of the Charter and action by air, sea, or land forces provided for in Article 42. The Charter also authorizes the use of force under Article 51 in the exercise of the right to self-defence in response to an act of aggression. The precise consequences of the unlawful use of force and the scope of the explicit exception of self-defence are still being worked out in state practice.

It should be emphasized that the powers conferred on the Security Council by Chapter VII of the Charter are designed as a means of maintaining or restoring peace, rather than establishing responsibility, which is only one of the factors to be taken into consideration by the Security Council in making what is essentially a political assessment.[4] The sanctions provided for under the UN Charter are not strictly criminal law sanctions.[5] Higgins shares the opinion of Pierre-Marie Dupuy, who argues that Articles 41 and 42 have 'the aim not of individually punishing the culprit of a wrongful act, but of terminating a *situation* that attacks peace or is a threat to it'.[6]

In reaching the conclusion in 1976 that states can be subject to a special regime of responsibility for criminal acts under international law, the ILC commented on state practice as follows:

It seems undeniable that today's unanimous and prompt condemnation of any direct attack on international peace and security is paralleled by almost universal disap-

---

³ See Chapter 1 above, s. 2(e).   ⁴ See also Chapter 2 above.
⁵ Cf. Chapter 13 above, s. 3.
⁶ P.-M. Dupuy, 'Implications of the Institutionalization of International Crimes of State', in H. H. Weiler, A. Cassese, and M. Spinedi (eds.) *International Crimes of State: A Critical Analysis of the ILC's Draft Article 19 on State Responsibility* (1989), 170, 176; and see R. Higgins, *Problems and Process* (1994), 166.

proval on the part of states towards certain other activities. Contemporary international law has reached the point of condemning outright the practice of certain states in forcibly keeping other peoples under colonial domination or forcibly imposing internal regimes based on discrimination and the most absolute racial segregation, in imperiling human life and dignity in other ways, or in so acting as gravely to endanger the preservation or conservation of the human environment. The international community as a whole, and not merely one or other of its members, now considers that such acts violate principles formally embodied in the Charter and, even outside the scope of the Charter, principles which are now so deeply rooted in the conscience of mankind that they have become particularly essential rules of general international law. There are enough manifestations of the views of states to warrant the conclusion that in the general opinion, some of these acts genuinely constitute 'international crimes', that is to say, international wrongs which are more serious than others and which, as such, should entail more severe legal consequences. This does not, of course, mean that all these crimes are equal—in other words, that they attain the same degree of seriousness and necessarily entail all the more severe consequences incurred, for example, by the supreme international crime, namely, a war of aggression.[7]

The status of aggression as an international crime is almost undisputed. Article V of the 1974 General Assembly consensus Resolution on a definition of aggression was designed to tackle the question of the legal consequences of aggression and states that: 'A war of aggression is a crime against international peace. Aggression gives rise to international responsibility'. The provision dealing with the criminal nature of aggression generated a great deal of contention. By 1973 there was agreement that 'aggression constitutes _____ against international peace, giving rise to responsibility under international law'.[8] Suggestions for filling in the blank included 'a grave violation', 'a crime', 'a criminal violation', or alternatively it was suggested that the subject be omitted completely. The UK felt that a reference merely to aggression without restricting it to aggressive war was objectionable.[9] The category of crimes set out in Article 6(a) of the Nuremberg Charter established criminal responsibility only for involvement in wars of aggression and not for participation in aggressive acts short of war.[10] The 1970 Declaration on Principles of International Law Concerning Friendly Relations and Cooperation Among States also describes a war of aggression as a crime against peace for which there is responsibility under international law.[11] Furthermore, the UK would not accept any form of state responsibility beyond the obligation to pay compensation for aggression, and the US and Japan supported the UK position.

The effort by a few powerful states to restrict the scope and impact of the

---

[7] (1976) *YrbkILC*, vol. 2, pt. 2, 109.

[8] See B. B. Ferencz, *Defining International Aggression* (1975), vol. 2, 43, and Document 24, 17.

[9] Ibid .

[10] Article 6 defines crimes against peace as 'planning, preparation, initiation, or waging of a war of aggression . . .'.

[11] GA Resolution 2625(XXV), 24 Oct. 1970; reproduced in (1971) 65 *AJIL* 243.

definition of aggression was viewed by many as an attempt to turn back the clock, and reverse not only the trend of the Nuremberg Trials but also the thinking of the ILC and the General Assembly.[12] Some of the judgments in the trials held after the Second World War under Control Council Law No. 10 had held that the invasion of Austria and Czechoslovakia were acts of aggression even though the countries surrendered without a war.[13] The ILC had never made a distinction between aggression and aggressive war, and this was manifested in its work on a Draft Code of Offences against the Peace and Security of Mankind.[14] In 1952, a General Assembly resolution referred to the crime of aggression without any reference to war.[15] Even the UN Charter avoids using the ambiguous term 'war'. The Soviet Union and non-aligned states eventually accepted the restrictive UK interpretation, but it was agreed to include an explanatory note in the definition saying 'the words international responsibility are used without prejudice to the scope of this term'.

In Article 5(2) the General Assembly confirmed a distinction between wars of aggression, which were considered to have a criminal status, and other acts of aggression short of war. All acts of aggression are international delicts entailing state responsibility. However, it seems that in 1974 only wars of aggression were accepted by the international community as being international crimes, although the Resolution does not explain the relationship between state and individual criminal responsibility in the context of wars of aggression. Equally, both the Nuremberg Charter and the UN Charter fail to address the issue. Moreover, Article 5(2) does not describe the regime of responsibility for a 'crime against international peace'. Such crimes are a special category, as they are the only violations of international law which permit the use of armed force in individual or collective self-defence to suppress them. A recent example of an act of aggression is the Iraqi invasion, occupation, and annexation of Kuwait in 1990, which could be described as a 'war' of aggression and consequently as an international crime.[16] An analysis of the response of the international community to this act might serve as an illustration of the possible legal consequences arising from aggression, and provide evidence that a special regime of consequences, characterized by its severity, is thought to be applicable in such instances.

The Security Council did not use the term 'aggression' in its first resolution on the matter, but referred instead to 'a breach of international peace and

---

[12] See Ferencz, *Defining International Aggression*, 43–4.
[13] See *In re* Von Weizsaecker *et al.* (Ministries Case), US Military Tribunal at Nuremberg, (1949) 16 *Annual Digest* 344, 347.   [14] See Chapter 12 above.
[15] Resolution 599 (VI), 31 Jan. 1952.
[16] See generally E. Lauterpacht *et al.* (eds.), *The Kuwait Crisis: Basic Documents* (1991), and M. Weller (ed.), *Iraq and Kuwait: The Hostilities and Their Aftermath* (1993).

security'.[17] The UN collective security system was immediately brought into operation and Resolution 660 (1990) condemned the 'Iraqi invasion of Kuwait', required that Iraq 'withdraw immediately and unconditionally all its forces to the positions in which they were located' before the invasion, and called for negotiations between Iraq and Kuwait to take place. Negotiations were ruled out when Iraq announced its annexation of Kuwait. This was rejected by the Security Council in Resolution 662 of 9 August 1990.

Several aspects of the subsequent reaction to the crisis may be highlighted. First, upon Iraq's failure to comply with the demands of Resolution 660, the Security Council, acting under Chapter VII of the UN Charter, adopted Resolution 661 of 6 August 1990, ordering all states to impose a strict economic embargo on Iraq. It is notable that the Resolution referred to all states, including non-members of the UN—a clear indication that the breach at hand had an effect *erga omnes*.[18] Never before had a response under the authority of Article 41 of the UN Charter been so immediate and so comprehensive, and compliance with Resolution 661 was surprisingly solid.

Second, when the Council had exhausted the catalogue of measures short of military hostilities against Iraq, it adopted Resolution 678 of 29 November 1990, which seemed to mark a retreat from the collective security or enforcement approach to the realm of self-defence.[19] By this Resolution, the Security Council authorized the forces cooperating with Kuwait, and commanded by the US, 'to use all necessary means to uphold and implement Security Council Resolution 660 and all subsequent relevant resolutions and to restore international peace and security in the area'. Despite Iraq's attempts to split the international community prior to the adoption of Resolution 678, the members of the General Assembly rose in unison against the 'Iraqi aggression and the continued occupation of Kuwait in flagrant violation of the Charter of the United Nations'.[20]

The third point is that aggression, like all breaches of international law, entails a duty to make restitution and reparation. Resolution 674 of 29 October 1990 reminded Iraq that 'under international law it is liable for any loss, damage or injury arising in regard to Kuwait and third states, and their nationals and corporations, as a result of the invasion and illegal occupation

---

[17] Resolution 660, 2 Aug. 1990. The Iraqi invasion was described as an 'act of aggression' in the original draft, but this reference was deleted at Soviet insistence. See C. Greenwood, 'New World Order or Old? The Invasion of Kuwait and the Rule of Law', (1992) 55 *Modern Law Review*, 153, 159.

[18] See also ibid. 160, and see further Chapter 15 above, s. 2(c), on the inapplicability of state neutrality in cases of crimes.

[19] See Greenwood, 'New World Order', 167–9, for the arguments relating to the legal basis for Resolution 678. Greenwood interprets Resolution 678 as providing for enforcement action.

[20] A/45/250, 10. See Lauterpacht et al., *The Kuwait Crisis*, 193, n. 30. See also M. Weller, 'The Kuwait Crisis: A Survey of Some Legal Issues', (1991) *African Journal of International and Comparative Law*, vol. 3, pt. 1, 1, 24.

of Kuwait by Iraq', and those concerned were invited to compile information regarding their claims. In a number of respects, the reparation claims in cases of aggression (as demonstrated by the Second World War[21]) differ from normal reparation claims. Graefrath and Mohr[22] list the following:

—the obligation of restitution and reparation and its size may be determined by decision of the Security Council;
—the obligation is not open to negotiation, it has to be accepted by the aggressor state;
—the methods of payment and the administration of the reparation procedure are under the supervision of the Security Council;
—to ensure that restitution and payment of damages is made, the whole economy of the country concerned may be subjected to international control.

A novel element was the demand by the Security Council in Resolution 686 of 7 March 1991 that a recognition of the duty to make reparation was a condition for ending military activities. The same Resolution also left open the option to use force if certain preconditions for an armistice were not met. This threat to use force in order to achieve the acceptance of the duty to make reparation, and the continuation of a general embargo to press for compliance with reparation claims, were also distinctive features of the response to the Gulf crisis. Resolution 687 of 3 April 1991, which was the closest approximation to a peace treaty, established a Compensation Commission as a subsidiary organ of the Security Council to evaluate losses, list claims and verify their validity, resolve disputes on reparation claims, and decide the mechanism for determining the level of contribution to the fund which would come mainly from Iraqi oil exports. The immense size of the claims made it virtually impossible to have all of them satisfied, but it is clear that the international community desired to teach Iraq a lesson. While in principle a demand for reparation is not punitive, the number of states and the amount of money involved suggests a punitive element.[23]

Finally, it is another consequence of aggression that limitations may be placed upon the exercise of the wrongdoing state's sovereign rights in order to ensure non-repetition of the crime. Resolution 687 established a demilitarized zone extending well into both Iraq and Kuwait. Iraq was also required to accept conditions relating to the destruction of weapons and the prohibition of the use of chemical, biological, or atomic weapons. The extensive control and verification procedures were clearly part of the sanction, as was the continuation of the weapons embargo. Such procedures mirror the ideas of 'corporate probation' and 'corporate rehabilitation' in corporate crime theory. Etzioni states:

---

[21] See Chapter 1 above, s. 3(i).
[22] B. Graefrath and M. Mohr, 'Legal Consequences of an Act of Aggression: The Case of the Iraqi Invasion and Occupation of Kuwait', (1992) 43 *Austrian Journal of Public and International Law*, 109, 121.   [23] See p. 195 above.

Imagine, for instance, a corporation that is found to have systematically neglected the safety of its consumers. It seems socially productive to put it on a five year diet of closer inspections. If it is found to have truly mended its ways, the inspectors should report that the firm has been rehabilitated and fully restore it to membership among decent and law abiding corporations.[24]

A similar policy, operating on an international level, would appear to have been behind the weapons inspections.

The missing link in this case was the failure to provide for war crimes trials. A request for the establishment of an international criminal court to punish Saddam Hussein was made by the EU as a whole at the instigation of the German Foreign Minister,[25] but it did not seem prudent or practicable in the long term for the coalition forces to go into Iraq, topple the Government, and try its leaders for war crimes,[26] and they did not have the mandate so to do. The only situation in which a mandate to remove an established government by military means has been authorized is that of North Korea in 1950. That year the General Assembly adopted a resolution containing implicit authorization for the forcible unification of Korea with reference to the establishment of a 'unified, independent and democratic'[27] Government of Korea.

Security Council Resolution 670 of 25 September 1990 confirmed the liability of Iraq and individual Iraqis for grave breaches of the Geneva Convention IV of 1949, and states were invited to gather relevant information and submit it to the Security Council. On 19 March 1993, the US transmitted a 'Report on Iraqi War Crimes'[28] to the President of the Security Council in accordance with Resolution 674, paragraph 2 of which invited states to collate substantiated information in their possession or submitted to them on the grave breaches by Iraq of Security Council decisions, the UN Charter, the 1949 Geneva Convention IV, the 1961 Vienna Convention on Diplomatic Relations, the 1963 Vienna Convention on Consular Relations, and international law. Iraq described the Report as full of arbitrary allegations, formulated with public relations assistance and given currency by the media for hostile purposes.[29] Most of the alleged crimes were such that they could only have been committed with the involvement of the state.[30] But war crimes trials in this particular situation seemed to fall outside the boundaries of

---

[24] A. Etzioni, 'The US Sentencing Commission on Corporate Crime: A Critique', in G. Geis and P. Jesilow (eds.), *White Collar Crime* (1993), 155.

[25] *Le Monde*, 17 Apr. 1991, 1 and 3. The Foreign Ministers of the EU countries requested that 'le dictateur de Bagdad soit jugé par un tribunal international pour crimes de guerre et tentative de génocide'.

[26] See also Conclusion below for some of the policy implications of such dramatic action.

[27] Resolution 376(V), 7 Oct. 1950.   [28] (1993) *YrbkUN*, 429–30.   [29] Ibid.

[30] The Report contained allegations of widespread and premeditated violations of the laws of war, including hostage-taking and the inhumane treatment of civilians. Also listed were indiscriminate Scud missile attacks against non-combatant civilians of Israel and Saudi-Arabia and the deliberate release of oil into the Persian Gulf and sabotage of oilfields.

political expediency and the survival of Saddam Hussein's dictatorship was perhaps not anticipated. In 1999, it emerged that the United States was still planning to pursue genocide and war crimes charges against Saddam Hussein, but the effort had little support from the Security Council. There was talk of establishing an international war crimes tribunal on Iraq or a commission of enquiry to gather evidence creating legal grounds for the detention of Saddam Hussein and other senior Iraqi officials should they travel abroad.[31]

It has been shown that the 1990–1 Gulf crisis brought into operation several novel features of the UN collective security system, the exercise of the right to self-defence, and the implementation of demands for reparation. Most of the decisions taken during the crisis were backed by virtual unanimity, and the message was that the crime of aggression would not be tolerated and would result in severe sanctions. The aim has been to demonstrate the attitude of states towards the unlawful use of force and to find evidence of the application of particularly severe consequences where an act is described as criminal. In the case of the Iraqi invasion of Kuwait, the international community acting with one voice passed judgment on a fellow-member of that community and applied sanctions of an unprecedented severity, some of which were arguably more akin to punishment than restitution.

Nevertheless, these developments are essentially within the sphere of collective security, and it cannot be said that Iraq was held criminally responsible for a state crime. No trials of individuals were held in which issues of criminal responsibility could be explored. The response to the Gulf Crisis was perhaps more to do with restoring the pre-existing situation and safeguarding Western interests than with establishing and advancing the legal scope of international responsibility for aggression. Thus, the significance of the Gulf Crisis is that it does provide evidence of the application of a special regime of severe measures by the political organs of the UN in cases of aggression, and to some extent supports the ILC's interpretation of advancements in state practice in 1976. When the ILC met in 1998, some members cited the Security Council's authorization of the bombardment of Iraq as an example of a criminal penalty rather than a civil sanction.[32]

---

[31] *International Herald Tribune*, 25–6 Sept. 1999 and 29 Oct. 1999.

[32] See Report of the ILC on the Work of its Fiftieth Session, GAOR, Fifty-Third session (1998), Suppl. No. 10, (A/53/10), para 270. Pellet has stated: 'Nazi Germany and Saddam Hussein's Iraq can be called "criminal states" and have been treated as such by the international community': A. Pellet, 'Can a State Commit a Crime? Definitely, Yes!', (1999) *EJIL*, vol. 10, no. 2, 425, 433.

3. REACTION OF STATES TO THE REGIME OF APARTHEID IN SOUTH AFRICA

The policy of apartheid was a state policy, and it was the racist regime of South Africa itself which was repeatedly described by the UN as being 'illegitimate'. Only the state could cause the majority of South Africans to live under a system which deprived them of their basic human rights, and the South African system of laws was designed and administered so as to prevent that majority from taking effective peaceful action to alter this condition of fundamental deprivation. The Apartheid Convention does not refer to the criminal responsibility of states, although it does stipulate that organizations and institutions may be criminal, thereby recognizing that apartheid is not merely a crime committed by individuals, despite the fact that only individual members of organizations and institutions may be punished under the Convention. It was perhaps considered best to leave it to the UN to take appropriate action against the state, and it may be argued that some of the action taken by the UN contained a punitive element.

In 1962 the General Assembly requested the Security Council to consider taking action against South Africa under Article 6 of the Charter which states: 'A member of the UN which has persistently violated the Principles contained in the present Charter may be expelled from the Organization by the General Assembly upon the recommendation of the Security Council.'[33] Such action was not pressed in the Security Council for over a decade; then in 1974 the General Assembly not only rejected the credentials of the South African delegation but also requested the Security Council to review relations between South Africa and the UN 'in the light of the constant violation by South Africa of the principles of the Charter and the Universal Declaration of Human Rights'.[34] The matter was left open, as no recommendation was forthcoming from the Security Council, but later the same year the General Assembly passed a resolution recommending that the South African regime should be 'totally excluded from participation in all international organizations and conferences under the auspices of the UN so long as it continues to practice apartheid',[35] and by 1975 South Africa was in effect excluded from all organs of the UN.

A Manifesto on Southern Africa, adopted by the Assembly of Heads of State and Government of the Organization of African Unity (OAU) in 1969, reads in part:

South Africa should be excluded from the UN agencies, and even from the UN itself. It should be ostracized by the world community. It should be isolated from world

---

[33] GA Resolution 1761 (XVII), 6 Nov. 1962.
[34] GA Resolution 3207 (XXIX), 30 Sept. 1974.
[35] GA Resolution 3324E (XXIX), 16 Dec. 1974.

trade patterns and left to be self-sufficient if it can. The South African Government cannot be allowed both to reject the very concept of mankind's unity and to benefit by the strength given through friendly international relations. And certainly Africa cannot acquiesce in the maintenance of the present policies against people of African descent.[36]

It was felt that the South African regime had no right to represent the people of South Africa, and that the liberation movements recognized by the OAU were 'the authentic representatives'[37] of the overwhelming majority of the South African people. The General Assembly requested all specialized agencies and other intergovernmental organizations to deny membership or privileges of membership to the South African regime, and to invite, in consultation with the OAU, representatives of the liberation movements of the South African people recognized by that organization to participate in their meetings.

The arguments against bringing South Africa to heel in this way were that South Africa would no longer be exposed to the expressions of abhorrence of mankind for apartheid if it were cast beyond the range of the voices of the international community. Expulsion could have indicated to the racist core in South Africa that the UN no longer wished to encourage hope of change. Perhaps the main reason why South Africa was never expressly expelled from the UN was that such action would have set a shattering precedent. Article 6 has a punitive element and could be construed as a criminal sanction. Wehberg has maintained that the equivalent provision of the League Covenant which allows the exclusion of a member violating 'any covenant of the League' is a measure that must be interpreted 'au premier chef comme une punition'.[38] The reluctance to utilize Article 6 demonstrates how severe this sanction is considered to be, and it can only realistically be applied against states guilty of crimes, otherwise the UN might disintegrate. The fact that it was proposed to take such action against South Africa suggests that the state itself was considered to be behaving in a criminal manner and deserved to be treated like an outcast.

The first resolutions of the Security Council calling for an arms embargo, adopted in 1963, were not mandatory. Then in 1977 the Security Council finally imposed a mandatory arms embargo upon South Africa under Chapter VII of the UN Charter.[39] The Resolution, the first imposing such mandatory sanctions against a member state under Chapter VII, called upon the South African Government to 'end violence against the African people and take urgent steps to eliminate apartheid and racial discrimination'. The

---

[36] UN Doc A/7754, 7 Nov. 1969; see United Nations, *The United Nations and Apartheid, 1948–1994*, Blue Books Series, vol. 1, Document 57, 309, 311.

[37] A/9061, 7 May 1973; see UN, *The United Nations and Apartheid*, Document 68, 319, 320.

[38] 'Le Problème de la mise de la guerre hors la loi', (1928–IV) 24 Hague *Recueil* 166.

[39] SC Resolution 418, 4 Nov. 1977.

Security Council also established a Committee consisting of all its members, to examine the progress of the implementation of Resolution 418, study ways in which the embargo could be made more effective, and make recommendations to the Security Council. In response to the worsening situation inside South Africa, the Security Council made further extensions to the embargo during the 1980s but these were not mandatory.

Stressing the significance of Resolution 418 (1977), the UN Secretary-General said that it was abundantly clear that the policy of apartheid, as well as the measures taken by the South African Government to implement that policy, were 'such a gross violation of human rights and so fraught with danger to international peace and security that a response commensurate with the gravity of the situation was required'.[40] He also felt it was significant that this momentous step was based on the unanimous agreement of the Council members. He declared that the UN had entered a 'new and significantly different phase' of the efforts to 'obtain redress' for the 'grievous wrongs' of apartheid.[41] Like Article 6, a mandatory arms embargo under Chapter VII of the UN Charter has a punitive element and is only to be applied in the gravest of situations. This is clear from the words of the Secretary-General, and arguably a 'gross violation of human rights fraught with danger to international peace and security' may also be described as a crime. Other significant responses to apartheid which could be construed as containing an element of punishment include the oil embargo and the sports and cultural boycotts which had a direct effect on the population in general.

In cases involving the possible commission of an international crime, the international community has had a tendency to be selective in its concerns and its condemnation. The international community was able to unite in its condemnation of South Africa because apartheid was a crime the perpetration of which was unthinkable to most states. This is not necessarily true of other flagrant violations of human rights including genocide. It would seem that South Africa was branded a criminal for almost half a century and that the severe sanctions directed against it encouraged if not created positive change. The case of apartheid in South Africa could therefore be described as one in which the state itself was punished for a crime by the international community, and although responsibility in this case was limited to cessation of the wrongful act of apartheid, this goal was ultimately achieved.

[40] S/PV.2046, 4 Nov. 1977; see *The United Nations and Apartheid*, Document 90, 348.
[41] Ibid.

4. INSTANCES OF STATE-SPONSORED TERRORISM

(a) The *Rainbow Warrior* Affair

The *Rainbow Warrior* sinking on 10 July 1985 in Auckland harbour, New Zealand, was an officially organized undercover French military operation with the strictly limited purpose of obstructing Greenpeace protests against French nuclear testing in the South Pacific. One member of the ship's crew, who was a citizen of the Netherlands, was killed in the operation. It emerged that explosives had been placed on the ship by agents of the Directorate General of External Security (DGSE), an arm of the French Ministry of Defence, and the French Government subsequently admitted responsibility. While it is an established principle that the state which sends agents to commit an illegal act abroad is liable rather than the agents themselves, in this case it was New Zealand's desire to secure both redress for the infringement of its sovereignty by France and the criminal conviction under municipal law of the captured agents themselves. The two DGSE agents who were arrested in New Zealand were sentenced to a total of ten years' imprisonment each for manslaughter and wilful damage by the national courts.[42] It was held that the offences were terrorist acts and that military personnel acting under official orders were not exempt from personal responsibility for crimes. Following negotiations between France and New Zealand it was agreed to refer all outstanding disputes between them regarding the *Rainbow Warrior* affair to the UN Secretary-General whose ruling they promised to observe.

In the Memorandum of the Government of New Zealand to the Secretary-General,[43] it was argued that the attack on the *Rainbow Warrior* constituted a serious violation of basic norms of international law, in particular, both New Zealand's sovereignty and the Charter of the UN had been violated, and these violations were neither accidental nor technical:

International law and New Zealand's sovereignty were violated deliberately and contemptuously. There is no room for doubt that the attack was both authorized and funded at a high level. The purpose of the operation was to prepare the ground for and to execute *a criminal act of violence* against property in New Zealand. This was done without regard for innocent civilians. That purpose was achieved and one of its consequences was the death of an innocent civilian.[44]

New Zealand went on to talk of the 'international legal responsibility' of the French Government for an incident which France admitted was '*a criminal outrage* committed on [New Zealand] territory, an outrage which nothing can excuse'.[45]

---

[42] *R v Mafart and Prieur*, New Zealand, High Court, Auckland Registry, 22 Nov. 1985, (Davison CJ) in 74 ILR 241.   [43] 74 ILR 257.

[44] Ibid. 258 (emphasis added).

[45] Letter of 8 Aug. 1985 from the President of France to the Prime Minister of New Zealand, 74 ILR 263 (emphasis added).

In its Memorandum France did present a half-hearted attempt to justify its actions on the basis that there had been a history of 'hostile action' by Greenpeace in the form of 'illegal' penetrations into waters around the Mururoa nuclear test site in 1973 and 1982, and that New Zealand had intervened in the internal affairs of France with respect to nuclear testing.[46] In the words of President Mitterrand, New Zealand had been a 'platform and a relay for initiatives hostile to France'.[47] However, France did not put forward a strong case that it had acted in 'anticipatory self-defence', and indeed it would have been difficult to argue that France was under attack, or faced with an instant, overwhelming threat, leaving no choice of means, by a non-violent environmentalist group.

The Secretary-General ruled that France should offer New Zealand an apology and that it should pay $7,000,000 in compensation.[48] In addition, compensation was to be paid to the relatives of the deceased crew member. It was decided that the two French officers serving prison sentences in New Zealand should be transferred to a French military facility on the isolated island of Hao in French Polynesia for a period of three years. The question of state criminality was not addressed, although it could be argued that the sum that France was required to pay amounted to punitive damages or a fine.[49] As part of the Secretary-General's settlement, France undertook to pay compensation to Greenpeace. France accepted liability and negotiations took place regarding the quantum of damages, but these failed and arbitration resulted.[50]

The *Rainbow Warrior* affair is significant in several respects. First, although the incident was an isolated act of terrorism which had no particular consequences for world peace, it was treated as a serious 'international delinquency' involving consequences which are consistent with the notion of criminal responsibility. Second, it is notable that New Zealand obtained justice with regard both to the agents and to the state which sent them, and while it is true that the agents in this case were not held criminally responsible under international law, a dual system of individual and state responsibility was found to operate effectively.

(b) The Lockerbie Incident

On 21 December 1988 a Pan Am flight bound from London to New York exploded over the Scottish town of Lockerbie, killing all 259 people on board and eleven local residents. The Security Council immediately called upon all

---

[46] 74 ILR 265.   [47] *Keesing* (1986), vol. 32, no. 8, 34565.
[48] *Rainbow Warrior* (New Zealand v. France), 6 July 1986, 74 ILR 241, 271.
[49] See further p. 195 above.
[50] The award dealt with exemplary damages, but is unpublished due to a special clause preventing publication without prior agreement.

states to assist in the apprehension and prosecution of those responsible for the tragedy.[51] Three years later it was announced by the Lord Advocate of Scotland that two Libyan nationals, alleged to be officers of the Libyan Intelligence Services and also working for Libyan Airlines, had been charged with conspiracy, murder, and contravention of the Aviation Security Act of 1982 for their role in placing explosives on board the Pan Am flight.[52] Warrants for their arrest were also issued in the US. A joint statement was subsequently put forward by the UK and the US requesting the Government of Libya: to surrender for trial all those charged with the crime and accept responsibility for the actions of Libyan officials; to disclose all knowledge of the crime, including the names of all those responsible, and allow full access to all witnesses, documents and other material evidence; and to pay appropriate compensation.[53] The British Foreign Secretary went on to assert that the accused individuals had acted as part of a conspiracy to further the purposes of the Libyan Intelligence Services by criminal means which amounted to terrorism. He described the Lockerbie incident as a case of 'mass murder, which is alleged to involve the organs of government of a state'.[54]

Libya denied the allegations made by the US and the UK, but offered to cooperate by allowing those states to scrutinize the facts relating to its own investigations. Libya appeared to be acting in accordance with the 1971 Montreal Convention for the Suppression of Unlawful Acts of Violence against the Safety of Civil Aviation, which provides that interested states can request the extradition of alleged offenders, but the requested state is not legally bound to comply. However, in the Security Council the UK contended that 'what we are concerned with here is the proper reaction of the international community to the situation arising from Libya's failure, thus far, to respond effectively to the most serious accusations of state involvement in acts of terrorism'.[55] This statement preceded Resolution 731 of 21 January 1992, adopted under Chapter VI of the Charter, in which the Security Council expressed concern over the results of investigations which 'implicate officials of the Libyan Government' in the Lockerbie incident, deplored the fact that the Libyan Government had not yet responded effectively to the requests of the US, the UK, and France to 'cooperate fully in establishing responsibility for the terrorist acts' which had been committed, and urged the Libyan Government 'immediately to provide a full and effective response to those

[51] SC Resolution 5057, 30 Dec. 1988.

[52] Announcement by the Lord Advocate of Scotland, 13 Nov. 1991, reproduced in a letter dated 20 Dec. 1991 from the Permanent Representative of the United Kingdom of Great Britain and Northern Ireland to the United Nations addressed to the Secretary-General, S/23307, 31 Dec. 1991, Annex I; *Keesing* (1991), vol. 37, no. 11, 38599.

[53] Ibid. Annex III, and letter dated 20 Dec. 1991 from the Permanent Representative of the United States of America to the United Nations addressed to the Secretary-General, S/23308, 31 Dec. 1992; (1992) *Yrbk UN*, 52.   [54] (n. 52 above) Annex II.

[55] S/PV.3033, 21 Jan. 1992, 104.

requests so as to contribute to the elimination of international terrorism'. A Special Envoy was subsequently sent to Libya by the Secretary-General to monitor the implementation of Resolution 731.

On 3 March 1992 Libya instituted proceedings in the ICJ relating to a dispute with the UK and the US respectively 'over the interpretation or application of the Montreal Convention'.[56] Libya alleged that while it had complied fully with its obligations, the US and the UK were in breach of the Convention, and that those states were legally obliged to halt such breaches and to desist from all violations of the sovereignty, territorial integrity, and political independence of Libya including the threat or use of force. Libya requested the ICJ to adjudicate on this matter and to provide provisional measures pending its judgment. It is noteworthy that in Libya's opinion the Montreal Convention applied to 'state' as well as 'ordinary' terrorism.[57] It was the contention of the US and the UK, on the other hand, that the alleged involvement of the state placed the case outside the framework of the Convention.[58]

Shortly after the conclusion of the oral arguments on interim measures, the US and the UK pressed for the adoption of a second Security Council resolution, this time under Chapter VII of the Charter. In the opinion of the UK:

> The Court is dealing with claims under the Montreal Convention and the Security Council is dealing with its appreciation of whether Libya's failure to respond to the . . . demands [put forward by the United States and United Kingdom] concerning terrorism constitutes a threat to international peace.[59]

In Resolution 748 of 31 March 1992, the Security Council expressed its concern over Libya's failure to provide a full and effective response to Resolution 731 and decided that the 'Libyan Government must commit itself definitively to cease all forms of terrorist action'. It also determined that Libya's failure to renounce terrorism and comply with the Security Council's demand constituted a threat to international peace and security which justified the imposition of enforcement measures under Chapter VII of the Charter. This Resolution resulted in the refusal of the ICJ to grant provisional measures, on the basis that a state's obligations under the UN Charter prevailed over its obligations under any other international agreement, including the Montreal Convention.[60]

The US and the UK continued to insist that the trial of the accused individuals should take place in either Scotland or the US until eventually, in

---

[56] *Case Concerning Questions of Interpretation and Application of the 1971 Montreal Convention Arising from the Aerial Incident at Lockerbie*, Provisional Measures, (1992) ICJ Reports 3.

[57] See M. Weller, 'The Lockerbie Case: A Premature End to the "New World Order"?', (1992) 4 *African Journal of International and Comparative Law*, 302, 318.

[58] See F. Beveridge, 'The Lockerbie Cases', (1999) 48 *ICLQ* 658, 660.   [59] CR 96/6, 17.

[60] See n. 56 above.

1998, a compromise was reached whereby the trial would take place in the Netherlands, under Scots criminal law and procedure and before a panel of Scottish judges sitting without a jury.[61] The accused have been extradited to Scottish jurisdiction at Camp Zeist and the case came before the court in May 2000. At the first public hearing the judge, Lord Sutherland, appeared to agree with the Crown that it was a matter for the evidence whether the accuseds' membership of the Libyan Intelligence Services was a crucial factor in the ultimate weighing of the evidence by the court.[62] The case should provide an opportunity for the relationship between state responsibility and individual responsibility for international crimes to be explored in some depth.

The Lockerbie incident, and its treatment by the ICJ and the Security Council, raises the issue of responsibility on two levels. First, the responsibility of the individuals concerned was invoked for what was in principle a crime under international law and certainly a crime under municipal law. Second, the incident gave rise to state responsibility for an internationally unlawful act, on the assumption that the individuals were Libyan agents acting on behalf of Libya, which could be described as the criminal responsibility of the state of Libya for what amounted to the crime of terrorism. Both forms of responsibility were invoked simultaneously, but Libya vigorously denied any involvement. The American and British demands that Libya pay compensation could therefore be viewed as a prejudgment, supported by the Security Council, as the responsibility of the Libyan state was premised on the guilt of the accused individuals which had not been established. The closest Libya came to admitting responsibility was during dealings with the UN Secretary-General, where it stated that it would be willing to 'guarantee the payment of compensation awarded as a result of the responsibility of its suspected citizens' if they were unable to pay it themselves.[63]

In his Dissenting Opinion in the Provisional Measures phase of the *Case Concerning Questions of Interpretation and Application of the 1971 Montreal Convention Arising from the Aerial Incident at Lockerbie*, Judge Bedjaoui argued that the Lockerbie incident raised two distinct disputes, one legal, the other practical. The question of the extradition of the two Libyan nationals was a legal issue to be dealt with by the ICJ, while the wider question of state

---

[61] The compromise was put forward in a letter dated 24 Aug. 1998 from the UK and US missions at the UN to the Secretary-General. The Security Council subsequently adopted Resolution 1192 welcoming the proposal, requiring all states to cooperate in the trial and declaring the suspension of the sanctions regime upon the surrender of the accused. In contrast to the UK, the US maintained its sanctions against Libya.

[62] The defence had argued that the Libyan intelligence services were not an illegal organization and were not accused of having an illegal purpose at the relevant time. See the materials at www.law.gla.uk/lockerbie/index.htm.

[63] Letter from the Secretary of the People's Committee for External Liaison and International Cooperation, 27 Feb. 1992; see Weller, 'The Lockerbie Case', 317.

terrorism, including the international responsibility of the Libyan state, was being dealt with politically by the Security Council.[64] One of the difficulties with Security Council action in this case was that the label 'threat to international peace and security' was attached to an act which was not considered to pose such a threat when it occurred three years earlier. There was no question of a genuine threat to international peace and security at the point at which the Security Council invoked Chapter VII of the Charter, but the Council was convinced that Libya itself was responsible for terrorism, and needed a basis upon which to take affirmative action. In the ICJ, the UK contended that Libya's request for provisional measures was 'designed to fetter the Security Council . . . in the exercise of its proper powers and to preclude the Security Council from acting in relation to a wider dispute involving allegations that the Libyan state was guilty of state terrorism'.[65] But the question whether an analysis of the legal factors relevant to the Lockerbie case would have led to a result incompatible with the Security Council decision remained unanswered.[66]

The Lockerbie incident and Judge Bedjaoui's comment raise the question of the link between UN Charter mechanisms for the maintenance of international peace and security and the legal institution of state responsibility in cases involving international crimes. It is not clear whether the Security Council's response in the Lockerbie case was an attempt to restore peace or a vindication of the law.[67] The fact that there was no existing threat to peace when the Security Council passed Resolution 748 points towards the latter suggestion, although there is a possibility that the US and the UK were pursuing mainly political objectives. The ICJ's judgment on the merits of the *Case Concerning Questions of Interpretation and Application of the 1971 Montreal Convention* may help to clarify some of the issues.[68]

The response of the Security Council to the Lockerbie incident provides some evidence of acceptance of the concept of state criminality, but also demonstrates a certain level of confusion over the appropriate legal and

---

[64] (1992) ICJ Reports 3, 33–4.   [65] Ibid. 11.

[66] On 27 Feb. 1998 the ICJ rejected the Preliminary Objections to its jurisdiction raised by the UK and the US and decided that the Application filed by Libya was admissible; see *Case Concerning Questions of Interpretation and Application of the 1971 Montreal Convention Arising from the Aerial Incident at Lockerbie (Libyan Arab Jamahiriya v UK)*, (1998) ICJ Reports 9; (*Libyan Arab Jamahiriya v US*), (1998) ICJ Reports 115.

[67] The case is further complicated by the fact that the US threatened to use force against Libya in response to its failure to comply with the Security Council Resolutions. It should also be recalled that on 15 Apr. 1986 the US, with the participation of the UK, bombed cities in Libya in response to alleged terrorist acts against US nationals and property, which resulted in civilian casualties. This action was not condemned by the Security Council due to the exercise of the veto by the US and the UK. The punitive raid on Baghdad by the US on 26 June 1993 in response to Iraq's alleged role in a plot to assassinate President Bush was a similar incident. The UN did not condemn the act, and the US was supported by the UK, the Russian Federation, and France, but this does not provide proof of legality; see (1993) *YrbkUN*, 431.

[68] Written pleadings are expected to be submitted by the parties early in 2001.

political consequences. The argument seemed to be that Libya's failure to extradite the suspected terrorists meant that it was supporting terrorism, which constituted a threat to the peace and also a continuation of the crime of state-sponsored terrorism, for which sanctions needed to be implemented. There was nothing extraordinary about the sanctions themselves,[69] and it is the explicit recognition of a state's involvement in an international crime by the Security Council, a body which is deemed to represent the international community, that is significant.

The Lockerbie incident and the *Rainbow Warrior* affair entailed very different responses. This is probably because France admitted responsibility for the attack on the ship belonging to Greenpeace and hoped to secure the release of its agents as a result, whereas Libya denied responsibility for the placing of explosives aboard the Pan Am aeroplane and attempted to pin the blame on the individuals who were allegedly involved. The pattern which emerges from these cases is that although the international community is beginning to recognize certain acts as criminal even when committed by the state, it has been reluctant expressly to give this legal substance. The effort to do so was largely successful in the *Rainbow Warrior* case, perhaps because of the relatively small-scale nature of the crime.

5. STATE OPINION

One of the requirements for the formation of a rule of customary international law is the acceptance by states that the rule is binding in law (*opinio juris sive necessitatis*). The opinions of states also play a vital role in the process of the codification and progressive development of international law by the ILC. There is consequently a considerable amount of evidence of what states actually think of Article 19 of the Draft Articles on State Responsibility. This provides some indication of whether or not states recognize and accept the concept of state criminality which Article 19 attempts to embody, but it must be emphasized that the comments of states relate essentially to the status of the concept within the remit of the Draft Articles and not to any status it may have otherwise in international law.[70] However, states have not always kept these two separate questions distinct.

Upon its adoption by the ILC, Article 19 met with a generally favourable

---

[69] These included the cessation of all air links with Libya, the prohibition of trade in arms and related material, and the reduction of the staff in Libyan diplomatic missions abroad. When these sanctions proved to be ineffective by Nov. 1993, the Security Council adopted Resolution 883, which extended the range of sanctions to include the freezing of all Libyan funds held abroad (with the exception of petroleum related assets), the banning of trade in oil-related equipment, and the cessation of all dealings with the Libyan Arab Airline.

[70] See also pp. 183–4 above.

response from developing and East European states in the Sixth Committee of the General Assembly.[71] India felt that the distinction between international crimes and delicts was bound to promote international solidarity because it recognized the fundamental interests of the international community as a whole.[72] Article 19 was also a 'matter of the greatest importance'[73] for the Kenyan delegation. The Soviet Union considered that the distinction made in Article 19 between international crimes and delicts was of 'fundamental importance', and the fact that the members of the ILC adopted its text unanimously on first reading was particularly significant.[74]

In contrast, the reaction of Western states was more cautious, and most spoke against the idea of the criminal responsibility of states. France recognized that Draft Article 19 was one of the most delicate but important articles of the whole study, and its main concern was the fact that this article, with the exception of paragraph 1, contained solely rules of progressive development. In its view the ILC had espoused a trend which was far from constituting an established or generally recognized rule, and which was consequently premature.[75] The UK thought that the most crucial issue was whether contemporary international law recognized a distinction between different types of internationally wrongful acts on the basis of the subject-matter of the international obligation breached. The UK delegation stated:

> Although there was growing evidence of the existence of such a distinction between civil and criminal responsibility based on the importance attached by the international community as a whole to certain international obligations of a fundamental nature, the difficulty lay in defining such international obligations and assessing the consequences of such a distinction.[76]

The US could find no compelling argument for the inclusion of the concept of criminal responsibility in the ILC's Draft at the present stage of development of international legal institutions. The US did not feel that the perception that some acts affected a wider class than others compelled the conclusion that an international law of the criminal responsibility of states must be created. What it supported was the need for an analysis of ways to measure damages to the wider class, and if the ILC were determined to ensure that particularly grave breaches gave rise to a level of responsibility which exceeded *restitutio ad integrum*, a mention of exemplary damages would have been significant.[77] Israel agreed with the doubts expressed on the advisability of retaining Draft Article 19, and warned that a document concerned with the objective criteria of state responsibility should not be injected with a political element and be allowed to reflect the deficiencies of the UN

---

[71] GAOR 31st session (1976), Sixth Committee, and see generally Weiler et al., *Crimes of State*, 45–79. [72] A/C.6/31/SR.29.
[73] A/C.6/31/SR.22. [74] A/C.6/31/SR.26. [75] Ibid. [76] A/C.6/31/SR.18.
[77] A/C.6/31/SR.17.

system.[78] There was therefore a significant divergence of state opinion concerning the desirability of Article 19, with most Western states doubting the existence of the concept of state criminality as part of positive international law.

It is valuable to compare the views of states in 1976 with their current views. In the Sixth Committee, at the fifty-first session of the General Assembly in 1996, the states of the Southern African Development Community remained in favour of the retention of the distinction between international crimes and delicts.[79] Japan merely stated that it felt 'further debate [was] necessary in such areas as the treatment of international crimes', without questioning the existence of a category of international crimes as such.[80] Ireland did not reject outright the concept of the criminal responsibility of states but argued:

There is not always a neat fit between domestic law concepts and those of international law, and this is clearly one of those cases where the proposed transposition of domestic law concepts into the international law field requires careful thought and reflection.

Ireland felt that the concept was conceivable as a theoretical construct, it being possible to give a general definition of an international crime and to identify some examples; however, its usefulness was queried.[81] Germany maintained the position it adopted when the distinction between crimes and delicts was first introduced, namely 'one of considerable scepticism regarding both the legal feasibility and the political desirability of the concept, combined with a cautious attitude of "wait and see" until not only draft article 19 of Part I but the entire system of legal consequences of crimes would be on the table', and suggested putting 'the genie of international crimes back into the bottle from where it was released twenty years ago'.[82] The French delegation did not contest the existence of internationally unlawful acts which were more serious than others, but felt that the distinction was still too vague.[83] The US and the UK were typically dismissive of the concept. The US had 'fundamental concerns about the very concept of state crimes. This concept does not find support in state practice. It confuses, rather than clarifies, the analysis of particular situations.'[84] Similarly, the UK argued that

---

[78] A/C.6/31/SR.28.

[79] Statement by A. Hoffmann on behalf of the states of the Southern African Development Community on Agenda Item 146: Report of the International Law Commission on the Work of its Forty-Eighth Session (Sixth Committee), UNGA, 51st Session, 7 Nov. 1996.

[80] Statement by M. Nakamura, Representative of Japan, on Item 146, 8 Nov. 1996.

[81] Statement by A. Connelly, Representative of Ireland, on Item 146, 7 Nov. 1996.

[82] Statement by B. Simma, Representative of Germany, on Item 146, 7 Nov. 1996.

[83] Interventions prononcées par M. Perrin de Brichambaut, Directeur des affaires juridiques, on Item 146, 4 and 7 Nov. 1996.

[84] Remarks of J. R. Crook, Office of the Legal Advisor, US Department of State, Sixth Committee, 7 Nov. 1996.

'the concept of "state crime" has not gained the broad international accept-ance that would be required for the introduction into the law of a new con-cept with such wide-ranging consequences'. The concept was found to be 'inchoate and lacking the modalities of implementation'. In essence, the UK felt that the concept lacked 'an adequate juridical basis and should not be retained'.[85]

More recently, in 1998, Ireland argued that the development of a dual clas-sification of internationally wrongful acts into international crimes and inter-national delicts was not desirable *de lege ferenda* for a number of reasons. First, the concept of crime as developed in national legal systems carried con-notations which could not be transposed easily into international law. Sec-ond, the application of penal sanctions to a state may be inherently unjust. Third, criminal liability was essentially about individual moral responsibility, and the best way to proceed was through individual criminal responsibility. Fourth, 'proposals for the progressive development of international law are unlikely to be successful if they are far removed from state practice'.[86] France proposed that Article 19 be deleted on the basis that it 'gives the unquestion-ably false impression that the aim is to "criminalize" public international law'[87] when in fact 'State responsibility is neither criminal nor civil' but 'sim-ply *sui generis*'.[88] The US continued strongly to oppose the provisions in the Draft Articles dealing with state crimes believing there to be no support for them under customary international law.[89] The US stated:

Existing international institutions and regimes already contain a system of law for responding to violations of international obligations which the Commission might term 'crimes'. Indeed, serious violations of humanitarian law, for instance, should be addressed through a coherent body of law applied by appropriate institutions. The Security Council has taken important steps in this direction through the creation of the International Criminal Tribunals for the Former Yugoslavia and Rwanda. Inten-sive international efforts are now under way to establish a permanent international criminal court. Avenues such as these clarify and strengthen the rule of law. By con-trast, the enunciation of a category of 'State crimes' would not strengthen the rule of law but could add unnecessary confusion.[90]

The UK remained 'firmly persuaded that it would be damaging and undesir-able to attempt to distinguish in the draft articles between international delicts in general and so-called "international crimes"',[91] and Austria expressed the view that there was little to be gained from the notion of state

---

[85] Statement to the Sixth Committee by I. Brownlie, Representative of the United Kingdom, on Item 146, 7 Nov. 1996.

[86] Comments and Observations received from Governments, A/CN.4/488, 25 Mar. 1998; Comments by Ireland under 'Article 19. International crimes and international delicts'.

[87] A/CN.4/488, Comments by France under Article 19.   [88] Ibid.

[89] A/CN.4/488, Comments by the United States under Article 19.   [90] Ibid.

[91] A/CN.4/488, Comments by the United Kingdom under Article 19.

crimes and that it had 'thus far not been accepted in State practice'.[92] Switzerland felt that the distinction between crimes and delicts amounted to 'an attempt by the international community to conceal the ineffectiveness of the conventional rules on State responsibility behind an ideological mask'.[93]

In contrast, the Nordic countries have consistently supported the ILC's distinction between crimes and delicts, and refer to the element of 'system criminality' in acts such as aggression and genocide. In their opinion, a state could be held responsible for these acts through punitive damages or measures affecting the dignity of the state.[94] Mongolia stood for the 'retention in the draft articles of both the concept of international crimes and the distinction of international wrongdoing between crimes and delicts',[95] and pointed out: 'The most important and appropriate requirement is that the determination of the commission of an international crime not be left to the decision of one State, but be attributed to the competence of international judicial bodies.'[96] The Czech Republic has maintained 'its consistent position in favour of maintaining a dichotomy of different types of internationally wrongful acts and, consequently, differentiating between the two regimes of State responsibility that such a dichotomy implies'.[97] The Czech Republic also stated: 'The idea of a specific regime for State responsibility for certain particularly serious acts is to be found in positive law and in State practice, although at the current stage no doubt in a relatively fragmentary, unsystematic or indirect form, or merely in outline.'[98] Italy supported the distinction between the most serious internationally wrongful acts and other wrongful acts, but argued that the special regime of state responsibility to be elaborated had 'nothing in common with penal sanctions such as those imposed under national criminal laws, and the use of some other term than "international crimes" could perhaps be envisaged'.[99] This seemed also to be the approach of the Czech Republic. Finally, Uzbekistan proposed a new version of Article 19, linking the concept of state crimes to that of a threat to international peace and security.[100]

In conclusion, it must be said that in the twenty-four years since the adoption by the ILC of a distinction between international crimes and delicts, the views of states have remained strikingly consistent. Overall, the mood is one of scepticism. Nevertheless, most states seem keen to continue the debate, and it should be remembered that the question facing the ILC is not so much whether international crimes of state exist as whether their existence should

---

[92] A/CN.4/488, Comments by Austria under Article 19.
[93] A/CN.4/488, Comments by Switzerland under Article 19.
[94] Written comments submitted to the UN Secretary-General by Denmark on behalf of the Nordic countries, 15 Jan. 1998.   [95] A/CN.4/488, Comments by Mongolia under Article 19.
[96] Ibid.   [97] A/CN.4/488, Comments by the Czech Republic under Article 19.
[98] Ibid.   [99] A/CN.4/448/Add. 2, Comments by Italy under Article 19.
[100] A/CN.4/448, Comments by Uzbekistan under Article 19.

be recognized in the Draft Articles on State Responsibility, and how. It should also be noted that the diverse comments so far received are not necessarily representative of the view of the international community as a whole.

6. DOCTRINE

The ILC commentary to Article 19[101] contains a detailed analysis of the development of the law relating to state responsibility up to 1976 in an attempt to find evidence in the literature of a distinction between two separate types of internationally wrongful act which depends on the subject-matter of the obligation breached, with each type entailing the application of a different regime of responsibility. This idea appears in a number of learned works; however, few writers openly advocate the adoption of a distinction between international crimes and international delicts. After the Second World War, Hersch Lauterpacht raised the question whether international law should make a distinction between two different categories of internationally wrongful acts of a state according to the gravity of the act in question and argued:

The comprehensive notion of international delinquency ranges from ordinary breaches of treaty obligations, involving no more than pecuniary compensation, to violations of international law amounting to a criminal act in the generally accepted meaning of the term.[102]

Verzijl viewed international crimes as distinct from delicts in that they not only created an obligation on the part of the offending state to restore the previously existing situation, or to indemnify the victim of the offence, but also entailed the application of sanctions by the international community.[103]

More recent doctrine provides a mixed response to the question of the existence of the concept of state criminality in international law, and often the comments relate directly to Article 19. Brownlie finds it doubtful whether the evidence adduced by the ILC gives more than very equivocal support for the existence of a category of state crimes as part of positive law.[104] Marek writes that the ILC Report 'itself bears witness to the complete absence of any penal elements in either the theory or the practice of international responsibility. The reader can therefore be referred to it for all the abundant material which directly contradicts its main proposition . . .'[105] In Gilbert's opinion the

---

[101] (1976) *YrbkILC*, vol. 2, pt. 2, 95–122.
[102] Oppenheim's *International Law*, i: *Peace*, 8th edn. (1955), 339.
[103] J. H. W. Verzijl, *International Law in Historical Perspective*, vi (1973), 741–2.
[104] I. Brownlie, *System of the Law of Nations: State Responsibility, pt. 1* (1983), 32.
[105] K. Marek, 'Criminalizing State Responsibility', (1978–9) 14 *Revue Belge de Droit International*, 460, 462.

nub of the issue is that '[a]cademics can generalize about, and Article 19 can even attempt to create international crimes, but until the breach thereof gives rise to different forms of liability it adds nothing to the development of any new trend in state responsibility'.[106] Cassese suggests that even though breaches of the rules referred to in Article 19(3), subparagraphs (a)–(c), have been considered by states to be delinquencies warranting a different legal response from that typical of international delicts, the international community has not gone so far as to regard them as crimes of state proper and to respond accordingly.[107] René-Jean Dupuy regards the concept of state crime as embodied in Article 19 as 'une œuvre d'innovation remarquable qui dépasse largement le concept prudent de "développement progressif"'.[108] Zemanek views the concept as an exercise in progressive development and advises against its adoption, believing that 'International law suffers already from too many notions which raise popular expectations that cannot be met'.[109]

On the other hand, Jiménez de Aréchaga describes Article 19 as a progressive development which has been generally well received by states in the General Assembly and by doctrinal opinion, and constitutes a basic response to the present needs of the international community.[110] Dugard does not find the difficulties inherent in Article 19 insurmountable and argues that 'state practice . . . lends support to the notion of state criminal responsibility', and that 'state criminal responsibility as a concept, albeit not as a developed programme of action, is today a part of international law'.[111] Pellet has been a consistent supporter of the notion of state crimes,[112] and Allott, in an otherwise scathing critique of the ILC's approach to the topic of state responsibility, favours the idea of attaching liability to states for criminal behaviour. He argues:

The most heinous international behavior will not be discouraged by attaching liability to individual human beings if it has the effect of removing legal and moral liability from the whole society which makes such behavior possible and for whose benefit

---

[106] 'The Criminal Responsibility of States', (1990) *ICLQ* 345, 366–7.

[107] A. Cassese, 'Remarks on the Present Legal Regulation of Crimes of States', in *Le Droit international à l'heure de sa codification: études en l'honneur de Roberto Ago*, iii (1987), 49, 50, 63–4.

[108] 'Communauté internationale et disparités de développement', (1979–IV) 165 Hague *Recueil* 13, 205.

[109] K. Zemanek, 'General Course on Public International Law', (1997) 266 Hague *Recueil*, 13, 257–9, 258.

[110] E. Jiménez de Aréchaga, 'General Course in Public International Law', (1978–I) 159 Hague *Recueil* 3, 273–5; see also E. Jiménez de Aréchaga and A. Tanzi, 'International State Responsibility', in M. Bedjaoui (ed.), *International Law: Achievements and Prospects* (1991), 356–8.

[111] 'The Criminal Responsibility of States', in M. C. Bassiouni (ed.), *International Criminal Law* i: *Crimes*, 2nd edn., 246 and 251.

[112] A. Pellet, 'Vive le crime! remarques sur les degrés de l'illicite en droit international', in *International Law on the Eve of the Twenty-first Century: Views from the International Law Commission* (1997), 287; 'Can a State Commit a Crime?', 425.

the behavior may well be carried out . . . Executing a few international criminals is not likely to encourage moral and lawful behavior by whole societies.[113]

Abi-Saab is of the opinion that 'At least the first three examples in Article 19, paragraph 3 provide clear cases in positive international law of aggravated responsibility for violations of certain fundamental norms.'[114] The latest edition of Oppenheim's *International Law*, edited by Jennings and Watts, which also appears to be the most recent authoritative opinion on the matter, provides unequivocal support for the notion of the criminal responsibility of states. The editors submit:

The liability of states is not limited to restitution or penal damages. Certain internationally wrongful acts attract, by reason of the special importance of the subject matter of the obligation which has been breached, a special and more severe degree of responsibility. The state, and those acting on its behalf, bear criminal responsibility for such violations of international law as by reason of their gravity, their ruthlessness, and their contempt for human life place them within the category of criminal acts as generally understood in the law of civilized countries.[115]

7. CONCLUSION

When the ILC adopted Draft Article 19 it was convinced that general international law differentiated between various types of internationally wrongful act and, consequently, between various regimes of international responsibility, although there was perhaps a tendency to conclude that positive law included little in support of the ILC's thesis, but that a different interpretation could yield the desired result. If the status of the concept of state criminality in contemporary international law is analysed in terms of the formation of custom, it could fall into one of four categories. First, it may be ahead of its time and non-existent as a concept outside the confines of the Draft Articles on State Responsibility. Second, it could have been an established part of customary international law which was merely codified by the ILC. Third, it may have become a part of customary law upon or since the adoption of Article 19. Finally, it might constitute an emerging category of customary international law.

To assert that the concept of state criminality does not exist would be to ignore the evidence of its existence that has been highlighted in the preceding chapters. But to go to the opposite extreme and argue that the concept was

---

[113] P. Allott, 'State Responsibility and the Unmaking of International Law', (1988) 29 *Harvard International Law Journal*, 1, 15.

[114] 'The Uses of Article 19', (1999) *EJIL*, vol. 10, no. 2, 339, 341–2.

[115] R. Y. Jennings and A. Watts (eds.), Oppenheim's *International Law*, i: *Peace*, 9th edn. (1996), 533–4.

strictly *lex lata* at the time of the adoption of Article 19 might mean artificially construing this evidence. It is therefore difficult to treat Article 19 as a problem of codifying existing law.

In the *North Sea Continental Shelf* cases Denmark and the Netherlands argued that even if at the date of the Continental Shelf Convention no rule of customary international law in favour of the equidistance principle existed, and no such rule was crystallized in Article 6, nevertheless such a rule had come into being since the Convention, partly because of its own impact and partly on the basis of subsequent state practice.[116] According to the Court these submissions involved treating Article 6 as a norm-creating provision which constituted the foundation of, or generated a rule which, while only conventional or contractual in its origin, had since passed into the general corpus of international law and was now accepted as such by the *opinio juris* of states.[117] The Court felt that this result was not lightly to be regarded as having been attained, and two main requirements would need to be satisfied. First, the provision would need to be of a fundamentally norm-creating character, such as could be regarded as forming the basis of a general rule of law. Regarding the provision under consideration by the Court, the very considerable and still unresolved controversies as to its exact meaning and scope raised doubts as to its potentially norm-creating character. Second, state practice in relation to the norm should be both extensive and virtually uniform, and should have occurred in such a way as to show a general recognition that a rule of law or legal obligation was involved.[118]

Judge Lachs has pointed out that '[e]ven unratified treaties may constitute a point of departure for legal practice',[119] and the Draft Articles have had some influence on the development of the customary law of state responsibility. However, it is improbable that Article 19 has had such an impact that the ICJ's two-stage test is now satisfied. States have rarely made reference to a category of international crimes except in connection with the work of the ILC, and these references fail to confirm the existence of a new normative conception, rather, they have tended to be rhetorical and polemical. Moreover, the ILC is considering abandoning the reference to state criminality altogether in order to produce a set of Draft Articles on State Responsibility which is acceptable to most states.[120] Therefore, it would be unwise to rely on the law-creating impact of Article 19. An unsuccessful attempt at progressive development may leave the law in a worse state than it would have been in if no attempt had been made, and it has been suggested that the issue of the criminal responsibility of states should not have been introduced into a set of draft articles that are essentially directed to other problems.[121]

---

[116] (1969) ICJ Reports 42.   [117] Ibid.   [118] Ibid.

[119] Dissenting Opinion, *North Sea Continental Shelf* cases, ibid. 225.

[120] See note to Article 40, A/CN.4/L.524, 13, and see First Report on State Responsibility by James Crawford, Special Rapporteur, A/CN.4/490 and Adds 1–3.   [121] See Brownlie, *System*, 32.

Another contention of Denmark and the Netherlands in the *North Sea Continental Shelf* cases was that, although prior to the Geneva Conference continental shelf law was only in its formative stage and state practice lacked uniformity, 'the process of the definition and consolidation of the *emerging customary law* took place through the work of the ILC, the reaction of governments to that work and the proceedings of the Geneva Conference', and this emerging customary law became 'crystallized in the adoption of the Continental Shelf Convention by the Conference'.[122] The Court agreed that rules of international law could be formed in this way, and there is a small chance that the concept of state responsibility for international crimes will one day become 'crystallized' by the adoption of a convention on state responsibility in which it is retained. But its current status as an 'emergent rule of customary international law'[123] can be supported even if the most that can be said with certainty is that some international wrongs are considered to be more serious than others and provoke more widespread and severe condemnation. Thus, if the question posed is whether positive law currently recognizes the concept of state responsibility for international crimes, the answer is probably 'no'. However, it is suggested that state practice since the Second World War confirms that the concept is gradually crossing the threshold between *lex ferenda* and *lex lata*, but that the final leg of its logical evolution still remains. Consequently, the concept will continue to raise issues which are both important and urgent. The final chapter will consider whether the threshold has already been crossed in relation to the crime of genocide.

---

[122] (1969) ICJ Reports 38 (emphasis added).   [123] Ibid. 39, 41.

17

State Criminality and the Significance of the 1948 Genocide Convention

1. INTRODUCTION

International jurisprudence relating to the concept of state criminality is relatively sparse. There are several reasons why international tribunals have not had occasion to deal with this issue. First, they are generally not competent to pronounce upon the consequences of the breach of an international obligation other than to determine whether reparation is due and, if so, to fix the amount to be paid. This limitation applies in particular to the ICJ which is empowered by Article 36(2)(d) of its Statute only to determine the nature or extent of any reparation due, although arguably this could extend to an assessment of punitive damages.[1] Second, the jurisdiction of international tribunals always has its origins in consent, and where the commission of a possible international crime is at issue, states are reluctant to submit to the judgment of a third party. Moreover, when a state injured by such an act considers itself entitled under international law to apply a sanction, it will not normally ask an international tribunal for the authority to do so or for confirmation that the application of the sanction was justified in the case in question.

The recent *Case Concerning the Application of the Genocide Convention* between Bosnia-Herzegovina and Yugoslavia has forced the ICJ to confront the question of state responsibility for criminal acts and it is proposed to analyse this case in some depth.

2. THE *CASE CONCERNING THE APPLICATION OF THE GENOCIDE CONVENTION (BOSNIA AND HERZEGOVINA V YUGOSLAVIA)*

On 20 March 1993, the Government of the Republic of Bosnia-Herzegovina filed in the Registry of the ICJ an Application instituting proceedings against the Government of the Federal Republic of Yugoslavia in respect of a dispute concerning alleged violations of the 1948 Genocide Convention.[2] The Application invoked Article IX of the Genocide Convention as the jurisdictional basis of the Court. Bosnia-Herzegovina requested the ICJ to adjudge and declare that Yugoslavia had *inter alia* violated several provisions of the

---

[1] See further Chapter 14 above   [2] (1993) ICJ Reports 3.

Genocide Convention. Bosnia-Herzegovina also requested the Court to indicate provisional measures to the effect that Yugoslavia should cease all acts of genocide against the people and state of Bosnia-Herzegovina. On 8 April 1993 the Court ruled: 'The Government of the Federal Republic of Yugoslavia should immediately, in the pursuance of its undertaking in the [1948 Genocide Convention], take all measures within its power to prevent commission of the crime of genocide.'[3] It would seem that the undertaking to which the Court is referring can only be that in Article I of the Genocide Convention, which imposes an obligation on states to prevent and punish the crime of genocide.

On 27 July 1993, Bosnia-Herzegovina made a second request for the indication of provisional measures to the effect that it should have the means to prevent acts of genocide and defend its people and state from such acts and from partition by means of genocide, including the ability to obtain weapons, equipment, and supplies. Meanwhile, on 10 August 1993, Yugoslavia requested the Court to indicate provisional measures requiring Bosnia-Herzegovina to take all measures within its power to prevent acts of genocide against the Bosnian Serbs. The Court responded by demanding the immediate implementation of provisional measures indicated in the April Court Order.[4] A Judgment on the Preliminary Objections raised by Yugoslavia was reached on 11 July 1996. Before considering the Court's Judgment, it is proposed to analyse the arguments presented by the two parties relating to the application and interpretation of the Genocide Convention.

In its Memorial,[5] Bosnia-Herzegovina requests the ICJ to adjudge and declare the following:

1. That . . . Yugoslavia . . . directly, or through the use of its surrogates, has violated and is violating the [Genocide Convention], by destroying in part, and attempting to destroy in whole, national, ethnical or religious groups within the, but not limited to the, territory of the Republic of Bosnia-Herzegovina, including in particular the Muslim population, by
— killing members of the group;
— causing deliberate bodily or mental harm to members of the group;
— deliberately inflicting on the group conditions of life calculated to bring about its physical destruction in whole or in part;
— imposing measures intended to prevent births within the group.
2. That . . . Yugoslavia . . . has violated and is violating the [Genocide Convention] by conspiring to commit genocide, by complicity in genocide, by attempting to commit genocide and by incitement to commit genocide;
3. That . . . Yugoslavia . . . has violated and is violating the [Genocide Convention] by aiding and abetting individuals and groups engaged in acts of genocide;

---

[3] Ibid. 24.   [4] Ibid. 349.
[5] Memorial of the Government of the Republic of Bosnia and Herzegovina, 15 Apr. 1994 (hereinafter Memorial).

4. That . . . Yugoslavia . . . has violated and is violating the [Genocide Convention] by virtue of having failed to prevent and punish acts of genocide;

5. That . . . Yugoslavia . . . must immediately cease the above conduct and take immediate and effective steps to ensure full compliance with its obligations under the [Genocide Convention].

6. That . . . Yugoslavia . . . must wipe out the consequences of its international wrongful acts and must restore the situation existing before the violations of the [Genocide Convention] were committed.

7. That, as a result of the international responsibility incurred for the above violations of the [Genocide Convention] . . . Yugoslavia . . . is required to pay and . . . Bosnia-Herzegovina is entitled to receive, in its own right and as *parens patriae* for its citizens, full compensation for the damage and losses caused, in the amount to be determined by the Court in a subsequent phase of the proceedings in this case.[6]

Bosnia-Herzegovina based its arguments on Article IX of the Genocide Convention, which it regarded as establishing state responsibility on three levels. First, it argued that a state may be guilty of genocide if it, or its officials or agents, commit genocide as defined in Article II of the Convention, or any of the acts enumerated in Article III. Second, it asserted that a state may be guilty of a breach of its obligations under Articles I, IV, V, and VI of the Convention if it fails to activate the organs and instruments of its domestic legal system to prohibit and prevent individuals from committing acts of genocide. Third, it added that the state commits a wrongful act according to Articles I and IV of the Convention when it fails to bring to trial and punish individuals who have committed acts of genocide.[7]

Bosnia-Herzegovina stated categorically that such responsibilities arise from a literal reading of the text of Article IX: 'the Convention defines genocide and corollary offences and establishes that these offences may be attributable to a broad range of individuals, high and low, *and also to states.*'[8] This, it was alleged, was 'no mere drafter's whim'.[9] Bosnia-Herzegovina recognized that it is necessary to have recourse to the *travaux préparatoires* leading up to the adoption of the Genocide Convention in order to determine the spirit and objectives of the drafters. Bosnia-Herzegovina concluded that it is 'absolutely clear from the *travaux* that the draft of Article IX was deliberately amended by the Assembly's Sixth Committee to include in the Convention a specific provision making states, in addition to individuals and groups, liable for the prohibited acts'.[10]

Throughout, Bosnia-Herzegovina emphasized that the question of a state's failure to prevent and punish genocide is completely separate from that of whether the state itself committed genocide. In attempting further to clarify

---

[6] See Memorial, 293, and (1996) ICJ Reports, para. 14.   [7] Memorial, 200–1.
[8] Ibid. 200.   [9] Ibid. 202.   [10] Ibid. 203–4.

its position regarding the nature of the action before the Court, Bosnia-Herzegovina stated:

The present action is not criminal in nature . . . The Genocide Convention, in describing genocide as 'a crime [under] international law' does so for a limited, specific purpose: to assert that states, in ratifying the Convention, 'undertake to prevent and to punish' the *persons* who commit such crimes. This provision does not purport to criminalize violations committed by states against other states.[11]

This was said to be the position under the terms of the Genocide Convention and the Statute of the ICJ, and it was claimed the *travaux* also make this clear. Article 19 of the ILC's Draft Articles on State Responsibility was referred to, but its relevance to the case at hand was deemed to be limited to the fact that it recognizes the possibility of genocide being committed by a state as such, and that this constitutes a 'wrongful act' taking the form of a state's breach of a fundamental treaty obligation.[12]

Yugoslavia challenged this interpretation of Article IX of the Genocide Convention, essentially on the ground that the Article uses the words 'including' rather than 'as well as' when referring to disputes relating to the responsibility of a state for genocide, which, it is argued, does not extend the jurisdiction of the Court as it appears in the first part of the Article:

In referring to the responsibility of a state, Article IX merely defines more closely the scope of the wording preceding the term 'including'. In the light of Articles I to VII this wording unquestionably refers to acts of genocide committed by individuals. The responsibility of the state as envisaged in Article IX is therefore responsibility resulting from any failure by the state to comply with the obligations spelled out in Articles I to VII concerning genocide committed by individuals. It is therefore a responsibility of omission, arising from a failure to react when confronted with genocide committed by individuals.[13]

Put simply, this means that a state is responsible for its failure to prevent or punish acts of genocide committed by individuals but is not responsible as such for acts of genocide. Yugoslavia argued that this interpretation is supported by the *travaux* and produced evidence to demonstrate that the responsibility envisaged is 'civil' as opposed to 'criminal', although Bosnia-Herzegovina did not appear to dispute this issue. Furthermore, Yugoslavia argued that the conflict occurring in certain parts of the territory of Bosnia-Herzegovina was of a domestic nature and that Yugoslavia did not exercise jurisdiction over that territory at the time in question. These assertions form the basis of Yugoslavia's Fifth Preliminary Objection:

[11] Ibid. 209.   [12] Ibid. 236–7.
[13] Verbatim Record, CR 96/5 (translation), 29 Apr. 1996, 51.

the case in point is an internal conflict between three sides in which . . . Yugoslavia was not taking part and . . . Yugoslavia did not exercise any jurisdiction within the region of Bosnia and Herzegovina at the material time,
. . . the Memorial of the Applicant State is based upon a fundamentally erroneous construction of the 1948 [Genocide Convention] and, in consequence the claims contained in the 'submissions' are based on allegations of state responsibility which fall outside the scope of the Convention and of its compromissory clause . . . there is no international dispute under Article IX of the Convention . . . and, consequently, the Court has no jurisdiction over this case.[14]

One major inconsistency in the arguments of Bosnia-Herzegovina was to refer to direct responsibility of the contracting parties to the Genocide Convention for criminal acts, while maintaining that such responsibility is 'civil'. In its Memorial, Bosnia-Herzegovina states:

genocide and other related wrongful acts which have been committed by Yugoslavia . . . according to the Government of Bosnia-Herzegovina amount to international crimes—in the sense international law gives to this expression. This follows clearly from Article 19 of the Draft Articles of the ILC on State Responsibility. . . .[15]

Bosnia-Herzegovina later declares that 'the present action is not criminal in nature and does not involve criminal procedure or rules of evidence and proof'.[16] This argument is difficult to sustain. Genocide, as defined in the Genocide Convention, is a crime, and it is difficult to see why it should necessarily involve different rules of evidence and proof when committed by states as opposed to individuals. It seems that Bosnia-Herzegovina was attempting to lower the standard of proof by shifting the burden to Yugoslavia and allowing inferences to be drawn from the patterns of proven facts, as is usual in civil proceedings. This raises the special problem of proving genocidal intent. Bosnia-Herzegovina stated that this '"intent" requirement would create undeniable problems in the present case if it were read to require that . . . Bosnia-Herzegovina . . . must demonstrate the individual or collective state of mind of the perpetrators of the atrocities'.[17] But this may be exactly what is required, precisely because it is a higher standard than that invoked in civil cases, where the general rule is that an actor is presumed to intend the natural consequences of his conduct. The requirement of intent is the distinguishing feature of genocide, and it must be shown that the intention is to eradicate a specified group.

Bosnia-Herzegovina's interpretation of Article 19 of the ILC's Draft Articles on State Responsibility is also misleading. It claimed that the term 'international crime' in Article 19 refers to matters which are irrelevant to the current litigation: 'Among them are the duty of states to criminalize acts of

---

[14] (1996) ICJ Reports, para. 14.   [15] Memorial, 187.   [16] Ibid. 209.
[17] Ibid. 223.

genocide committed by persons over whom they have jurisdiction.'[18] But this corresponds to a state's duty to prevent and punish genocide, a duty which Bosnia-Herzegovina alleged Yugoslavia had failed to perform. Bosnia-Herzegovina went on to say that 'the draft confirms Bosnia-Herzegovina's claim that the Genocide Convention's Article IX is applicable to states, as a wrong effected by the breach of a fundamental, inescapable treaty obligation, for which states may be held responsible by this Court'.[19] This statement is not supported by Article 19, which deals with state crimes and makes no reference to the ICJ.

The ICJ was therefore called upon to determine whether it had jurisdiction to entertain the case on the basis of Article IX of the Genocide Convention. Its conclusion was that the reference in Article IX to 'the responsibility of a state for genocide or for any of the other acts enumerated in Article III' did not exclude any form of state responsibility, nor was the responsibility of a state for acts of its organs excluded by Article IV of the Convention which contemplates the commission of an act of genocide by 'rulers' or 'public officials'.[20] The Court also decided that the applicability of the Genocide Convention was not restricted to a particular type of conflict, and that a state's obligation to prevent and punish the crime of genocide was not territorially limited by Article VI of the Convention. The ICJ rejected the Fifth Preliminary Objection of Yugoslavia by eleven votes to four, and determined that it had jurisdiction to hear the case on the merits, being in no doubt that there existed a dispute between the parties with respect to the meaning and legal scope of several provisions of the Genocide Convention, including Article IX, which thus related to 'the interpretation, application or fulfilment of the . . . Convention, including . . . the responsibility of a state for genocide'. Hence, the Court did not rule out the possibility that a state could be held directly responsible for genocide, but it was not necessary at this stage to comment on the form or extent of such responsibility.

3. THE INTERNATIONAL COURT OF JUSTICE'S INTERPRETATION OF THE GENOCIDE CONVENTION

The ICJ's interpretation of Article IX of the Genocide Convention raises the issue of intertemporal law. The intertemporal problem in international law relates to the delimitation of the temporal sphere of the application of norms while attempting to achieve a balance between the requirements of development and stability.[21] Fitzmaurice described the general principle in these terms:

---

[18] Ibid. 236.   [19] Ibid. 237.   [20] (1996) ICJ Reports, para. 32.
[21] See generally T. O. Elias, 'The Doctrine of Intertemporal Law', (1980) 74 *AJIL* 285; R. Higgins, 'Some Observations on the Inter-Temporal Rule in International Law', in J. Makarczyk (ed.), *Theory of International Law at the Threshold of the Twenty-First Century* (1996), 173.

In a considerable number of cases, the rights of States (and more particularly of parties to an international dispute) depend or derive from rights, or a legal situation, existing at some time in the past, or on a treaty concluded at some comparatively remote date ... It can now be regarded as an established principle of international law that in such cases the situation in question must be appraised, and the treaty interpreted, in the light of the rules of international law as they existed at the time, and not as they exist today. In other words, it is not permissible to import into the legal evaluation of a previously existing situation, or of an old treaty, doctrines of modern law that did not exist or were not accepted at the time, and only resulted from the subsequent development or evolution of international law.[22]

In the ninth edition of Oppenheim's *International Law*, Jennings and Watts state the general principle, but qualify it with the following:

Nevertheless, in some respects the interpretation of a treaty's provisions cannot be divorced from developments in the law subsequent to its adoption ... the concepts embodied in a treaty may be not static but evolutionary ... 'Moreover, an international instrument has to be interpreted and applied within the framework of the entire legal system prevailing at the time of the interpretation.'[23]

This qualification of the general principle is based to a significant extent on the ICJ's Advisory Opinion in the *Namibia* case, from which the quotation derives.[24] In its discussion of the mandates conferred by the League of Nations the Court also declared:

'the strenuous conditions of the modern world' and 'the well-being and development' of the peoples concerned—were not static, but were by definition evolutionary ... The parties to the Covenant must consequently be deemed to have accepted them as such. That is why, viewing the institutions of 1919, the Court must take into consideration the changes which have occurred in the supervening half-century, and its interpretation cannot remain unaffected by the subsequent development of law, through the Charter of the United Nations and by way of customary law.[25]

The question whether the general intertemporal principle was applicable in cases involving human rights was implicitly raised by the ICJ in its Judgment on Preliminary Objections in the *South-West Africa* cases.[26] Judges Spender and Fitzmaurice, who filed a Joint Dissenting Opinion, could find no justification for 'judicial rectification'[27] of the mistaken policy relating to South-West Africa

---

[22] G. G. Fitzmaurice, 'The Law and Procedure of the International Court of Justice', (1953) 30 *BYIL* 1, 5.

[23] R. Y. Jennings and A. Watts (eds.), Oppenheim's *International Law*, i: *Peace*, 9th edn. (1992) 1282.

[24] *Legal Consequences for States of the Continued Presence of South Africa in Namibia (South West Africa) notwithstanding Security Council Resolution 276 (1970)*, (1971) ICJ Reports 3.

[25] Ibid. 31.   [26] (1962) ICJ Reports 319.   [27] Ibid. 540.

and did not favour the application of a 'principle of "hindsight"'.[28] Thirlway describes the technique of judging not the actual intention of the parties concerned, but what ought to have been their intention with the benefit of hindsight, as 'intertemporal renvoi'.[29] In the *Aegean Sea Continental Shelf* case, the Court applied a presumption that the meaning of a generic term is 'intended to follow the evolution of the law and to correspond with the meaning attached to the expression by the law in force at any given time'.[30]

The European Court of Human Rights has emphasized that the European Convention on Human Rights is a living instrument and that human rights should be interpreted by reference to developing ideas and 'in the light of present day conditions'.[31] Higgins argues that '"generic clauses" and human rights provisions are not really random exceptions to a general rule. They are an application of a wider principle—intention of the parties, reflected by reference to the objects and purpose—that guides the law of treaties.'[32] She states that this was also the approach of the *Institut de Droit International* which took up the idea that any interpretation of a treaty must take into account all relevant rules of international law binding the parties at the time of application in its 1975 resolution concerning 'The Intertemporal Problem in International Law'.[33] The 1969 Vienna Convention on the Law of Treaties contains no provision dealing directly with the intertemporal issue as it relates to the interpretation of treaties.

The intertemporal issue is clearly relevant to an interpretation of the Genocide Convention half a century after its adoption, but it was not addressed by the Court in its 1996 Judgment. The *travaux* and the literature indicate that at the time of its adoption, Article IX almost certainly excluded the criminal responsibility of a state for genocide and was probably limited to the civil responsibility of a state for its failure to fulfil the obligation to prevent and punish acts of genocide. Yet the Court states that Article IX does not exclude any form of state responsibility. This result could still have been achieved without ignoring the intertemporal problem and it is proposed to examine some of the possible arguments.

Although in some senses it could be argued that the Genocide Convention was not of an evolutionary character, as it addressed a specific type of act

---

[28] Ibid.

[29] H. Thirlway, 'The Law and Procedure of the International Court of Justice', (1989) 60 *BYIL* 1, 135–43.   [30] (1978) ICJ Reports 3, 32.

[31] *Tyrer* case, Judgment, (1978), Series A, no. 26, para. 31.

[32] Higgins, 'Some Observations', 181.

[33] A proposal by Fitzmaurice to delete this statement was defeated. *Annuaire de L'Institut de Droit International* (1975), 339 and 367–70; *Annuaire de l'Institut de Droit International* (1992), Résolutions 1957–91, 111–13; see also Higgins, 'Some Observations', 180 and Thirlway (n. 29 above), 138.

which had occurred in the past, this would ignore the subsequent development of customary law relating to genocide and the classification of the rule prohibiting genocide as *jus cogens*. The Court does make some reference to these developments and to the customary and *erga omnes* character of the rights and obligations enshrined by the Convention,[34] but fails to explain how the responsibility of states for genocide may have evolved. One criticism of the *Namibia* decision was that no evidence was produced to show that the parties in fact accepted the concepts at issue to be evolutionary, and in his Dissenting Opinion, Fitzmaurice found that there could not have been such an intention even though he accepted the principle of allowing recourse to modern law in this way.[35] With respect to the Genocide Convention, there is evidence that the drafters and signatories did consider the issue of state responsibility to be evolutionary.[36] Many of the drafters were keen to include the direct responsibility of a state for genocide in the Convention and Article IX seems to have been left deliberately vague so as to allow for future developments.[37] Moreover, the scope of Article IX was debated by signatory states, and it seems that states were open to interpret it narrowly or broadly. In the light of the *Namibia* decision, it would appear that the Court is at liberty to interpret or reinterpret Article IX in a manner which reflects the developments which have taken place since the adoption of the Genocide Convention, and it seems appropriate to do so given the continued occurrence of genocidal acts and the corresponding worldwide concern. Indeed, because genocide is typically committed by a state against its own citizens, it is particularly important to allow for the evolution of the law of state responsibility in this sphere.

4. COUNTER-CLAIMS IN THE *CASE CONCERNING THE APPLICATION OF THE GENOCIDE CONVENTION* [38]

On 17 December 1997, the ICJ decided by thirteen votes to one that the counter-claims submitted by Yugoslavia in its Counter-Memorial fulfilled the conditions governing counter-claims laid down in Article 80 of the Rules of

---

[34] (1996) ICJ Reports, para. 31.

[35] (1971) ICJ Reports 3, 277; and see Thirlway, 'Law and Procedure', 137–8.

[36] Indeed, the crime of genocide as such was considered to be evolutionary. This is borne out by the Preamble to the Convention, which states that genocide has marred all periods of history, and in the ad hoc Committee the Soviet representative pointed out that the Convention would apply not only to then existing forms of genocide but also 'to any method that might be evolved in the future with a view to destroying the physical existence of a group'. See Letter dated 24 May 1994 from the Secretary-General to the President of the Security Council, S/1994/674, including Final Report of the Commission of Experts Established pursuant to SC Resolution 780 (1992), para. 89.   [37] See also Chapter 2 above, s. 3(b).

[38] See http://www.icj-cij.org/idocket/ibhy/ibhyorders/ibhyorder971217.html.

Court and were consequently admissible. The Court must therefore consider the following claims made by Yugoslavia:

1. In view of the fact that no obligations established by the [Genocide Convention] have been violated with regard to Muslims and Croats
—since the acts alleged by the Applicant have not been committed at all, or not to the extent and in the way alleged by the Applicant, or
—if some have been committed, there was absolutely no intention of committing genocide, and/or
—they have not been directed specifically against the members of one ethnic or religious group, i.e., they have not been committed against individuals just because they belong to some ethnic or religious group,
consequently, they cannot be qualified as acts of genocide or other acts prohibited by the [Genocide Convention], and/or
2. In view of the fact that the acts alleged by the Applicant in its submissions cannot be attributed to [Yugoslavia],
—since they have not been committed by the organs of [Yugoslavia],
—since they have not been committed on the territory of [Yugoslavia],
—since they have not been committed by the order or under control of the organs of [Yugoslavia],
—since there is no other grounds based on the rules of international law to consider them as 'acts of [Yugoslavia]'
therefore the Court rejects all claims of the Applicant, and
3. Bosnia and Herzegovina is responsible for the acts of genocide committed against the Serbs in Bosnia and Herzegovina and for other violations of the obligations established by the [Genocide Convention]. . . .[39]

Among others, these claims specifically raise the question of a state's genocidal intent which will have to be examined by the Court.

In his Separate Opinion, Judge ad hoc Lauterpacht pointed to the problems posed by the operation of Article IX of the Genocide Convention, and stated that they are 'of an entirely different kind from those normally confronting an international tribunal of essentially civil, as opposed to criminal, jurisdiction'.[40] Judge Weeramantry, who dissented from the Court's decision, argued that the concept of a counter-claim is inapplicable to criminal offences, thus clearly interpreting the dispute as something other than a civil claim. In his opinion, the Genocide Convention 'takes us beyond the realm of crimes against any particular State, and into the realm of crimes against humanity, where the notion of balancing of individual State interests is unthinkable'.[41] His statement echoes that of the ICJ in the *Reservations to the Convention on Genocide* case,[42] where, in discussing the objects of the Genocide Convention, the Court stated: 'In such a Convention the contracting states do not have any interests of their own; they merely have, one and all, a

---

[39] Ibid. 6 (para. 5).   [40] Ibid. 30 (para. 23).
[41] Ibid. 34.   [42] (1951) ICJ Reports, 15.

common interest, namely, the accomplishment of those high purposes which are the *raison d'être* of the convention.'[43]

5. POSSIBLE IMPLICATIONS OF THE JUDGMENT IN THE *CASE CONCERNING THE APPLICATION OF THE GENOCIDE CONVENTION*

The possibility that the ICJ could decide to hold Yugoslavia and/or Bosnia-Herzegovina directly responsible for genocide raises the question of the future position regarding other acts which currently entail the criminal responsibility of individuals, as opposed to states, under international law. The Geneva Conventions of 1949 and the additional Protocols which form the basis of international humanitarian law differ from the Genocide Convention in that they do not contain a compromissory clause conferring jurisdiction on the ICJ and they do not envisage the trial of offenders by an international criminal tribunal. This is somewhat surprising given that the Genocide Convention had been negotiated just a few months earlier. In the second Provisional Measures phase of the *Case Concerning the Application of the Genocide Convention*, Bosnia-Herzegovina invoked as additional grounds of jurisdiction the customary and conventional international laws of war and international humanitarian law, including, but not limited to, the four Geneva Conventions of 1949, Protocol I, the Hague Regulations on Land Warfare of 1907, and the Nuremberg Charter, Judgment, and Principles. The Court dismissed this on the grounds that

the applicant has not brought to the attention of the Court any provision in the texts enumerated conferring upon the Court jurisdiction to deal with a dispute between the Parties concerning matters to which those acts relate . . . such jurisdiction is not *prima facie* established.[44]

Thus, it seems that a similar case could not have been brought alleging state responsibility for war crimes alone on the basis of the instruments dealing with such crimes. However, Article 91 of Protocol I does address state responsibility:

A party to the conflict which violates the provisions of the Conventions or of this Protocol shall, if the case demands, be liable to pay compensation. It shall be responsible for all acts committed by persons forming part of its armed forces.

The provisions to which the Article refers relate primarily to the repression of breaches by individuals although the scope of the Article is unclear. Article 3

---

[43] (1951) ICJ Reports, 23　　　　[44] (1993) ICJ Reports 325, 341.

of the earlier Hague Convention (No. IV) Respecting the Laws and Customs of War on Land states similarly:

A belligerent party which violates the provisions of the said Regulations shall, if the case demands, be liable to pay compensation. It shall be responsible for all acts committed by persons forming part of its armed forces.

This provision suggests that the state itself may be liable for breaches of the Convention, but it is difficult to see how state responsibility could be established in the case of a dispute if there is no recourse to the ICJ. The issue of whether state responsibility in such instances is civil or criminal was never discussed, which perhaps indicates that it was assumed to be civil.

Common Article 1 of the 1949 Geneva Conventions state that the 'High Contracting Parties undertake to respect and ensure respect for the present Convention in all circumstances'. This Article is often viewed as providing a basis for international implementation of the Conventions.[45] The words 'ensure respect' seem to indicate that all states, whether or not they are involved in a particular conflict, have a duty to help secure the implementation of the Conventions in any situation where there is a violation. This was the interpretation put forward in Pictet's commentary to the Conventions, where he said 'that in the event of a Power failing to fulfil its obligations, the other Contracting Parties (neutral, allied or enemy) may, and should, endeavour to bring it back to an attitude of respect for the Convention'.[46] This interpretation seems to have developed since the negotiation of the Conventions. Previously, the words to 'ensure respect' meant that the whole population of a country which was a party to the Conventions should respect the law in all circumstances. In contrast, the modern interpretation implies the existence of an obligation *erga omnes* to comply with the Conventions.

The Apartheid Convention of 1973 contains a standard compromissory clause in Article XII:

Disputes between states parties arising out of the interpretation, application or implementation of the present Convention which have not been settled by negotiation shall, at the request of the states parties to the dispute, be brought before the ICJ. . . .

The Convention provides for the suppression and punishment of the crime of apartheid when committed by individuals, members of organizations and institutions, and representatives of the state. It is likely that as regards international crimes which are not the subject of a specific convention, a state would in most circumstances have to rely on the *erga omnes* character of the obligation in order to bring an action against another state. In the *Case Concerning the Application of the Genocide Convention* the ICJ does affirm that

---

[45] See A. Roberts, 'The Laws of War: Problems of Implementation in Contemporary Conflicts', (1995) *Duke Journal of Comparative and International Law*, vol. 6, no. 1, 29.

[46] J. Pictet, *The Geneva Conventions of 12 August 1949: Commentary*, i (1952), 26.

the rights and obligations enshrined by the Genocide Convention are rights and obligations *erga omnes*,[47] but it is doubtful whether the Court would have assumed jurisdiction on this basis alone. [48]

6. THE *CASE CONCERNING THE LEGALITY OF THE USE OF FORCE*

On 29 April 1999, Yugoslavia instituted proceedings in the ICJ against ten NATO countries for violations of the obligation not to use force against another state.[49] Yugoslavia invoked Article IX of the Genocide Convention as a possible basis for the jurisdiction of the Court. Yugoslavia's contention was that

> the sustained and intensive bombing of the whole of its territory, including the most heavily populated areas, constitutes 'a serious violation of Article II of the Genocide Convention' ... that 'the pollution of soil, air and water, destroying the economy of the country, contaminating the environment with depleted uranium, inflicts conditions of life on the Yugoslav nation calculated to bring about its physical destruction' ... that it is the Yugoslav nation as a whole and as such that is targeted ... that the use of certain weapons whose long-term hazards to health and the environment are already known, and the destruction of the largest part of the country's power system, with catastrophic consequences of which the Respondent must be aware, 'impl[y] the intent to destroy, in whole or in part', the Yugoslav national group as such.[50]

In its Orders in relation to Yugoslavia's request for the indication of provisional measures, the Court held that it did not have *prima facie* jurisdiction under Article IX to hear the case on its merits.[51] The Court referred to Article II of the Genocide Convention and concluded that the threat or use of force against a state could not in itself constitute an act of genocide and that there was no evidence of the necessary element of intent.[52] The Court did confirm, however, that disputes relating to 'the interpretation, application or fulfilment' of the Convention included disputes 'relating to the responsibility of a state for genocide or for any of the other acts enumerated in article III', even though in this case the acts complained of by Yugoslavia were incapable of coming within the provisions of the Genocide Convention.[53]

[47] (1996) ICJ Reports, para. 31.
[48] See the case of *East Timor* (Portugal v. Australia), (1995) ICJ Reports 90 and pp. 221–2 above.   [49] See ICJ web site: http://www.icj-cij.org.
[50] See *Yugoslavia v Canada*, http://www.icj-cij.org/icjwww/idocket/iyca/iycaorders/Iyca_iroder_19990602.htm, para. 34.   [51] Ibid. para. 41.
[52] Ibid. para. 39.   [53] Ibid. para. 36.

7. CONCLUSION

The *travaux préparatoires* of the Genocide Convention indicate a certain amount of confusion among the drafters of the Genocide Convention, who were keen to reflect the popular spirit of the age but hampered by the conservatism of states.[54] As Fitzmaurice pointed out during the debates in the Sixth Committee: 'Whilst everyone agreed that an act of genocide, if committed by a state or government, was a breach of the Convention, there appeared to be considerable difficulty in expressing that idea in the text of the Convention itself.'[55] While it would seem that the criminal responsibility of states was excluded given that few states supported such a notion in 1948, the wording of Article IX is nevertheless ambiguous, and the issue of the role of the state in the perpetration of genocide ought surely to be a question of criminality. It is arguable that Article IX was deliberately left ambiguous as the question of state responsibility was so difficult to settle. Had it been clear that the reference to state responsibility was to civil responsibility for the failure of a state to keep in force legislation intended to prevent and suppress acts of genocide, and for its failure to punish genocide committed on its territory against aliens, Article IX is unlikely to have generated so much debate. The precise wording of that Article is 'the responsibility of a state for genocide or for any of the other acts enumerated in article III'. If it had meant to say 'the responsibility of a state for failing to prevent or punish genocide', it is surprising that nobody pointed out the ambiguity. Thus, there is nothing in the Convention to exclude the direct responsibility of a state for genocide, and nothing to prevent its interpretation in a new light so that it reflects developments in international law.

The establishment of international criminal tribunals to try those accused of genocide and other international crimes committed in the former Yugoslavia and in Rwanda[56] has brought to life the ideals of the Genocide Convention in relation to individual responsibility. On 2 September 1998 the International Criminal Tribunal for Rwanda found Jean-Paul Akayesu guilty of genocide.[57] In its Judgment the Tribunal concluded that 'genocide was, indeed, committed in Rwanda in 1994 against the Tutsi as a group. Furthermore, in the opinion of the Chamber, this genocide appears to have been

---

[54] See also Chapter 2 above.

[55] See Official Records of the Third Session of the General Assembly, Part I, Sixth Committee, Legal Questions, Summary Records of Meetings, 21 Sept.–10 Dec. 1948, 96th Meeting, 352.

[56] Statute for the International Criminal Tribunal for the Former Yugoslavia, 22 Feb. 1993 (1993) 32 *ILM* 1159; Statute for the International Criminal Tribunal for Rwanda, 8 Nov. 1994 (1994) 33 *ILM* 1598.

[57] *The Prosecutor v Jean-Paul Akayesu*, Case No. ICTR–96–4–T, (1998) 37 *ILM* 1399 (summary); See also International Criminal Tribunal for Rwanda web site: http://www.un.org/ictr.

meticulously organized.'[58] The Tribunal also pointed out that 'an accused person could be declared innocent of the crime of genocide even when it is established that genocide had indeed taken place, but also ... a person could be found guilty of genocide without necessarily having to establish that genocide had taken place throughout the country concerned'.[59] In other words, the Tribunal's task is to assess solely individual criminal responsibility. It is the ICJ's task to consider the question whether the Genocide Convention is also equipped to deal with state responsibility for genocide in cases in which genocide has occurred 'throughout the country concerned'.

The ICJ plays an important role in developing international law,[60] and a judgment that Yugoslavia and/or Bosnia-Herzegovina are directly responsible for genocide could have significant repercussions. In his Dissenting Opinion in the Judgment on Preliminary Objections, Judge ad hoc Kreca uttered the warning that such a judgment could propel the Court into a quasi-legislative arena.[61] His fear related to the possibility that the Court might accept the concept of the criminal responsibility of a state which he believed had 'not yet found a place within positive international law'.[62]

It is suggested, however, that the advances in relation to the crime of genocide may represent the crystallization of the concept of state criminality in a first stage of development. It would seem that a state can be held responsible, albeit primarily in a civil sense, for what is expressly recognized to be a criminal act even when committed by the state. In the *Case Concerning the Application of the Genocide Convention* the criminal character of genocide is not disputed, even though it is the state's responsibility for genocide that is under examination. In his Dissenting Opinion in relation to the Court's Order on Counter-Claims, Judge Weeramantry describes the case before the Court in criminal terms, although his approach is perhaps progressive.[63] However, there is a possibility that the ICJ might consider awarding punitive damages even if it is not within its powers expressly to determine that a state is *criminally* responsible for genocide.

The *Case Concerning the Application of the Genocide Convention* [64] has given both the Genocide Convention and the concept of state criminality renewed impetus, and signifies the re-emergence since the Second World War of the concept of state criminality as relevant and potentially workable. It would seem that state responsibility for genocide is undergoing a process of adaptation to the needs and expectations of today's international community and may be entering a *sui generis* domain.

---

[58] *The Prosecutor v Jean-Paul Akayesu*, para. 125.   [59] Ibid. n. 61.
[60] See also Conclusion to Part IV above.   [61] (1996) ICJ Reports, para. 103.   [62] Ibid.
[63] Order of 17 Dec. 1997: http://www.icj-cij.org/idocket/ibhy/ibhyorders/ibhyorder971217. html, 30.
[64] It should be noted that on 2 July 1999 Croatia instituted proceedings against Yugoslavia for violations of the Genocide Convention committed between 1991 and 1995. See ICJ web site: http://www.icj-cij.org.

Conclusion

A hundred and fifty years ago an English Admiralty judge, Dr Lushington, refused to accept that a state could not be a pirate.[1] It has always been the argument in the domain of international crime that the rules and principles are not static, but must develop so that they correspond to the needs of the international community of states as this community advances. In Part I of this book, it was argued that the concept of state criminality has a history that stretches back at least as far as the First World War, and that it has been a significant issue in the codification and development of the law relating to international crimes and state responsibility. The concept was found to be juridically feasible in Part II, and in attempting to give it greater specificity in Part III, a general principle of international law was revealed. The purpose of Part IV was to look more closely at the practical feasibility of the general principle, and to determine the extent to which this aspect lent support to the contention that the notion of state responsibility for international crimes was making its way across the boundary between *lex ferenda* and *lex lata*. Finally, in Part V it was suggested that both history and more recent state practice show that state responsibility for international crimes is an emerging category of customary international law. The conclusion to be derived from this discussion is that states can, in principle, commit crimes ranging from their earliest to their most modern manifestations, and be held criminally responsible, and that this is an emergent general principle of international law.

Some of the most significant developments since the Second World War relate to the crime of genocide and it may be that genocide is now in a special category.[2] The 1948 Genocide Convention and the concept of state criminality have been given contemporary relevance by the *Case Concerning the Application of the Genocide Convention*, and it is therefore possible that the general principle will emerge fully in relation to genocide in the first instance.

The major characteristics of the concept of state criminality and the elements of the existing framework for imposing criminal responsibility upon states under international law may be summarized as follows:

1. The concept of state criminality is an emergent general principle of international law.

---

[1] Referred to by Shawcross in his opening speech before the Nuremberg Tribunal: *The Trial of German Major War Criminals: Opening Speeches of the Chief Prosecutors* (1946), 57–8.

[2] See Chapter 17 above.

2. The emergent general principle of state criminality may also be described as an emerging category of customary international law.[3]

3. Crimes and delicts constitute two qualitatively different types of internationally wrongful act. Eight candidate criteria and indicia have been put forward in Part III as evidence of this conceptual distinction. This does not mean that a continuum of international responsibility is inconceivable, but simply that along such a continuum international responsibility passes through different stages. These stages relate both to the quality of the wrongful act (ranging from minor to exceptionally serious) and to the kind of actor (i.e. whether it is a state or an individual).

4. The concept of state responsibility for international crimes is juridically feasible and may be analysed in terms of a criminal organization model or a corporate crime model.[4]

5. Measures that correspond to punishment can be applied against a state,[5] and this sometimes occurs but on a pragmatic basis.[6]

6. The best response to state crimes which is available under the current international legal system may be a combination of:

(a) a declaratory judgment and/or an award of punitive damages[7] against the state by the ICJ or an international tribunal or commission. The ICJ could also play a role in settling disputes arising out of any action taken by the political organs of the UN. (In most cases involving the commission of a crime by a state, condemnation and collective action by the organs of the UN will occur immediately and will have the primary aim of stopping the wrongful act and restoring the pre-existing situation, although it may to some extent constitute a preliminary assessment as to the quality of the wrongful act. However, if the political organs wish to make a conclusive determination as to the quality of the wrongful act, without having recourse to the ICJ, they should establish a subsidiary body to serve a judicial function.)[8]
(b) trials of the individual leaders in the crime before an international criminal tribunal.

7. Possible alternative frameworks for imposing criminal responsibility on states in the future include:

(a) the extension of the jurisdiction of the proposed International Criminal Court to include states, or the establishment of a criminal division in the ICJ.[9]
(b) the creation of a complete regime of state criminal responsibility by the ILC in its Draft Articles on State Responsibility.[10] (The ILC has so far failed to produce a proper regime of state criminal responsibility. However, the

---

[3] The terminology derives from the *North Sea Continental Shelf* cases, (1969) ICJ Reports 4, 38–9 and 41; see Chapter 16 above, s. 7.   [4] See Chapters 3 and 4 above.
[5] See Chapters 13 and 14 above.   [6] See Chapter 16 above.   [7] See Chapter 14 above.
[8] See Chapter 15 above, s. 2(b).   [9] See above, Chapter 15, s. 3(a), and Chapter 2, s. 2(a).
[10] See Chapter 13 above, s. 5.

work of the ILC is significant in that it recognizes that the concept of state criminality will become a feature of international law.)

8. Apart from the above, the future development of the concept of state criminality may occur through:

(a) a 'common law' approach to the concept by judges in national, regional, or international courts and tribunals.[11] The concept contains elements that conduce to its development in this way.
(b) maturation of the concept of obligations *erga omnes*.[12]

9. By analogy with the concept of obligations *erga omnes*, the emergent general principle of state criminality may crystallize in a first stage of development before all the modalities of giving it practical and legal substance are worked out.

The question of the moral and political feasibility of the concept of state criminality has been touched upon. It was suggested in Chapter 8 that there is such a thing as a 'conscience of mankind' which is a source of positive morality in international law. Morality or ethics may be viewed as a body of higher rules designed to ensure harmonious social relations. The question arises as to whether morality as such can be ascribed to a state or to the international community (in accordance with the corporate crime model). It has been shown that under international law responsibility may be imputed to a state for the activities of the individuals by whom it is governed. Arguably, if conduct can be attributed in this way, so might morality. As Kelsen has pointed out, 'if it is possible to impute physical acts performed by individuals to the State although the State has no body, it must be possible to impute psychic acts to the State although the State has no soul. Imputation to the State is a juristic construction, not a description of natural reality.'[13] A state's activities are inevitably judged on the basis of human ideas and ideals of morality and the difficulty with the classical view of criminal law as a moral code is that it tends to assume a unitary view of morality.

It could be argued, on the other hand, that since the essence of the concept of state criminality is that the state itself is responsible, this is not a form of vicarious liability but original responsibility (in accordance with the organizational criminality model). Therefore, not only those persons exercising authority in a state but the state as a legal person in its own right must be shown to be the subject of a moral code. Given that each state has its own moral code reflected in its criminal law, international morality could be said to exist to the extent that the moral codes of individual states overlap. The

---

[11] See above, Chapter 15, s. 3(c), and Conclusion to Part IV.
[12] See above, Chapter 6 and Chapter 15, s. 3(b).
[13] H. Kelsen, 'Collective and Individual Responsibility in International Law with Particular Regard to the Punishment of War Criminals', (1942–3) 31 *California Law Rev.*, 530, 533.

state would then be the subject of this higher, more universal without being unitary, moral code.

The institution of a regime of state criminal responsibility fosters complex policy implications. Justice Jackson, Chief Prosecutor for the US at the Nuremberg Tribunal, made the following bold declaration:

let me make it clear that while this law is first applied against German aggressors, the law includes, and if it is to serve a useful purpose it must condemn, aggression by any other nations, including those which sit here now in judgment.[14]

However, there is clearly a danger that the notion of state criminality could be used as a political weapon, and the Security Council has a tendency to be selective in its concerns and fickle in its responses. ('What know the laws that thieves do pass on thieves?'[15]) In some situations a state accused of a crime could legitimately argue *tu quoque* if it is judged by a single state or by states with shared goals. Were the concept to fall under the dominant influence or control of a few states, it could be used and abused to further their policy interests, and there would be the risk of discrimination and embarrassment to states. Furthermore, criminalizing an aspect of state responsibility could undermine rather than strengthen international political and legal security. If a state were accused of committing an act of aggression, for example, and military sanctions implemented against it and its unconditional surrender demanded, the collapse of the government and break-up of the social structure could cause internal strife and ever more serious threats to world peace. Today it seems that the greatest divisions between people and the dominating source of conflict is cultural:

The people of different civilizations have different views on the relations between God and man, the individual and the group, the citizen and the state, parents and children, husband and wife, as well as differing views of the relative importance of rights and responsibilities, liberty and authority, equality and hierarchy. These differences are the product of centuries. They will not soon disappear.[16]

It is submitted that despite these very real political issues, so long as the concept of state criminality takes care to reinforce the commonalities between cultures rather than the differences—and criminal law in any society is regarded as a necessary and unifying force—it can be a workable concept.

The concept of state criminality may be a means of ensuring that international consensus develops and endures, and in this sense it is an ennobling concept. Adding some vision and imagination to positive law need not be destructive; it may be a source of renewal of international law. It has been said: 'The law, like the traveler, must be ready for the morrow. It must have a

---

[14] *Opening Speeches* (n. 1 above), 45.
[15] Shakespeare, *Measure for Measure*, Act II, Scene 1.
[16] S. P. Huntingdon, 'The Clash of Civilizations?', *Foreign Affairs* (Summer 1993), 22, 25.

principle of growth.'[17] This book has taken the form of a journey through a variety of sources which has resulted in the uncovering of the *general principle* of the criminal responsibility of states. It seems plausible to suggest that this principle is now on the threshold, and it is 'ready for the morrow'.

[17] B. N. Cardozo, *The Growth of the Law* (1924), 20.

Appendix 1

Text of the 1948 Convention on the Prevention and Punishment of the Crime of Genocide

The Contracting Parties having considered the declaration made by the General Assembly of the United Nations in its resolution 96(I) dated 11 December 1946 that genocide is a crime under international law, contrary to the spirit and aims of the United Nations and condemned by the civilized world; recognizing that at all periods of history genocide has inflicted great losses on humanity; and being convinced that, in order to liberate mankind from such an odious scourge, international cooperation is required; hereby agree as hereinafter provided

ARTICLE I

The Contracting Parties confirm that genocide, whether committed in time of peace or in time of war, is a crime under international law which they undertake to prevent and punish.

ARTICLE II

In the present Convention, genocide means any of the following acts committed with intent to destroy, in whole or in part, a national, ethnical, racial, or religious group, as such:
- (a) Killing members of the group;
- (b) Causing serious bodily or mental harm to members of the group;
- (c) Deliberately inflicting on the group conditions of life calculated to bring about its physical destruction in whole or in part;
- (d) Imposing measures intended to prevent births within the group;
- (e) Forcibly transferring children of the group to another group.

ARTICLE III

The following acts shall be punishable:
- (a) Genocide;
- (b) Conspiracy to commit genocide;
- (c) Direct and public incitement to commit genocide;
- (d) Attempt to commit genocide;
- (e) Complicity in genocide.

ARTICLE IV

Persons committing genocide or any of the other acts enumerated in article III shall be punished, whether they are constitutionally responsible rulers, public officials, or private individuals.

ARTICLE V

The Contracting Parties undertake to enact, in accordance with their respective Constitutions, the necessary legislation to give effect to the provisions of the present Convention and, in particular, to provide effective penalties for persons guilty of genocide or of any of the other acts enumerated in article III.

ARTICLE VI

Persons charged with genocide or any of the other acts enumerated in article III shall be tried by a competent tribunal of the State in the territory of which the act was committed, or by such international penal tribunal as may have jurisdiction with respect to those Contracting Parties which shall have accepted its jurisdiction.

ARTICLE VII

Genocide and other acts enumerated in article III shall not be considered as political crimes for the purpose of extradition.

The Contracting Parties pledge themselves in such cases to grant extradition in accordance with their laws and treaties in force.

ARTICLE VIII

Any Contracting Party may call upon the competent organs of the United Nations to take such action under the Charter of the United Nations as they consider appropriate for the prevention and suppression of acts of genocide or any of the other acts enumerated in article III.

ARTICLE IX

Disputes between the Contracting Parties relating to the interpretation, application or fulfilment of the present Convention, including those relating to the responsibility of a State for genocide or any of the other acts enumerated in article III, shall be submitted to the International Court of Justice at the request of any of the parties to the dispute.

ARTICLE X

The present Convention, of which the Chinese, English, French, Russian and Spanish texts are equally authentic, shall bear the date of 9 December 1948.

ARTICLE XI

The present Convention shall be open until 31 December 1949 for signature on behalf of any Member of the United Nations and of any non-member State to which an invitation to sign has been addressed by the General Assembly. The present Convention shall be ratified, and the instruments of ratification shall be deposited with the Secretary-General of the United Nations.

After January 1950, the present Convention may be acceded to on behalf of any Member of the United Nations and of any non-member State which has received an invitation as aforesaid. Instruments of accession shall be deposited with the Secretary-General of the United Nations.

ARTICLE XII

Any Contracting Party may at any time by notification addressed to the Secretary-General of the United Nations, extend the application of the present Convention to all or any of the territory for the conduct of whose foreign relations that Contracting Party is responsible.

ARTICLE XIII

On the day when the first twenty instruments of ratification or accession have been deposited, the Secretary-General shall draw up a *procès-verbal* and transmit a copy of it to each Member of the United Nations and to each of the non-member states contemplated in article XI.

The present Convention shall come into force on the ninetieth day following the date of deposit of the twentieth instrument of ratification or accession. Any ratification or accession effected subsequent to the latter date shall become effective on the ninetieth day following the date of deposit of the twentieth instrument of ratification or accession effected subsequent to the latter date shall become effective on the ninetieth day following the deposit of the instrument of ratification or accession.

ARTICLE XIV

The present Convention shall remain in effect for a period of ten years as from the date of its coming into force. It shall remain thereafter in force for successive periods of five years for such Contracting Parties as have not denounced it at least six months before the expiration of the current period. Denunciation shall be effected by a written notification addressed to the Secretary-General of the United Nations.

ARTICLE XV

If, as a result of denunciations, the number of Parties to the present Convention should become less than sixteen, the Convention shall cease to be in force as from the date on which the last of these denunciations shall become effective.

ARTICLE XVI

A request for the revision of the present Convention may be made at any time by any Contracting Party by means of a notification in writing addressed to the Secretary-General.

The General Assembly shall decide upon the steps, if any, to be taken in respect of such request.

ARTICLE XVII

The Secretary-General of the United Nations shall notify all Members of the United Nations and the non-member States contemplated in article XI of the following:

(a) Signatures, ratifications, and accession received in accordance with article XI;
(b) Notifications received in accordance with article XII;
(c) The date upon which the present Convention comes into force in accordance with article XIII;
(d) Denunciations received in accordance with article XIV;
(e) The abrogation of the Convention in accordance with article XV;
(f) Notifications received in accordance with article XVI.

ARTICLE XVIII

The original of the present Convention shall be deposited in the archives of the United Nations.

A certified copy of the Convention shall be transmitted to all Members of the United Nations and to the non-member States contemplated in article XI.

ARTICLE XIX

The present Convention shall be registered by the Secretary-General of the United Nations on the date of its coming into force.

Appendix 2

Draft Articles on State Responsibility: Articles 15 to 19 on the Substantive and Instrumental Consequences of International Crimes Formulated by Mr Arangio-Ruiz, Special Rapporteur, in 1995[1]

ARTICLE 15

Without prejudice [In addition] to the legal consequences entailed by an international delict under articles 6 to 14 of the present Part, an international crime as defined in article 19 of Part I entails the special or supplementary consequences set forth in Articles 16 to 19 below.

ARTICLE 16

1. Where an internationally wrongful act of a state is an international crime, every state is entitled, subject to the condition set forth in paragraph 5 of article 19 below, to demand that the state which is committing or has committed the crime should cease its wrongful conduct and provide full reparation in conformity with articles 6 to 10 bis, as modified by paragraphs 2 and 3 below.

2. The right of every injured state to obtain restitution in kind as provided in article 7 shall not be subject to the limitations set forth in subparagraphs (c) and (d) of paragraph 1 of the said article,[2] except where restitution in kind would jeopardize the existence of the wrongdoing state as an independent member of the international community, its territorial integrity or the vital needs of its people.

3. Subject to the preservation of its existence as an independent member of the international community and to the safeguarding of its territorial integrity and the vital needs of its people, a state which has committed an international crime is not entitled to benefit from any limitations of its obligation to provide satisfaction and guarantees of non-repetition as envisaged in articles 10 and 10 bis, relating to the respect of its dignity, or from any rules or principles of international law relating to the protection of its sovereignty and liberty.

---

[1] See A/CN.4/469/Add.1.

[2] Article 7 relates to the injured state's entitlement to obtain restitution in kind provided this: (c) would not involve a burden out of all proportion to the benefit which the injured state would gain from obtaining restitution in kind instead of compensation; or (d) would not seriously jeopardize the political independence or economic stability of the state which has committed the internationally wrongful act, whereas the injured state would not be similarly affected if it did not obtain restitution in kind.

ARTICLE 17

1. Where the internationally wrongful act of a state is an international crime, every
   state whose demands under article 16 have not met with an adequate response
   from the state which has committed or is committing the crime is entitled, subject to the condition set forth in paragraph 5 of article 19 below, to resort to
   countermeasures under the conditions and restrictions set forth in articles 11, 13
   and 14 as modified by paragraphs 2 and 3 of the present article.[3]
2. The condition set forth in paragraph 5 of article 19 below does not apply to such
   urgent, interim measures as are required to protect the rights of an injured state
   or to limit the damage caused by the international crime.
3. The requirement of proportionality set forth in article 13 shall apply to countermeasures taken by any state so that such measures shall not be out of proportion to the gravity of the international crime.

ARTICLE 18

1. Where an internationally wrongful act is an international crime, all states shall,
   subject to the condition set forth in paragraph 5 of article 19 below:
   (a) refrain from recognizing as legal or valid, under international or national
       law, the situation created by the international crime;
   (b) abstain from any act or omission which may assist the wrongdoing state in
       maintaining the said situation;
   (c) assist each other in carrying out their obligations under subparagraphs (a)
       and (b) and, in so far as possible, coordinate their respective reactions
       through available international bodies or ad hoc arrangements;
   (d) refrain from hindering in any way, by act or omission, the exercise of the
       rights or powers provided for in articles 16 and 17;
   (e) fully implement the *aut dedere aut judicare* principle, with respect to any
       individuals accused of crimes against the peace and security of mankind
       the commission of which has brought about the international crime of the
       state or contributed thereto;
   (f) take part, jointly or individually, in any lawful measures decided or recom-
       mended by any international organization of which they are members against
       the state which has committed or is committing the international crime;
   (g) facilitate, by all possible means, the adoption and implementation of any
       lawful measures intended to remedy any emergency situations caused by
       the international crime.
2. Subject to the conditions set forth in paragraph 5 of article 19 below, the state
   which has committed or is committing an international crime shall not oppose

---

[3] In particular, Article 14 lists 'prohibited countermeasures' such as the threat or use of force
in breach of the UN Charter; any other conduct susceptible of endangering the territorial
integrity or political independence of the state against which it is taken; any conduct which is not
in conformity with the rules of international law on the protection of fundamental human rights,
is of serious prejudice to the normal operation of bilateral or multilateral diplomacy, is contrary
to a peremptory norm of general international law, consists of a breach of an obligation towards
any state other than the state which has committed the internationally wrongful act.

fact-finding operations or observer missions in its territory for the verification of compliance with its obligations of cessation or reparation.

ARTICLE 19

1. Any state member of the UN party to the present Convention claiming that an international crime has been or is being committed by one or more states shall bring the matter to the attention of the General Assembly or the Security Council of the UN in accordance with Chapter VI of the UN Charter.
2. If the General Assembly or the Security Council resolves by a qualified majority of the members present and voting that the allegation is sufficiently substantiated as to justify the grave concern of the international community, any member state of the UN party to the present Convention, including the state against which the claim is made, may bring the matter to the ICJ by unilateral application for the Court to decide by a judgment whether the alleged international crime has been or is being committed by the accused state.
3. The qualified majority referred to in the preceding paragraph shall be, in the General Assembly, a two-thirds majority of the members present and voting, and in the Security Council, nine members present and voting including permanent members, provided that any members directly concerned shall abstain from voting.
4. In any case where the ICJ is exercising its competence in a dispute between two or more member states of the UN parties to the present Convention, on the basis of a title of jurisdiction other than paragraph 2 of the present article, with regard to the existence of an international crime of state, any other member state of the UN which is a party to the present Convention shall be entitled to join, by unilateral application, the proceedings of the Court for the purpose of paragraph 5 of the present article.
5. A decision of the ICJ that an international crime has been or is being committed shall fulfil the condition for the implementation, by any member state of the UN party to the present Convention, of the special or supplementary legal consequences of international crimes of states as contemplated in articles 16, 17 and 18 of the present Part.

ARTICLE 20

The provisions of the articles of the present Part are without prejudice to:
  (i) any measures decided upon by the Security Council of the United Nations in the exercise of its functions under the provisions of the Charter;
  (ii) the inherent right of self-defence as provided in Article 51 of the Charter.

Appendix 3

State Responsibility: Titles and texts of the draft articles on Responsibility of States for internationally wrongful acts adopted by the Drafting Committee on second reading[1]

RESPONSIBILITY OF STATES FOR INTERNATIONALLY
WRONGFUL ACTS

PART ONE

THE INTERNATIONALLY WRONGFUL ACT OF A STATE

CHAPTER I: General Principles

Article 1
Responsibility of a State for its internationally wrongful acts

Every internationally wrongful act of a State entails the international responsibility of that State.

Article 2
Elements of an internationally wrongful act of a State

There is an internationally wrongful act of a State when conduct consisting of an action or omission:
  (a) Is attributable to the State under international law; and
  (b) Constitutes a breach of an international obligation of the State.

Article 3
Characterization of an act of a State as internationally wrongful

The characterization of an act of a State as internationally wrongful is governed by international law. Such characterization is not affected by the characterization of the same act as lawful by internal law.

---

[1] A/CN.4/L.602/Rev.1, 26 July 2001.

Chapter II: Attribution of Conduct to a State

Article 4
Conduct of organs of a State

1. The conduct of any State organ shall be considered an act of that State under international law, whether the organ exercises legislative, executive, judicial or any other functions, whatever position it holds in the organization of the State, and whatever its character as an organ of the central government or of a territorial unit of the State.
2. An organ includes any person or entity which has that status in accordance with the internal law of the State.

Article 5
Conduct of persons or entities exercising elements of governmental authority

The conduct of a person or entity which is not an organ of the State under article 4 but which is empowered by the law of that State to exercise elements of the governmental authority shall be considered an act of the State under international law, provided the person or entity is acting in that capacity in the particular instance.

Article 6
Conduct of organs placed at the disposal of a State by another State

The conduct of an organ placed at the disposal of a State by another State shall be considered an act of the former State under international law if the organ is acting in the exercise of elements of the governmental authority of the State at whose disposal it is placed.

Article 7
Excess of authority or contravention of instructions

The conduct of an organ of a State or of a person or entity empowered to exercise elements of the governmental authority shall be considered an act of the State under international law if the organ, person or entity acts in that capacity, even if it exceeds its authority or contravenes instructions.

Article 8
Conduct directed or controlled by a State

The conduct of a person or group of persons shall be considered an act of a State under international law if the person or group of persons is in fact acting on the instructions of, or under the direction or control of, that State in carrying out the conduct.

Article 9
Conduct carried out in the absence or default of the official authorities

The conduct of a person or group of persons shall be considered an act of a State under international law if the person or group of persons is in fact exercising elements of the governmental authority in the absence or default of the official authorities and in circumstances such as to call for the exercise of those elements of authority.

Article 10
Conduct of an insurrectional or other movement

1. The conduct of an insurrectional movement which becomes the new government of a State shall be considered an act of that State under international law.
2. The conduct of a movement, insurrectional or other, which succeeds in establishing a new State in part of the territory of a pre-existing State or in a territory under its administration shall be considered an act of the new State under international law.
3. This article is without prejudice to the attribution to a State of any conduct, however related to that of the movement concerned, which is to be considered an act of that State by virtue of articles 4 to 9.

Article 11
Conduct acknowledged and adopted by a State as its own

Conduct which is not attributable to a State under the preceding articles shall nevertheless be considered an act of that State under international law if and to the extent that the State acknowledges and adopts the conduct in question as its own.

CHAPTER III: Breach of an International Obligation

Article 12
Existence of a breach of an international obligation

There is a breach of an international obligation by a State when an act of that State is not in conformity with what is required of it by that obligation, regardless of its origin or character.

Article 13
International obligation in force for a State

An act of a State does not constitute a breach of an international obligation unless the State is bound by the obligation in question at the time the act occurs.

Article 14
Extension in time of the breach of an international obligation

1. The breach of an international obligation by an act of a State not having a continuing character occurs at the moment when the act is performed, even if its effects continue.
2. The breach of an international obligation by an act of a State having a continuing character extends over the entire period during which the act continues and remains not in conformity with the international obligation.
3. The breach of an international obligation requiring a State to prevent a given event occurs when the event occurs and extends over the entire period during which the event continues and remains not in conformity with that obligation.

Article 15
Breach consisting of a composite act

1. The breach of an international obligation by a State through a series of actions or omissions defined in aggregate as wrongful, occurs when the action or omission occurs which, taken with the other actions or omissions, is sufficient to constitute the wrongful act.
2. In such a case, the breach extends over the entire period starting with the first of the actions or omissions of the series and lasts for as long as these actions or omissions are repeated and remain not in conformity with the international obligation.

CHAPTER IV: Responsibility of a State in Connection with the Act of Another State

Article 16
Aid or assistance in the commission of an internationally wrongful act

A State which aids or assists another State in the commission of an internationally wrongful act by the latter is internationally responsible for doing so if:
  (a) That State does so with knowledge of the circumstances of the internationally wrongful act; and
  (b) The act would be internationally wrongful if committed by that State.

Article 17
Direction and control exercised over the commission of an internationally wrongful act

A State which directs and controls another State in the commission of an internationally wrongful act by the latter is internationally responsible for that act if:
  (a) That State does so with knowledge of the circumstances of the internationally wrongful act; and
  (b) The act would be internationally wrongful if committed by that State.

Article 18
Coercion of another State

A State which coerces another State to commit an act is internationally responsible for that act if:
  (a) The act would, but for the coercion, be an internationally wrongful act of the coerced State; and
  (b) The coercing State does so with knowledge of the circumstances of the act.

Article 19
Effect of this Chapter

This Chapter is without prejudice to the international responsibility, under other provisions of these articles, of the State which commits the act in question, or of any other State.

CHAPTER V: Circumstances Precluding Wrongfulness

Article 20
Consent

Valid consent by a State to the commission of a given act by another State precludes the wrongfulness of that act in relation to the former State to the extent that the act remains within the limits of that consent.

Article 21
Self-defence

The wrongfulness of an act of a State is precluded if the act constitutes a lawful measure of self-defence taken in conformity with the Charter of the United Nations.

Article 22
Countermeasures in respect of an internationally wrongful act

The wrongfulness of an act of a State not in conformity with an international obligation towards another State is precluded if and to the extent that the act constitutes a countermeasure taken against the latter State in accordance with Chapter II of Part Three.

Article 23
Force majeure

1. The wrongfulness of an act of a State not in conformity with an international obligation of that State is precluded if the act is due to *force majeure*, that is the occurrence of an irresistible force or of an unforeseen event, beyond the control of the State, making it materially impossible in the circumstances to perform the obligation.
2. Paragraph 1 does not apply if:
   (a) The situation of *force majeure* is due, either alone or in combination with other factors, to the conduct of the State invoking it; or
   (b) The State has assumed the risk of that situation occurring.

Article 24
Distress

1. The wrongfulness of an act of a State not in conformity with an international obligation of that State is precluded if the author of the act in question has no other reasonable way, in a situation of distress, of saving the author's life or the lives of other persons entrusted to the author's care.
2. Paragraph 1 does not apply if:
   (a) The situation of distress is due, either alone or in combination with other factors, to the conduct of the State invoking it; or
   (b) The act in question is likely to create a comparable or greater peril.

Article 25
Necessity

1. Necessity may not be invoked by a State as a ground for precluding the wrongfulness of an act not in conformity with an international obligation of that State unless the act:
    (a) Is the only way for the State to safeguard an essential interest against a grave and imminent peril; and
    (b) Does not seriously impair an essential interest of the State or States towards which the obligation exists, or of the international community as a whole.
2. In any case, necessity may not be invoked by a State as a ground for precluding wrongfulness if:
    (a) The international obligation in question excludes the possibility of invoking necessity; or
    (b) The State has contributed to the situation of necessity.

Article 26
Compliance with peremptory norms

Nothing in this Chapter precludes the wrongfulness of any act of a State which is not in conformity with an obligation arising under a peremptory norm of general international law.

Article 27
Consequences of invoking a circumstance precluding wrongfulness

The invocation of a circumstance precluding wrongfulness in accordance with this Chapter is without prejudice to:
    (a) Compliance with the obligation in question, if and to the extent that the circumstance precluding wrongfulness no longer exists;
    (b) The question of compensation for any material loss caused by the act in question.

PART TWO

CONTENT OF THE INTERNATIONAL RESPONSIBILITY OF A STATE

Chapter I: General Principles

Article 28
Legal consequences of an internationally wrongful act

The international responsibility of a State which is entailed by an internationally wrongful act in accordance with the provisions of Part One involves legal consequences as set out in this Part.

Article 29
Continued duty of performance

The legal consequences of an internationally wrongful act under this Part do not affect the continued duty of the responsible State to perform the obligation breached.

Article 30
Cessation and non-repetition

The State responsible for the internationally wrongful act is under an obligation:
(a) To cease that act, if it is continuing;
(b) To offer appropriate assurances and guarantees of non-repetition, if circumstances so require.

Article 31
Reparation

1. The responsible State is under an obligation to make full reparation for the injury caused by the internationally wrongful act.
2. Injury includes any damage, whether material or moral, caused by the internationally wrongful act of a State.

Article 32
Irrelevance of internal law

The responsible State may not rely on the provisions of its internal law as justification for failure to comply with its obligations under this Part.

Article 33
Scope of international obligations set out in this Part

1. The obligations of the responsible State set out in this Part may be owed to another State, to several States, or to the international community as a whole, depending in particular on the character and content of the international obligation and on the circumstances of the breach.
2. This Part is without prejudice to any right, arising from the international responsibility of a State, which may accrue directly to any person or entity other than a State.

Chapter II: Reparation for Injury

Article 34
Forms of reparation

Full reparation for the injury caused by the internationally wrongful act shall take the form of restitution, compensation and satisfaction, either singly or in combination, in accordance with the provisions of this Chapter.

Article 35
Restitution

A State responsible for an internationally wrongful act is under an obligation to make restitution, that is, to re-establish the situation which existed before the wrongful act was committed, provided and to the extent that restitution:
  (a) Is not materially impossible;
  (b) Does not involve a burden out of all proportion to the benefit deriving from restitution instead of compensation.

Article 36
Compensation

1. The State responsible for an internationally wrongful act is under an obligation to compensate for the damage caused thereby, insofar as such damage is not made good by restitution.
2. The compensation shall cover any financially assessable damage including loss of profits insofar as it is established.

Article 37
Satisfaction

1. The State responsible for an internationally wrongful act is under an obligation to give satisfaction for the injury caused by that act insofar as it cannot be made good by restitution or compensation.
2. Satisfaction may consist in an acknowledgement of the breach, an expression of regret, a formal apology or another appropriate modality.
3. Satisfaction shall not be out of proportion to the injury and may not take a form humiliating to the responsible State.

Article 38
Interest

1. Interest on any principal sum due under this Chapter shall be payable when necessary in order to ensure full reparation. The interest rate and mode of calculation shall be set so as to achieve that result.
2. Interest runs from the date when the principal sum should have been paid until the date the obligation to pay is fulfilled.

Article 39
Contribution to the injury

In the determination of reparation, account shall be taken of the contribution to the injury by wilful or negligent action or omission of the injured State or any person or entity in relation to whom reparation is sought.

Chapter III: Serious Breaches of Obligations under Peremptory Norms of General International Law

Article 40
Application of this Chapter

1. This Chapter applies to the international responsibility which is entailed by a serious breach by a State of an obligation arising under a peremptory norm of general international law.
2. A breach of such an obligation is serious if it involves a gross or systematic failure by the responsible State to fulfil the obligation.

Article 41
Particular consequences of a serious breach of an obligation under this Chapter

1. States shall cooperate to bring to an end through lawful means any serious breach within the meaning of article 40.
2. No State shall recognize as lawful a situation created by a serious breach within the meaning of article 40, nor render aid or assistance in maintaining that situation.
3. This article is without prejudice to the other consequences referred to in this Part and to such further consequences that a breach to which this Chapter applies may entail under international law.

PART THREE

THE IMPLEMENTATION OF THE INTERNATIONAL RESPONSIBILITY OF A STATE

Chapter I: Invocation of the Responsibility of a State

Article 42
Invocation of responsibility by an injured State

A State is entitled as an injured State to invoke the responsibility of another State if the obligation breached is owed to:
  (a) That State individually; or
  (b) A group of States including that State, or the international community as a whole, and the breach of the obligation:
     (i) Specially affects that State; or
     (ii) Is of such a character as radically to change the position of all the other States to which the obligation is owed with respect to the further performance of the obligation.

Article 43
Notice of claim by an injured State

1. An injured State which invokes the responsibility of another State shall give notice of its claim to that State.
2. The injured State may specify in particular:

(a) The conduct that the responsible State should take in order to cease the wrongful act, if it is continuing;

(b) What form reparation should take in accordance with the provisions of Part Two.

Article 44
Admissibility of claims

The responsibility of a State may not be invoked if:

(a) The claim is not brought in accordance with any applicable rule relating to the nationality of claims;

(b) The claim is one to which the rule of exhaustion of local remedies applies and any available and effective local remedy has not been exhausted.

Article 45
Loss of the right to invoke responsibility

The responsibility of a State may not be invoked if:

(a) The injured State has validly waived the claim;

(b) The injured State is to be considered as having, by reason of its conduct, validly acquiesced in the lapse of the claim.

Article 46
Plurality of injured States

Where several States are injured by the same internationally wrongful act, each injured State may separately invoke the responsibility of the State which has committed the internationally wrongful act.

Article 47
Plurality of responsible States

1. Where several States are responsible for the same internationally wrongful act, the responsibility of each State may be invoked in relation to that act.

2. Paragraph 1:
   (a) Does not permit any injured State to recover, by way of compensation, more than the damage it has suffered;
   (b) Is without prejudice to any right of recourse against the other responsible States.

Article 48
Invocation of responsibility by a State other than an injured State

1. Any State other than an injured State is entitled to invoke the responsibility of another State in accordance with paragraph 2 if:
   (a) The obligation breached is owed to a group of States including that State, and is established for the protection of a collective interest of the group; or
   (b) The obligation breached is owed to the international community as a whole.

2. Any State entitled to invoke responsibility under paragraph 1 may claim from the responsible State:
   (a) Cessation of the internationally wrongful act, and assurances and guarantees of non-repetition in accordance with article 30; and

(b) Performance of the obligation of reparation in accordance with the preceding articles, in the interest of the injured State or of the beneficiaries of the obligation breached.

3. The requirements for the invocation of responsibility by an injured State under articles 43, 44 and 45 apply to an invocation of responsibility by a State entitled to do so under paragraph 1.

CHAPTER II: *Countermeasures*

Article 49
Object and limits of countermeasures

1. An injured State may only take countermeasures against a State which is responsible for an internationally wrongful act in order to induce that State to comply with its obligations under Part Two.
2. Countermeasures are limited to the non-performance for the time being of international obligations of the State taking the measures towards the responsible State.
3. Countermeasures shall, as far as possible, be taken in such a way as to permit the resumption of performance of the obligations in question.

Article 50
Obligations not affected by countermeasures

1. Countermeasures shall not affect:
   (a) The obligation to refrain from the threat or use of force as embodied in the Charter of the United Nations;
   (b) Obligations for the protection of fundamental human rights;
   (c) Obligations of a humanitarian character prohibiting reprisals;
   (d) Other obligations under peremptory norms of general international law.
2. A State taking countermeasures is not relieved from fulfilling its obligations:
   (a) Under any dispute settlement procedure applicable between it and the responsible State;
   (b) To respect the inviolability of diplomatic or consular agents, premises, archives and documents.

Article 51
Proportionality

Countermeasures must be commensurate with the injury suffered, taking into account the gravity of the internationally wrongful act and the rights in question.

Article 52
Conditions relating to resort to countermeasures

1. Before taking countermeasures, an injured State shall:
   (a) Call on the responsible State, in accordance with article 43, to fulfil its obligations under Part Two;
   (b) Notify the responsible State of any decision to take countermeasures and offer to negotiate with that State.

2. Notwithstanding paragraph 1(b), the injured State may take such urgent countermeasures as are necessary to preserve its rights.
3. Countermeasures may not be taken, and if already taken must be suspended without undue delay if:
   (a) The internationally wrongful act has ceased, and
   (b) The dispute is pending before a court or tribunal which has the authority to make decisions binding on the parties.
4. Paragraph 3 does not apply if the responsible State fails to implement the dispute settlement procedures in good faith.

Article 53
Termination of countermeasures

Countermeasures shall be terminated as soon as the responsible State has complied with its obligations under Part Two in relation to the internationally wrongful act.

Article 54
Measures taken by States other than an injured State

This Chapter does not prejudice the right of any State, entitled under article 48, paragraph 1 to invoke the responsibility of another State, to take lawful measures against that State to ensure cessation of the breach and reparation in the interest of the injured State or of the beneficiaries of the obligation breached.

PART FOUR

GENERAL PROVISIONS

Article 55
Lex specialis

These articles do not apply where and to the extent that the conditions for the existence of an internationally wrongful act or the content or implementation of the international responsibility of a State are governed by special rules of international law.

Article 56
Questions of State responsibility not regulated by these articles

The applicable rules of international law continue to govern questions concerning the responsibility of a State for an internationally wrongful act to the extent that they are not regulated by these articles.

Article 57
Responsibility of an international organization

These articles are without prejudice to any question of the responsibility under international law of an international organization, or of any State for the conduct of an international organization.

Article 58
Individual responsibility

These articles are without prejudice to any question of the individual responsibility under international law of any person acting on behalf of a State.

Article 59
Charter of the United Nations

These articles are without prejudice to the Charter of the United Nations.

Bibliography

ABI-SAAB, G., 'The Uses of Article 19', (1999) *EJIL*, vol. 10, no. 2, 339–51.

AGO, R., 'Délit international', (1939–II) 68 Hague *Recueil*, 419–554.

ALEXIDZE, L., 'Legal Nature of *Jus Cogens* in Contemporary International Law', (1981–III) 172 Hague *Recueil*, 223–70.

ALLOTT, P., 'State Responsibility and the Unmaking of International Law', (1988) 29 *Harvard International Law Journal*, 1–26.

AMERICAN LAW INSTITUTE, *Restatement of the Law Third: The Foreign Relations Law of the United States*, ii. Washington, DC: American Law Institute Publishers, 1987.

ANAND, R. P., *Studies in International Adjudication*. Dobbs Ferry, NY: Oceana, 1969.

ANDERSON, M. R., 'State Obligations in a Transnational Dispute: The Bhopal Case', in Butler (1991: 83–95).

ANDREWS, J., 'Reform in the Law of Corporate Liability', (1973) *Criminal Law Review*, 91–7.

ANON., 'Genocide: A Commentary on the Convention', (1948–9) 58 *Yale Law Journal*, 1142–60.

APOLLIS, G., 'Le Règlement de l'affaire du "Rainbow Warrior"', (1987) 91 *RGDIP*, 9–43.

APPLEMAN, J. A., *Military Tribunals and International Crimes*. Westport, Conn: Greenwood Press, 1954.

ARNULL, A., *The General Principles of EEC Law and the Individual*. Leicester: Leicester University Press, 1990.

BARAK, G. (ed.), *Crimes by the Capitalist State: An Introduction to State Criminality*. Albany, NY: State University of New York Press, 1991.

BASSIOUNI, M. C., *Substantive Criminal Law*. Springfield, Ill: Charles C. Thomas, 1978.

—— *International Criminal Law: A Draft International Criminal Code*. Alphen aan den Rijn, Netherlands Sijthoff & Noordhoff, 1980.

—— 'The Penal Characteristics of Conventional International Criminal Law', (1983) *Case Western Reserve Journal of International Law*, vol. 15, 27–37.

—— (ed.) *International Criminal Law*. 3 vols. Dobbs Ferry, NY: Transnational, 1986.

—— (ed.) *International Criminal Law*, i: *Crimes* 2nd edn. Ardsley, NY: Transnational, 1999.

—— *A Draft International Criminal Code and Draft Statute for an International Criminal Tribunal*. Dordrecht: Martinus Nijhoff, 1987.

—— 'The Commission of Experts Established Pursuant to Security Council Resolution 780: Investigating Violations of International Humanitarian Law in the Former Yugoslavia', (1996) Occasional Paper No. 2, International Human Rights Law Institute, De Paul University, Chicago.

—— *The Statute of the International Criminal Court: A Documentary History*. Ardsley, NY: *Transnational*, 1998.

—— and DERBY, D. H., 'Final Report on the Establishment of an International Criminal Court for the Implementation of the Apartheid Convention and Other Relevant International Instruments', (1981) 9 *Hofstra Law Rev.*, 523–92.

BEDJAOUI, M. (ed.), *International Law: Achievements and Prospects*. Dordrecht: Martinus Nijhoff, 1991.

BENTON, W. E., and GRIMM, G., *Nuremberg: German Views of the War Trials*. Dallas: Southern Methodist University Press, 1955.

BERGSMO, M., 'Etnisk rensing og internasjonal rett', (1993) *Nordisk Tidskrift om Menneskerettigheter*, vol. 11, no. 2, 176–94.

BERNHARDT, R. (ed.), *Encyclopaedia of Public International Law*. 12 instalments and 2 separate vols. Amsterdam: North-Holland, 1981–92.

BEVERIDGE, F., 'The Lockerbie Affair', (1992) 41 *ICLQ*, 907–20.

BIANCHI, A., 'Immunity versus Human Rights: The Pinochet Case', (1999) *EJIL*, vol. 10, no. 2, 237–77.

BIRNIE, P. W., and BOYLE, A. E., *International Law and the Environment*. Oxford: Clarendon Press, 1992.

BISHOP, W. W. Jr, *International Law Cases and Materials*, 2nd edn. Boston: Little, Brown, 1962.

BORCHARD, E. M., 'Important Decisions of the Mixed Claims Commission, United States and Mexico', (1927) 21 *AJIL*, 516–22.

BORTZ, S. I., 'Avoiding a Collision of Competence: The Relationship Between the Security Council and the International Court of Justice in Light of *Libya v United States*', (1993) *Journal of Transnational Law and Policy*, vol. 2: 643, 353–78.

BOURQUIN, M., 'Règles générales du droit de la paix', (1931–I) 35 Hague *Recueil*, 1–232.

BOWETT, D., 'Reprisals Involving Recourse to Armed Force', (1972) 66 *AJIL*, 1–36.

—— 'Crimes of State and the 1996 Report of the International Law Commission on State Responsibility', (1998) 9 *EJIL*, 163–73.

BOYLE, A. E., 'International Law and the Protection of the Global Atmosphere: Concepts, Categories and Principles', in R. Churchill and D. Freestone (eds.), *International Law and Global Climate Change*. London/Dordrecht: Graham & Trotman/ Martinus Nijhoff, 1991, 7–19.

BRAITHWAITE, J., and FISSE, B., *Corporations, Crime and Accountability*. Cambridge: Cambridge University Press, 1993.

—— and GEIS, G., 'On Theory and Action for Corporate Crime Control', in A. Duff (ed.), *Punishment*. Aldershot: Dartmouth, 1993, 292–314.

BRIERLY, J. L., 'The Theory of Implied State Complicity in International Claims', (1928) 9 *BYIL*, 42–9.

BRIGGS, H. W. (ed.), *The Law of Nations: Cases, Documents and Notes*, 2nd edn. London: Stevens, 1953.

BRÖHMER, J., *State Immunity and the Violation of Human Rights*. The Hague: Martinus Nijhoff Publishers, 1997.

BROWNLIE, I., *International Law and the Use of Force by States*. Oxford: Clarendon Press, 1963

—— *System of the Law of Nations: State Responsibility*, pt. 1. Oxford: Clarendon Press, 1983.

—— *Principles of Public International Law*, 4th edn. Oxford: Clarendon Press, 1990.

—— 'The Decisions of Political Organs of the United Nations and the Rule of Law', in MacDonald, R. St J. (ed.), *Essays in Honour of Wang Tieya*. Dordrecht: Martinus Nijhoff, 1994, 91–102.

—— *Basic Documents in International Law*. Oxford: Clarendon Press, 1995.

—— 'General Course on Public International Law', (1995) 255 Hague *Recueil*, 9–227.

BRUECK, O., *Les Sanctions en droit international*. Paris: A. Pedone, 1933.

BRYANT, R. D., *A World Rule of Law, a Way to Peace*. San Francisco, Calif.: 1977.

BURCHELL, E. M. (ed.), *South African Criminal Law and Procedure*, i: *General Principles of Criminal Law*. Kenwyn: Juta, 1997.

BURNETT, P. M., *Reparation at the Paris Peace Conference from the Standpoint of the American Delegation*. 2 vols. New York: Columbia University Press, 1940.

BUTLER, W. E. (ed.), *Control over Compliance with International Law*. Dordrecht: Kluwer Academic, 1991.

BYERS, M., 'Conceptualizing the Relationship between *Jus Cogens* and *Erga Omnes* Rules', (1997) *Nordic Journal of International Law*, 1–29.

CALOYANNI, M. A., 'L'Organisation de la cour permanente de justice et son avenir', (1931–IV) 38 Hague *Recueil*, 655–778.

CALVOCORESSI, P. N., *Nuremberg: The Facts, the Law and the Consequences*. London: Chatto & Windus, 1947.

CARDOZO, B. N., *The Growth of the Law*. New Haven, Conn.: Yale University Press, 1924.

CARON, D. D., 'State Crimes in the ILC Draft Articles on State Responsibility: Insights from Municipal Experience with Corporate Crimes', (1998) 92 *American Society of International Law Proceedings*, 307–12.

CASSESE, A. (ed.), *United Nations Law / Fundamental Rights*. Alphen aan den Rijn, Netherlands: Sijthoff & Noordhoff, 1979.

—— *Violence and Law in the Modern Age*. Cambridge: Polity Press, 1986.

—— 'Remarks on the Present Legal Regulation of Crimes of States', in *International Law at the Time of Its Codification: Essays in Honour of Roberto Ago*, iii. Milan: Giuffrè, 1987, 49–64.

—— and WEILER, J. H. H. (eds.), *Change and Stability in International Law-Making*. Berlin: Walter de Gruyter, 1988.

CASTRÉN, E., *The Present Law of War and Neutrality*. Helsinki: Annales Academiae Scientiarum Fennicae, 1954.

CHALK, F., and JONASSOHN, K. (eds.), *The History and Sociology of Genocide: Analyses and Case Studies*. New Haven, Conn.: Yale University Press, 1990.

CHARNY, I., *How Can We Commit the Unthinkable? Genocide: The Human Cancer*. Epping: Bowker, 1982.

CHENG, B., *General Principles of Law as Applied by International Courts and Tribunals*. London: Stevens, 1953; repr. Cambridge: Cambridge University Press, 1993.

CHINKIN, C., *Third Parties in International Law*. Oxford: Clarendon Press, 1993.

CLARK, R. S., 'Does the Genocide Convention Go Far Enough? Some Thoughts on the Nature of Criminal Genocide in the Context of Indonesia's Invasion of East Timor', (1981) 8 *Ohio Northern University Law Review*, 321–8.

—— 'Crimes against Humanity', in Gingsburgs and Kudriavtsev (eds.), *The Nuremberg Trial and International Law* (1990: 177–212).

CLEMENTS, L. J., *European Human Rights: Taking a Case Under the Convention*. London: Sweet & Maxwell, 1994.

COHEN, S., 'Human Rights and Crimes of the State: The Culture of Denial', in Muncie et al. (1996: 489–507).

COHN, G., *Kriegsverhütung und Schuldfrage*. Universitätsverlag von Robert Noske in Leipzig, 1931. Reviewed by U. Kersten (1931–2), *Harvard Law Review*, vol. 45, 1286–8.

COMMISSION ON GLOBAL GOVERNANCE, *Our Global Neighbourhood*. Oxford: Oxford University Press, 1995.

CONOT, R. E., *Justice at Nuremberg*. London: Weidenfeld & Nicolson, 1983.

COSNARD, M., 'Quelques observations sur les décisions de la chambre des Lords du 25 novembre 1998 et du 24 mars 1999 dans l'affaire Pinochet', (1999) 103 *RGDIP*, 309–28.

CRAIG BARKER, J., 'The Future of Former Head of State Immunity after Ex Parte Pinochet', (1999) 48 *ICLQ*, 937–49.

CRAWFORD, J., *The Creation of States in International Law*. Oxford: Clarendon Press, 1979.

CURTIN, D., 'Effective Sanctions and the Equal Treatment Directive: The *Von Colson* and *Harz* Cases', (1985) 22 *Common Market Law Review*, 505–32.

DANCHEV, A., and HALVERSON, T. (eds.), *International Perspectives on the Yugoslav Conflict*. London: Macmillan, 1996.

DAUBE, D., *The Defence of Superior Orders in Roman Law*. Oxford: Clarendon Press, 1956.

DAVIDSON, S., *The Inter-American Human Rights System*. Aldershot: Dartmouth, 1997.

DEKKER, I. F., and POST, H. H., 'The Gulf War from the Point of View of International Law: An Ordinary War of Aggression Inspired by Territorial Ambition?', (1986) 17 *Netherlands Yearbook of International Law*, 75–105.

DENZA, E., 'Ex Parte Pinochet: Lacuna or Leap?', (1999) 48 *ICLQ*, 949–58.

DEPARTMENT OF STATE, *Report of Robert H. Jackson, US Representative to the International Conference on Military Trials, London, 1945*. Washington, DC: US Govt. Printing Office, 1949.

—— *A Decade of American Foreign Policy: Basic Documents 1941–1949*, rev, edn. Washington, DC: US Govt. Printing Office, 1985.

DEUTSCH, K. W., and HOFFMAN, S. (eds.), *The Relevance of International Law: Essays in Honour of Leo Gross*. Cambridge, Mass.: Schenkman, 1968.

DINSTEIN, Y., *The Defence of Obedience to Superior Orders*. Leyden: A.W. Sijthoff, 1965.

—— (ed.), *International Law at a Time of Perplexity: Essays in Honour of Shabtai Rosenne*. Dordrecht: Martinus Nijhoff, 1989.

—— 'The *Erga Omnes* Applicability of Human Rights', (1992) *Archiv des Volkerrechts*, vol. 30, 16–21.

—— and TABORY, M. (eds), *War Crimes in International Law*. The Hague: Martinus Nijhoff, 1996.

DOELDER, H. DE, and TIEDEMANN, K. (eds.), *Criminal Liability of Corporations*. The Hague: Kluwer Law International, 1996.

DOMINICÉ, C., 'The International Responsibility of States for Breach of Multilateral Obligations', (1999) *EJIL* vol. 10, no. 2, 353–63.

—— 'Quelques observations sur l'immunité de juridiction pénale de l'ancien chef d'état', (1999) 103 *RGDIP*, 297–308.

DROST, P. N., *The Crime of State*, i: *Humanicide*; ii: *Genocide*. Leyden: A.W. Sythoff, 1959.

DUMAS, J., 'De la résponsabilité internationale des États: à raison de crimes où de délits commis sur leurs térritoires au préjudice d'étrangers', (1929) 6 *Revue Internationale de Droit Pénal*.

DUNN, F. S., *The Protection of Nationals*. Baltimore: Johns Hopkins Press, 1932.

DUNNE, M., and BONAZZI, T. (eds.), *Citizenship and Rights in Multicultural Societies*. Keele: Keele University Press, 1995.

DUPUY, P-M., 'Observations sur le "crime international de l'état"', (1980) 84 *RGDIP*, 449–86.

—— 'Crimes et immunités, ou dans quelle mesure la nature des premiers empêche l'exercice des secondes', (1999) 103 *RGDIP*, 289–296.

DUPUY, R-J., 'Communauté international et disparités de développement', (1979–IV) 165 Hague *Recueil*, 13–231.

DURKHEIM, E., *The Division of Labour in Society*. New York: Free Press, 1964.

EAGLETON, C., 'Measure of Damages in International Law', (1929–30) 39 *Yale Law Journal*, 52–75.

—— 'An Attempt to Define Aggression', (1950) *International Conciliation*, no. 264, 581–652.

EDWARDS, R. W. Jr, 'Contributions of the Genocide Convention to the Development of International Law', (1981) 8 *Ohio Northern University Law Review*, 300–14.

EHARD, H., 'The Nuremberg Trial against the Major War Criminals and International Law', (1949) 43 *AJIL*, 223–45.

EIDE, A., *FN's fredsbevarende aksjoner* [The UN's Peacekeeping Operations]. Oslo: Pax, 1966.

EIRIKSSON, G., 'The Work of the International Law Commission at Its Forty-Sixth Session', (1995) 64 *Nordic Journal of International Law*, 59–127.

EISENBERG, C., *Drawing the Line: The American Decision to Divide Germany 1944–1949*. Cambridge: Cambridge University Press, 1996.

ELAGAB, O. Y., *The Legality of Non-Forcible Counter-Measures in International Law*. Oxford: Clarendon Press, 1988.

ELIAS, R., *The Politics of Victimization: Victims, Victimology and Human Rights*. Oxford: Oxford University Press, 1986.

ELIAS, T. O., 'The Doctrine of Intertemporal Law', (1980) 74 *AJIL*, 285–307.

EMERSON, R., 'The New Higher Law of Anti-Colonialism', in Deutsch and Hoffman (1968: 153–74).

ETZIONI, A., 'The US Sentencing Commission on Corporate Crime: A Critique', in G. Geis and P. Jesilow (eds.), *White-Collar Crime*, Special Issue of the Annals of the American Academy of Political and Social Science, 525 (Jan.). Newbury Park, Calif.: Sage, 1993, 147–56.

EUSTATHIADES, C. TH., 'Les Sujets du droit international et la responsabilité internationale: nouvelle tendences', (1953–III) 84 Hague *Recueil*, 434–633.

FALK, R. A., KOLKO, G., and LIFTON, R. J., *Crimes of War: A Legal, Political-Documentary, and Psychological Inquiry into the Responsibility of Leaders, Citizens, and Soldiers for Criminal Acts in Wars*. New York: Random House, 1971.

FERENCZ, B. B., *Defining International Aggression*. 2 vols. Dobbs Ferry, NY: Oceana, 1975.

FERENCZ, B. B., *An International Criminal Court: A Step Towards World Peace—A Documentary History and Analysis.* 2 vols. London: Oceana, 1980.

—— 'An International Criminal Code and Court: Where They Stand and Where They're Going', (1992) 30 *Columbia Journal of Transnational Law*, 375.

FINCH, G. A., 'The Peace Conference of Paris', (1919) 13 *AJIL*, 159–86.

—— 'Retribution for War Crimes', (1943) 37 *AJIL*, 81–103.

—— 'The Genocide Convention', (1949) 43 *AJIL*, 732–9.

FISCHER, H., 'The Suppression of Slavery in International Law', (1950) 3 *ILQ*, 28–51, 508–22.

FITZMAURICE, G. G., 'The Law and Procedure of the International Court of Justice: General Principles and Substantive Law', (1950) 27 *BYIL*, 1–41.

—— 'The General Principles of International Law Considered from the Standpoint of the Rule of Law', (1957–II) 92 Hague *Recueil*, 1–227.

—— 'Judicial Innovation, Its Uses and Its Perils', in *Cambridge Essays in International Law: Essays in Honour of Lord McNair.* Dobbs Ferry, NY: Oceana; London: Stevens, 1965, 24–47.

FOX, H. M., 'Reparations and State Responsibility: Claims Against Iraq Arising out of the Invasion and Occupation of Kuwait', in Rowe (1993: 261–86).

—— 'The First Pinochet Case: Immunity of a Former Head of State', (1999) 48 *ICLQ*, 207–16.

—— 'The Pinochet Case No. 3', (1999) 48 *ICLQ*, 687–702.

FREEMAN, A. V., *The International Responsibility of States for Denial of Justice.* London: Longmans, Green, 1938.

FRIEDLANDER, R. A., 'The Foundations of International Criminal Law: A Present Day Inquiry', (1983) 15 *Case Western Reserve Journal of International Law*, 13–25.

FRIEDRICHS, D. O. (ed.), *State Crime*, i: *Defining, Delineating and Explaining State Crime*; ii: *Exposing, Sanctioning and Preventing State Crime.* Aldershot: Ashgate, 1998.

GAFFIKIN, B., 'The International Court of Justice and the Crisis in the Balkans', (1995) *Sydney Law Review*, vol. 17, no. 3, 458–72.

GAJA, G., '*Jus Cogens* Beyond the Vienna Convention', (1981–III) 172 Hague *Recueil*, 273–316.

—— 'Should All References to International Crimes Disappear from the ILC Draft Articles on State Responsibility?', (1999) *EJIL*, vol. 10, no. 2, 365–70.

GARCIA-AMADOR, F. V., 'State Responsibility: Some New Problems', (1958–II) 94 Hague *Recueil*, 365–487.

—— SOHN, L. B., and BAXTER, R. R., *Recent Codification of the Law of State Responsibility for Injuries to Aliens.* Dobbs Ferry, NY: Oceana; Leiden: A. W. Sijthoff, 1974.

GARLAND, D., and YOUNG, P., *The Power to Punish: Contemporary Penalty and Social Analysis.* London: Heinemann Educational, 1983.

GARNER, J. W., 'Community Fines and Collective Punishment', (1917) 2 *AJIL*, 511–37.

GATTINI, A., 'Smoking/No Smoking: Some Remarks on the Current Place of Fault in the ILC Draft Articles on State Responsibility', (1999) *EJIL*, vol. 10, no. 2, 397–404.

GENTILI, A., *De Iure Belli Libri Tres*, ii, trans. of edn. of 1612 by C. J. Rolfe. Oxford: Clarendon Press/London: Humphrey Milford, 1933.

GILBERT, G., 'The Criminal Responsibility of States', (1990) *ICLQ*, 345–69.

—— 'The "Law" and "Transnational Terrorism"', (1995) 26 *Netherlands Yearbook of International Law*, 3–32.

GINGSBURGS, G., *Moscow's Road to Nuremberg: The Soviet Background to the Trial*. The Hague: Martinus Nijhoff, 1996.

—— and KUDRIAVTSEV, V. N. (eds.), *The Nuremberg Trial and International Law*. Dordrecht: Martinus Nijhoff, 1990.

GIRAUD, E., 'La Théorie de la légitime défense', (1934–III) 49 Hague *Recueil*, 691–860.

GLASER, S., 'L'État en tant que personne morale est-il pénalement responsable?', (1949) 29 *Revue de Droit Pénal et de Criminologie*, no. 5, 425–52.

GOLDHAGEN, D. J., *Hitler's Willing Executioners: Ordinary Germans and the Holocaust*. London: Little, Brown, 1996.

GOOCH, G. P., and TEMPERLEY, H. (eds.), *British Documents on the Origins of the War*, 1898–1914. 11 vols. London: HMSO, 1927–38.

GOODWIN-GILL, G. S., and TALMON, S. (eds.), *The Reality of International Law: Essays in Honour of Ian Brownlie*. Oxford: Clarendon Press, 1999.

GOTANDA, J. Y., 'Awarding Punitive Damages in International Commercial Arbitrations in the Wake of *Mastrobuono v Shearson Lehman Hutton, Inc*', (1997) *Harvard International Law Journal*, vol. 38, no. 1, 59–112.

GOUNELLE, M., 'Quelques remarques sur la notion de "crime international" et sur l'évolution de la responsabilité international de l'état', in *Mélanges offerts à Paul Reuter: le droit international: unité et diversité*. Paris: A. Pedone, 1981, 315–26.

GOWLAND-DEBBAS, V., 'Security Council Action and Issues of State Responsibility', (1994) 43 *ICLQ*, 54–94.

GRAEFRATH, B., 'Responsibility and Damages Caused: Relationship Between Responsibility and Damages', (1984–II) 185 Hague *Recueil*, 9–149.

—— and MOHR, M. 'Legal Consequences of an Act of Aggression: The Case of the Iraqi Invasion and Occupation of Kuwait', (1992) 43 *Austrian Journal of Public and International Law*, 109–38.

GRAVEN, J., 'Les Crimes contre l'humanité', (1950) 76 Hague *Recueil*, 433–605.

GRAY, C. D., *Judicial Remedies in International Law*. Oxford: Clarendon Press, 1987 (paperback cdn. 1990).

GREEN, L. C., *Superior Orders in National and International Law*. Leiden: A. W. Sijthoff, 1976.

—— 'New Trends in International Criminal Law', (1981) *Israel Yearbook on Human Rights*, vol. 11, 9–40.

—— 'Command Responsibility in International Law', (1995) *Transnational Law and Contemporary Problems*, vol. 5, no. 2, 319.

—— 'Enforcement of the Law in International and Non-International Conflicts: the Way Ahead', (1996) *Denver Journal of International Law and Policy*, vol. 24, no. 2/3, 285–320.

GREENWOOD, C. J., 'New World Order or Old? The Invasion of Kuwait and the Rule of Law', (1992) 55 *Modern Law Review*, 153–78.

—— 'The International Tribunal for Former Yugoslavia', (1993) 69 *International Affairs*, 641–55.

GROTIUS, H., *De Jure Belli ac Pacis Libri Tres*, ii, trans. F.W. Kelsey. Oxford: Clarendon Press/London: Humphrey Milford, 1925.

HAENSEL, C., 'The Nuremberg Trial Revisited', (1963–4) 13 *De Paul Law Rev.*, 248–59.

HAILBRONNER, K., 'Sanctions and Third Parties and the Concept of International Public Order', (1992) *Archiv des Volkerrechts*, vol. 30, 2–13.

HALL, W. E., *International Law*, 8th edn. Oxford: Clarendon Press, 1924.

HAMPSON, F. J., 'Liability for War Crimes', in Rowe (1993: 241–60).

HANNIKAINEN, L., *Peremptory Norms (Jus Cogens) in International Law*. Helsinki: Lakimiesliiton Kustannus 'Finnish Lawyers' Publishing Co., 1988.

HARRIS, D. J., *Cases and Materials on International Law*, 5th edn. London: Sweet & Maxwell, 1998.

—— O'BOYLE, M., and WARBRICK, C., *Law of the European Convention on Human Rights*. London: Butterworth, 1995.

HASSAN, F., 'The Theoretical Basis of Punishment in International Criminal Law', (1983) 15 *Case Western Reserve Journal of International Law*, 39–60.

HEFFTER, A. W., *Le Droit international de l'Europe*. Berlin: Schroeder; Paris: Cotillon, 1873.

HIGGINS, R. H., *Problems and Process: International Law and How We Use It*. Oxford: Clarendon Press, 1994.

—— 'Some Observations on the Inter-Temporal Rule in International Law', in Makarczyk (1996: 173–81).

HOCHSTEDLER, E. (ed.), *Corporations as Criminals*. Beverly Hills, Calif.: Sage, 1984.

HOOGH, A. J .J. DE, 'The Relationship Between *Jus Cogens*, Obligations *Erga Omnes* and International Crimes: Peremptory Norms in Perspective', (1991) 42 *Austrian Journal of Public and International Law*, 183–214.

—— *Obligations Erga Omnes and International Crimes: A Theoretical Inquiry into the Implementation and Enforcement of the International Responsibility of States*. The Hague: Kluwer Law International, 1996.

HOROWITZ, I. L., *Taking Lives: Genocide and State Power*. New Brunswick, NJ: Transaction, 1980.

HOSOYA, C., ANDO, N., and ONUMA, Y. (eds.), *The Tokyo War Crimes Trial: An International Symposium*. Tokyo: Kodansha International, 1986.

HUDSON, M. O., *International Tribunals: Past and Future*. Washington, DC: Carnegie Endowment for International Peace, 1944.

—— 'The Twenty-Ninth Year of the World Court', (1951) 45 *AJIL*, 1–36.

HUNTINGTON, S. P., 'The Clash of Civilizations?', (Summer 1993) *Foreign Affairs*, 22–49.

HUTCHINSON, D. N., 'Solidarity and Breaches of Multilateral Treaties', (1988) 110 *BYIL*, 151–215.

HYDE, C. C., 'The Adjustment of the I'm Alone Case', (1935) 29 *AJIL*, 296–301.

ITO, T., 'Japan's Settlement of the Post-World War II Reparations and Claims', (1994) *Japanese Annual of International Law*, no. 37, 38–71.

JENNINGS, R. Y., 'Judicial Legislation in International Law', (1938) *Kentucky Law Journal*, vol. 26, no. 2, 112–27.

—— 'General Course on Principles of International Law', (1967–II) 121 Hague *Recueil*, 323–600.

—— and WATTS, A. (eds.), Oppenheim's *International Law*, i, *Peace*, 9th edn. Harlow: Longman, 1992 (paperback edn. 1996).

JESSUP, P. C., 'Responsibility of States for Injuries to Individuals', (1946) *Columbia Law Review*, vol. 46, no. 6, 903–28.

—— *A Modern Law of Nations: An Introduction*. Hamden, Conn.: Archon, 1968.

JIA, B. B., 'The Differing Concepts of War Crimes and Crimes against Humanity', in Goodwin-Gill and Talmon (1999: 243–71).

JIMÉNEZ DE ARÉCHAGA, E., 'General Course in Public International Law', (1978–I) 159 Hague *Recueil*, 3–343.

—— and TANZI, A., 'International State Responsibility', in Bedjaoui (1991: 347–80).

JODL, A., 'A Short Historical Consideration of German War Guilt', in *Nazi Conspiracy and Aggression*, viii. Washington, DC: USGPO, 1946, 662–9.

JOHNSON, D. H. N., 'The Draft Code of Offences against the Peace and Security of Mankind', (1955) *ICLQ*, 445–68.

KELSEN, H., 'Collective and Individual Responsibility in International Law with Particular Regard to the Punishment of War Criminals', (1942–3) 31 *California Law Review*, 530–71.

—— *Peace through Law*. Chapel Hill: University of North Carolina Press, 1944.

—— 'Will the Judgment in the Nuremberg Trial Constitute a Precedent in International Law?', (1947) 1 *ILQ*, 153–71.

—— *Principles of International Law*. New York: Holt, Rinehart & Winston, 1966.

KEMP, D., *Damages for Personal Injury and Death*, 5th edn. London: Pearson Professional, 1995.

KLEE, E., DRESSEN, W., and RIESS, V., *'Those Were the Days': The Holocaust through the Eyes of the Perpetrators and Bystanders*. London: Hamish Hamilton, 1991.

KOPELMANAS, L., 'The Problem of Aggression and the Prevention of War', (1937) 31 *AJIL*, 244–57.

KOROVIN, E. A., 'The Second World War and International Law', (1946) 40 *AJIL*, 742–55.

KRANZBUHLER, O., 'Nuremberg Eighteen Years Afterward', (1964–5) 14 *De Paul Law Rev*. 333–47.

KRAUS, H., 'The Nuremberg Trial of the Major War Criminals: Reflections After Seventeen Years', (1963–4) 13 *De Paul Law Rev.*, 233–47.

KRITZ, N. J. (ed.), *Transitional Justice*, i. Washington, DC: United States Institute of Peace Press, 1995.

KUNZ, J. L., 'L'Article XI du Pacte de la Société de Nations', (1932–I) Hague *Recueil*, 681–790.

—— 'The United Nations Convention on Genocide', (1949) 43 *AJIL*, 738–46.

—— 'Sanctions in International Law', (1960) 54 *AJIL*, 324–47.

KUPER, L., *Genocide*. London: Penguin, 1981.

—— 'International Action against Genocide', Minority Rights Group, Report 53, rev. edn. London: Minority Rights Group, 1984.

—— *The Prevention of Genocide*. New Haven, Conn.: Yale University Press, 1985.

LACHS, M., 'General Course on International Law', (1980–IV) 169 Hague *Recueil*.

LAMBERT-FAIVRE, Y., *Droit de dommage corporel: systèmes d'indemnisation*, 3rd edn. Paris: Dalloz, 1996.

LAUTERPACHT, E., *Aspects of the Administration of International Justice*. Cambridge: Grotius, 1991.

—— (ed.), *The Kuwait Crisis: Basic Documents*. Cambridge International Documents Series, 1. Cambridge: Grotius, 1991.

LAUTERPACHT, H., 'Règles générales du droit de la paix', (1937–IV) Hague *Recueil*, 99–422.

—— (ed.), *International Law: A Treatise by L. Oppenheim*, ii: *Disputes, War and Neutrality*, 7th edn. London: Longman, 1952.

—— *The Development of International Law by the International Court*. London: Stevens & Sons, 1958.

LEISER, B. M., 'Victims of Genocide', (1981) 8 *Ohio Northern University Law Review*, 315–20.

LEMKIN, R., *Axis Rule in Occupied Europe*. Washington, DC: Carnegie Endowment for International Peace, 1944.

—— 'Genocide as a Crime under International Law', (1947) 41 *AJIL*, 145–51.

LEVENTHAL, H., 'The Nuremberg Verdict', (1947) 60 *Harvard Law Review*, 857–907.

LLOYD GEORGE, D., *The Truth about the Peace Treaties*, i. London: Gollancz, 1938.

LUARD, E., *Basic Texts in International Relations*. Basingstoke: Macmillan, 1992.

LUCKAU, A., *The German Delegation at the Paris Peace Conference*. New York: Columbia University Press, 1941.

LYSÉN, G., *State Responsibility and International Liability of States for Lawful Acts: A Discussion of Principles*. Skrifter från Juridiska Fakulteten i Uppsala. 59, Juridiska Föreningen i Uppsala, 1997.

MACARTHUR, D., *Reminiscences*. London: Heinemann, 1964.

MACBRIDE, S., *Israel in Lebanon: Report of the International Commission to Enquire into Reported Violations of International Law by Israel during Its Invasion of the Lebanon*. London: Ithaca Press, 1983.

MCDOUGAL, M. S., LASWELL, H. D., and CHEN, L. (eds.), *Human Rights and World Public Order*. New Haven, Conn.: Yale University Press, 1980.

MCGREGOR, H., 'Personal Injury and Death', in Tunc (1986: ch. 9).

MCINTOSH, D., and HOLMES, M. (eds.), *Personal Injury Awards in EU and EFTA Countries: An Industry Report*, 2nd edn. London: Lloyd's of London Press, 1994.

MCLENNAN, G., HELD, D., and HALL, S. (eds.), *The Idea of the Modern State*. Milton Keynes: Open University Press, 1984.

MAISON, R., 'Le Crime de génocide dans les premiers jugements du Tribunal Pénal International pour le Rwanda', (1990) 103 *RGDIP*, 129–145.

MAKARCZYK, J. (ed.), *Theory of International Law at the Threshold of the 21st Century: Essays in Honour of Krzysztof Skubiszewski*. The Hague: Kluwer Law International, 1996.

MAMDANI, M., 'From Conquest to Consent as the Basis of State Formation: Reflections on Rwanda', (1996) 216 *New Left Review*, 3–36.

MANTAUX, P., *Paris Peace Conference 1919: Proceedings of the Council of Four*. Geneva: Institut Universitaire de Hautes Études Internationales, 1964.

MAREK, K., 'Criminalizing State Responsibility', (1978–9) 14 *Revue Belge de Droit International*, 460–85.

MARKESINIS, B., and DEAKIN, S. F., *Tort Law*, 3rd edn. Oxford: Clarendon Press, 1994.

MARQUARDT, P. D., 'Law Without Borders: The Constitutionality of an International Criminal Court', (1995) 33 *Columbia Journal of Transnational Law*, 73.

MERON, T., *Human Rights Law-Making in the United Nations*. Oxford: Clarendon Press, 1986.

MINEAR, R. H., *Victors' Justice: The Tokyo War Crimes Trial*. Princeton, NJ: Princeton University Press, 1971.

MIOTLA, A., 'The Case for an International Criminal Court', (May 1994) UN and Conflict Programme, London.

MOHR, M., 'The International Law Commission's Distinction Between "International Crimes" and "International Delicts" and Its Implications', in Spinedi and Simma (1987: 115–41).

MOORE, J. B., *A Digest of International Law*. 8 vols. Washington, DC: Govt. Printing Office, 1906.

MOORE, M. S., *Placing Blame: A General Theory of the Criminal Law*. Oxford: Clarendon Press, 1997.

MUELLER, G. O. W., and WISE, E. M. (eds.), *International Criminal Law*. London: Sweet & Maxwell/South Hackensack, NJ: Fred B. Rothman, 1965.

MULLINS, C., *The Leipzig Trials*. London: H. F. & G. Witherby, 1921.

MUNCH, F., 'Criminal Responsibility of States', in Bassiouni (1986: 123–9).

MUNCIE, J., McLAUGHLIN, E., and LANGAN, M. (eds.), *Criminological Perspectives: A Reader*. London: Sage, 1996.

NAPEL, H. M. TEN, 'The Concept of International Crimes of States: Walking the Thin Line between Progressive Development and Disintegration of the International Legal Order', (1988) *Leiden Journal of International Law*, vol. 1, no. 2, 149–69.

O'BRIEN, J. C., 'The International Tribunal for Violations of International Humanitarian Law in the Former Yugoslavia', (1993) 87 *AJIL*, 639–59.

O'CONNELL, D. P., *International Law*, 2nd edn., 2 vols. London: Stevens & Sons, 1970.

ODA, H., *Japanese Law*. London: Butterworth, 1992.

OPPENHEIM, L., *International Law*, i: *Peace*. London: Longmans, 1905.

ORLAND, L., and CACHERA, C., 'Corporate Crime and Punishment in France: Criminal Responsibility of Legal Entities (Personnes Morales) under the New French Criminal Code (Nouveau Code Pénal)', (1995) 11 *Connecticut Journal of International Law*, 111–68.

OSIANDER, A., *The States System of Europe, 1640–1990*. Oxford: Clarendon Press, 1994.

PAL, R. B., *International Military Tribunal for the Far East, Dissentient Judgment*. Calcutta: Sanyal, 1953.

PARRY, C., 'Some Considerations upon the Protection of Individuals in International Law', (1956–II) 90 Hague *Recueil*, 653–725.

PAUST, J. J., 'The Link Between Human Rights and Terrorism and Its Implications for the Law of State Responsibility', (1987) 11 *Hastings International and Comparative Law Review*, 41–54.

PEASLEE, A. J., 'The Sanction of International Law', (1916) 10 *AJIL*, 328–36.

PELLA, V. V., *La Criminalité collective des états et le droit pénal de l'avenir*. Bucharest: Imp. de l'État, 1925.

—— 'Fonctions pacificatrices du droit pénal supranational et fin du système traditionnel des traités de paix', (1947) *RGDIP*, vol. 51, 1–27.

—— 'Towards an International Criminal Court', (1950) 44 *AJIL*, 37–68.

—— *La Guerre-crime et les criminels de guerre*. Neuchatel: La Baconnière, 1964.

PELLET, A., 'Vive le crime! Remarques sur les degrés de l'illicite en droit internationale', in *International Law on the Eve of the Twenty-first Century: Views from the International Law Commission*. New York: United Nations, 1997, 287–315.

PELLET, A., 'Can a State Commit a Crime? Definitely, Yes!', (1999) *EJIL*, vol. 10, no. 2, 425–34.

PHILLIMORE, R. J., *Commentaries upon International Law*, 3rd edn., 4 vols. London: Butterworth, 1879–89.

—— 'An International Criminal Court and the Resolutions of the Committee of Jurists', (1922–3) *BYIL*, 79–86.

PHILLIPSON, C., *International Law and the Great War*. London: T. Fisher Unwin, 1915.

PICTET, J., *The Geneva Conventions of 12 August 1949: Commentary*, i. Geneva: International Committee of the Red Cross, 1952.

POLITIS, N., *The New Aspects of International Law*. Washington, DC: Carnegie Endowment for International Peace, 1928.

POMORSKI, S., 'Conspiracy and Criminal Organization', in Ginsburgs and Kudriavtsev (1990: 213–48).

PRITT, D. N., 'War Criminals', (1945) *Labour Monthly*.

PUFENDORF, S., *De Jure Naturae et Gentium Libri Octo*, ii, trans. of 1688 edn. by C. H. Oldfather and W. A. Oldfather. Oxford: Clarendon Press/London: Humphrey Milford, 1934.

PUGH, M., 'Legal Aspects of the Rainbow Warrior Affair', (1987) 36 *ICLQ*, 655–69.

QUADRI, R., 'Cours général de droit international public', (1964–III) 113 Hague *Recueil*, 237–483.

QUIGLEY, J., 'The International Law Commission's Crime–Delict Distinction: A Toothless Tiger?', (1988) 66 *Revue de Droit International de Sciences Diplomatiques et Politiques*, 117–61.

RAGAZZI, M., *The Concept of International Obligations* Erga Omnes. Oxford: Clarendon Press, 1997.

RAMCHARAN, B. G., *The Right to Life in International Law*. Dordrecht: Martinus Nijhoff, 1985.

RICE, W. G. Jr, 'State Responsibility for Failure to Vindicate the Public Peace', (1934) 28 *AJIL*, 246–54.

RIGAUX, F., 'Le Crime d'état: réflexions sur l'article 19 du projet d'articles sur la résponsabilité des états', in *International Law at the Time of Its Codification: Essays in Honour of Roberto Ago*, iii. Milan: Giuffrè, 1987, 301–25.

ROBERTS, A., 'The Laws of War: Problems of Implementation in Contemporary Conflicts', (1995) *Duke Journal of Comparative and International Law*, vol. 6, no. 1, 11–78.

ROBINSON, N., *The Genocide Convention*. New York: Jewish Institute of Foreign Affairs, 1960.

ROBLEDO, G., 'Le *Jus cogens* international: sa genèse, sa nature, ses fonctions', (1981–III) 172 Hague *Recueil*, 9–217.

RÖLING, B. V. A., and CASSESE, A., *The Tokyo Trial and Beyond: Reflections of a Peacemonger*. Cambridge: Polity Press, 1993.

—— and RÜTER, C. F. (eds.), *The Tokyo Judgement: The International Military Tribunal for the Far East, 29 April 1946–12 November 1948*. 2 vols. Amsterdam: APA-University Press Amsterdam, 1977.

ROOT, E., 'The Outlook for International Law', (1916) 10 *AJIL*, 2–11.

ROSENNE, S., 'War Crimes and State Responsibility', (1994) *Israel Yearbook on Human Rights*, vol. 24, 63–102.

ROSS, J. I. (ed.), *Controlling State Crime: An Introduction*. London: Garland, 1995.

ROWE, P. (ed.), *The Gulf War 1990–91 in International and English Law*. London: Sweet & Maxwell and Routledge, 1993.

ROXBURGH, R. F., 'The Sanction of International Law', (1920) 14 *AJIL*, 26–37.

ROZAKIS, C. L., *The Concept of Jus Cogens in the Law of Treaties*. Amsterdam: North-Holland, 1976.

RUBINSTEIN, A., 'The Enforcement of Morals in a Secular Society', (1972) *Israel Yearbook. on Human Rights*, vol. 2, 57–98.

RUHASHYANKIKO, N., *Study of the Question of the Prevention and Punishment of the Crime of Genocide*, prepared for the UN Sub-Commission on Prevention of Discrimination and Protection of Minorities, ECOSOC, Commission on Human Rights, E/CN.4/Sub.2/416, 4 July 1978.

RUSSELL OF LIVERPOOL, LORD, *The Trial of Adolph Eichmann*. London: Heinemann, 1962.

RUTTER, M. F., *Handbook on Damages for Personal Injuries and Death in Singapore and Malaysia*. Singapore: Butterworth, 1988.

SACHARIEW, K., 'State Responsibility for Multilateral Treaty Violations: Identifying the Injured State and Its Legal Status', (1988) 35 *Netherlands International Law Review*, 273–89.

SAHOVIC, M., 'Le Concept du crime international de l'état et le développement du droit international', in *International Law at the Time of Its Codification: Essays in Honour of Roberto Ago*, iii. Milan: Giuffrè, 1987, 363–9.

SALDAÑA, Q., 'La Justice pénale internationale', (1925–V) 10 Hague *Recueil*, 223–424.

SAROOSHI, D., 'The Legal Framework Governing United Nations Subsidiary Organs', (1996) *BYIL*, 413–78.

SAWYER, R., *Slavery in the Twentieth Century*. London: Routledge & Kegan Paul, 1986.

SCHACHTER, O., *International Law in Theory and Practice*. Dordrecht: Martinus Nijhoff, 1991.

SCHWARZENBERGER, G., 'The Problem of an International Criminal Law', (1950) 3 *Current Legal Problems*, 263.

—— *International Law as Applied by International Courts and Tribunals*, i, 3rd edn. London: Stevens & Sons, 1957.

—— 'International *Jus Cogens*?', (1965) 43 *Texas Law Review*, 455–78.

—— *International Law and Order*. London: Stevens & Sons, 1971.

SCHWELB, E., 'Some Aspects of International *Jus Cogens* as Formulated by the International Law Commission', (1967) 61 *AJIL*, 946–75.

—— 'The *Actio Popularis* and International Law', (1972) *Israel Yearbook on Human Rights*, vol. 2, 46–56.

SHAW, M. N., 'Genocide and International Law', in Dinstein (1989: 797–820).

—— *International Law*. Cambridge: Grotius, 1997.

SIBERT, M., *Traité de droit international public: le droit de la paix*. Paris: Dalloz, 1951.

SIEGHART, P., *The International Law of Human Rights*. Oxford: Clarendon Press, 1983.

SIMMA, B., 'Bilateralism and Community Interest in the Law of State Responsibility', in Dinstein (1989: 821–44).

SIMMA, B., 'From Bilateralism to Community Interest in International Law', (1994–VI) 250 Hague *Recueil*, 217–384.

SINCLAIR, I. M., *The Vienna Convention on the Law of Treaties*. Manchester: Manchester University Press, 1984.

SLAPPER, G., and TOMBS, S., *Corporate Crime*. Harlow: Longman, 1999.

SMITH, B. F., *Reaching Judgment at Nuremberg*: London: André Deutsch, 1977.

—— *The American Road to Nuremberg: The Documentary Record 1944–1945*. Stanford, Calif.: Hoover Institution Press, 1982.

SOBOLEWSKI, E., 'Essay on International Criminal Law', London: White Eagle Press, 1962.

SØRENSEN, M. (ed.), *Manual of Public International Law*. London: Macmillan, 1968.

SPINEDI, M., 'Protection of the Environment through Criminal Law', (1991) 2 *Yearbook of International Environmental Law*, 99–101.

—— and SIMMA, B. (eds.), *United Nations Codification of State Responsibility*. New York: Oceana, 1987.

STARACE, V., 'La Responsabilité résultant de la violation des obligations à l'égard de la communauté internationale', (1976–V) 153 Hague *Recueil*, 267–317.

STEINER, H. J., and ALSTON, P., *International Human Rights in Context: Law, Politics, Morals*. Oxford: Clarendon Press, 1996.

STESSENS, G., 'Corporate Criminal Liability: A Comparative Perspective', (1994) 43 *ICLQ*, 493–520.

STIMSON, H. L., 'Nuremberg: Landmark in Law', (1947) 25 *Foreign Affairs*, 179–80, 188–9.

STOLL, H., 'Consequences of Liability: Remedies', in Tunc (1986: ch. 8).

STONE, J., *Aggression and World Order*. London: Stevens & Sons, 1958.

SWEENEY, J. M., OLIVER, C. T., and LEECH, N. E., *The International Legal System: Cases and Materials*. Mineola, NY: Foundation Press, 1981.

TAYLOR, A. J. P., *The Origins of the Second World War*. London: Hamish Hamilton, 1961.

TAYLOR, T., 'Guilt, Responsibility, and the Third Reich', Churchill College Overseas Fellowship Lectures 6. Cambridge: Heffer, 1970.

—— *The Anatomy of the Nuremberg Trials*. London: Bloomsbury, 1993.

TEMPERLEY, H. W. V. (ed.), *A History of the Peace Conference of Paris*. 6 vols. H. Frowde and Hodder & Stoughton, 1920–4.

TERNON, Y., *L'État criminel: les génocides au xxᵉ siècle*. Paris: Seuil, 1995.

THIRLWAY, H., 'The Law and Procedure of the International Court of Justice', (1989) 60 *BYIL*, 1–157; (1990) 61 *BYIL*, 1–133.

TOGNI, L., *The Struggle for Human Rights: An International and South African Perspective*. Kenwyn, South Africa: Juta, 1994.

TOMUSCHAT, C. (ed.), *The United Nations at Age Fifty: A Legal Perspective*. The Hague: Kluwer Law International, 1995.

TOSI, J.-P., *Le Droit des obligations au Sénégal*. Paris: Librarie Générale de Droit et de Jurisprudence, 1981.

TRAININ, A. N., *Hitlerite Responsibility under International Law*. London: Hutchinson, 1944.

TREVAN, T., *Saddam's Secrets: The Hunt for Iraq's Hidden Weapons*. London: Harper-Collins, 1999.

TRIFFTERER, O., 'Prosecution of States for Crimes of State', in Bassiouni (1986: 99–107); repr. in (1996) 67 *Revue Internationale de Droit Pénal*, 341–64.

TSKHOVREBOV, Z., 'An Unfolding Case of Genocide: Chechnya, World Order and the "Right to Be Left Alone"', (1995) 64 *Nordic Journal of International Law*, 501–55.

TUNC, A. (ed.), *International Encyclopaedia of Comparative Law: Torts*, xi/2. Dordrecht: Martinus Nijhoff, 1986.

TUNKIN, G. I., *Theory of International Law*. London: George Allen & Unwin, 1974.

UNITED NATIONS. *The United Nations and Apartheid, 1948–1994*. Blue Books Series 1. New York: Dept. of Public Information, 1994.

UNITED NATIONS WAR CRIMES COMMISSION, *History of the United Nations War Crimes Commission and the Development of the Laws of War*. London: HMSO, 1948.

VABRES, D. DE, *Les principes modernes du droit pénal international*. Paris: Sirey, 1928.

—— 'Le Procès de Nuremberg devant les principes modernes du droit pénal international', (1947–I) Hague *Recueil*, 481–580.

VAN DIJK, P., and VAN HOOF, G. J. H., *Theory and Practice of the European Convention on Human Rights*. Deventer, Netherlands: Kluwer Law and Taxation Publishers, 1984.

VATTEL, E. DE, *The Law of Nations*. London: S. Sweet, Stevens & Sons, A. Maxwell, 1834.

VERDROSS, A., 'Forbidden Treaties in International Law', (1937) 31 *AJIL*, 571–7.

—— '*Jus Dispositivum* and *Jus Cogens* in International Law', (1966) 60 *AJIL*, 55–63.

VERZIJL, J. H. W., *International Law in Historical Perspective*, vi. Leiden: A.W. Sijthoff, 1973.

VISSCHER, C. DE, *Théories et réalités en droit international public*, 4th edn. Paris: Pedone, 1970.

—— 'Positivisme et "jus cogens"', (1971) 75 *RGDIP*, 5–11.

VISSER, P. J., and POTGIETER, J. M., *Law of Damages*. Cape Town: Juta, 1981.

VON HIRSCH, A., and JAREBORG, N., 'Gauging Criminal Harm: A Living-Standard Analysis', (1991) *Oxford Journal of Legal Studies*, vol. 2, no. 1, 1–38.

WALDOCK, H., 'General Course on Public International Law', (1962–II) 106 Hague *Recueil*, 5–251.

WEBBER, F., 'The Pinochet Case: The Struggle for the Realization of Human Rights', (1999) *Journal of Law and Society*, vol. 26, no. 4, 523–37.

WEHBERG, H., 'Le Problème de la mise de la guerre hors la loi', (1928–IV) 24 Hague *Recueil*, 151–306.

WEIL, P., 'Towards Relative Normativity in International Law', (1983) 77 *AJIL*, 413–42.

WEILER, J. H. H., CASSESE, A., and SPINEDI, M. (eds.), *Crimes of State: A Critical Analysis of the International Law Commission's Draft Article 19 on State Responsibility*. Berlin: Walter de Gruyter, 1989.

WELLER, M., 'The Kuwait Crisis: A Survey of Some Legal Issues', (1991) 3 *African Journal of International and Comparative Law*, 1–40.

—— 'The Lockerbie Case: A Premature End to the "New World Order"', (1992) 4 *African Journal of International and Comparative Law*, 302–24.

—— (ed.), *Iraq and Kuwait: The Hostilities and Their Aftermath*. Cambridge International Documents Series 3. Cambridge: Grotius, 1993.

WESTON, B. H., FALK, R. A., and D'AMATO, A. A. (eds.), *International Law and World Order*. Minnesota: West Publishing Company, 1980.

WHITAKER, B., *Revised and Updated Report on the Question of the Prevention and Punishment of the Crime of Genocide*, prepared for the UN Sub-Commission on Prevention of Discrimination and Protection of Minorities, ECOSOC, Commission on Human Rights, E/CN.4/Sub.2/1985/6, 2 July 1985.

WHITEMAN, M. M., *Damages in International Law*, i. Washington, DC: US Govt. Printing Office, 1937.

—— *Digest of International Law*. 15 vols. Washington, DC: Dept. of State, 1963–73.

WILLIS, J. F., *Prologue to Nuremberg: The Politics and Diplomacy of Punishing War Criminals of the First World War*. Westport, Conn.: Greenwood Press, 1982.

WRIGHT, Q., 'War Crimes under International Law', (1946) 62 *LQR*, 40–52.

—— 'The Law of the Nuremberg Trial', (1947) 41 *AJIL*, 38–72.

—— 'The Corfu Channel Case', (1949) *AJIL*, 491–4.

—— 'International Law and Guilt by Association', (1949) 43 *AJIL*, 746–55.

YEE, S., 'A Proposal to Reformulate Article 23 of the ILC Draft Statute for an International Criminal Court', (1996) *Hastings International and Comparative Law Review*, vol. 19, no. 3, 529–37.

ZEMANEK, K., 'General Course on Public International Law', (1997) 266 Hague *Recueil*, 13–335.

Index